Changing Texas

# Changing Texas

## Implications of Addressing or Ignoring the Texas Challenge

Steve H. Murdock
Michael E. Cline
Mary Zey
P. Wilner Jeanty
Deborah Perez

Texas A&M University Press
College Station

Library of Congress Cataloging-in-Publication Data

Murdock, Steve H.
Changing Texas : Implications of addressing or ignoring the Texas
    challenge / Steve H. Murdock.
        p. cm.
    Includes bibliographical references and index.
    ISBN 978-1-62349-159-8 (pbk. : alk. paper)—ISBN 978-1-62349-166-6
(e-book) 1. Population forecasting—Texas. 2. Social change—Texas.
3. Economic forecasting—Texas. 4. Education—Texas—Forecasting.
5. Texas—Population. 6. Texas—Social conditions—21st century.
7. Texas—Economic conditions—21st century. I. Title.
    HB3525.T4M868 2014
    304.609764—dc23
                        2013036274

To Diana and William P. Hobby, Jr., who have dedicated their lives to improving conditions for the current and future populations of Texas.

# Contents

# List of Figures

# List of Tables

# Preface

In the early 1990s a set of researchers in the Department of Rural Sociology at Texas A&M University began to monitor and project the growth of the population of Texas. This group led by Steve Murdock and including Patricia Bramwell, Darrell Fannin, Rita Hamm, Nazrul Hoque, Beverly Pecotte, and Steve White (who contributed to both of the first two Texas Challenge volumes [Murdock et al. 1997; Murdock et al. 2003]) and Jennifer Balkan, Andrea Chrietzberg, Sheila Dos Santos-Dierking, Jeffrey Jordan, Martha Michael, Teresa Ray, Xuihong You, Hongwei Wang, and Xiadong Wang (who contributed to one of the volumes) noted that Texas was among the most rapidly growing states in the nation. These researchers also established that this rapid growth was increasingly composed of minority population groups: nonHispanic Black, Hispanic, and nonHispanic Asian and Other groups. Finally, they established that two patterns impacting populations across the nation were impacting Texas. These were the aging of the population (particularly the nonHispanic White population) and the growing diversity in the types of households being created.

These fastest growing population and household groups were those that, due to a variety of historical, discriminatory, and other factors, also had the lowest incomes, highest rates of poverty, and lowest levels of education. Using trends current at the time, Murdock et al. (1997, 2003) projected that if the socioeconomic differentials among such groups and the majority nonHispanic White population did not change, and the population of the state continued to increase in the future as it had in the past, the population of Texas would become increasingly poorer and less well educated, with extensive implications for both the public and private sectors.

Such changes would have dramatic implications for the State of Texas, reducing aggregate household incomes, leading to a less well educated labor force, and resulting in larger populations in Texas prisons and more people on Medicaid, TANF, and similar programs. All of these trends, if continued, would lead to a generally less competitive and prosperous Texas.

These findings were presented first in a set of applied research reports provided to state agencies and legislative leaders (Murdock et al. 1995, 1996) and then in the two previous volumes published by the Texas A&M University Press, *The Texas Challenge* (1997) and *The New Texas Challenge* (2003). These publications informed the discussion with extensive data from the 1990 and the 2000 Census, data from state agencies, and through projections of future populations and their likely socioeconomic characteristics. They impacted the discussion at all levels of government, and former Lieutenant Governor William P. Hobby, Jr., and State Senator Teel Bivens, then Chair of the Senate Education Committee, both noted that they were among the most important volumes affecting their views of Texas' future and the public policy needs challenging Texas. For example, Senator Bivens in discussing the second of the two books (Murdock et al. 2003: xxxiv) noted that:

> I know of no work that offers a clearer vision of what is at stake for our state than the book you currently hold in your hands. *The New Texas Challenge* has had a greater impact on me as a legislator than any other scholarly work I have received. In a resounding fashion, it underscores the need for our state to continue building on the progress we have made toward increasing the quality and accessibility of our educational system from prekindergarten through all levels of higher education.

## THE INTELLECTUAL AND POLICY IMPERATIVES FOR *CHANGING TEXAS: IMPLICATIONS OF ANSWERING OR IGNORING THE TEXAS CHALLENGE*

The current volume represents the third volume in this series, but it is much more than simply a continuation of a series. It not only presents extensive data for more recent periods than the last volumes and projections for mid-century (through 2050), it also extends the analysis of the earlier volumes in several ways. This volume provides and discusses new population projections for the time periods from 2010 to 2050. These projections allow for an examination of Texas at the middle of the 21st century. How large will its population be and where will that population live? How diverse will that population be and how old will it be? How will its household structure change? What effects will the aging and diversification of the population and the change in households have on the service and socioeconomic characteristics of Texas?

Second, this volume, more than the former volumes, provides detailed discussions of the implications of population-related change for the people of Texas. It examines how the state could alter those population-related changes that are likely to negatively impact Texas residents and how it could further enhance those changes with positive impacts. How will increases in minority populations' incomes, assets, and educational attainment levels alter Texas' future? What will be the levels of educational attainment, the income and poverty levels, the levels of employment and unemployment, and the occupational distribution of the Texas labor force? How will the projected demographic changes impact the demand for health care and the overall level of specific health conditions in Texas? How will the demands on elementary, secondary, and higher education change and how will the levels of need for financial assistance for students in higher education change? What will be the effects of demographic change on levels of business activity and asset accumulation and for business development? What effects will the projected change have on state revenues and expenditures in the coming decades? These and similar questions are addressed in this volume.

Finally, this volume, more than the earlier volumes, examines the implications of alternative policies and their likely effects on population-related socioeconomic change. It evaluates policy changes that could alter the course of the population-related effects to enhance their positive and reduce their negative impacts. These include changes that will likely be seen as overly conservative by some and overly liberal by others. However, we take no stand concerning what paths should be followed. Policy formation and imposition remain the responsibility of the state's policy makers. We do, however, believe that objective information, when appropriately analyzed, suggests that governmental and private-sector policies will have different socioeconomic effects on diverse population groups with implications for the future of Texas.

In sum, although no single volume can thoroughly address all of the implications of population change for Texas for the next 40 years, this volume provides an attempt that we believe is useful in both raising key questions about Texas' future and answering many of them under alternative courses of action and policies. Our ultimate hope is that it will be useful to Texas decision makers and to the people of Texas.

# Acknowledgments

We express our gratitude to those who assisted us in a variety of ways in the completion of this work. We wish to thank the Meadows Foundation and the Greater Texas Foundation for their financial support. In particular, Mr. Bruce Esterline and Mr. Mike McCoy from the Meadows Foundation and Dr. Wynn Rosser from the Greater Texas Foundation were instrumental in ensuring we had the resources to complete this effort. Without their support the work you hold in your hands would not exist.

We also express our appreciation to Susan Brown, Assistant Commissioner for Planning Accountability at the Texas Higher Education Coordinating Board, and Billy Hamilton, former Deputy Controller of Texas, for their careful reviews and helpful suggestions for the critically important education and economic impact chapters, respectively.

We also wish to thank our mentor and friend, former Lt. Governor William P. Hobby, Jr., for his financial support, his continuing encouragement, and for his efforts for the State of Texas in ensuring that thousands of students and others have opportunities that would not have existed without his stewardship as lieutenant governor. Similarly, we wish to acknowledge the financial support and friendship of James Adams. Mr. Adams has used, promoted, and encouraged others to use the challenge documents and has often provided essential advice to the senior author in obtaining support for our work.

Several colleagues were also instrumental in the completion of this work, including Dr. Nazrul Hoque, who worked with us to complete population projections for Texas, and Mr. John Womack who assisted us in numerous ways in regard to analytical and computer-related efforts without which we would not have been able to complete this volume. Both have been friends and colleagues for more than 25 years. We also wish to thank Dr. George Hough who worked with us at the beginning of the project that produced this work and produced products we continue to use. We express special appreciation to our technical editor, Karen White, who ensured greater consistency and readability in this work than would otherwise have occurred.

We also express appreciation to Erma Hunter who ensured we had all the materials necessary to complete the work and worked with us in numerous ways to ease our burden. We wish to also thank Dr. Mary Lenn Dixon, our editor at Texas A&M University Press, for all her assistance and support.

We also thank those who worked on earlier published versions of the related works and who thus made our work easier. These include Patricia Bramwell, Sheila Dos-Santos Dierking, Darrell Fannin, Jeffrey Jordan, Nazrul Hoque, Beverly Pecotte, Steve White, and Xuihong You.

We wish to express special appreciation to our families, who suffered with us during long hours, missed weekends and holidays, and continuing pressure to meet deadlines. We owe them more than we can ever repay.

Finally, we wish to thank the countless number of Texans who have encouraged our work and provided insight into how Texas was changing. It is ultimately for them that this work has been completed and to whom it is dedicated.

Changing Texas

CHAPTER 1

# Introduction: The Conceptual and Empirical Basis for the Work

Texans have a deep affection for their state believing, like people from many other states, that it is unique and superior in many ways to all others. Texans, however, have a particularly strong belief in the uniqueness of the state because of its heritage as a separate nation and the fact that parts of it were parts of several different nations before its existence as a separate republic (Haynes 2013; Murdock et al. 2013). Similarly, the sheer size and the differences in the Texas climate and topography from one region to another and the variety of social and cultural heritages of the people that became encompassed in the State of Texas required residents to have resilience in order to survive and prosper in a region that periodically produced droughts and floods as well as blizzards, tornadoes, and hurricanes. Its diverse topographies and climates produced ways of life that revolved around a variety of enterprises including farming, ranching, hunting and fishing, and commerce of a wide variety of types. These differences resulted in conflicts between new and longtime residents that sometimes led to the total destruction of historically unique and socially and culturally distinct ways of life. Given this heritage, it is not surprising that Texans have also developed a wide variety of different perspectives on what are likely to be the most important factors impacting the future of Texas.

In recent decades Texas has shown substantial growth and rapid change in the characteristics of its population. It has also experienced substantial economic expansion. These changes are placing it among those states that are likely to play especially critical roles in shaping the future of the United States.

The growth in the total size of Texas' population and the increasing racial/ethnic diversity of the population, coupled with increasing proportions of young minority and older nonHispanic White residents and an increasing diversity of households, are likely to produce a state in which population change may result in a variety of generally desirable as well as less desirable socioeconomic outcomes.

Among the reasons for such impacts are the differences in socioeconomic resources associated with the changing characteristics of the state's population. For example, Texas' population and households (see Chapters 2 and 3) are projected to show dramatic increases in the size of minority (especially Hispanic) populations and households. As shown in Table 1.1, incomes in 2010 varied dramatically among racial/ethnic groups, when nonHispanic Black and Hispanic households had median household incomes of roughly $35,000 to $37,000, while nonHispanic White and nonHispanic Asian and Other households had income levels of roughly $60,000 to $64,000. Texas is also projected to have increases in the number and proportion of young minority populations and elderly nonHispanic White populations, and both the young and the old have clear income limitations. Table 1.1 shows that those households with a householder who was less than 25 years of age in 2010 had median incomes of roughly $24,000 and those with householders 65 years of age or older had incomes of roughly $34,000. Households with middle-aged adult householders had incomes varying from $51,000 to more than $59,000. In addition, Texas is projected to have a larger proportion of married couple and a smaller proportion of nonfamily households in the future than today. As shown in Table 1.1, married couple households had a median income of nearly $70,000 in 2010. Female householder households had a median income of about $28,000, male householder households had a median income of about $40,000, and nonfamily households had a median income of roughly $31,000.

Such socioeconomic differences are not inherent in the demographic differences associated with them, but these and other factors that interact with population change make it clear that understanding how the new demographic characteristics of Texas may change the state's economy and its service structure is of critical importance. It is essential for the state's decision makers and residents to understand how the change in such characteristics may impact the levels of demand for, and utilization of, specific types of private and public sector services and may change the socioeconomic characteristics of Texas. Exploring these changes is the central purpose of this volume.

We have previously argued that change in the size and rate of growth in the racial/ethnic, age, and household composition of Texas' population is forming critical challenges for this state (Murdock et al. 1997, 2003). These challenges are those of providing the social and economic resources that will allow all Texans to obtain the skills and education necessary to become competitive in increasingly socially and culturally diverse, and

Table 1.1

Median Household Income in Texas by
Age of Householder, Race/Ethnicity of
Householder, and Household Type, 2010

| Characteristic of Householder | Median Income |
|---|---|
| **Age of Householder** | |
| Total | $ 48,615 |
| Under 25 | 23,656 |
| 25 to 44 | 50,837 |
| 45 to 64 | 59,538 |
| 65 and over | 34,178 |
| **Race/Ethnicity of Householder** | |
| Total | $ 48,615 |
| NH* White | 59,772 |
| NH Black | 35,674 |
| Hispanic | 37,087 |
| NH Asian | 64,191 |
| **Household Type** | |
| Total | $ 48,615 |
| Family households | 56,575 |
| Married couple | 69,888 |
| Female householders | 28,415 |
| Male householders | 40,274 |
| Nonfamily households | 30,800 |

*Source*: U.S. Census Bureau 2011a.
*NH refers to nonHispanic; values for categories labeled
NH are only for the nonHispanic persons in each race
category. Hispanic includes Hispanics of all races.

economically competitive, national and international economies. In our
earlier works, we described what could happen to the socioeconomic characteristics of the Texas population depending on what occurs or does not
occur to increase the skills and education of the state's increasingly diverse
population. In this work, we extend that analysis by both describing and
evaluating past demographic and related socioeconomic change and ex-

amining the future of Texas' population through 2050. This work is both a report card, of sorts, on our earlier works and a continuing explication of the future of Texas depending on how its population changes and how the state adapts to and develops the population and related socioeconomic resources resulting from such change.

## THE STATE OF KNOWLEDGE: POPULATION, EDUCATION, AND SOCIOECONOMIC CHANGE

The assertions noted above about the interrelationships of demographic and socioeconomic factors are more than simply our assertions but are supported by a wide variety of work in the demographic, economic, and sociological literature. In this section we provide a brief summary of some of this work while acknowledging that the breadth and depth of such work cannot be adequately addressed given our space limitations. Nevertheless, we believe the review below clearly substantiates the existence and importance of such relationships.

The important interrelationships among demographic, education, and socioeconomic dimensions are well established. For example, a November 2005 "Policy Alert" published by the National Center for Public Policy and Higher Education and drawing upon a report by Kelly (2005a: 1) warned that "if current population trends continue and states do not improve the education of all racial/ethnic groups, the skills of the workforce and the incomes of U.S. residents are projected to decline." This warning (also see Kelly 2005b) is based on several demographic and socioeconomic trends and interrelationships that have established the following:

1. The U.S. workforce is becoming more racially and ethnically diverse;
2. The racial and ethnic groups that are less well educated (e.g., Hispanics) are the fastest growing due to higher rates of natural increase and immigration;
3. The increasing rate of retirement of "baby boomers"—the most highly educated generation in United States history—is expected to lead to a drop in the average level of education of the U.S. workforce now and for the next two decades;
4. If these current population trends continue and states do not improve the education levels and graduation rates from high school and college for all racial and ethnic groups, the knowledge and skill levels of the U.S. workforce will decline;
5. If the knowledge and skill levels of the workforce decline, occupational achievement will be lower;

6. If occupational achievement declines, the income of U.S. residents will decline;
7. If the levels of knowledge and skills of the U.S. workforce decline, more jobs will be exported off-shore;
8. As jobs are exported off-shore and U.S. residents' incomes decline, the taxes paid by U.S. residents will decline; and
9. As taxes decline, revenue for state and federal support of state and federal services will decline, including support for education.

This chain of interrelationships is dependent on the validity of three key demographic and socioeconomic trends:

1. The rate of increase in minority populations with reduced socio-economic resource bases;
2. The relationship between the demographic characteristics of populations and the education level of the population; and
3. The relationships between education and income (both personal and household) and between education and poverty and other types of socioeconomic change.

A summary of the state of knowledge regarding these factors is examined below.

### Growth in Minority Populations
The increasing racial and ethnic diversity of Texas will be clearly delineated in Chapters 2 and 3. Such data were provided for earlier time periods in previous works (Murdock et al. 1997, 2003). Similarly, clear documentation of national patterns are evident in work by Passel and Cohn (2008a, 2008b), Perez and Hirschman (2009), and Johnson and Lichter (2010: 151) who note, based on U.S. Census Bureau projections (U.S. Census Bureau 2008a), that by 2042 "everyone but non-Hispanic Whites. . .will become the majority population. The size of the minority population is projected to grow to 235.7 million or 54 percent of the total United States population by 2050". Even more recent projections by the Census Bureau (U.S. Census Bureau 2012b; 2012c) show the minority population (the population other than the nonHispanic White) increasing to more than 241 million by 2060. Immigration and high fertility are the major contributors to growing racial and ethnic diversity among American children and youth.

Among minority groups, Hispanic children (especially those 0–4 years of age) are the largest contributors to this growth (Perez and Hirschman 2009; Cohn and Bahrampour 2006; Mather 2009; Murdock et al. 2012), while the absolute number of nonHispanic White children in these ages is declining.

Johnson and Lichter (2010) and Murdock et al. (2012) further demonstrate
that these trends manifest themselves unevenly over U.S. counties, with major concentrations in the Southwest. Such groups are leading the trends in
these patterns by exhibiting rates of growth in "majority-minority" populations of children considerably higher than those for the United States
population overall (Johnson and Lichter 2010:152; Murdock et al. 2012).

At the same time, although higher levels of minority population growth
are more concentrated in some regions of the nation than in others, there
is little doubt that patterns of minority population growth are increasingly
pervasive across the United States. Thus Murdock et al. (2012) reported
that while only four states showed increases in their numbers of non-
Hispanic White children from 2000 to 2010, all 50 states reported increases
in their numbers of Hispanic children.

The growth in minority populations has created a new "generational
rift" along racial and ethnic lines—between a slow-growing older non-
Hispanic White population and a faster growing younger Hispanic population (Mather 2009). These conflicts are not only between ethnic and racial
groups, but also between the old and young, and even more importantly
between those who are economically mobile and those who are not, due
to cultural, educational, and language differences. Mather argues that increased racial and ethnic diversity among American children has height-
ened the need for appropriate public policy responses to improve and ex-
pand specialized school programs, especially pre-kindergarten programs,
English as a second language (ESL), limited English proficiency (LEP),
and community educational services in reading and math, to accelerate
learning among such youth.

*Race/Ethnicity and Education*
Substantial evidence shows that educational attainment varies across racial
and ethnic groups in the U.S. According to 2009 census data, 90 percent
of nonHispanic White adults report that they have at least a high school
level of education, while only 61 percent of Hispanics have a high school
diploma or equivalent (Ryan and Seibens 2012). Asians reported the highest percentage with bachelor's, master's and professional, and doctorate
degrees. NonHispanic Blacks were more likely to have completed some
college than any of the other groups, however they were less likely to have
completed a bachelor's, master's, doctorate, or professional degree than
those who were nonHispanic White. Similarly, results from the National
Assessment of Educational Progress (NAEP) have for some time shown
that reading and writing skills of Black and Hispanic children are substantially below those of nonHispanic White children at grade levels 3, 7, and
11 (Beaton 1986; Milne et al. 1986; Milne and Gombert 1983; NAEP 1985;
Baretz-Snowden et al.1988).

What lies at the base of educational differences is educational disadvantage that, due to a variety of historical, discriminatory, and other factors, varies by race/ethnicity (Psacharopoulos and Tilak 1992). Among the demographic factors that are predictive of such educational disadvantage are: 1) minority racial/ethnic status, 2) living in a poverty household, 3) having a poorly educated mother (or surrogate), 4) living in a single parent family, or 5) having a non-English-language family background. Children who are disadvantaged on several of these indicators are generally at greater risk of educational failure—performing poorly on standardized tests, dropping out of high school, or never attaining a higher education degree. As a result, children who come from poor families, and especially those who have the additional disadvantage of having parents who are not fluent in English, are especially disadvantaged (Ekstrom et al. 1986; Denny et al. 2000; Duncan et al. 2007; Gottschalk 2008; Gordon and Becker 2012).

*Education, Income, and Socioeconomic Change*
Among the most frequently studied relationships in economics and sociology, across numerous countries (Mincer 1974; Ashenfelter and Rouse 1999; Card 1999; Abdullah et al. 2011;) and multiple time periods (Becker 1967; Hanoch 1967; Schultz 1968) to post–2000 periods (U.S. Census Bureau and U.S. Bureau of Labor Statistics 2011), is the relationship between an individual's education and income (Rosen 1989; Romer 1990; Reardon 2011). These studies document that increased education results in increased wages and higher incomes. For example, United States Census Bureau data (2002) show that, in 2000, college graduates could expect to earn an average of $2.1 million over their working lives, compared to $1.0 million for high school dropouts (Cheeseman Day and Newburger 2002). A similar analysis based on 2010 data (Julian and Kominski 2011) provided lifetime earnings estimates for males and females by both educational attainment and race/ethnicity. This analysis clearly showed that increased levels of education increase lifetime earnings. For example, the authors find that among nonHispanic White males a graduate degree leads to a lifetime income advantage of nearly $1.9 million compared to a nonHispanic White male with less than a high school degree. The differences for the same educational levels were $1.6 million for an Hispanic male, $1.4 million for a nonHispanic Black male, and $2.3 million for a nonHispanic Asian male. Although clear racial/ethnic (and gender, as shown in other parts of this book) differences exist, it is evident that, for all racial/ethnic and gender groups, education pays.

Additionally, educated individuals not only earn more, they also experience less unemployment and work in higher paying occupations than their less well-educated counterparts. Higher levels of education result in the creation of higher levels of skills and human capital that increase productivity, which increases market demand and higher occupational achievement and results in higher incomes (see Cohn and Addison 1998 and Abdullah et al. 2011 for selective reviews describing such effects). Such analyses show that children's future incomes are largely determined by the education they attain. Children from poor families are less likely to achieve in school, and low levels of educational attainment lead to future low occupational attainment and thus low income. The 2010 Current Population Survey data (U.S. Census Bureau and U.S. Bureau of Labor Statistics 2011) demonstrate a strong positive correlation between education and income. They show that among adults 24 to 64 years of age, as education increases, median income increases.

Still other analysts have studied macro-level relationships at the state and national levels. These aggregative analyses (Denison 1962; Bowman and Anderson 1963; Schultz 1963) have estimated the contribution of education expenditures to national income and how state educational expenditures affect state income. They have consistently found that increased levels of education contribute to higher state and national income (Tolley and Olson 1971; Davern and Fisher 2001). In fact, an analysis by McKinsey & Company (2009) asserts that the persistent achievement gap between Hispanic and nonHispanic Black compared to nonHispanic White students in the United States will over time have the economic effect of a "permanent national recession." They argue that if the achievement gap had not existed between Black and Hispanic and nonHispanic Whites so that all earned at the level of nonHispanic Whites, GDP in 2008 would have been $310 to $525 billion higher (2–4 percent). If the gap between (all) low-income students and their peers had been narrowed, GDP in the same year would have been $400 billion to $670 billion higher (3–5 percent).

In a comprehensive quantitative review of the extant econometrics literature through a meta-regression analysis of 64 empirical studies that collectively reported 868 estimates of the effects of education on income, Abdullah et al. (2011) found that education is, on average, an effective tool for reducing income differences among social and racial/ethnic groups. They conclude that the distribution of education is critically important and that ensuring fair and equitable access to education is an important means of increasing individual, household, and national income levels.

The effects of education on income are pervasive even during periods of economic decline and/or stagnation. Between 2008 and 2010, during the depth of the "Great Recession," people with the highest educational attainment were the least likely to be unemployed (Ryan and Siebens 2012:15). These authors also found that for any given month, those without a high school diploma were the most likely to be unemployed, while high school graduates were more likely to be unemployed than those with bachelor's degrees. In August 2010, the unemployment rate for people with less than a high school education was 13.1 percent, while the unemployment rate for people with an advanced degree was 4.1 percent. The rates for these two groups in March 2008, before the recession, were 9.5 percent and 1.5 percent, respectively. In August of 2012 the national unemployment rate was 8.3 percent overall, while the unemployment rate for those with a college education was 4.1 percent.

It is evident that poorly educated persons experience long-term economic impacts (Isaacs 2010, 2011, 2012). Children and youth from families with low family income and low maternal education do poorly. They perform less well on standardized tests compared with advantaged youth and are less likely to graduate from high school and complete college. These lower levels of academic achievement and educational attainment result in lower levels of economic success as adults. For example, children born into families with family incomes in the bottom 20 percent are twice as likely as middle-class children to be in the bottom income brackets as adults.

Education plays a key role. The likelihood of being school ready is increased 9 percent by children attending preschool before starting kindergarten (Isaacs 2012). In addition, such analyses suggest that expanding preschool programs to focus on four-year-olds from poor families has a high potential for increasing school readiness.

Efforts to improve economic prospects of children from low-income families have often focused on the existing formal educational system as it is presently structured, but often with disappointing results (Jacob and Ludwig 2009). Research has demonstrated that disparities in academic skills are apparent well before children begin their formal schooling, suggesting that efforts targeted earlier than kindergarten may well be effective in preventing the disparities that schools and policy makers seek to remediate.

Scholars have recommended that policy makers emphasize early childhood education programs to remediate the intricate economic causes of poor academic achievement that keep children from low-income families at low-income levels as adults (Isaacs and Magnuson 2011). Bartik et al. (2011) in Chapter 8 of *Investing in Kids* suggest that the evidence is strong that early childhood education can significantly increase the future earnings and income of low-income children. They estimate that half-day prekindergarten programs for 4-year-olds, if such programs are high quality, can raise the future income among those from households with earnings in the lowest income quintile by 7 percent. Their analysis suggests that with even one year of a full-time high quality child care and preschool program, from shortly after birth to age 5, children from the lowest income quintile would increase their annual incomes as adults by 35 percent, a six times greater return than that obtained from a half-day one year early childhood education program.

It must be acknowledged, of course, that not only does education affect income but income also affects education. This issue is generally examined as an intergenerational query beginning with individual education achievement and asking the question: What parental background (education, occupation, and income) and demographic/contextual characteristics (region of the county, urban versus rural residence, family structure) lead to various levels of educational attainment? These analyses find that mothers' education and family income are generally the strongest predictors of their children's level of educational attainment. Combining these findings with those above suggests that mother's education and family of origin's income disproportionately determine a child's education and the child's education determines his or her future income. A recent analysis (see Maralani 2013) using sophisticated models has provided evidence that demographic factors work interactively with education and other factors to effect intergenerational change in socioeconomic levels of minority households.

The lack of adequate income as experienced in poverty households has particularly negative impacts on education. Poor children in the U.S. start school at a disadvantage in terms of their skills. Less than half (48 percent) of poor children, according to Isaacs (2012), are ready for school at age 5, compared to 75 percent of children from middle and higher income families. The importance of demographic variables is evident in that this 27 percent gap is reduced to roughly 7 percent when key demographic characteristics (such as household composition and racial/ethnic status) are controlled.

That income and education disparities are not historical but current in their effects is evident in several recent analyses. For example, a recent analysis by Acs et al. (2013) shows that the socioeconomic characteristics of nonHispanic Black and Hispanic populations in the United States continue to lag behind those of nonHispanic Whites. Nearly 50 years after Moynihan's famous study of the Black family, analyses by Acs et al. (2013) suggest that there has been a lack of substantial progress in closing socioeconomic differences between nonHispanic Black and nonHispanic White Americans and show that Hispanics in the United States show similar patterns of continuing disparity. Similarly, a recent analysis by Turner et al. (2013) indicates that although such disparity has been reduced substantially compared to earlier decades, disparity is still evident with nonHispanic Black and Hispanic customers receiving disparate treatment in housing relative to nonHispanic Whites.

The literature reviewed above provides substantial support for the major underlying premises of the present effort. This literature indicates that there is a substantial nation-wide increase in Hispanic and other minority populations and households and that, due to a variety of historical, discriminatory, and other factors, these populations have low levels of education.

These low levels of education lead, in turn, to reduced levels of income and to reduced levels of other socioeconomic factors linked to income. The interrelationships between demographic, educational, and socioeconomic factors have substantial interactive impacts on the social and economic events impacting society. Thus, levels of change in education among segments of the state's population may have substantial and significant effects on the socioeconomic characteristics of individuals, households, communities, and the State of Texas as a whole.

## CONTENT OF, DEFINITIONS AFFECTING, AND LIMITATIONS IMPACTING THIS WORK

### Organization

This work proceeds with a discussion concerning the current and future demographic change likely to impact Texas in the coming years (Chapter 2). This involves an examination of several key elements, including the past and likely future levels of population growth in the state and change in several population characteristics. Although numerous characteristics are discussed, emphasis is placed on the specific effects of change in the age structure and racial/ethnic composition on Texas' population and households. An examination of change in the size, the diversity, and the age structure of Texas' population form three of the four key elements of future population change examined in the text.

Chapter 3 examines the fourth major demographic factor impacting socioeconomic and other factors in Texas: that is, the number, size, and composition of households in Texas. In the same manner as in Chapter 2, both historical and projected future patterns are examined.

Chapters 2 and 3 present and discuss the critical size, diversity, and age dimensions of projected change in Texas' population and in characteristics of households with specific emphasis on the total level and rate of population and household growth, change in household types, and change in the racial/ethnic composition and age structure of the current and projected future population and households in Texas. Together Chapters 2 and 3 provide the demographic base underlying analyses presented in all other chapters.

Given the demographic base provided in Chapters 2 and 3, we proceed with a series of chapters that examine the effects of population growth and change in age, race/ethnicity, and household structure on specific socioeconomic dimensions and factors critical to the determination of the future of Texas. Each of the following chapters examines one or more economic, service, or policy areas.

Chapter 4 examines the effects of population and household change on the size and characteristics of the labor force. It includes analysis of effects on skill levels, earnings, and the occupational structure and levels of education of the labor force. It also provides data on enrollment in workforce training programs in Texas.

Chapter 5 examines the impacts of population growth, increasing racial/ethnic diversity, the aging of the population, and change in household composition on several key components of the private and public sectors. These include examinations of income differentials, poverty rates, consumer expenditures, asset accumulation and net worth, housing and housing demand (both owner and renter), housing expenditures, and state tax revenues.

Chapter 6 evaluates the effects of demographic change on both elementary and secondary and higher education. It examines the effects on enrollment levels, the need for specific types of programs, financial assistance, and other factors impacting education.

Chapter 7 examines the impacts of demographic change on health, on health care, on human services, and on correctional programs in Texas. It describes both the likely change in service populations and the associated costs.

Chapter 8 examines the effects of future demographic change on transportation in Texas. It includes a discussion of the effects on the demand for highways and roads, commuting and transit patterns, and the effects on the characteristics of drivers in the state.

The final chapter, Chapter 9, provides a summary of the work and examines key trends that must be addressed by policy makers to meet the needs of future populations and enhance the impacts of demographic and socioeconomic change on the public and private sectors of Texas. It delineates the key issues of whether current patterns, if continued, will produce a prosperous and competitive Texas or whether steps to enhance the competitiveness of Texas' fastest growing and less prosperous population segments are necessary and could lead to a more competitive and prosperous Texas.

The intent of this work is to provide its readers with a view of the potential characteristics of Texas' future populations and households and of the effects of change in these characteristics on the private and public sectors. It provides an analysis of what may occur, depending on what happens or does not happen to impact the socioeconomic and other characteristics historically associated with the size, distribution, and composition of its population.

*Cautions and Clarifications*
As readers examine this third volume in a series of works describing the state's demographic future and its implications, they should be aware of changes that have occurred in demographic dimensions and definitions

over the 1990 to 2010 period (during which these three analyses were completed), the extent to which changes in policies related to eligibility and forms of service delivery have altered service usage rates, and the inherent limitations of any analysis that attempts to project future events. Understanding these factors is critical to understanding how and why some socioeconomic and service characteristics are changing in unexpected ways and the implications of demographic and household change for the socioeconomic and public service future of Texas. Understanding changes in demographic definitions, changes in public policy, and limitations of projections is critical to the use and evaluation of data such as those described in this volume.

### Definitional Changes

One set of changes in the definition of racial/ethnic characteristics occurred with effects that are small and impossible to completely identify but may have caused some inconsistencies in racial/ethnic counts for 2000. In 1980 and 1990, census respondents (whose responses were used in our analysis of patterns of current and future socioeconomic change in the first Texas Challenge document [1997]) were asked to indicate to which racial group—White; African American or Black; Asian or Pacific Islander; American Indian, Aleutian or Native Hawaiian; or Other racial group, etc.—they belonged. They were allowed to select only one (a single) race category. They were also asked whether they were of Hispanic ethnicity. For the 1997 work, our projections used 1980 to 1990 patterns of change to make projections through 2030 using these consistent values. Although subject to the limitation of all projections, there were no technical definitional issues in the racial/ethnic categories utilized in the 1997 Texas Challenge volume.

In completing the New Texas Challenge (2003), we used the results of the 2000 Census, but respondents to this census were allowed (for the first time in Census history) to check multiple race categories if they had origins from more than one racial group while still responding to a single ethnic question (whether they were or were not of Hispanic Origin). Because the response categories in 2000 were different from those in 1990, making the racial/ethnic results for 2000 comparable to those for 1990 required making assumptions about what persons who indicated more than one race in 2000 would have indicated as their single race category in the 1990 Census and adjusting 2000 Census results accordingly. This assumption was essential so that 1990 to 2000 patterns of change could be measured. Although only about 5 percent of respondents in 2000 indicated being members of more than one racial group, it was still necessary to make adjustments for the change in census response patterns for persons in the multiple race groups in 2000. These adjustments are described in *The New Texas Challenge* (2003).

The 2010 Census employed the same response categories that were used in the 2000 Census, making it possible to clearly identify 2000 to 2010 changes within the census racial/ethnic categories. The analysis presented in this volume (based on 2000 to 2010 changes) thus uses completely comparable racial/ethnic categories.

In sum, categories used to measure change in racial and ethnic groups were entirely consistent in the 1980 and 1990 periods used in *The Texas Challenge* (1997) and in the 2000 and 2010 categories used in this volume. The only potential for differences in racial/ethnic counts is when comparing *The New Texas Challenge* (2003) to the current volume, and any such differences are likely to be quite small.

### Change in Terminology Related to Race/Ethnicity

Another change has been made in the current volume to ensure compatibility with other volumes published by demographers. In previous Texas Challenge volumes, we employed the Texas and Southwestern terms referring to nonHispanic Whites as Anglos and shortened terms for nonHispanic Blacks and nonHispanic Asians and Other to Black and Asians and Others respectively. Because of the more common usage of the nonHispanic precedent terms and the fact that the common usage was confusing to readers from outside the Southwest, the full nonHispanic White, nonHispanic Black, nonHispanic Asian and Other, and Hispanic (of all races) terms are employed in this volume. It is essential to note that the nonHispanic Asian and Other category as used here includes not only persons of Asian heritage but also persons who indicated they were members of some other racial group and those who indicated that they identified their heritage to two or more racial/ethnic groups.

### Change in Policy

It is important to note that the number of persons involved in different state services is altered by administrative and legislative changes in such programs as well as by change in underlying population characteristics. Change in laws related to incarceration have periodically affected rates of incarceration, change in Medicaid rules have impacted Medicaid enrollment levels, and change in Medicaid and Medicare will be impacted by the changes likely to result from the Affordable Care Act (2010; also see Cline and Murdock 2012). Whenever possible we attempt to make it clear when rule or legislated changes are likely to impact service usage, but in some cases it is difficult to delineate such effects. We wish to make the reader aware that changing procedural and legislative requirements as well as demographic change must be taken into account when examining change in the number and characteristics of persons enrolled in some programs.

*The Uncertainty of Projections*
We clearly acknowledge that the projected values presented here are directly dependent on demographic characteristics and trends changing in expected ways and continuing to have the relationships to private sector demand and public service requirements that existed in 2010 (or that change in the manner projected). If Texas population characteristics change, public sector program enrollment criteria change, or the relationships between demographic and service and socioeconomic factors change in unexpected ways, then the projected effects may not occur or may be attenuated or accentuated. As with any projections, the validity of the assumptions on which the projections are based form the critical elements influencing the accuracy of the findings.

## CONCLUSION

In this chapter we have presented the rationale for the work, reviewed literature establishing the conceptual and empirical base supporting it, provided an outline of its content, and indicated assumptions and limitations of which the reader should be aware. We are aware of the potential limitations of this work but believe that it provides important reading for those who wish to understand Texas' demographic future and its implications for the public and private sectors. This work does not assume that demography is destiny but only that demography forms a key dimension of critical importance in understanding the future of Texas.

# CHAPTER 2

# Recent and Projected Population Change in Texas

## HISTORIC PATTERNS OF POPULATION CHANGE

Texas has experienced rapid, continuous, and substantial population growth since 1850, the first time in which it was included as a state in the decennial census. It had only 212,592 people (Table 2.1). In fact, in every decade since becoming part of the United States, Texas has shown a higher rate of population growth than the nation as a whole. It became the second largest state (behind California) by 1994.

Recent population growth has been particularly extensive. Texas' population increased from 16,986,510 in 1990, to 20,851,820 in 2000, to 25,145,561 in 2010 (Table 2.1), and it was estimated to be 26,059,203 as of July 1, 2012 (the most recent date for which estimates are available at the time of this publication). Texas was the fastest growing state in numerical terms both from 2000 to 2010 with an increase of 4,293,741 and from 2010 to 2012 with an increase of 913,642, the fifth fastest growing in percentage terms from 2000 to 2010 with an increase of 20.6 percent, and the second fastest growing in percentage terms from 2010 to 2012 with an increase of 3.6 percent.

Growth has not been uniformly distributed across the state, however. The state had three of the ten largest cities in the nation in 2010 with Houston being the fourth largest, San Antonio the seventh largest, and Dallas the ninth largest. Texas also had the county with the smallest population in the United States (Loving, with 82 people in 2010). Seventy-nine of its 254 counties showed population declines from 2000 to 2010 and 96 from 2010 to 2012. Texas remains a state of diversity in population growth rates as in other characteristics.

The population of Texas has also become increasingly racially and ethnically diverse. In 1990, the state's population was 60.6 percent nonHispanic

Table 2.1

Total Population and Percent Population Change
in Texas and the United States, 1850–2010

| Year | Total Population | | Percent Change from Previous Time Period | |
|------|------------------|------|------|------|
| | Texas | U.S. | Texas | U.S. |
| 1850 | 212,592 | 23,191,876 | — | — |
| 1860 | 604,215 | 31,443,321 | 184.2 | 35.6 |
| 1870 | 818,579 | 39,818,449 | 35.5 | 26.6 |
| 1880 | 1,591,749 | 50,155,783 | 94.5 | 26.0 |
| 1890 | 2,235,527 | 62,947,714 | 40.4 | 25.5 |
| 1900 | 3,048,710 | 75,994,575 | 36.4 | 20.7 |
| 1910 | 3,896,542 | 91,972,266 | 27.8 | 21.0 |
| 1920 | 4,663,228 | 105,710,620 | 19.7 | 14.9 |
| 1930 | 5,824,715 | 122,775,046 | 24.9 | 16.1 |
| 1940 | 6,414,824 | 131,669,275 | 10.1 | 7.2 |
| 1950 | 7,711,194 | 150,697,361 | 20.2 | 14.5 |
| 1960 | 9,579,677 | 179,323,175 | 24.2 | 19.0 |
| 1970 | 11,196,730 | 203,302,031 | 16.9 | 13.4 |
| 1980 | 14,229,191 | 226,545,805 | 27.1 | 11.4 |
| 1990 | 16,986,510 | 248,709,873 | 19.4 | 9.8 |
| 2000 | 20,851,820 | 281,421,906 | 22.8 | 13.2 |
| 2010 | 25,145,561 | 308,745,538 | 20.6 | 9.7 |

*Source*: Carter et al. 2006; and U.S. Census Bureau 2011b.
*Note*: April 1 of reported year.

White, 11.6 percent nonHispanic Black, 25.6 percent Hispanic, and 2.2 percent nonHispanic Asian and Other. By 2010, Texas population was 45.3 percent nonHispanic White (decreasing from 52.4 percent nonHispanic White in 2000 and is estimated to have become less than 50 percent nonHispanic White sometime between 2003 and 2004), 11.5 percent nonHispanic Black, 37.6 percent Hispanic (including Hispanics of all races), and 5.6 percent nonHispanic Asian and Other (Table 2.2). By 2010, Texas was only one of four states (with Hawaii, California, and New Mexico) in which less than 50 percent of the population was nonHispanic White. Texas is a majority minority state.

Because minority populations tend to have younger age structures and Texas has a large minority population, the state has a younger age structure

Table 2.2

Population, Population Change, Percent Population Change, Proportion of Population,
and Proportion of Net Change in Population in Texas, by Race/Ethnicity, 1990–2010

| Race/Ethnicity | Population | | | Numerical Change | | Percent Change | |
| | 1990 | 2000 | 2010 | 1990–2000 | 2000–2010 | 1990–2000 | 2000–2010 |
|---|---|---|---|---|---|---|---|
| NH* White | 10,291,680 | 10,933,313 | 11,397,345 | 641,633 | 464,032 | 6.2 | 4.2 |
| NH Black | 1,976,360 | 2,364,255 | 2,886,825 | 387,895 | 522,570 | 19.6 | 22.1 |
| Hispanic | 4,339,905 | 6,669,666 | 9,460,921 | 2,329,761 | 2,791,255 | 53.7 | 41.8 |
| NH Asian/Other | 378,565 | 884,586 | 1,400,470 | 506,021 | 515,884 | 133.7 | 58.3 |
| Total | 16,986,510 | 20,851,820 | 25,145,561 | 3,865,310 | 4,293,741 | 22.8 | 20.6 |

| Race/Ethnicity | Proportion of Population | | | Proportion of Net Change | |
| | 1990 | 2000 | 2010 | 1990–2000 | 2000–2010 |
|---|---|---|---|---|---|
| NH White | 60.6 | 52.4 | 45.3 | 16.6 | 10.8 |
| NH Black | 11.6 | 11.3 | 11.5 | 10.0 | 12.2 |
| Hispanic | 25.6 | 32.0 | 37.6 | 60.3 | 65.0 |
| NH Asian/Other | 2.2 | 4.2 | 5.6 | 13.1 | 12.0 |
| Total | 100.0 | 100.0 | 100.0 | 100.0 | 100.0 |

*Source*: U.S. Census Bureau 1991a, 2001a, 2011b.
*NH refers to nonHispanic; values for categories labeled NH are only for the nonHispanic persons in each race
category. Hispanic includes Hispanics of all races.

than the nation as a whole. Texas has consistently shown a median age of
2 to 4 years less than that of the nation with a median age of 33.6 years
compared to 37.2 years for the nation in 2010 (Table 2.3). This younger age
structure has significant implications for numerous state services, such as
education and youth services.

## PROJECTED POPULATION

The Texas population is projected to grow rapidly, become increasingly
diverse, and grow older. Table 2.4 shows the state's projected population
under alternative levels (assumptions about long-term patterns) of age,
sex, and race/ethnicity specific fertility, mortality, and migration (including
both international and domestic migration). Fertility, mortality, and migration are the three processes determining population change. These projections were made using a cohort-component projection model. In this model
population counts from the 2010 Census for each of 85 age groups for

Table 2.3

Median Age in the United States and Texas, 1900–2010

| Year | United States | Texas |
|------|---------------|-------|
| 1900 | 22.9 | 18.7 |
| 1910 | 24.1 | 20.2 |
| 1920 | 25.3 | 22.0 |
| 1930 | 26.5 | 23.7 |
| 1940 | 29.0 | 26.8 |
| 1950 | 30.1 | 27.9 |
| 1960 | 29.5 | 27.0 |
| 1970 | 28.1 | 26.4 |
| 1980 | 30.0 | 28.0 |
| 1990 | 32.9 | 30.8 |
| 2000 | 35.3 | 32.3 |
| 2010 | 37.2 | 33.6 |

*Source*: Carter et al. 2006; and U.S. Census Bureau 2011c.

each sex for each of the four, nonHispanic White, nonHispanic Black, and nonHispanic Asian and Other racial/ethnic groups, and Hispanics (from all races) (a total of 680 individual cohorts) for each county and the state were employed. Assumptions were made about fertility (for females ages 15–49 for each of the four racial/ethnic groups) and about mortality and migration (for all single year age, sex, and race/ethnicity specific cohorts) for all individual years 2011 though 2050. These projections were prepared in a cooperative project between the Hobby Center for the Study of Texas at Rice University and the Texas State Data Center at the University of Texas at San Antonio.

Because fertility and mortality can generally be more accurately projected than migration, these projections assume the same levels of fertility and mortality within each age (85 age groups), sex (both sexes), and racial/ethnicity (4 racial/ethnic groups) specific cohort (680 total individual cohorts for each county and the state for each year from 2011 to 2050) but use alternative scenarios based on differences in levels of age, sex, and race/ethnicity migration. The first scenario, assuming zero migration, provides a base set of values indicating what the population will be if there is no migration but only change as a result of the difference between fertility and mortality rates (the difference between the number of births and deaths, referred to as natural increase). Although the probability of this scenario characterizing future patterns of growth in Texas is low, given

Table 2.4

Population in Texas by Race/Ethnicity in 2000 and 2010 and
Projected to 2050 Assuming Alternative Projection Scenarios
of Age, Sex, and Race/Ethnicity-Specific Net Migration

| Year | NH* White | NH Black | Hispanic | NH Asian & Other | Total |
|------|-----------|----------|----------|------------------|-------|
| 2000 | 10,933,313 | 2,364,255 | 6,669,666 | 884,586 | 20,851,820 |
| 2010 | 11,397,345 | 2,886,825 | 9,460,921 | 1,400,470 | 25,145,561 |
| **Assuming Zero Net Migration (0.0 Scenario)** | | | | | |
| 2020 | 11,576,595 | 3,122,637 | 11,137,672 | 1,536,693 | 27,373,597 |
| 2030 | 11,501,020 | 3,280,941 | 12,869,753 | 1,638,249 | 29,289,963 |
| 2040 | 11,182,576 | 3,355,500 | 14,570,851 | 1,714,232 | 30,823,159 |
| 2050 | 10,766,622 | 3,366,528 | 16,191,150 | 1,728,206 | 32,052,506 |
| **Assuming Net Migration Equal to One-Half of 2000–2010 (0.5 Scenario)** | | | | | |
| 2020 | 11,752,530 | 3,295,198 | 12,031,059 | 1,825,130 | 28,903,917 |
| 2030 | 11,850,180 | 3,658,997 | 15,082,058 | 2,309,763 | 32,900,998 |
| 2040 | 11,676,157 | 3,951,909 | 18,489,803 | 2,881,525 | 36,999,394 |
| 2050 | 11,376,576 | 4,182,155 | 22,268,390 | 3,483,178 | 41,310,299 |
| **Assuming Net Migration Equal to 2000–2010 (1.0 Scenario)** | | | | | |
| 2020 | 11,931,815 | 3,477,928 | 13,003,159 | 2,170,409 | 30,583,311 |
| 2030 | 12,211,664 | 4,080,453 | 17,702,132 | 3,288,536 | 37,282,785 |
| 2040 | 12,194,151 | 4,653,725 | 23,514,974 | 4,953,861 | 45,316,711 |
| 2050 | 12,024,913 | 5,195,861 | 30,701,208 | 7,283,548 | 55,205,530 |

Source: Projections by the authors and data and rates from U.S. Census Bureau 2001b,
2011c.
*NH refers to nonHispanic; values for categories labeled NH are only for the non-
Hispanic persons in each race category. Hispanic includes Hispanics of all races.
Note: Race/ethnicity specific counts for 2000 are adjusted from previous volumes
using different allocations for two race combinations. All two race combinations are
included in the NH Asian & Other category.

the state's history of continuous inmigration, compared to the projections in the other two scenarios, it allows one to identify the amount of change due to natural increase and that due to migration. A second scenario, referred to as the 2000–2010 projection scenario (also referred to as the 1.0 scenario), assumes age, sex, and race/ethnicity specific net migration rates equal to the cohort rates from 2000–2010. It provides values that indicate what Texas' population will be if the rates for fertility, mortality, and migration of the last decennial census decade continue for the next 40 years. The scenario assuming migration rates that are one-half (the 0.5 scenario) the rates of 2000 to 2010 provides an intermediate growth scenario, one in which projections are made under the assumption that the 2000–2010 rates of age, sex and race/ethnicity specific net migration slow from those that occurred from 2000 to 2010.

The data in Table 2.4 show projections of the Texas population under alternative scenarios. Although emphasis will be placed on the 2000–2010 net migration scenario in many parts of the analysis, it is important to note that Texas population will increase even in the absence of growth through migration. With no inmigration, Texas population will increase by about 6.9 million over the period from 2010 to 2050. However, growth with continued 2000 to 2010 levels of migration (the 1.0 scenario) will exceed 30 million during the same 40-year period, with the state's population being more than 55 million by the middle of the century. Also evident in this table and those that follow (Tables 2.5–2.7) is that growth will be largely due to minority populations. Under the scenario assuming no net migration (also referred to as the 0.0 scenario), the nonHispanic White population will decline from 2010 to 2050, while under the scenarios assuming one half and a continuation of 2000–2010 patterns of age, sex, and race/ethnicity specific net migration (the 0.5 and 1.0 scenarios), this population grows in the early decades and then declines in the later decades of the projection period. Even under the high growth scenario in which the total population increases to more than 55 million people in 2050 with an increase of more than 30 million people from 2010 to 2050 (Table 2.7), only 2.1 percent of the population increase will be due to the nonHispanic White population, while 7.7 percent will be due to the nonHispanic Black population, 19.5 percent to the nonHispanic Asian and Other population, while the overwhelming majority, 70.7 percent, will be due to growth in the Hispanic population (Table 2.7).

As a result of such patterns, under the 0.5 and 1.0 scenarios (Table 2.6), Texas population will become 50 percent or more Hispanic by 2040. It will become more than 50 percent Hispanic by 2050 under the 0.0 scenario, while being 21.8 percent nonHispanic White by 2050 and as much as 13.2 percent Asian and Other (under the 1.0 scenario).

Table 2.5

Percent Change in the Population in Texas for 2000–2010 and Projected
to 2050 Using the Projections of the Population That Assume Alternative
Scenarios of Age, Sex, and Race/Ethnicity-Specific Net Migration

| Time Period | NH* White | NH Black | Hispanic | NH Asian & Other | Total |
|---|---|---|---|---|---|
| 2000–2010 | 4.2 | 22.1 | 41.8 | 58.3 | 20.6 |
| **Assuming Zero Net Migration (0.0 Scenario)** | | | | | |
| 2010–2020 | 1.6 | 8.2 | 17.7 | 9.7 | 8.9 |
| 2020–2030 | −0.7 | 5.1 | 15.6 | 6.6 | 7.0 |
| 2030–2040 | −2.8 | 2.3 | 13.2 | 4.6 | 5.2 |
| 2040–2050 | −3.7 | 0.3 | 11.1 | 0.8 | 4.0 |
| 2010–2050 | −5.5 | 16.6 | 71.1 | 23.4 | 27.5 |
| **Assuming Net Migration Equal to One-Half of 2000–2010 (0.5 Scenario)** | | | | | |
| 2010–2020 | 3.1 | 14.1 | 27.2 | 30.3 | 14.9 |
| 2020–2030 | 0.8 | 11.0 | 25.4 | 26.6 | 13.8 |
| 2030–2040 | −1.5 | 8.0 | 22.6 | 24.8 | 12.5 |
| 2040–2050 | −2.6 | 5.8 | 20.4 | 20.9 | 11.7 |
| 2010–2050 | −0.2 | 44.9 | 135.4 | 148.7 | 64.3 |
| **Assuming Net Migration Equal to 2000–2010 (1.0 Scenario)** | | | | | |
| 2010–2020 | 4.7 | 20.5 | 37.4 | 55.0 | 21.6 |
| 2020–2030 | 2.3 | 17.3 | 36.1 | 51.5 | 21.9 |
| 2030–2040 | −0.1 | 14.0 | 32.8 | 50.6 | 21.5 |
| 2040–2050 | −1.4 | 11.6 | 30.6 | 47.0 | 21.8 |
| 2010–2050 | 5.5 | 80.0 | 224.5 | 420.1 | 119.5 |

Source: Projections by the authors and data and rates from U.S. Census Bureau 2001b, 2011c.
*NH refers to nonHispanic; values for categories labeled NH are only for the non-Hispanic persons in each race category. Hispanic includes Hispanics of all races.

Table 2.6

Percent of the Population by Race/Ethnicity in Texas for 2000 and 2010
and Projected to 2050 Using the Projections of the Population That Assume
Alternative Scenarios of Age, Sex, and Race/Ethnicity-Specific Net Migration

| Year | NH* White | NH Black | Hispanic | NH Asian & Other | Total |
|------|-----------|----------|----------|------------------|-------|
| 2000 | 52.4 | 11.3 | 32.0 | 4.3 | 100.0 |
| 2010 | 45.3 | 11.5 | 37.6 | 5.6 | 100.0 |
| **Assuming Zero Net Migration (0.0 Scenario)** | | | | | |
| 2020 | 42.3 | 11.4 | 40.7 | 5.6 | 100.0 |
| 2030 | 39.3 | 11.2 | 43.9 | 5.6 | 100.0 |
| 2040 | 36.3 | 10.9 | 47.2 | 5.6 | 100.0 |
| 2050 | 33.6 | 10.5 | 50.5 | 5.4 | 100.0 |
| **Assuming Net Migration Equal to One-Half of 2000–2010 (0.5 Scenario)** | | | | | |
| 2020 | 40.7 | 11.4 | 41.6 | 6.3 | 100.0 |
| 2030 | 36.0 | 11.1 | 45.8 | 7.1 | 100.0 |
| 2040 | 31.6 | 10.7 | 50.0 | 7.7 | 100.0 |
| 2050 | 27.5 | 10.2 | 53.9 | 8.4 | 100.0 |
| **Assuming Net Migration Equal to 2000–2010 (1.0 Scenario)** | | | | | |
| 2020 | 39.0 | 11.4 | 42.5 | 7.1 | 100.0 |
| 2030 | 32.8 | 10.9 | 47.5 | 8.8 | 100.0 |
| 2040 | 26.9 | 10.3 | 51.9 | 10.9 | 100.0 |
| 2050 | 21.8 | 9.4 | 55.6 | 13.2 | 100.0 |

*Source*: Projections by the authors and U.S. Census Bureau 2001b, 2011c.
*NH refers to nonHispanic; values for categories labeled NH are only for the non-
Hispanic persons in each race category. Hispanic includes Hispanics of all races.

Such patterns are consistent with those projected for the nation. In a
recent report, the U.S. Census Bureau (2012b, 2012c) projects an absolute
decline in the nonHispanic White population of the United States from
2010 to 2060 (so that all growth will be due to minority populations) and
indicates that over 60 percent of the net growth will be due to the Hispanic
population.

The projections in Table 2.8 show that the overall age of the population

Table 2.7

Number and Percent of Net Change in the Texas Population Due to Each Race/
Ethnicity Group, Assuming Alternative Projection Scenarios, 2010–2050

| Race/Ethnicity | Number | Percent |
|---|---|---|
| **Assuming Rates of Net Migration Equal to** | | |
| **Zero Net Migration (0.0 Scenario)** | | |
| NH* White | −630,723 | −9.1 |
| NH Black | 479,703 | 6.9 |
| Hispanic | 6,730,229 | 97.4 |
| NH Asian & Other | 327,736 | 4.8 |
| Total | 6,906,945 | 100.0 |
| **Assuming Rates of Net Migration Equal to** | | |
| **One-Half of 2000–2010 (0.5 Scenario)** | | |
| NII White | −20,769 | −0.1 |
| NH Black | 1,295,330 | 8.0 |
| Hispanic | 12,807,469 | 79.2 |
| NH Asian & Other | 2,082,708 | 12.9 |
| Total | 16,164,738 | 100.0 |
| **Assuming Rates of Net Migration Equal** | | |
| **to 2000–2010 (1.0 Scenario)** | | |
| NH White | 627,568 | 2.1 |
| NH Black | 2,309,036 | 7.7 |
| Hispanic | 21,240,287 | 70.7 |
| NH Asian & Other | 5,883,078 | 19.5 |
| Total | 30,059,969 | 100.0 |

*Source*: Projections by the authors and 2010 data and rates from U.S. Census Bureau 2011c.
*NH refers to nonHispanic; values for categories labeled NH are only for the non-Hispanic persons in each race category. Hispanic includes Hispanics of all races.

will increase over time. Only 10.3 percent of the population of Texas was 65 years of age or older in 2010, but at least 16.9 percent, and perhaps 20.9 percent of the total population will be 65 years of age or older by 2050. At the same time, the percentage under 18 years of age will decrease from 27.3 percent in 2010 to between 23 and 24 percent under the alternative scenarios. The proportions in other ages remain relatively similar

Table 2.8

Percent of the Population by Age Group and Race/Ethnicity
in 2010 and Projected for 2050 Using the Projections of the
Population That Assume Alternative Scenarios of Age, Sex,
and Race/Ethnicity-Specific Net Migration for Texas

| Age | NH* White | NH Black | Hispanic | NH Asian & Other | Total |
|-----|-----------|----------|----------|------------------|-------|
| **2010** | | | | | |
| <18 | 20.4 | 28.1 | 35.1 | 29.6 | 27.3 |
| 18–24 | 8.7 | 11.2 | 11.7 | 10.2 | 10.2 |
| 25–44 | 25.7 | 29.1 | 30.1 | 32.3 | 28.2 |
| 45–64 | 29.8 | 24.0 | 17.5 | 21.4 | 24.0 |
| 65+ | 15.4 | 7.6 | 5.6 | 6.5 | 10.3 |
| **Assuming Zero Net Migration (0.0 Scenario) 2050** | | | | | |
| <18 | 18.5 | 21.2 | 28.2 | 16.7 | 23.6 |
| 18–24 | 7.6 | 8.6 | 10.0 | 6.9 | 8.9 |
| 25–44 | 23.3 | 25.7 | 25.3 | 22.0 | 24.5 |
| 45–64 | 23.6 | 25.1 | 20.3 | 24.4 | 22.1 |
| 65+ | 27.0 | 19.4 | 16.2 | 30.0 | 20.9 |
| **Assuming Net Migration Equal to One-Half 2000–2010 (0.5 Scenario) 2050** | | | | | |
| <18 | 18.3 | 20.9 | 27.8 | 19.7 | 23.8 |
| 18–24 | 7.5 | 8.8 | 10.3 | 7.9 | 9.2 |
| 25–44 | 23.2 | 25.6 | 26.5 | 26.6 | 25.5 |
| 45–64 | 23.6 | 25.3 | 20.9 | 25.2 | 22.5 |
| 65+ | 27.4 | 19.4 | 14.5 | 20.6 | 19.0 |
| **Assuming Net Migration Equal to 2000–2010 (1.0 Scenario) 2050** | | | | | |
| <18 | 18.2 | 20.7 | 27.3 | 21.9 | 24.0 |
| 18–24 | 7.4 | 8.9 | 10.6 | 8.6 | 9.4 |
| 25–44 | 23.0 | 25.5 | 27.8 | 30.5 | 26.9 |
| 45–64 | 23.7 | 25.6 | 21.4 | 24.9 | 22.8 |
| 65+ | 27.7 | 19.3 | 12.9 | 14.1 | 16.9 |

*Source*: Projections by the authors and data and rates from U.S. Census Bureau 2011c.
*NH refers to nonHispanic; values for categories labeled NH are only for the non-Hispanic persons in each race category. Hispanic includes Hispanics of all races.

across scenarios. The percentage of persons 65 years of age or older decreases as the growth in Hispanic and nonHispanic Asian and Other populations increase because of the younger age structure of these populations. Growth in minority populations generally reduces the percentage of elderly persons, and therefore the impact of the elderly population, in the coming decades.

## SUMMARY

In this chapter we have examined the past and projected future characteristics of the population in Texas. The change in the size, age, race/ethnicity, and related characteristics of the population were discussed. The key points of this chapter are as follows:

1.  Texas' population was 25,145,561 in 2010, making it the second largest state (behind California, which had a population of 37,253,956). Texas was the fastest growing state in numerical terms from 2000 to 2010, increasing its population by 4,293,741, and the fifth fastest growing in percentage terms, increasing by 20.6 percent. From April 1, 2010, to July 1, 2012 the Texas population increased by more than 900,000, making it the fastest growing state in the nation in numerical terms and the second fastest growing (after North Dakota) in percentage terms.

2.  Texas counties and cities show substantial differences in size and rates of growth. Texas has the county with the smallest population in the nation, Loving County, with 82 people in 2010, and yet the state's largest county, Harris County, had more than 4 million people in 2010. It has three of the 10 largest cities in the United States: Houston, the fourth largest in the nation with more than 2.1 million people in 2010, San Antonio, the seventh largest with 1.3 million in 2010, and Dallas, with about 1.2 million in 2010. Despite extensive growth overall, 79 of 254 counties showed population declines from 2000 to 2010 and 96 from 2010 to 2012.

3.  Texas is a state with racial/ethnic diversity. By 2010 it was one of only four states (including California, Hawaii, and New Mexico) that was less than 50.0 percent nonHispanic White, and in 2010, its population was 45.3 percent nonHispanic White, 11.5 percent nonHispanic Black, 37.6 percent Hispanic, and 5.6 percent nonHispanic Asian and Other.

4.  Texas, similar to the rest of the nation, has a population that is getting older but is younger than the nation as a whole. The median age of the population of Texas was 18.7 years of age in 1900, 27.9 in 1950, 32.3 in 2000, and 33.6 years of age in 2010. The nation's median ages for these pe-

riods were 22.9, 30.1, 35.3, and 37.2, respectively. The populations both in Texas and in the nation are expected to show continued aging in the future.

5.   Using projections of the number of births, deaths, and net migration for each of 85 age groups and both sexes for all years from 2011 to 2050 for each of the nonHispanic White, nonHispanic Black, Hispanic, and nonHispanic Asian and Other population groups, projections were made of the state's future population. Under the scenario that assumes the age, sex, and race/ethnicity specific net migration levels of the 2000 to 2010 period continue into the future (1.0 scenario), Texas is projected to have a population of 55,205,530 in 2050 (an increase of more than 30 million people, a 119.5 percent increase from 2010 to 2050). This population will be composed of 12,024,913 nonHispanic White, 5,195,861 nonHispanic Black, 30,701,208 Hispanic, and 7,283,548 nonHispanic Asian and Other persons, representing respectively 21.8, 9.4, 55.6, and 13.2 percent of the total population of Texas in 2050. Of the state's total growth between 2010 and 2050, 2.1 percent will be due to the nonHispanic White, 7.7 percent to the nonHispanic Black, 70.7 percent to the Hispanic, and 19.5 percent to the nonHispanic Asian and Other populations.

6.   Texas' population will also grow older but the extent of aging will be different in different population segments due to differences in birth, death, and migration rates. In 2010, 15.4 percent of the nonHispanic White population, 7.6 percent of the nonHispanic Black population, 5.6 percent of the Hispanic population, and 6.5 percent of the nonHispanic Asian and Other population were 65 years of age or older. By 2050 the comparable figures for these groups will be 27.7, 19.3, 12.9, and 14.1 percent, respectively.

The data in this chapter document a rapidly growing, racially/ethnically diversifying, and aging population. These are patterns that first appeared in earlier decades but are projected to continue, and in some cases to be accentuated, in the coming years. As the data in Table 1.1 indicate, if these demographic changes occur and the associated socioeconomic concomitants do not change, the implications of such changes and those projected for households may markedly impact the socioeconomic future of Texas. It is these factors that we examine in detail in the chapters that follow.

CHAPTER 3

# Recent and Projected Household Change in Texas

Texas households, like Texas' population, have shown patterns of substantial change in recent decades. In this chapter we examine both recent patterns of change and projected patterns of future change in the number of Texas households. For both periods the change in the number and characteristics of households, the change by race/ethnicity, the aging of householders (those persons in whose name a housing unit is owned or rented), and the change in household types are examined. As with the analysis of population in Chapter 2, our purpose is to establish the base, in this case the base of households, whose numbers and characteristics impact the socioeconomic characteristics and service usage rates in Texas both now and in the future.

## RECENT PATTERNS OF HOUSEHOLD CHANGE

The increase in the number of households closely follows the increase in the population. The number of households in Texas increased by 1,529,579 from 2000 to 2010 (Table 3.1), while the population increased by 4,293,741, for a 20.7 percent increase in the number of households and a 20.6 percent increase in the total population.

Similarly, the increase in the number of households by race/ethnicity of householder also generally reflects population change. However, because households are units of population and those heading them (statistically creating a household) must be 15 years of age or older, populations with higher proportions of persons 15 years of age or older tend to have larger numbers of householders per unit of population, and hence larger numbers of households, while those population groups with young age distributions tend to have lower numbers of households per unit of population.

These patterns are reflected in Table 3.2. Texas population in 2010

Table 3.1

Number and Percent Change in Households in the
United States and Texas, 1970–2010

|  | 1970 | 1980 | 1990 | 2000 | 2010 |
|---|---|---|---|---|---|
| | | | Number of Households | | |
| United States | 63,616,135 | 80,467,427 | 91,947,410 | 105,480,101 | 116,716,292 |
| Texas | 3,433,996 | 4,934,936 | 6,070,937 | 7,393,354 | 8,922,933 |

| | Percent Change in Households | | | |
|---|---|---|---|---|
| | 1970–1980 | 1980–1990 | 1990–2000 | 2000–2010 |
| United States | 26.5 | 14.3 | 14.7 | 10.7 |
| Texas | 43.7 | 23.0 | 21.8 | 20.7 |

*Source*: Carter et al. 2006; and U.S. Census Bureau 2011d.

consisted of 45.3 percent nonHispanic White, 11.5 percent nonHispanic Black, 37.6 percent Hispanic, and 5.6 percent nonHispanic Asians and Other persons, while the 8,922,933 households in Texas in 2010 were composed of 53.8 percent nonHispanic White households, 12.0 percent nonHispanic Black households, 29.3 percent Hispanic households, and 4.9 percent nonHispanic Asian and Other households.

The data in Table 3.2 also show that the growth in the number of households does reflect total population change. From 1990 to 2010, Hispanic and nonHispanic Asian and Other groups had the largest percentage increases in the number of households; 1990 to 2010 change was 16.4 percent for nonHispanic White, 58.9 percent for nonHispanic Black, 125.7 percent for Hispanic, and 286.2 percent for nonHispanic Asian and Other households. Whereas the percentage of all households with a nonHispanic White householder decreased from 68.0 percent of all households in 1990 to 53.8 percent by 2010, the percentage of households with a Black householder increased from 11.1 percent to 12.0 percent, the percentage with an Hispanic householder increased from 19.1 to 29.3 percent, and the percentage with an Asian or Other householder increased from 1.8 percent in 1990 to 4.9 percent in 2010.

Change in Texas households has reflected national patterns with the size

Table 3.2

Number and Percent of Households and Change in Households in Texas by Race/Ethnicity of Householder, 1990–2010

Households

| Year | NH* White | | NH Black | | Hispanic | | NH Asian & Other | | Total | |
|---|---|---|---|---|---|---|---|---|---|---|
| | Number | % | Number | % | Number | % | Number | % | Number | % |
| 1990 | 4,127,371 | 68.0 | 672,366 | 11.1 | 1,158,010 | 19.1 | 113,190 | 1.8 | 6,070,937 | 100.0 |
| 2000 | 4,540,078 | 61.4 | 843,712 | 11.4 | 1,789,623 | 24.2 | 219,941 | 3.0 | 7,393,354 | 100.0 |
| 2010 | 4,803,580 | 53.8 | 1,068,108 | 12.0 | 2,614,157 | 29.3 | 437,088 | 4.9 | 8,922,933 | 100.0 |

Number and Percent Change in Households

| Years | NH* White | | NH Black | | Hispanic | | NH Asian & Other | | Total | |
|---|---|---|---|---|---|---|---|---|---|---|
| | Number | % | Number | % | Number | % | Number | % | Number | % |
| 1990–2000 | 412,707 | 10.0 | 171,346 | 25.5 | 631,613 | 54.5 | 106,751 | 94.3 | 1,322,417 | 21.8 |
| 2000–2010 | 263,502 | 5.8 | 224,396 | 26.6 | 824,534 | 46.1 | 217,147 | 98.7 | 1,529,579 | 20.7 |
| 1990–2010 | 676,209 | 16.4 | 395,742 | 58.9 | 1,456,147 | 125.7 | 323,898 | 286.2 | 2,851,996 | 47.0 |

*Source:* U.S. Census Bureau 1991c, 2001c, 2011d.
*NH refers to nonHispanic; values shown are only for the nonHispanic persons in each race category. Hispanic includes Hispanics of all races.

Table 3.3

Number, Percent of, and Percent Change in Texas Households by Size and Type, 1980–2010

| Size/Type of Household | Households | | | | Percent Change in Number of Households | | |
|---|---|---|---|---|---|---|---|
| | 1980 | 1990 | 2000 | 2010 | 1980–1990 | 1990–2000 | 2000–2010 |
| Total Households (in thousands) | 4,935 | 6,071 | 7,393 | 8,923 | 23.0 | 21.8 | 20.7 |
| Households by Size | | | | | | | |
| One-person | 21.6 | 23.9 | 23.7 | 24.2 | 36.1 | 20.8 | 23.5 |
| Two-person | 30.8 | 30.1 | 30.5 | 30.3 | 20.2 | 23.4 | 19.9 |
| Three-person | 17.5 | 17.3 | 17.1 | 16.6 | 21.6 | 20.4 | 17.2 |
| Four-person | 15.6 | 15.7 | 15.3 | 14.7 | 23.8 | 18.7 | 16.1 |
| Five-person | 8.0 | 7.5 | 7.8 | 8.0 | 15.3 | 26.7 | 24.2 |
| Six or more person | 6.5 | 5.5 | 5.6 | 6.1 | 4.1 | 24.0 | 31.5 |
| Households by Type | | | | | | | |
| Family | 74.6 | 71.6 | 71.0 | 69.9 | 18.1 | 20.8 | 18.8 |
| Married Couple Family | 62.6 | 56.6 | 54.0 | 50.6 | 11.2 | 16.2 | 13.1 |
| Male Householder | 2.5 | 3.4 | 4.3 | 5.2 | 67.3 | 54.0 | 47.0 |
| Female Householder | 9.5 | 11.6 | 12.7 | 14.1 | 50.2 | 33.3 | 33.6 |
| Nonfamily | 25.4 | 28.4 | 29.0 | 30.1 | 37.5 | 24.4 | 25.3 |

*Source*: U.S. Census Bureau 1991c, 2001c, 2011d.

of households generally decreasing and the percentage of family households (consisting of two or more people related by kinship, marriage, or adoption) decreasing as a proportion of all households. For the nation, the percentage of family households decreased from 68.1 percent in 2000 to 66.4 percent in 2010. The change in Texas households was a decrease from 71 percent family households in 2000 to 69.9 percent in 2010 (Table 3.3). Similarly, when data for different types of family households are examined, 50.6 percent of all family households in Texas consisted of married couple households in 2010, while 48.4 percent were such households nationally. Although Texas patterns are somewhat different from those for the nation, the trends in these patterns in Texas are similar to those in the nation. The data on household size in Table 3.3 also show Texas having larger percentages of one person households over time and decreasing percentages of two, three, or more person households. This trend follows the national pattern.

　　Household change in Texas shows a rapidly increasing number and proportion of minority households. Data from Texas, as well as for the nation, display patterns of change toward smaller and more diverse household forms.

## PROJECTIONS OF HOUSEHOLDS AND HOUSEHOLD CHARACTERISTICS

Tables 3.4 through 3.8 provide projections of the total number of households in Texas by age and race/ethnicity of householder in 2010 and projected through 2050. Due to space limitations, data are presented only for the scenario assuming one-half of 2000–2010 rates of net migration and that assuming 2000–2010 rates of net migration.

Table 3.4

Number of Households in Texas by Race/Ethnicity in 2010 and Projected to 2050 Using the Projections That Assume Alternative Scenarios of Age, Sex, and Race/Ethnicity-Specific Net Migration for Texas

| Year | NH* White | NH Black | Hispanic | NH Asian & Other | Total |
|------|-----------|----------|----------|--------|-------|
| 2010 | 4,803,580 | 1,068,108 | 2,614,157 | 437,088 | 8,922,933 |

**Assuming Rates of Net Migration Equal to One-Half of 2000–2010 (0.5 Scenario)**

| Year | NH* White | NH Black | Hispanic | NH Asian & Other | Total |
|------|-----------|----------|----------|--------|-------|
| 2020 | 5,046,309 | 1,260,767 | 3,511,692 | 613,500 | 10,432,268 |
| 2030 | 5,205,251 | 1,437,627 | 4,521,072 | 822,651 | 11,986,601 |
| 2040 | 5,251,394 | 1,591,672 | 5,683,255 | 1,035,677 | 13,561,998 |
| 2050 | 5,196,147 | 1,717,042 | 7,025,821 | 1,280,378 | 15,219,388 |

**Assuming Rates of Net Migration Equal to 2000–2010 (1.0 Scenario)**

| Year | NH* White | NH Black | Hispanic | NH Asian & Other | Total |
|------|-----------|----------|----------|--------|-------|
| 2020 | 5,151,937 | 1,338,099 | 3,837,880 | 724,367 | 11,052,283 |
| 2030 | 5,425,724 | 1,616,386 | 5,363,033 | 1,163,454 | 13,568,597 |
| 2040 | 5,575,149 | 1,894,395 | 7,336,093 | 1,768,575 | 16,574,212 |
| 2050 | 5,605,710 | 2,163,639 | 9,880,494 | 2,655,253 | 20,305,096 |

*Source*: Projections by the authors and 2010 data and rates derived from U.S. Census Bureau 2011d.
*NH refers to nonHispanic; values for categories labeled NH are only for the non-Hispanic persons in each race category. Hispanic includes Hispanics of all races.

*Racial/Ethnic Diversity and Increasing Elderly*
The data in Tables 3.4 through 3.8 show that the number of households is
projected to increase substantially and households will become increasingly
diverse and older. The data in Table 3.4 show that under the scenario assuming 2000–2010 rates of net migration the total number of households
will increase from 8.9 million in 2010 to 20.3 million in 2050, an increase of
11.5 million households or 127.6 percent (see Tables 3.4 and 3.5). Minority
household growth will be particularly extensive under the scenario assuming 2000–2010 rates of net migration. The number of nonHispanic White
households will increase by 802,130 or 16.7 percent from 2010 to 2050,
but nonHispanic Black households will increase by nearly 1.1 million or

Table 3.5

Percent Change in the Number of Households in Texas in 2010 and
Projected to 2050 Using the Projections That Assume Alternative Scenarios
of Age, Sex, and Race/Ethnicity-Specific Net Migration for Texas

| Time Period | NH*<br>White | NH<br>Black | Hispanic | NH<br>Asian &<br>Other | Total |
|---|---|---|---|---|---|
| | **Assuming Rates of Net Migration Equal to<br>One-Half of 2000–2010 (0.5 Scenario)** | | | | |
| 2010–2020 | 5.1 | 18.0 | 34.3 | 40.4 | 16.9 |
| 2020–2030 | 3.1 | 14.0 | 28.7 | 34.1 | 14.9 |
| 2030–2040 | 0.9 | 10.7 | 25.7 | 25.9 | 13.1 |
| 2040–2050 | −1.1 | 7.9 | 23.6 | 23.6 | 12.2 |
| 2010–2050 | 8.2 | 60.8 | 168.8 | 192.9 | 70.6 |
| | **Assuming Rates of Net Migration Equal<br>to 2000–2010 (1.0 Scenario)** | | | | |
| 2010–2020 | 7.3 | 25.3 | 46.8 | 65.7 | 23.9 |
| 2020–2030 | 5.3 | 20.8 | 39.7 | 60.6 | 22.8 |
| 2030–2040 | 2.8 | 17.2 | 36.8 | 52.0 | 22.2 |
| 2040–2050 | 0.5 | 14.2 | 34.7 | 50.1 | 22.5 |
| 2010–2050 | 16.7 | 102.6 | 278.0 | 507.5 | 127.6 |

*Source*: Projections by the authors and 2010 data and rates derived from U.S. Census
Bureau 2011d.
*NH refers to nonHispanic; values for categories labeled NH are only for the non-
Hispanic persons in each race category. Hispanic includes Hispanics of all races.

Table 3.6

Percent of Households in Texas by Race/Ethnicity of Householder in 2010
and Projected to 2050 Using the Projections That Assume Alternative
Scenarios of Age, Sex, and Race/Ethnicity-Specific Net Migration for Texas

| Year | NH* White | NH Black | Hispanic | NH Asian & Other |
|------|-----------|----------|----------|------------------|
| 2010 | 53.8 | 12.0 | 29.3 | 4.9 |
| **Assuming Rates of Net Migration Equal to One-Half of 2000–2010 (0.5 Scenario)** | | | | |
| 2020 | 48.4 | 12.1 | 33.7 | 5.8 |
| 2030 | 43.4 | 12.0 | 37.7 | 6.9 |
| 2040 | 38.7 | 11.7 | 41.9 | 7.5 |
| 2050 | 34.1 | 11.3 | 46.2 | 8.4 |
| **Assuming Rates of Net Migration Equal to 2000–2010 (1.0 Scenario)** | | | | |
| 2020 | 46.6 | 12.1 | 34.7 | 6.6 |
| 2030 | 40.0 | 11.9 | 39.5 | 8.6 |
| 2040 | 33.6 | 11.4 | 44.3 | 10.7 |
| 2050 | 27.6 | 10.7 | 48.7 | 13.0 |

*Source*: Projections by the authors and 2010 data and rates derived from U.S. Census Bureau 2011d.
*NH refers to nonHispanic; values for categories labeled NH are only for the non Hispanic persons in each race category. Hispanic includes Hispanics of all races.

102.6 percent, Hispanic households will increase by nearly 7.3 million or 278.0 percent, and nonHispanic Asian and Other households will increase by 2.2 million or 507.5 percent (see Tables 3.4 and 3.5).

As a result of such patterns the racial/ethnic compositions of households will change substantially (see Table 3.6). Whereas 53.8 percent of all households in 2010 had a nonHispanic White householder and 12.0 percent had a nonHispanic Black householder, 29.3 percent had an Hispanic householder and 4.9 percent a householder who was nonHispanic Asian or from an Other racial/ethnic group; by 2050 under the scenario assuming 2000–2010 rates of net migration, only 27.6 percent of households will have a nonHispanic White householder and 10.7 percent a nonHispanic

Black householder, while the percentage of all households with an Hispanic householder will increase to 48.7 percent and the percentage with a householder who is Asian or from some Other racial/ethnic group will increase to 13.0 percent. By 2050, 72.4 percent of all households in Texas will have a minority population householder. In fact, as shown in Table 3.7, 93.0 percent of the net increase in the number of households will result from the growth in the number of minority households.

Households in Texas will also become older (see Table 3.8). Although the median age of householders in 2010 was 48.0 years, under the scenario assuming 2000–2010 rates of net migration, the median age will increase to 51.3 years by 2050. The percentage of households with a householder who was 65 years of age or older of age will increase substantially from 18.3 percent in 2010 to 27.6 percent (under the scenario assuming 2000–2010 rates

Table 3.7

Number and Percent of Net Change in Texas Households Due to Each Race/ Ethnicity Group, Using the Projections That Assume Alternative Scenarios of Age, Sex, and Race/Ethnicity-Specific Net Migration for Texas, 2010–2050

| Race/Ethnicity | Number | Percent |
|---|---|---|
| **Assuming Rates of Net Migration Equal to One-Half of 2000–2010 (0.5 Scenario)** | | |
| NH* White | 392,567 | 6.2 |
| NH Black | 648,934 | 10.3 |
| Hispanic | 4,411,664 | 70.1 |
| NH Asian & Other | 843,290 | 13.4 |
| Total | 6,296,455 | 100.0 |
| **Assuming Rates of Net Migration Equal to 2000–2010 (1.0 Scenario)** | | |
| NH White | 802,130 | 7.0 |
| NH Black | 1,095,531 | 9.6 |
| Hispanic | 7,266,337 | 63.8 |
| NH Asian & Other | 2,218,165 | 19.6 |
| Total | 11,382,163 | 100.0 |

*Source*: Projections by the authors and 2010 data and rates derived from U.S. Census Bureau 2011d.
*NH refers to nonHispanic; values for categories labeled NH are only for the non-Hispanic persons in each race category. Hispanic includes Hispanics of all races.

Table 3.8

Percent of Households in Texas by Age and Race/Ethnicity of the Householder
and Median Age of Householders by Race/Ethnicity in 2010 and Projected
for 2020 and 2050 Using the Projection Scenario That Assumes 2000–2010
Age, Sex, and Race/Ethnicity-Specific Net Migration for Texas

| Age Group | NH* White | NH Black | Hispanic | NH Asian & Other | Total |
|---|---|---|---|---|---|
| **2010** | | | | | |
| 15 to 24 years | 4.9 | 6.3 | 6.9 | 6.3 | 5.7 |
| 25 to 44 years | 30.9 | 40.9 | 47.8 | 47.7 | 37.9 |
| 45 to 64 years | 40.5 | 38.9 | 33.7 | 36.2 | 38.1 |
| 65 years and over | 23.7 | 13.9 | 11.6 | 9.8 | 18.3 |
| Median Age | 51.7 | 46.2 | 43.1 | 43.1 | 48.0 |
| **2020** | | | | | |
| 15 to 24 years | 4.3 | 5.6 | 6.6 | 6.4 | 5.4 |
| 25 to 44 years | 28.5 | 37.1 | 43.8 | 44.0 | 35.9 |
| 45 to 64 years | 36.4 | 38.4 | 35.2 | 36.4 | 36.2 |
| 65 years and over | 30.8 | 18.9 | 14.4 | 13.2 | 22.5 |
| Median Age | 55.6 | 48.8 | 44.8 | 44.9 | 49.8 |
| **2050** | | | | | |
| 15 to 24 years | 3.7 | 4.3 | 5.1 | 4.7 | 4.6 |
| 25 to 44 years | 25.5 | 30.9 | 37.5 | 39.9 | 33.8 |
| 45 to 64 years | 30.4 | 35.1 | 35.0 | 36.8 | 34.0 |
| 65 years and over | 40.4 | 29.7 | 22.4 | 18.6 | 27.6 |
| Median Age | 59.4 | 53.4 | 48.7 | 47.2 | 51.3 |

*Source*: Projections by the authors and 2010 data and rates derived from U.S. Census
Bureau 2011d.
*NH refers to nonHispanic; values shown are only for the nonHispanic persons in
each race category. Hispanic includes Hispanics of all races.

of net migration) by 2050. On the other hand, the percentage of younger
households will decline. The percentage of households with a householder
under 25 years of age will decrease from 5.7 percent in 2010 to 4.6 percent by 2050. Similarly the percent in the 25–44 age group will decline
from 37.9 percent in 2010 to 33.8 percent by 2050 and the number in the

45–64 age group will decline from 38.1 percent in 2010 to 34.0 percent by 2050.

These data also show that there will be substantial differences in the age structure of the different racial/ethnic groups, with nonHispanic White households having the oldest age structure. For example, 40.4 percent of all nonHispanic White householders, but 29.7 percent of nonHispanic Black householders, 22.4 percent of Hispanic householders, and 18.6 percent of householders from Asian and Other groups will be 65 years of age or older by 2050. Of householders in the key working ages of 25 to 44, 25.5 percent will be nonHispanic White, while 30.9 percent will be nonHispanic Black, 37.5 percent will be Hispanic, and 39.9 percent will be nonHispanic Asian and Other by 2050. Such data make it clear that the working age population in Texas will increasingly be from minority households.

### Growing Diversity in Household Forms

Another implication of the change in Texas households can be seen when alternative household types are examined. The data in Table 3.9 show the change that will occur in the forms of households from 2010 to 2050 if the 2010 rates of different types of households within each of the racial/ethnic groups prevail in 2050.

The data in the first panel of Table 3.9 for 2010 show that rates of family household formation are highest for Hispanic households (79.5 percent) followed by nonHispanic Asian and Other (72.1 percent), nonHispanic White (65.5 percent), and nonHispanic Black (64.9 percent) households. Within family households there is substantial variation, with the percentage of family households that consist of married-couple families being highest for nonHispanic Asian and Other (57.5 percent) and for Hispanic (53.2) households, followed by nonHispanic White (52.8 percent), and nonHispanic Black (31.2 percent) households. The percentage of nonfamily households is highest for nonHispanic Black (35.1 percent), followed by nonHispanic White (34.5 percent), nonHispanic Asian and Other (27.9 percent), and Hispanic (20.5 percent) households.

When the numbers of households by race/ethnicity (in the second panel of Table 3.9, showing data for 2050) are compared to those in the first panel, the data show that current demographic trends will lead to further changes in household composition by 2050. Households will clearly reflect change in the population. In 2010, 53.8 percent of all households had a nonHispanic White householder, 12.0 percent had a nonHispanic Black householder, 29.3 percent had an Hispanic householder, and 4.9 percent had a nonHispanic Asian and Other householder. These 2010 rates when applied to the projected number of households show 27.6 percent non-Hispanic White, 10.6 percent nonHispanic Black, 48.7 percent Hispanic, and 13.1 percent nonHispanic Asian and Others households in 2050. As a

Table 3.9

Number and Percent of Households in Texas by Type of Household and Race/Ethnicity of Householder in 2010 and Projections for 2050 Assuming 2000–2010 Rates of Age, Sex, and Race/Ethnicity Specific Net Migration

| Family Type | NH* White | | NH Black | | Hispanic | | NH Asian & Other | | Total | |
|---|---|---|---|---|---|---|---|---|---|---|
| | Number | % | Number | % | Number | % | Number | % | Number | % |
| **2010** | | | | | | | | | | |
| Family households | 3,149,737 | 65.5 | 693,216 | 64.9 | 2,079,254 | 79.5 | 314,941 | 72.1 | 6,237,148 | 69.9 |
| Married couple family | 2,538,801 | 52.8 | 333,487 | 31.2 | 1,391,404 | 53.2 | 251,321 | 57.5 | 4,515,013 | 50.6 |
| With own children | 960,886 | 20.0 | 156,242 | 14.6 | 856,910 | 32.8 | 141,460 | 32.4 | 2,115,498 | 23.7 |
| No own children | 1,577,915 | 32.8 | 177,245 | 16.6 | 534,494 | 20.4 | 109,861 | 25.1 | 2,399,515 | 26.9 |
| Other family | 610,936 | 12.7 | 359,729 | 33.7 | 687,850 | 26.3 | 63,620 | 14.6 | 1,722,135 | 19.3 |
| Male householder, spouse absent | 177,289 | 3.7 | 62,350 | 5.9 | 207,728 | 7.9 | 20,064 | 4.6 | 467,431 | 5.2 |
| With own children | 85,648 | 1.8 | 29,617 | 2.8 | 102,175 | 3.9 | 7,364 | 1.7 | 224,804 | 2.5 |
| No own children | 91,641 | 1.9 | 32,733 | 3.1 | 105,553 | 4.0 | 12,700 | 2.9 | 242,627 | 2.7 |
| Female householder, spouse absent | 433,647 | 9.0 | 297,379 | 27.8 | 480,122 | 18.4 | 43,556 | 10.0 | 1,254,704 | 14.1 |
| With own children | 222,145 | 4.6 | 172,510 | 16.1 | 297,692 | 11.4 | 23,411 | 5.4 | 715,758 | 8.1 |
| No own children | 211,502 | 4.4 | 124,869 | 11.7 | 182,430 | 7.0 | 20,145 | 4.6 | 538,946 | 6.0 |
| Nonfamily households | 1,653,843 | 34.5 | 374,892 | 35.1 | 534,903 | 20.5 | 122,147 | 27.9 | 2,685,785 | 30.1 |
| 1-person | 1,348,369 | 28.1 | 321,315 | 30.1 | 401,358 | 15.4 | 92,224 | 21.1 | 2,163,266 | 24.2 |
| 2 or more persons | 305,474 | 6.4 | 53,577 | 5.0 | 133,545 | 5.1 | 29,923 | 6.8 | 522,519 | 5.9 |
| Total Households | 4,803,580 | 100.0 | 1,068,108 | 100.0 | 2,614,157 | 100.0 | 437,088 | 100.0 | 8,922,933 | 100.0 |

Table 3.9, continued

| Family Type | NH* White | | NH Black | | Hispanic | | NH Asian & Other | | Total | |
|---|---|---|---|---|---|---|---|---|---|---|
| | Number | % | Number | % | Number | % | Number | % | Number | % |
| **2050** | | | | | | | | | | |
| Family households | 3,548,326 | 63.2 | 1,372,042 | 63.4 | 7,726,653 | 78.3 | 1,934,473 | 72.9 | 14,581,494 | 71.8 |
| Married couple family | 2,879,631 | 51.3 | 676,743 | 31.3 | 5,196,780 | 52.6 | 1,555,570 | 58.6 | 10,308,724 | 50.8 |
| With own children | 1,089,884 | 19.4 | 317,061 | 14.7 | 3,200,489 | 32.4 | 875,577 | 33.0 | 5,483,011 | 27.0 |
| No own children | 1,789,747 | 31.9 | 359,682 | 16.6 | 1,996,291 | 20.2 | 679,993 | 25.6 | 4,825,713 | 23.8 |
| Other family | 668,695 | 11.9 | 695,299 | 32.1 | 2,529,873 | 25.7 | 378,903 | 14.3 | 4,272,770 | 21.0 |
| Male householder, spouse absent | 185,594 | 3.3 | 120,126 | 5.5 | 735,693 | 7.5 | 115,685 | 4.4 | 1,157,098 | 5.7 |
| With own children | 89,660 | 1.6 | 57,061 | 2.6 | 361,865 | 3.7 | 42,459 | 1.6 | 551,045 | 2.7 |
| No own children | 95,934 | 1.7 | 63,065 | 2.9 | 373,828 | 3.8 | 73,226 | 2.8 | 606,053 | 3.0 |
| Female householder, spouse absent | 483,101 | 8.6 | 575,173 | 26.6 | 1,794,180 | 18.2 | 263,218 | 9.9 | 3,115,672 | 15.3 |
| With own children | 247,479 | 4.4 | 333,659 | 15.4 | 1,112,453 | 11.3 | 141,478 | 5.3 | 1,835,069 | 9.0 |
| No own children | 235,622 | 4.2 | 241,514 | 11.2 | 681,727 | 6.9 | 121,740 | 4.6 | 1,280,603 | 6.3 |
| Nonfamily households | 2,057,384 | 36.8 | 791,597 | 36.6 | 2,153,841 | 21.7 | 720,780 | 27.1 | 5,723,602 | 28.2 |
| 1-Person | 1,744,525 | 31.2 | 697,107 | 32.2 | 1,702,265 | 17.1 | 570,464 | 21.4 | 4,714,361 | 23.2 |
| 2 or more Person | 312,859 | 5.6 | 94,490 | 4.4 | 451,576 | 4.6 | 150,316 | 5.7 | 1,009,241 | 5.0 |
| Total Households | 5,605,710 | 100.0 | 2,163,639 | 100.0 | 9,880,494 | 100.0 | 2,655,253 | 100.0 | 20,305,096 | 100.0 |

*Source:* Derived by applying age, sex and race/ethnicity-specific householder rates from 2011d to author derived projections of the population. *NH refers to nonHispanic; values shown are only for the nonHispanic persons in each race category. Hispanic includes Hispanics of all races

result of such changes and the differences in household types among racial/
ethnic groups, the percentage of family households will increase overall
from 69.9 percent in 2010 to 71.8 percent in 2050, with a corresponding decrease in nonfamily households from 30.1 percent in 2010 to 28.2 in 2050.
This shift is largely due to the racial/ethnic composition of households,
however, rather than revealing a change in the propensity for different
household types. Whereas there was an increase in the overall percentage
of family households and a decrease in the percentage of nonfamily households, the percentage of family households decreased among all racial/eth-
nic groups and the percentage of nonfamily households increased across
all racial/ethnic groups. The overall increase in the percentage of family
households is a result of the large percentage of the total increase that is
due to Hispanic and nonHispanic Asian and Other households, which have
higher rates of family to nonfamily households. Changes in factors such
as the racial/ethnic composition of the population have implications for a
variety of factors, including the prevalence of different household types.

As a final factor impacting future households, we examine how the types
of households are likely to change due to changing racial/ethnic composition. This is simulated by multiplying the percentage of households by type
as projected using race/ethnicity specific household type values for 2010 by
the 2050 projected numbers of households by race/ethnicity and comparing them to the 2050 values assuming that the total number of projected
households for 2050 are distributed by household type according to the
rates by type for nonHispanic Whites in 2010. The results of this simulation
are shown in Table 3.10.

The first column of numbers in Table 3.10 shows changes projected to
occur in 2050 given the actual projected households by race/ethnicity in
2050 and the 2010 distributions of household types within each racial/eth-
nic group. Those in the second column indicate the distribution assuming
that the nonHispanic White rates in 2010 applied to all racial/ethnic groups
in 2050. The total number of households in each of the columns equals the
total number projected for 2050 but they are differentially distributed. In
column one they are distributed on the basis of the actual race/ethnicity
composition expected in 2050. In column two they are distributed as if the
distribution of households by type for nonHispanic Whites in 2010 applied
to all race/ethnicity groups in 2050. A comparison of these two columns of
values indicates how the state's more diverse base of households is likely to
impact the relative types of future households in Texas.

As is evident in the difference between the columns shown in Table 3.10,
the diversification of the population will increase the number of family
households by 1,911,654 and decrease the number of nonfamily households by an identical amount. Within these types, the number of married-
couple households will increase by more than 295,000 and the number of

Table 3.10

Total Number of Households by Type in 2050 Under the Projection Scenario That
Assumes 2000–2010 Rates of Net Migration and Alternatively Assumes That the NH*
White Rates of Households by Household Type Apply to All Race/Ethnicity Groups

| Household Type | Assuming Race/ Ethnicity Specific Rates for 2010 Apply in 2050 | Assuming NH* White Rates for 2010 Apply to All Race/Ethnicity Groups in 2050 | Difference between Projections |
|---|---|---|---|
| Family households | 14,581,494 | 12,669,840 | 1,911,654 |
| Married couple family | 10,308,724 | 10,013,384 | 295,340 |
| With own children | 5,483,011 | 3,789,867 | 1,693,144 |
| No own children | 4,825,713 | 6,223,517 | −1,397,804 |
| Other family | 4,272,770 | 2,656,456 | 1,616,314 |
| Male householder, no spouse | 1,157,098 | 756,353 | 400,745 |
| With own children | 551,045 | 365,393 | 185,652 |
| No own children | 606,053 | 390,960 | 215,093 |
| Female householder, no spouse | 3,115,672 | 1,900,103 | 1,215,569 |
| With own children | 1,835,069 | 973,369 | 861,700 |
| No own children | 1,280,603 | 926,734 | 353,869 |
| Nonfamily households | 5,723,602 | 7,635,256 | −1,911,654 |
| Total Households | 20,305,096 | 20,305,096 | — |

*Source*: Projections by the authors and 2010 data and rates derived from U.S. Census Bureau
2011d.
*NH refers to nonHispanic; values shown are only for the nonHispanic persons in each race
category. Hispanic includes Hispanics of all races.

female-headed households will increase by more than 1.2 million due to
the changing underlying demographics (assuming that rates of households
by type within racial and ethnic groups do not change between 2010 and
2050). The number of "other" families will increase, as will married couple
households; within "other" family types, the number with own children
(adding those for male and female householders) will increase by more
than 1.0 million.

   The results in Table 3.10 suggest that future household composition will
lead both to growth in family households and to a growth in single parent
family households. The complexity of Texas households will continue and
perhaps increase in the coming decades.

## SUMMARY

This chapter has provided a description of recent and projected future patterns of household change in Texas. The data in this chapter indicate that:

1. The number of Texas households increased by 80.8 percent between 1980 and 2010, from 4,934,936 in 1980 to 8,922,933 in 2010. The rate of household growth in Texas has exceeded that in the United States as a whole in every decade since 1980.

2. Household size varies among racial/ethnic groups, with nonHispanic Black and Hispanic households having larger average sizes. Texas households were 53.8 percent nonHispanic White, 12.0 percent nonHispanic Black, 29.3 percent Hispanic, and 4.9 percent Asian and Other in 2010, while the population was 45.3, 11.5, 37.6, and 5.6 percent, respectively.

3. Household forms have become more diverse. Whereas 74.6 percent of all Texas households were family households and 25.4 percent were nonfamily in 1980, 69.9 percent were family and 30.1 percent nonfamily households by 2010. The percentage of married-couple households declined from 62.6 to 50.6 percent and single parent households increased from 12.0 to 19.3 percent of all households from 1980 to 2010.

4. Projections of the number of future Texas households indicate that households will increase substantially from 8.9 million in 2010 to 20.3 million in 2050, an increase of 127.6 percent (under the scenario assuming 2000–2010 rates of net migration). The increase will be largest for minority populations, with the number of nonHispanic White households increasing by 802,130 and accounting for 7.0 percent of the net growth from 2010 to 2050, while 1,095,531 or 9.6 percent of the growth will be due to nonHispanic Black households, 7,266,337 or 63.8 percent due to Hispanic households, and 2,218,165 or 19.6 percent due to nonHispanic Asian and Other households. NonHispanic White households will be 27.6 percent of all households, nonHispanic Black will be 10.7 percent, Hispanic will be 48.7 percent or nearly one-half of all households, and nonHispanic Asian and Others will be 13.0 percent of all households in 2050, compared to 53.8, 12.0, 29.3, and 4.9 percent in 2010.

5. Texas householders will also become older. Although 18.3 percent of all households in 2010 had a householder who was 65 years of age or older, in 2050, 27.6 percent of householders will be 65 years of age or older. This will vary by race/ethnicity with 40.4 percent of nonHispanic White, 29.7 percent of nonHispanic Black, 22.4 percent of Hispanic, and 18.6 percent of nonHispanic Asian and Other having a householder who is 65 years of age or older in 2050.

6. The diversification of the racial/ethnic backgrounds of householders is, in the absence of other factors, likely to lead to increases in

the percentage of family households (increasing from 69.9 percent in 2010 to 71.8 percent in 2050) and households with children (increasing from 34.3 percent in 2010 to 38.7 percent in 2050). These changes are largely among the groups that have access to the fewest socioeconomic resources. They represent changes in family types that will substantially change the trends of the past few decades. Texas households will become more traditional in form, with an increased number of family households.

Overall, the data in this chapter demonstrate that the number and the types of Texas households, like the population, will change substantially in the coming years. These households will become increasingly diverse racially and ethnically, will become older, and will display an array of forms substantially different than those that have characterized the state in the past. As with the changing population, these changing households will present challenges for Texas as it manages its future.

CHAPTER 4

# Effects of Demographic Change on the Size, Race/ Ethnicity, and Socioeconomic Characteristics of the Texas Labor Force

Among the most critical elements shaping the future of Texas are the characteristics of its labor force. In this chapter we examine recent trends in the growth of the Texas labor force and the implications of the state's changing demographics for the size and characteristics of the future labor force, including implications for the occupation of workers, their educational levels, and their wages and salaries. By so doing, we examine both the opportunities and challenges presented by the future characteristics of Texas' labor force.

### RECENT TRENDS IN LABOR FORCE CHARACTERISTICS

As shown in Table 4.1, the Texas labor force increased by 50.1 percent from 1990 to 2010 compared to an increase of 27.1 percent for the nation. This reflects the 48.0 percent growth of the state's population over the same time period and the 24.1 percent rate of growth in the population of the United States. The data in Table 4.2 show that the industries and occupations of workforce members are similar for the nation and Texas. The most notable differences in the distributions of employment by occupation and industry are in terms of the larger employment of Texas workers in natural resources (e.g., gas and oil, etc.), construction, and maintenance related occupations and in the agricultural, forestry, fishing and hunting, and mining (which includes many activities related to gas and oil exploration and development),

Table 4.1

Civilian Labor Force in the United States and Texas, 1990–2010

| Civilian Labor Force | 1990 | 2000 | 2010 | Percent Change | | |
|---|---|---|---|---|---|---|
| | | | | 1990–2000 | 2000–2010 | 1990–2010 |
| United States | 123,478,450 | 137,668,798 | 156,968,894 | 11.5 | 14.0 | 27.1 |
| Texas | 8,219,028 | 9,830,559 | 12,338,033 | 19.6 | 25.5 | 50.1 |

*Source*: U.S. Census Bureau 1992, 2002, 2011c, 2011e.

construction, and transportation industries. In sum, employment growth in the state has been extensive and concentrated in many of the energy and related industries commonly associated with Texas.

## CURRENT AND PROJECTED FUTURE PATTERNS OF CHANGE IN THE LABOR FORCE

In this section, we examine the future labor force in Texas. Projections of the labor force were made by assuming that 2010 age, sex, and race/ethnicity specific rates of labor force participation will apply in 2050. These rates were multiplied by the number of persons 16 years of age and older by sex and race/ethnicity in years from 2010 to 2050 to obtain the projections discussed below.

Tables 4.3 through 4.7 present data on the demographic characteristics of the Texas workforce in 2010 and projected characteristics through 2050. Table 4.3 shows that the workforce consisted of 5,993,750 nonHispanic White workers, 1,388,071 nonHispanic Black workers, 4,280,954 Hispanic workers, and 675,258 nonHispanic Asian and Other workers, representing 48.6, 11.3, 34.7, and 5.4 percent, respectively (see Table 4.5), of the total workforce of 12,338,033 in 2010.

Under the scenario assuming that 2000 to 2010 rates of net migration continue, the total labor force will increase to 26,115,127 in 2050 (by 111.7 percent), while the nonHispanic White labor force will decrease to 5,650,708 workers, a decline of 5.7 percent (see Tables 4.3 and 4.4). The nonHispanic Black labor force will increase to 2,390,368 workers (an increase of 72.2 percent from 2010), the number of Hispanic workers will increase to 14,414,381 (an increase of 236.7 percent), and the number of Asian and Other workers will increase to 3,659,670 (an increase of 442.0 percent). In 2050, under this scenario, 21.6 percent of all workers

Table 4.2

Percent of Employed Persons 16 Years of Age or Older in the United States and Texas in 2010 by Occupation and Industry of Employment

| Occupation/Industry | Percent | | Percent Difference |
|---|---|---|---|
| | United States | Texas | |
| **Occupation** | | | |
| Civilian employed population 16 years and over | 139,033,928 | 11,271,851 | — |
| Management, business, science, & arts | 35.9 | 34.3 | −1.6 |
| Service | 18.0 | 17.8 | −0.2 |
| Sales & office | 25.0 | 25.1 | 0.1 |
| Natural resources, construction, & maintenance | 9.1 | 11.2 | 2.1 |
| Production, transportation, and material moving | 11.9 | 11.7 | −0.2 |
| **Industry** | | | |
| Civilian employed population 16 years and over | 139,033,928 | 11,271,851 | — |
| Ag., forestry, fishing & hunting, & mining | 1.9 | 2.9 | 1.0 |
| Construction | 6.2 | 8.0 | 1.8 |
| Manufacturing | 10.4 | 9.3 | −1.1 |
| Wholesale trade | 2.8 | 2.9 | 0.1 |
| Retail trade | 11.7 | 11.5 | −0.2 |
| Transportation & warehousing, & utilities | 4.9 | 5.5 | 0.6 |
| Information | 2.2 | 1.9 | −0.3 |
| Finance & ins., & real estate & rental/ leasing | 6.7 | 6.6 | −0.1 |
| Professional, scientific, & management, & administrative & waste management services | 10.6 | 10.8 | 0.2 |
| Educational services & health care & social assist. | 23.2 | 21.8 | −1.4 |
| Arts, entertainment, & recreation, & accommodation & food services | 9.2 | 8.6 | −0.6 |
| Other services (except public administration) | 5.0 | 5.3 | 0.3 |
| Public administration | 5.2 | 4.8 | −0.4 |

*Source*: U.S. Census Bureau 2011e.

Table 4.3

Civilian Labor Force in Texas by Race/Ethnicity in 2010 and
Projected to 2050 Assuming Alternative Projection Scenarios
of Age, Sex, and Race/Ethnicity-Specific Net Migration

| Year | NH* White | NH Black | Hispanic | NH Asian & Other | Total |
|------|-----------|----------|----------|------------------|-------|
| 2010 | 5,993,750 | 1,388,071 | 4,280,954 | 675,258 | 12,338,033 |
| **Assuming Rates of Net Migration Equal to One-Half of 2000–2010 (0.5 Scenario)** | | | | | |
| 2020 | 5,827,798 | 1,563,078 | 5,558,283 | 895,420 | 13,844,579 |
| 2030 | 5,588,030 | 1,689,749 | 6,918,690 | 1,165,339 | 15,361,808 |
| 2040 | 5,511,007 | 1,815,800 | 8,372,348 | 1,412,932 | 17,112,087 |
| 2050 | 5,352,597 | 1,915,049 | 10,083,203 | 1,673,661 | 19,024,510 |
| **Assuming Rates of Net Migration Equal to 2000–2010 (1.0 Scenario)** | | | | | |
| 2020 | 5,916,367 | 1,653,940 | 6,094,479 | 1,067,868 | 14,732,654 |
| 2030 | 5,758,919 | 1,894,218 | 8,318,397 | 1,689,242 | 17,660,776 |
| 2040 | 5,753,788 | 2,147,111 | 10,986,752 | 2,520,127 | 21,407,778 |
| 2050 | 5,650,708 | 2,390,368 | 14,414,381 | 3,659,670 | 26,115,127 |

*Source*: Projections by the authors and 2010 data and rates derived from U.S. Census
Bureau 2011d, 2011e.
*NH refers to nonHispanic; values shown are only for the nonHispanic persons in
each race category. Hispanic includes Hispanics of all races.

will be nonHispanic White, 9.2 percent nonHispanic Black, 55.2 percent
Hispanic, and 14.0 percent nonHispanic Asian and Other (Table 4.5). The
Texas labor force will grow substantially and become increasingly diverse.

The magnitude of the projected change in the composition of the labor force is particularly evident in Table 4.6. Under either of the scenarios
shown, there will be substantial change in the race/ethnicity composition
of the labor force. For example, under the scenario assuming 2000–2010
rates of net migration, the total increase in the labor force from 2010 to
2050 will be 13,777,094 with 73.6 percent of this increase or 10,133,427
workers resulting from an increase in the Hispanic labor force, 21.6 percent

Table 4.4

Percent Change in Civilian Labor Force in Texas by Race/Ethnicity
Assuming Alternative Projection Scenarios, 2010–2050

| Year | NH* White | NH Black | Hispanic | NH Asian & Other | Total |
|------|-----------|----------|----------|------------------|-------|
| **Assuming Rates of Net Migration Equal to One-Half of 2000–2010 (0.5 Scenario)** | | | | | |
| 2010–2020 | −2.8 | 12.6 | 29.8 | 32.6 | 12.2 |
| 2020–2030 | −4.1 | 8.1 | 24.5 | 30.1 | 11.0 |
| 2030–2040 | −1.4 | 7.5 | 21.0 | 21.2 | 11.4 |
| 2040–2050 | −2.9 | 5.5 | 20.4 | 18.5 | 11.2 |
| 2010–2050 | −10.7 | 38.0 | 135.5 | 147.9 | 54.2 |
| **Assuming Rates of Net Migration Equal to 2000–2010 (1.0 Scenario)** | | | | | |
| 2010–2020 | −1.3 | 19.2 | 42.4 | 58.1 | 19.4 |
| 2020–2030 | −2.7 | 14.5 | 36.5 | 58.2 | 19.9 |
| 2030–2040 | −0.1 | 13.4 | 32.1 | 49.2 | 21.2 |
| 2040–2050 | −1.8 | 11.3 | 31.2 | 45.2 | 22.0 |
| 2010–2050 | −5.7 | 72.2 | 236.7 | 442.0 | 111.7 |

*Source*: Projections by the authors and 2010 data and rates derived from U.S. Census Bureau 2011d, 2011e.
*NH refers to nonHispanic; values shown are only for the nonHispanic persons in each race category. Hispanic includes Hispanics of all races.

or 2,984,412 from an increase in the Asian and Other labor force, and 1,002,297 or 7.3 percent from an increase in the nonHispanic Black labor force. These increases will be offset in part by a 343,042 decline in the number of nonHispanic White workers. It is evident that the future of the Texas labor force will be increasingly determined by change in the labor force resulting from its minority populations.

The age structure of the labor force of Texas will also change but with less substantial effects than the change in the total population. For example, the data in Table 4.7 indicate that in 2010, 8.7 percent of the labor force was 60 years of age or older and that 11.3 percent will be of those ages in 2050; 78.4 percent of workers are in the key workforce ages of 20 to 54

Table 4.5

Percent of Civilian Labor Force in Texas by Race/Ethnicity in 2010
and Projected to 2050 Assuming Alternative Projection Scenarios

| Year | NH* White | NH Black | Hispanic | NH Asian & Other |
|------|-----------|----------|----------|------------------|
| 2010 | 48.6 | 11.3 | 34.7 | 5.4 |
| **Assuming Rates of Net Migration Equal to One-Half of 2000–2010 (0.5 Scenario)** | | | | |
| 2020 | 42.1 | 11.3 | 40.1 | 6.5 |
| 2030 | 36.4 | 11.0 | 45.0 | 7.6 |
| 2040 | 32.2 | 10.6 | 48.9 | 8.3 |
| 2050 | 28.1 | 10.1 | 53.0 | 8.8 |
| **Assuming Rates of Net Migration Equal to 2000–2010 (1.0 Scenario)** | | | | |
| 2020 | 40.2 | 11.2 | 41.4 | 7.2 |
| 2030 | 32.6 | 10.7 | 47.1 | 9.6 |
| 2040 | 26.9 | 10.0 | 51.3 | 11.8 |
| 2050 | 21.6 | 9.2 | 55.2 | 14.0 |

*Source*: Projections by the authors and 2010 data and rates derived from U.S. Census Bureau 2011d, 2011e.
*NH refers to nonHispanic; values shown are only for the nonHispanic persons in each race category. Hispanic includes Hispanics of all races.

in 2010 and 76.5 percent will be in 2050 assuming 2000–2010 rates of age, sex, and race/ethnicity specific net migration.

What is evident is that, under the same scenario, there will be substantial change in the age structure of workers in some racial/ethnic groups. The percentage of nonHispanic White workers who are 60 years of age or older, which was 12.1 percent in 2010, will be 18.2 percent in 2050. Similarly, the percentage of nonHispanic Black workers in this age group was 6.4 percent in 2010 but will be 12.5 percent in 2050. The extent of change is less substantial for other groups. Among Hispanic workers the percentage who are 60 years of age or older will increase from 5.0 to 8.5 percent and the change for nonHispanic Asian and Other workers will be from 7.0 to 10.7 percent. The labor force will age overall, but because of the age differentials among

Table 4.6

Number and Percent of Net Change in the Civilian Labor
Force in Texas Due to Each Race/Ethnicity Group, Assuming
Alternative Projection Scenarios, 2010–2050

| Race/Ethnicity | Number | Percent |
|---|---|---|
| **Assuming Rates of Net Migration Equal to One-Half of 2000–2010 (0.5 Scenario)** | | |
| NH* White | −641,153 | −9.6 |
| NH Black | 526,978 | 7.9 |
| Hispanic | 5,802,249 | 86.8 |
| NH Asian & Other | 998,403 | 14.9 |
| Total | 6,686,477 | 100.0 |
| **Assuming Rates of Net Migration Equal to 2000–2010 (1.0 Scenario)** | | |
| NH White | −343,042 | −2.5 |
| NH Black | 1,002,297 | 7.3 |
| Hispanic | 10,133,427 | 73.6 |
| NH Asian & Other | 2,984,412 | 21.6 |
| Total | 13,777,094 | 100.0 |

*Source*: Projections by the authors and 2010 data and rates derived from U.S. Census
Bureau 2011d, 2011e.
*NH refers to nonHispanic; values shown are only for the nonHispanic persons in
each race category. Hispanic includes Hispanics of all races.

the members of different racial/ethnic groups, the age structure of the total
population of workers will vary across racial/ethnic groups.

## SOCIOECONOMIC IMPLICATIONS OF THE
## DEMOGRAPHIC CHANGE IN THE LABOR FORCE

In the absence of change in the relationships between racial/ethnic characteristics and socioeconomic characteristics, the Texas labor force will have
substantially different socioeconomic characteristics in the future than it
does today. One of the impacts is that the overall level of educational attainment of the workforce will likely decline.

Tables 4.8 and 4.9 allow demographic changes impacting educational
attainment to be examined. Table 4.8 shows the number of workers by

Table 4.7

Percent of Civilian Labor Force in Texas by Race/Ethnicity in 2010
and Projected for 2050 Assuming Alternative Projection Scenarios

| Age Group | Percent of Labor Force | | | | |
| | NH* White | NH Black | Hispanic | NH Asian & Other | Total |
| --- | --- | --- | --- | --- | --- |
| **2010** | | | | | |
| 16–19 | 3.8 | 5.1 | 6.2 | 3.6 | 4.8 |
| 20–24 | 8.6 | 11.1 | 13.3 | 9.1 | 10.5 |
| 25–34 | 19.8 | 23.9 | 27.2 | 25.7 | 23.1 |
| 35–44 | 20.6 | 23.7 | 24.4 | 26.5 | 22.7 |
| 45–54 | 24.8 | 22.5 | 18.4 | 20.8 | 22.1 |
| 55–59 | 10.3 | 7.3 | 5.5 | 7.3 | 8.1 |
| 60–64 | 6.9 | 4.0 | 3.1 | 4.5 | 5.1 |
| 65+ | 5.2 | 2.4 | 1.9 | 2.5 | 3.6 |
| **Assuming Rates of Net Migration Equal to One-Half of 2000–2010 (0.5 Scenario)** | | | | | |
| **2050** | | | | | |
| 16–19 | 3.7 | 3.8 | 5.1 | 2.9 | 4.4 |
| 20–24 | 8.3 | 9.4 | 11.8 | 7.0 | 10.2 |
| 25–34 | 20.0 | 21.5 | 23.8 | 18.4 | 22.0 |
| 35–44 | 20.5 | 22.4 | 22.2 | 25.2 | 22.0 |
| 45–54 | 20.2 | 21.2 | 20.1 | 23.5 | 20.5 |
| 55–59 | 9.4 | 9.1 | 7.3 | 8.6 | 8.2 |
| 60–64 | 7.4 | 6.0 | 4.7 | 6.4 | 5.7 |
| 65+ | 10.5 | 6.6 | 5.0 | 8.0 | 7.0 |
| **Assuming Rates of Net Migration Equal to 2000–2010 (1.0 Scenario)** | | | | | |
| **2050** | | | | | |
| 16–19 | 3.7 | 3.9 | 4.9 | 3.0 | 4.3 |
| 20–24 | 8.2 | 9.5 | 11.7 | 7.3 | 10.1 |
| 25–34 | 19.8 | 21.1 | 24.3 | 20.0 | 22.4 |
| 35–44 | 20.5 | 22.4 | 22.9 | 27.9 | 23.0 |
| 45–54 | 20.2 | 21.5 | 20.6 | 23.2 | 21.0 |
| 55–59 | 9.4 | 9.1 | 7.1 | 7.9 | 7.9 |
| 60–64 | 7.5 | 5.9 | 4.3 | 5.5 | 5.3 |
| 65+ | 10.7 | 6.6 | 4.2 | 5.2 | 6.0 |

*Source*: Projections by the authors and 2010 data and rates derived from U.S. Census Bureau 2011d, 2011e.
*NH refers to nonHispanic; values shown are only for the nonHispanic persons in each race category. Hispanic includes Hispanics of all races.

Table 4.8

Civilian Labor Force in Texas by Level of Education and Race/Ethnicity in 2010 and Projected for 2050 Using the Population Projection That Assumes 2000–2010 Rates of Net Migration (Percents Computed within Level of Educational Attainment)

| Level of Attainment | NH* White | | NH Black | | Hispanic | | NH Asian & Other | | Total |
|---|---|---|---|---|---|---|---|---|---|
| | Number | % | Number | % | Number | % | Number | % | Total Number |
| **2010** | | | | | | | | | |
| Less than 9th grade | 53,677 | 7.9 | 23,170 | 3.4 | 580,812 | 85.1 | 24,787 | 3.6 | 682,446 |
| 9th to 12th grade, no dip. | 365,527 | 29.5 | 146,807 | 11.8 | 687,958 | 55.5 | 38,705 | 3.2 | 1,238,997 |
| High school graduate | 1,940,151 | 48.3 | 502,146 | 12.5 | 1,427,126 | 35.5 | 148,468 | 3.7 | 4,017,891 |
| Some college | 1,145,651 | 48.8 | 339,389 | 14.5 | 752,148 | 32.1 | 109,532 | 4.7 | 2,346,720 |
| Associate degree | 503,869 | 57.2 | 101,217 | 11.5 | 231,241 | 26.3 | 44,054 | 5.0 | 880,381 |
| Bachelor's degree | 1,353,910 | 62.2 | 193,098 | 8.9 | 435,847 | 20.0 | 195,196 | 8.9 | 2,178,051 |
| Graduate/Professional | 630,965 | 63.5 | 82,244 | 8.3 | 165,822 | 16.7 | 114,516 | 11.5 | 993,547 |
| Total | 5,993,750 | 48.6 | 1,388,071 | 11.3 | 4,280,954 | 34.6 | 675,258 | 5.5 | 12,338,033 |
| **2050** | | | | | | | | | |
| Less than 9th grade | 62,096 | 2.4 | 54,065 | 2.1 | 2,350,226 | 89.4 | 161,441 | 6.1 | 2,627,828 |
| 9th to 12th grade, no dip. | 257,334 | 11.3 | 188,329 | 8.3 | 1,677,223 | 73.8 | 149,876 | 6.6 | 2,272,762 |
| High school graduate | 1,960,381 | 21.9 | 949,777 | 10.6 | 5,200,353 | 58.0 | 858,057 | 9.5 | 8,968,568 |
| Some college | 914,551 | 22.6 | 496,277 | 12.3 | 2,145,672 | 53.1 | 482,182 | 12.0 | 4,038,682 |
| Associate degree | 501,038 | 27.6 | 192,961 | 10.6 | 864,659 | 47.6 | 258,893 | 14.2 | 1,817,551 |
| Bachelor's degree | 1,225,547 | 30.6 | 326,740 | 8.1 | 1,456,245 | 36.3 | 1,002,328 | 25.0 | 4,010,860 |
| Graduate/Professional | 729,761 | 30.7 | 182,219 | 7.7 | 720,002 | 30.3 | 746,894 | 31.3 | 2,378,876 |
| Total | 5,650,708 | 21.6 | 2,390,368 | 9.2 | 14,414,380 | 55.2 | 3,659,671 | 14.0 | 26,115,127 |

*Source:* Projections by the authors and 2010 data and rates derived from U.S. Census Bureau 2011d, 2011e.
*NH refers to nonHispanic; values shown are only for the nonHispanic persons in each race category. Hispanic includes Hispanics of all races.

Table 4.9

Civilian Labor Force in Texas by Level of Education and Race/Ethnicity in 2010 and Projected for 2050 Using the Population Projection That Assumes 2000–2010 Rates of Net Migration (Percents Computed within Race/Ethnic Group)

| Level of Attainment | NH* White | | NH Black | | Hispanic | | NH Asian & Other | | Total | |
|---|---|---|---|---|---|---|---|---|---|---|
| | Number | % | Number | % | Number | % | Number | % | Number | % |
| **2010** | | | | | | | | | | |
| Less than 9th grade | 53,677 | 0.9 | 23,170 | 1.7 | 580,812 | 13.6 | 24,787 | 3.7 | 682,446 | 5.5 |
| 9th to 12th grade, no dip. | 365,527 | 6.1 | 146,807 | 10.6 | 687,958 | 16.1 | 38,705 | 5.7 | 1,238,997 | 10.0 |
| High school graduate | 1,940,151 | 32.4 | 502,146 | 36.1 | 1,427,126 | 33.2 | 148,468 | 22.0 | 4,017,891 | 32.6 |
| Some college | 1,145,651 | 19.1 | 339,389 | 24.5 | 752,148 | 17.6 | 109,532 | 16.2 | 2,346,720 | 19.0 |
| Associate degree | 503,869 | 8.4 | 101,217 | 7.3 | 231,241 | 5.4 | 44,054 | 6.5 | 880,381 | 7.1 |
| Bachelor's degree | 1,353,910 | 22.6 | 193,098 | 13.9 | 435,847 | 10.2 | 195,196 | 28.9 | 2,178,051 | 17.7 |
| Graduate/Professional | 630,965 | 10.5 | 82,244 | 5.9 | 165,822 | 3.9 | 114,516 | 17.0 | 993,547 | 8.1 |
| Total | 5,993,750 | 100.0 | 1,388,071 | 100.0 | 4,280,954 | 100.0 | 675,258 | 100.0 | 12,338,033 | 100.0 |
| **2050** | | | | | | | | | | |
| Less than 9th grade | 62,096 | 1.1 | 54,065 | 2.3 | 2,350,226 | 16.3 | 161,441 | 4.4 | 2,627,828 | 10.1 |
| 9th to 12th grade, no dip. | 257,334 | 4.6 | 188,329 | 7.9 | 1,677,223 | 11.6 | 149,876 | 4.1 | 2,272,762 | 8.7 |
| High school graduate | 1,960,381 | 34.6 | 949,777 | 39.6 | 5,200,353 | 36.1 | 858,057 | 23.4 | 8,968,568 | 34.3 |
| Some college | 914,551 | 16.2 | 496,277 | 20.8 | 2,145,672 | 14.9 | 482,182 | 13.2 | 4,038,682 | 15.5 |
| Associate degree | 501,038 | 8.9 | 192,961 | 8.1 | 864,659 | 6.0 | 258,893 | 7.1 | 1,817,551 | 7.0 |
| Bachelor's degree | 1,225,547 | 21.7 | 326,740 | 13.7 | 1,456,245 | 10.1 | 1,002,328 | 27.4 | 4,010,860 | 15.3 |
| Graduate/Professional | 729,761 | 12.9 | 182,219 | 7.6 | 720,002 | 5.0 | 746,894 | 20.4 | 2,378,876 | 9.1 |
| Total | 5,650,708 | 100.0 | 2,390,368 | 100.0 | 14,414,380 | 100.0 | 3,659,671 | 100.0 | 26,115,127 | 100.0 |

*Source:* Projections by the authors and 2010 data and rates derived from U.S. Census Bureau 2011d, 2011e.

*NH refers to nonHispanic; values shown are only for the nonHispanic persons in each race category. Hispanic includes Hispanics of all races.

educational level in 2010 and projected for 2050 assuming that the percentage of workers by age and race/ethnicity in 2010 apply to 2050. It also
shows the percentages within educational categories across race/ethnicity
groups. These data point to the substantial growth in the number and percentage of the labor force that is minority. Across all educational levels, the
percentage of all workers who are nonHispanic White declines from 2010
to 2050. For example, in 2010, the percentages of workers with bachelor's
and graduate/professional degrees who were nonHispanic White were 62.2
and 63.5 percent, respectively, but by 2050 only 30.6 percent of those with
bachelor's degrees and 30.7 percent of those with graduate/professional
degrees will be nonHispanic White. Although nonHispanic White workers' numbers and proportions will still be disproportionately high at higher
levels of education compared to their share of the total labor force in these
groups, the increase in the number and proportion of workers at all levels
who will be minority population members is substantial. By 2050, Hispanics will account for 30 percent or more of workers at all education levels.

At the same time, these data make it clear that, in the absence of change in
the levels of educational attainment among minority population members,
minority workers, particularly Hispanic and nonHispanic Black workers,
will remain concentrated at lower educational levels. As shown in Table 4.9,
whereas 40.3 percent of nonHispanic White workers and 31.9 percent of
nonHispanic Asian and Other workers will have a high school degree or
less education in 2050, 64.0 percent of Hispanics and 49.8 percent of non-
Hispanic Black workers will have these educational levels. Only 5.0 percent
of Hispanic and 7.6 percent of nonHispanic Black workers are projected
to have graduate/professional degrees in 2050 compared to 20.4 percent of
Asian and Other workers and 12.9 percent of nonHispanic White workers.

The overall effect of demographic change on the Texas workforce is evident in the final column of Table 4.9. While 48.1 percent of all workers
in Texas had a high school education or less in 2010, without increases in
educational levels, 53.1 percent will have a high school level of education
or less in 2050. Although all projections of job requirements indicate that
increased levels of education will be required in the future compared to
today, the data here suggest that whereas 25.8 percent of all Texas workers
had a bachelor's or graduate/professional degree in 2010, that percentage
will decrease to 24.4 percent by 2050. This is a small difference, but when
future job qualifications will require increasingly higher levels of education
over time to remain competitive, this potential decline is problematic.

Analysis of the data in Table 4.10 shows the effects of changing demographic characteristics of the labor force on the occupational distribution
of the workforce in 2050 assuming that the occupational distribution by
race/ethnicity in 2010 applies in 2050. The data in this table demonstrate
the pervasive effects of demographic change in altering the racial/ethnic

Table 4.10

Civilian Labor Force in Texas by Occupation and Race/Ethnicity in 2010 and Projections for 2050 Using the Population Projection That Assumes 2000–2010 Rates of Net Migration (Percents Computed within Occupation)

| Occupation | NH* White Number | % | NH Black Number | % | Hispanic Number | % | NH Asian & Other Number | % | Total Number |
|---|---|---|---|---|---|---|---|---|---|
| **2010** | | | | | | | | | |
| Management, business, & financial | 1,058,172 | 66.6 | 132,846 | 8.4 | 302,324 | 19.0 | 95,176 | 6.0 | 1,588,518 |
| Computer, engineering, & science | 358,765 | 62.1 | 39,099 | 6.8 | 83,891 | 14.5 | 96,068 | 16.6 | 577,823 |
| Education, legal, community service, arts, & media | 724,002 | 62.4 | 122,384 | 10.6 | 257,046 | 22.2 | 56,288 | 4.8 | 1,159,720 |
| Healthcare practitioners & technical | 295,036 | 57.3 | 65,499 | 12.7 | 97,794 | 19.0 | 56,734 | 11.0 | 515,063 |
| Healthcare support | 79,146 | 31.7 | 60,785 | 24.4 | 99,450 | 39.9 | 9,902 | 4.0 | 249,283 |
| Protective service | 127,646 | 49.9 | 47,129 | 18.4 | 74,339 | 29.0 | 6,838 | 2.7 | 255,952 |
| Other services | 462,503 | 32.0 | 155,926 | 10.8 | 750,190 | 52.0 | 74,584 | 5.2 | 1,443,203 |
| Sales & related | 722,364 | 54.9 | 124,254 | 9.4 | 392,434 | 29.8 | 76,068 | 5.9 | 1,315,120 |
| Office & administrative support | 810,380 | 49.9 | 221,018 | 13.6 | 524,266 | 32.3 | 67,795 | 4.2 | 1,623,459 |
| Farming, fishing, & forestry | 21,091 | 32.5 | 2,906 | 4.5 | 39,248 | 60.5 | 1,648 | 2.5 | 64,893 |
| Construction & maintenance | 492,997 | 38.7 | 63,338 | 5.0 | 687,148 | 54.0 | 30,155 | 2.3 | 1,273,638 |
| Production occupations | 241,359 | 35.3 | 70,274 | 10.3 | 330,577 | 48.4 | 41,035 | 6.0 | 683,245 |
| Transportation & material moving | 275,774 | 38.4 | 121,232 | 16.9 | 302,554 | 42.1 | 18,379 | 2.6 | 717,939 |
| Unemployed | 324,515 | 37.3 | 161,381 | 18.5 | 339,693 | 39.0 | 44,588 | 5.2 | 870,177 |
| Total | 5,993,750 | 48.6 | 1,388,071 | 11.3 | 4,280,954 | 34.7 | 675,258 | 5.5 | 12,338,033 |

Table 4.10, continued

| Occupation | NH* White | | NH Black | | Hispanic | | NH Asian & Other | | Total |
|---|---|---|---|---|---|---|---|---|---|
| | Number | % | Number | % | Number | % | Number | % | Number |
| **2050** | | | | | | | | | |
| Management, business, & financial | 1,001,752 | 36.2 | 229,502 | 8.3 | 1,020,077 | 36.8 | 519,374 | 18.7 | 2,770,705 |
| Computer, engineering, & science | 343,241 | 27.8 | 69,473 | 5.6 | 287,370 | 23.3 | 533,181 | 43.3 | 1,233,265 |
| Education, legal, community service, arts, & media | 675,274 | 33.1 | 208,549 | 10.2 | 852,663 | 41.8 | 301,931 | 14.9 | 2,038,417 |
| Healthcare practitioners & technical | 273,935 | 27.1 | 110,322 | 10.9 | 324,432 | 32.1 | 301,401 | 29.9 | 1,010,090 |
| Healthcare support | 72,818 | 13.2 | 101,206 | 18.4 | 325,509 | 59.0 | 51,996 | 9.4 | 551,529 |
| Protective service | 122,168 | 24.5 | 83,349 | 16.7 | 255,290 | 51.2 | 37,947 | 7.6 | 498,754 |
| Other services | 432,821 | 12.0 | 269,127 | 7.4 | 2,512,037 | 69.5 | 399,115 | 11.1 | 3,613,100 |
| Sales & related | 682,003 | 26.0 | 214,593 | 8.2 | 1,315,798 | 50.1 | 413,694 | 15.7 | 2,626,088 |
| Office & administrative support | 751,006 | 23.3 | 376,378 | 11.7 | 1,739,956 | 53.9 | 361,604 | 11.1 | 3,228,954 |
| Farming, fishing, & forestry | 20,277 | 11.9 | 5,231 | 3.1 | 135,464 | 79.6 | 9,221 | 5.4 | 170,193 |
| Construction & maintenance | 476,297 | 15.1 | 116,141 | 3.7 | 2,389,153 | 75.8 | 170,324 | 5.4 | 3,151,915 |
| Production occupations | 231,270 | 13.5 | 125,133 | 7.3 | 1,128,992 | 66.0 | 225,458 | 13.2 | 1,710,853 |
| Transportation & material moving | 264,729 | 16.2 | 219,911 | 13.5 | 1,043,945 | 64.0 | 102,494 | 6.3 | 1,631,079 |
| Unemployed | 303,117 | 16.1 | 261,453 | 13.9 | 1,083,685 | 57.6 | 231,930 | 12.4 | 1,880,185 |
| Total | 5,650,708 | 21.6 | 2,390,368 | 9.2 | 14,414,381 | 55.2 | 3,659,670 | 14.0 | 26,115,127 |

*Source:* Projections by the authors and 2010 data and rates derived from Ruggles et al. 2010; U.S. Census Bureau 2011g.

*NH refers to nonHispanic; values shown are only for the nonHispanic persons in each race category. Hispanic includes Hispanics of all races.

characteristics of persons employed in virtually every occupation. For example, 66.6 percent of those employed in management occupations, 62.1 percent employed in computer/engineering occupations, 62.4 percent employed in education, legal, and other professions, 57.3 percent employed as healthcare practitioners, 54.9 percent employed as sales and related professionals, and 37.3 percent of the unemployed in Texas in 2010 were nonHispanic White. By 2050, nonHispanic White workers will make up 36.2 percent, 27.8 percent; 33.1 percent, 27.1 percent, 26.0 percent, and 16.1 percent, respectively, of the workforce in these categories. By contrast, Hispanic workers made up 19.0 percent, 14.5 percent, 22.2 percent, 19.0 percent, 29.8 percent, and 39.0 percent in 2010 and are projected to be 36.8 percent, 23.3 percent, 41.8 percent, 32.1 percent, 50.1 percent, and 57.6 percent in 2050. Levels of relative growth similar to those for Hispanics are expected for nonHispanic Asian and Other workers, except they will account for 43.3 percent of all engineers and 29.9 percent of healthcare practitioners although they will represent only 14 percent of the total workforce. NonHispanic Black members of the labor force are expected to retain roughly the same proportions of the employment in the occupational categories shown in 2050 as they did in 2010. The data for the total labor force make it clear that the labor force will be increasingly composed of minority population members with 51.4 percent in 2010 but 78.4 percent in 2050 being minority group members.

The data in Table 4.10 also reveal shifts in the percentage of Texans likely to be in different occupations. For example, 12.9 percent, 9.4 percent, and 4.2 percent of all workers were in management; education, legal, and related occupations; and healthcare practitioner professions in 2010. By 2050, the percentage in these occupations will be 10.6, 7.8, and 3.9 percent, respectively. On the other hand, the percentages in construction and maintenance, production, and transportation related occupations were 10.3, 5.5, and 5.8 percent, respectively, in 2010, but are projected to be 12.1, 6.6, and 6.3 percent of all those employed in 2050. Growth in employment will be more obvious in the occupations requiring fewer technical skills than in those requiring greater levels of skills.

The data in Tables 4.11 and 4.12 show the potential effects of demographic change in the labor force on the income distribution of employed persons in 2010 and projected for 2050. The data in Table 4.11 show that the higher proportions of workers in higher income positions among nonHispanic White workers compared to other population groups may continue. Comparing the percentage at each income level to the percentage of the total number of persons employed in each race/ethnicity group allows one to determine the relative distribution of income among race/ethnicity categories of workers. The percentage of all those employed at nearly all income levels who are nonHispanic White decreases between 2010 and 2050

Table 4.11

Wage and Salary of Civilian Labor Force in Texas by Race/Ethnicity in 2010 and Projected for 2050 (in 2010 Constant Dollars) Using the Population Projection That Assumes 2000–2010 Rates of Net Migration (Percent Computed within Income Group)

| Wage & Salary Earnings | NH* White Number | % | NH Black Number | % | Hispanic Number | % | NH Asian & Other Number | % | Total Number |
|---|---|---|---|---|---|---|---|---|---|
| **2010** | | | | | | | | | |
| <$10,000 | 1,202,388 | 44.3 | 305,565 | 11.3 | 1,068,508 | 39.4 | 137,075 | 5.0 | 2,713,536 |
| $10,000 to $24,999 | 985,222 | 34.8 | 313,673 | 11.1 | 1,393,273 | 49.2 | 137,753 | 4.9 | 2,829,921 |
| $25,000 to $34,999 | 674,300 | 45.0 | 191,802 | 12.8 | 562,926 | 37.5 | 70,110 | 4.7 | 1,499,138 |
| $35,000 to $49,999 | 922,756 | 55.2 | 197,626 | 11.8 | 465,333 | 27.8 | 86,188 | 5.2 | 1,671,903 |
| $50,000 to $74,999 | 935,394 | 63.4 | 144,548 | 9.8 | 301,504 | 20.4 | 93,565 | 6.4 | 1,475,011 |
| $75,000 to $99,999 | 401,139 | 69.5 | 43,252 | 7.5 | 83,891 | 14.5 | 48,721 | 8.5 | 577,003 |
| $100,000 or more | 548,036 | 78.1 | 30,224 | 4.3 | 65,826 | 9.4 | 57,258 | 8.2 | 701,344 |
| Unemployed | 324,515 | 37.3 | 161,381 | 18.5 | 339,693 | 39.0 | 44,588 | 5.2 | 870,177 |
| Total | 5,993,750 | 48.5 | 1,388,071 | 11.3 | 4,280,954 | 34.7 | 675,258 | 5.5 | 12,338,033 |
| **2050** | | | | | | | | | |
| <$10,000 | 1,130,630 | 18.9 | 530,523 | 8.9 | 3,592,098 | 59.9 | 739,330 | 12.3 | 5,992,581 |
| $10,000 to $24,999 | 922,648 | 13.4 | 540,192 | 7.8 | 4,704,377 | 68.1 | 743,198 | 10.7 | 6,910,415 |
| $25,000 to $34,999 | 633,200 | 19.4 | 332,145 | 10.2 | 1,911,706 | 58.7 | 379,915 | 11.7 | 3,256,966 |
| $35,000 to $49,999 | 868,093 | 26.6 | 343,310 | 10.5 | 1,580,935 | 48.5 | 468,343 | 14.4 | 3,260,681 |
| $50,000 to $74,999 | 885,683 | 33.1 | 253,047 | 9.4 | 1,028,169 | 38.4 | 511,129 | 19.1 | 2,678,028 |
| $75,000 to $99,999 | 382,281 | 37.7 | 76,061 | 7.5 | 287,370 | 28.4 | 267,410 | 26.4 | 1,013,122 |
| $100,000 or more | 525,056 | 46.7 | 53,637 | 4.8 | 226,041 | 20.1 | 318,415 | 28.4 | 1,123,149 |
| Unemployed | 303,117 | 16.1 | 261,453 | 13.9 | 1,083,685 | 57.5 | 231,930 | 12.4 | 1,880,185 |
| Total | 5,650,708 | 21.6 | 2,390,368 | 9.2 | 14,414,381 | 55.2 | 3,659,670 | 14.0 | 26,115,127 |

*Source:* Projections by the authors and 2010 data and rates derived from Ruggles et al. 2010; U.S. Census Bureau 2011g.
*NH refers to nonHispanic; values shown are only for the nonHispanic persons in each race category. Hispanic includes Hispanics of all races.

Table 4.12

Wage and Salary of Civilian Labor Force in Texas by Race/Ethnicity in 2010 and Projected for 2050 (in 2010 Constant Dollars) Using the Population Projection That Assumes 2000–2010 Rates of Net Migration (Percent Computed within Race/Ethnicity Groups)

| Wage & Salary Earnings | NH* White | | NH Black | | Hispanic | | NH Asian & Other | | Total | |
|---|---|---|---|---|---|---|---|---|---|---|
| | Number | % | Number | % | Number | % | Number | % | Number | % |
| **2010** | | | | | | | | | | |
| <$10,000 | 1,202,388 | 20.1 | 305,565 | 22.0 | 1,068,508 | 25.0 | 137,075 | 20.3 | 2,713,536 | 22.0 |
| $10,000 to $24,999 | 985,222 | 16.4 | 313,673 | 22.6 | 1,393,273 | 32.6 | 137,753 | 20.4 | 2,829,921 | 22.9 |
| $25,000 to $34,999 | 674,300 | 11.3 | 191,802 | 13.8 | 562,926 | 13.1 | 70,110 | 10.4 | 1,499,138 | 12.2 |
| $35,000 to $49,999 | 922,756 | 15.4 | 197,626 | 14.2 | 465,333 | 10.9 | 86,188 | 12.8 | 1,671,903 | 13.6 |
| $50,000 to $74,999 | 935,394 | 15.6 | 144,548 | 10.4 | 301,504 | 7.0 | 93,565 | 13.9 | 1,475,011 | 12.0 |
| $75,000 to $99,999 | 401,139 | 6.7 | 43,252 | 3.1 | 83,891 | 2.0 | 48,721 | 7.2 | 577,003 | 4.7 |
| $100,000 or more | 548,036 | 9.1 | 30,224 | 2.2 | 65,826 | 1.5 | 57,258 | 8.5 | 701,344 | 5.7 |
| Unemployed | 324,515 | 5.4 | 161,381 | 11.7 | 339,693 | 7.9 | 44,588 | 6.5 | 870,177 | 6.9 |
| Total | 5,993,750 | 100.0 | 1,388,071 | 100.0 | 4,280,954 | 100.0 | 675,258 | 100.0 | 12,338,033 | 100.0 |
| **2050** | | | | | | | | | | |
| <$10,000 | 1,130,630 | 20.0 | 530,523 | 22.2 | 3,592,098 | 25.0 | 739,330 | 20.2 | 5,992,581 | 22.9 |
| $10,000 to $24,999 | 922,648 | 16.3 | 540,192 | 22.6 | 4,704,377 | 32.7 | 743,198 | 20.3 | 6,910,415 | 26.5 |
| $25,000 to $34,999 | 633,200 | 11.2 | 332,145 | 13.9 | 1,911,706 | 13.3 | 379,915 | 10.4 | 3,256,966 | 12.5 |
| $35,000 to $49,999 | 868,093 | 15.4 | 343,310 | 14.4 | 1,580,935 | 11.0 | 468,343 | 12.8 | 3,260,681 | 12.5 |
| $50,000 to $74,999 | 885,683 | 15.7 | 253,047 | 10.6 | 1,028,169 | 7.1 | 511,129 | 14.0 | 2,678,028 | 10.3 |
| $75,000 to $99,999 | 382,281 | 6.8 | 76,061 | 3.2 | 287,370 | 2.0 | 267,410 | 7.3 | 1,013,122 | 3.9 |
| $100,000 or more | 525,056 | 9.3 | 53,637 | 2.2 | 226,041 | 1.6 | 318,415 | 8.7 | 1,123,149 | 4.3 |
| Unemployed | 303,117 | 5.3 | 261,453 | 10.9 | 1,083,685 | 7.3 | 231,930 | 6.3 | 1,880,185 | 7.1 |
| Total | 5,650,708 | 100.0 | 2,390,368 | 100.0 | 14,414,381 | 100.0 | 3,659,670 | 100.0 | 26,115,127 | 100.0 |

*Source:* Projections by the authors and 2010 data and rates derived from Ruggles et al. 2010; U.S. Census Bureau 2011g.

*NH refers to nonHispanic; values shown are only for the nonHispanic persons in each race category. Hispanic includes Hispanics of all races.

but their income advantages prevail. The percentage of workers who are nonHispanic White in 2050 is larger than the 21.6 percent that they make up of all individuals in the labor force in all income categories of $35,000 or more, while it is less than that percentage in all lower income categories. The percentage that nonHispanic Black workers represent is higher than their proportion of the total workforce (9.2 percent in 2050) only in the three income categories between $25,000 and $74,999 and among the unemployed. The representation of Hispanics is larger than their proportion of all those employed (55.2 percent) only at income levels below $35,000. The percentage of nonHispanic Asians and Others is higher than the 14.0 percent of the labor force that they represent in all income categories above $35,000. The data in Table 4.1 suggest that, in the absence of change in the income distribution of those groups who currently earn the lowest salary and wages, the growth projected in such labor force areas will not lead to the members of those groups obtaining higher wages and salaries. In the absence of change, it will lead to a generally lower income distribution among Texas workers.

The data in the final columns of Table 4.12 show the effects of demographic change on the overall income distribution. A comparison of these data for 2010 and 2050 (in 2010 constant dollars) shows that income levels will generally decline among Texas workers. Whereas 44.9 percent of workers earned less than $25,000 in 2010, 49.4 percent will earn less than $25,000 in 2050 (in 2010 constant dollars). At the same time the percentage of workers earning $50,000 or more was 22.4 percent in 2010 but would be 18.5 percent in 2050. Overall, the median income of workers will decline from $29,179 in 2010 to $25,479 in 2050 (in 2010 constant dollars).

The data on wages and salaries for Texas workers show that the average Texas worker in 2050 will be poorer than in 2010 if the income levels of Texas workers do not increase. Improved levels of education for Texas workers coupled with continued attempts to obtain employers who provide higher paying jobs are essential to creating a more prosperous future for Texas workers.

The data above clearly indicate that the future labor force of Texas may require assistance to become more competitive. One means of increasing the skills and hence the competitiveness of the Texas labor force is through the provision of additional training. Tables 4.13 and 4.14 provide data on such programs as reported from the Texas Workforce Commission. These are but a few of such programs in the state provided by the public sector. There are also numerous programs provided by the private sector. These data are best seen as a sample of workforce training programs serving the total Texas workforce. Nonetheless they provide some indication of the likely characteristics of persons in such programs.

Table 4.13

Participants in Selected Workforce Training Programs in Texas,
Percent Change in Projected Participants, and Percent of
Participants by Race/Ethnicity, Using the Population Projection
That Assumes 2000–2010 Rates of Net Migration, 2010–2050

| Year/ Period | NH* White | NH Black | Hispanic | NH Asian & Other | Total |
|---|---|---|---|---|---|
| **Panel A: Participants in Selected Workforce Training Programs** | | | | | |
| 2010 | 11,661 | 20,219 | 21,578 | 3,803 | 57,261 |
| 2020 | 11,510 | 24,092 | 30,719 | 6,014 | 72,335 |
| 2030 | 11,204 | 27,592 | 41,929 | 9,514 | 90,239 |
| 2040 | 11,194 | 31,275 | 55,378 | 14,193 | 112,040 |
| 2050 | 10,994 | 34,819 | 72,655 | 20,611 | 139,079 |
| **Panel B: Percent Change in Projected Participants in Selected Workforce Training Programs** | | | | | |
| 2010–2020 | −1.3 | 19.2 | 42.4 | 58.1 | 26.2 |
| 2020–2030 | −2.6 | 14.5 | 36.5 | 58.2 | 24.7 |
| 2030–2040 | −0.1 | 13.4 | 32.1 | 49.2 | 24.2 |
| 2040–2050 | −1.8 | 11.3 | 31.2 | 45.2 | 24.2 |
| 2010–2050 | −5.7 | 72.2 | 236.7 | 442.0 | 142.9 |
| **Panel C: Percent of Participants in Selected Workforce Training Programs by Race/Ethnicity** | | | | | |
| 2010 | 20.4 | 35.3 | 37.7 | 6.6 | 100.0 |
| 2020 | 15.9 | 33.3 | 42.5 | 8.3 | 100.0 |
| 2030 | 12.4 | 30.6 | 46.5 | 10.5 | 100.0 |
| 2040 | 10.0 | 27.9 | 49.4 | 12.7 | 100.0 |
| 2050 | 7.9 | 25.0 | 52.2 | 14.8 | 100.0 |

Source: Projections by the authors and 2010 data and rates derived from Texas Workforce Commission, Workforce Investment Act, Participant Demographics, July 2010.
Note: Excludes adult self-service only participants.
*NH refers to nonHispanic; values shown are only for the nonHispanic persons in
each race category. Hispanic includes Hispanics of all races.

Table 4.14

Total State Expenditures and State Expenditures for Selected Workforce
Training Programs in Texas (in 2010 Dollars) and Projections to 2050 Using
the Population Projection That Assumes 2000–2010 Rates of Net Migration

| Year | WIA Youth | WIA Adult* | WIA Dislocated Worker | Total State Expenditures |
|------|-----------|------------|------------------------|--------------------------|
| 2010 | $ 47,626,244 | $ 47,616,416 | $ 45,479,604 | $ 140,722,256 |
| 2020 | 62,174,312 | 59,601,304 | 56,704,848 | 178,480,464 |
| 2030 | 78,956,040 | 73,688,392 | 70,642,880 | 223,287,312 |
| 2040 | 98,800,880 | 90,816,592 | 88,130,688 | 277,748,160 |
| 2050 | 123,185,328 | 111,890,680 | 110,231,320 | 345,307,328 |

*Source*: Projections by the authors and 2010 data and rates derived from Texas Workforce Commission, Workforce Investment Act, Participant Demographics, July 2010; and per participant costs obtained from Texas Workforce Commission, Workforce Investment Act 2010 Annual Report.
*Excludes adult self-service only participants.

The data in Table 4.13 show persons in the Workforce Investment Act of 1998 (WIA) programs in 2010 and projections through 2050. The projections shown in this table indicate that the number of persons in this group will increase by more than 81,000, by 142.9 percent, from 2010 to 2050. The number of persons in such programs will thus increase more rapidly than the population (that is projected to increase by 119.5 percent) and the labor force (that is projected to increase by 111.7 percent) during the same time period.

The data in this table when compared to labor force data also show that members of the labor force in WIA programs are more likely to be minority workers. For example, whereas 20.4 percent of WIA workers were nonHispanic White, 35.3 percent nonHispanic Black, 37.7 percent Hispanic, and 6.6 percent nonHispanic Asian and Others in 2010, 48.6 percent in the workforce as a whole were nonHispanic White, 11.3 percent nonHispanic Black, 34.7 percent were Hispanic, and 5.4 percent were nonHispanic Asian and Other in 2010. Similarly, by 2050 the total Texas labor force is projected to be 21.6 percent nonHispanic White, 9.2 percent nonHispanic Black, 55.2 percent Hispanic, and 14.0 percent nonHispanic Asian and Other but those in WIA programs are projected to be 7.9 percent nonHispanic White, 25.0 percent nonHispanic Black, 52.2 percent Hispanic, and 14.8 percent nonHispanic Asian and Other. Clearly, these programs are addressing the employment needs of Texas populations with high levels of unemployment and underemployment and (as shown in Table 4.14) will cost the state a projected $345 million per year by 2050.

## SUMMARY

In this chapter we have examined the effects of the projected demographic change on the size and characteristics of the Texas labor force, on the educational levels of the workforce, on the likely occupational distribution of the labor force, and on the salary levels of the labor force. The results of the analysis suggest the following:

1.   The Texas labor force increased by more than 50 percent from 1990 to 2010 compared to a 27.1 percent increase for the nation. Texas workers were more likely to be employed in natural resources-related occupations, and in the agriculture, forestry, fishing and hunting, and mining, construction, and transportation industries than workers in the nation as a whole.

2.   Using age and race/ethnicity specific labor force participation rates for 2010 applied to the projected population (under the scenario assuming 2000–2010 rates of net migration) by age and race/ethnicity for labor force ages 16 and older, projections of the future labor force of Texas were completed for periods through 2050. These projections point to a labor force that will increase substantially from 12,338,033 in 2010 to 26,115,127 in 2050, an increase of 111.7 percent, or 13,777,094 workers.

3.   The projected labor force will become increasingly diverse. In 2010, 48.6 percent of the labor force was composed of workers who were non-Hispanic White, 11.3 percent nonHispanic Black, 34.7 percent Hispanic, and 5.4 percent nonHispanic Asian and Other. By 2050, the labor force is projected to become 21.6 percent nonHispanic White, 9.2 percent non-Hispanic Black, 55.2 percent Hispanic, and 14.0 percent nonHispanic Asian and Other. The change in the size of the labor force from 2010 to 2050 includes a decline of more than 343,000 nonHispanic White workers, an increase of more than 1 million nonHispanic Black workers, an increase of more than 10 million Hispanic workers, and an increase of nearly 3 million nonHispanic Asian and Other workers.

4.   The workforce will also become older, with 18.2 percent of non-Hispanic White workers, 12.5 percent of nonHispanic Black, 10.7 percent of nonHispanic Asian and Other, 8.5 percent of Hispanic, and 11.3 percent of all workers projected to be 60 years of age or older in 2050 compared to only 12.1 percent of nonHispanic White, 6.4 percent of nonHispanic

Black, 7.0 percent nonHispanic Asian and Other, 5.0 percent of Hispanic, and 8.7 percent of all workers in 2010.

5.  The results of the analysis relating to the educational, occupational, and income of workers show that, in the absence of change, the Texas labor force as a whole will be less well educated, work in lower status occupations, and have lower incomes in 2050 than in 2010. For example, 48.1 percent of all workers in Texas had a high school or lower level of education in 2010 but 53.1 percent will have those levels of education in 2050. Whereas 25.8 percent of all Texas workers in 2010 had a bachelor's or graduate/professional degree, 24.4 percent will have these levels of education in 2050. Educational levels and other factors will also impact the occupations of Texas workers; whereas 12.9 percent of all workers were in management positions, 9.4 percent in education, legal, and related fields, and 4.2 percent were healthcare practitioners in 2010, 10.6 percent, 7.8 percent, and 3.9 percent will be in these occupations in 2050. Workers' incomes will also decrease, in the absence of change in minority workers' income levels, with the percentage of all workers earning less than $25,000 (in 2010 constant dollars) increasing from 44.9 in 2010 to 49.4 percent in 2050, the percentage earning $50,000 or more declining from 22.4 percent in 2010 to 18.5 percent in 2050, and the median income of all workers declining from $29,179 in 2010 to $25,479 in 2050.

6.  Attempts are being made to provide additional training and other services to workers who need to develop or enhance their skills through Workforce Investment Act (WIA) training and other programs. By 2050 WIA programs are projected to be providing assistance to more than 139,000 additional workers (92.1 percent of whom will be nonHispanic Black, Hispanic, or nonHispanic Asian and Others). These and related data indicate that the state is attempting to assist workers in enhancing their skills and employability.

Overall, the data in this chapter clearly indicate that Texas must increase the skills and education of its labor force. In the absence of improvements in skills and education, the labor force will be less competitive and poorer in the future than it is today.

# CHAPTER 5

# Effects of Demographic Change on Selected Economic Factors Impacting the Private and Public Sectors of Texas

The characteristics of populations impact the private sector. The number and characteristics of populations affect the income and other economic resources of populations. Populations with larger proportions of adults in their most productive middle ages generally have greater economic resources for investment and higher levels of expenditures than those populations concentrated in youth, young adult, or elderly age groups. Similarly, levels of population growth are key components in the growth in overall markets, and the age, sex, and race/ethnicity characteristics of populations determine key market segments for different types of goods and services. The interrelationships are myriad and no single chapter can do justice to all of the interactive effects between demographic and economic factors.

In this chapter we provide a selective view of some of the effects of projected patterns of change in Texas population and households on factors impacting the economic characteristics of populations and the demands of population and household change on key socioeconomic parameters. We examine the effects of change in the extent of population growth and the population's age, sex, race/ethnicity, and household composition characteristics on income and poverty, on state tax revenues and expenditures, and on consumer expenditures in different sectors and product areas of the economy. We also examine the effects on household assets and net worth, on the number and rate of growth in owner and renter housing units, on the median value of owned housing units, and on the median rents for rented units. Although the analysis is quite extensive, it provides only a sampling of the important effects of demographic change on economic change in the public and private sectors.

### ECONOMIC CHANGE IN THE PRIVATE AND PUBLIC SECTORS FROM 2000 TO 2010

The data in Table 5.1 show that, despite extensive growth in Texas and its generally acknowledged lower rates of unemployment and reduced recessionary related changes compared to those that occurred in other parts of the nation, Texas maintained lower average incomes than the nation during the period from 1999 to 2010. Median income in the state increased (in constant dollars) relative to the nation from 89.9 percent in 1989 to 95.1 percent in 1999. By 2010 it had increased an additional 2.0 percent, with median household income levels increasing to 97.1 percent of the national median income level. Texas poverty rates remained higher than those for the nation. Poverty rates for persons in Texas were 117.0 percent of those in the nation in 2010, a decline from 124.2 percent in 1999 and 138.2 percent in 1989. Despite closure over time, in 2010, the percentage of persons in Texas in poverty was 17.9 percent, compared to 15.3 percent for the nation as a whole.

Table 5.2 shows additional income and poverty data for Texas by race/ethnicity of householder. The data in Table 5.2 show increases in income and also in overall poverty levels for all persons in all racial/ethnic groups over the period from 1999 to 2010. Whether examined in terms of median household, median family, or per capita income, incomes increased by between 24 and 37 percent from 1999 to 2010 for all racial/ethnic groups. Although the differences due to the recent recession are not totally encompassed in these data, it is evident that incomes increased in Texas from 1999 to 2010, and there were increases for all racial/ethnic groups.

The data in Table 5.2 also show clear income and poverty differences by race/ethnicity. Median household incomes for nonHispanic Black and Hispanic populations were 60 to 65 percent of the levels of nonHispanic Whites. Incomes for nonHispanic Asian and Others were approximately 95 to 98 percent of those for nonHispanic Whites in 1999, and similar differences persisted in 2010. In 1999 whereas nonHispanic White households had a median household income of $47,162, nonHispanic Black households had a median income of $29,321, Hispanic households a median income of $29,873, and nonHispanic Asian and Other households had a median income of $44,717. In 2010 these values were $61,049, $36,466, $37,019, and $60,110, respectively.

Due to differentials in family and household size (with larger household sizes being evident for some minority populations), differences in per capita incomes were larger (see Table 5.2). Per capita income in 1999 for the

Table 5.1

Median Household Income, Per Capita Income, Percent of Persons in Poverty in Texas
and the United States, and Texas Values as a Percent of United States Values, 1989–2010

| | | | | Percent Change | | |
|---|---|---|---|---|---|---|
| Income/Poverty | 1989 | 1999 | 2010 | 1989–1999 | 1999–2010 | 1989–2010 |
| **Texas** | | | **Panel A: Constant Dollars** | | | |
| Median Household Income | $45,867 | $52,246 | $48,615 | 13.9 | −7.0 | 6.0 |
| Per Capita Income | $21,908 | $25,670 | $23,863 | 17.2 | −7.0 | 8.9 |
| Percent of Persons in Poverty | 18.1 | 15.4 | 17.9 | −14.9 | 16.2 | −1.1 |
| | | | **Panel B: Current Dollars** | | | |
| Median Household Income | $27,016 | $39,927 | $48,615 | 47.8 | 21.8 | 79.9 |
| Per Capita Income | $12,904 | $19,617 | $23,863 | 52.0 | 21.6 | 84.9 |
| Percent of Persons in Poverty | 18.1 | 15.4 | 17.9 | −14.9 | 16.2 | −1.1 |
| **United States** | | | **Panel A: Constant Dollars** | | | |
| Median Household Income | $51,028 | $54,951 | $50,046 | 7.7 | −8.9 | −1.9 |
| Per Capita Income | $24,482 | $28,247 | $26,059 | 15.4 | −7.7 | 6.4 |
| Percent of Persons in Poverty | 13.1 | 12.4 | 15.3 | −5.3 | 23.4 | 16.8 |
| | | | **Panel B: Current Dollars** | | | |
| Median Household Income | $30,056 | $41,994 | $50,046 | 39.7 | 19.2 | 66.5 |
| Per Capita Income | $14,420 | $21,587 | $26,059 | 49.7 | 20.7 | 80.7 |
| Percent of Persons in Poverty | 13.1 | 12.4 | 15.3 | −5.3 | 23.4 | 16.8 |
| **Texas Values as a Percent of United States Values** | | | | | | |
| Median Household Income | 89.9 | 95.1 | 97.1 | 5.8 | 2.2 | 8.1 |
| Per Capita Income | 89.5 | 90.9 | 91.6 | 1.6 | 0.8 | 2.3 |
| Percent of Persons in Poverty | 138.2 | 124.2 | 117.0 | −10.1 | −5.8 | −15.3 |

*Source*: U.S. Census Bureau 2011e, 2002, 1992.

NonHispanic White population was $26,197. For the nonHispanic Black
population it was $14,324. For the Hispanic population it was $10,770 and
for the nonHispanic Asian and Other populations it was $19,113. The val-
ues for these groups in 2010 were $34,826, $18,545, $14,169, and $24,634,
respectively. For Hispanics, whereas median household incomes were 60 to
65 percent of those for nonHispanic Whites in 1999 and 2010, per capita

Table 5.2

Income and Poverty Characteristics of the Population in Texas by Race/Ethnicity, 1999–2010

| Race/Ethnicity | Median Household Income | Median Family Income | Per Capita Income | Number (in Thousands of Persons) and Percent in Poverty | | | | | | | |
|---|---|---|---|---|---|---|---|---|---|---|---|
| | | | | Persons | | Families | | Children | | Elderly | |
| | | | | Number | % | Number | % | Number | % | Number | % |
| **1999** | | | | | | | | | | | |
| NH[a] White | $ 47,162 | $ 57,194 | $ 26,197 | 826.5 | 7.8 | 156.2 | 5.2 | 205.7 | 8.3 | 113.6 | 8.0 |
| NH Black | 29,321 | 33,355 | 14,324 | 515.9 | 23.3 | 116.2 | 20.3 | 213.1 | 30.0 | 45.1 | 27.3 |
| Hispanic | 29,873 | 30,840 | 10,770 | 1,658.4 | 25.4 | 338.1 | 22.8 | 734.3 | 31.2 | 85.3 | 25.7 |
| NH Asian/Other[b] | 44,717 | 52,552 | 19,113 | 116.9 | 12.9 | 22.2 | 10.7 | 36.8 | 14.0 | 7.2 | 16.0 |
| Total | 39,927 | 45,861 | 19,617 | 3,117.6 | 15.4 | 632.7 | 12.0 | 1,189.9 | 20.5 | 251.2 | 12.8 |
| **2010** | | | | | | | | | | | |
| NH White | $ 61,049 | $ 76,350 | $ 34,826 | 981.9 | 8.7 | 173.5 | 5.6 | 225.4 | 9.6 | 114.9 | 6.8 |
| NH Black | 36,466 | 43,636 | 18,545 | 660.4 | 23.5 | 131.1 | 19.9 | 260.1 | 32.2 | 45.2 | 21.7 |
| Hispanic | 37,019 | 38,919 | 14,169 | 2,274.0 | 25.5 | 445.1 | 22.9 | 1,050.9 | 33.5 | 113.6 | 23.3 |
| NH Asian/Other | 60,110 | 71,716 | 24,634 | 168.1 | 13.0 | 29.4 | 10.1 | 51.6 | 13.6 | 12.5 | 15.4 |
| Total | 49,646 | 58,142 | 24,870 | 4,084.4 | 16.8 | 779.0 | 13.0 | 1,588.0 | 23.8 | 286.1 | 11.6 |

Table 5.2, continued

| | Percent Change 1999–2010 | | | Numeric and Percent Change 1999–2010 | | | | | | | |
|---|---|---|---|---|---|---|---|---|---|---|---|
| | % | % | % | Numeric | % | Numeric | % | Numeric | % | Numeric | % |
| NH White | 29.4 | 33.5 | 32.9 | 155.5 | 18.8 | 17.2 | 11.0 | 19.7 | 9.6 | 1.3 | 1.2 |
| NH Black | 24.4 | 30.8 | 29.5 | 144.5 | 28.0 | 14.9 | 12.8 | 46.9 | 22.0 | 0.1 | 0.2 |
| Hispanic | 23.9 | 26.2 | 31.6 | 615.5 | 37.1 | 107.0 | 31.6 | 316.6 | 43.1 | 28.3 | 33.2 |
| NH Asia/Other | 34.4 | 36.5 | 28.9 | 51.3 | 43.9 | 7.2 | 32.4 | 14.8 | 40.1 | 5.3 | 72.7 |
| Total | 24.3 | 26.8 | 26.8 | 966.8 | 31.0 | 146.3 | 23.1 | 398.1 | 33.5 | 35.0 | 13.9 |

*Source*: U.S. Census Bureau, 2002, 2011e.

[a]NH refers to nonHispanic; values shown are only for the nonHispanic persons in each race category. Hispanic includes Hispanics of all races.

[b]Median values for NH Asian & Others estimated from income distributions.

incomes for Hispanics were only about 41 percent of the per capita incomes for nonHispanic Whites in both years.

The data in Table 5.2 also show substantial differences in poverty levels across racial/ethnic groups but similarity in the differences between racial/ethnic groups during the two periods presented in the table. Poverty rates for persons who are nonHispanic Black and Hispanic were roughly three times as high as those for nonHispanic Whites in 2010, with poverty rates from 23 to 24 percent for nonHispanic Black and Hispanic persons compared to 8 to 9 percent for nonHispanic White and 13 percent for nonHispanic Asian and Others. Even larger relative differences are evident for families and for the elderly.

The differences in poverty rates for children are especially pronounced (see Table 5.2). For example, whereas 8.3 percent of nonHispanic White children lived in poverty households in 1999 and 9.6 percent did so in 2010, the values for nonHispanic Black children were 30.0 percent in 1999 and 32.2 percent in 2010, while those for Hispanic children were 31.2 percent in 1999 and 33.5 percent in 2010. NonHispanic Black and Hispanic children were three times more likely to live in poverty as nonHispanic White children in 2010.

The increases in the total number of persons in poverty were also substantial. Texas added more than 967,000 persons to its poverty population between 1999 and 2010, including more than 398,000 children. Of all persons added to the poverty population, nearly 616,000 were Hispanic, 156,000 nonHispanic White, 145,000 nonHispanic Black, and 51,000 nonHispanic Asian and Other.

Overall, these data show that incomes have increased in Texas, but that substantial disparities have persisted and relative poverty increased. Whereas Texas' population increased by 20.6 percent from 2000 to 2010, there was a 31 percent increase in the poverty population from 1999 (the reference year for income data for the 2000 census) to 2010. Texas continues to face socioeconomic challenges.

The data in Tables 5.3 and 5.4 show that growth in Texas governmental revenues and expenditures were limited due to recessionary pressures. The data in Table 5.3 show state tax collections from 1990 through 2010. Tax collections increased from $13.6 billion in 1990 when tax collections amounted to $801.01 per capita and represented 4.7 percent of personal income, to nearly $18.9 billion in 1995 when taxes were $997.40 per capita and nearly 5 percent of personal income, to $25.3 billion in 2000 when taxes were $1,209.84 per capita and represented 4.3 percent of personal income, to a maximum of nearly $41.4 billion in 2008 when they represented 4.3 percent of personal income and amounted to $1,705.77 per capita. Taxes declined to $35.4 billion in 2010 when they represented only 3.6 percent of personal income and $1,403.75 per capita.

Table 5.3

Total State Tax Collections and Per Capita Tax Collections in Texas, 1990–2010

| Fiscal Year | State Tax Collections | Resident Population | Per Capita Tax Collections | Percent Change from Previous Period | Taxes as a Percent of Personal Income |
|---|---|---|---|---|---|
| 1990 | $ 13,632,640,459 | 17,019,370 | $ 801.01 | — | 4.7 |
| 1995 | 18,858,790,042 | 18,907,964 | 997.40 | 24.5 | 4.8 |
| 2000 | 25,283,768,842 | 20,898,439 | 1,209.84 | 21.3 | 4.3 |
| 2005 | 29,838,277,614 | 22,767,257 | 1,310.58 | 8.3 | 4.0 |
| 2008 | 41,357,928,953 | 24,245,967 | 1,705.77 | 30.2 | 4.3 |
| 2010 | 35,368,901,064 | 25,196,099 | 1,403.75 | −17.7 | 3.6 |

*Source*: Texas Comptroller of Public Accounts 2012b.
*Note*: Population figures are for fiscal years.

Table 5.4 shows change in net expenditures for state services by category. The data show that increases in expenditures (in 2010 constant dollars) during the past decade were most extensive for health and human services (a 74 percent increase from 2000 to 2010, the latter partially reflecting the effects of the recession on households and families) and for the executive branch of the government (a 67.1 percent increase from 2000 to 2010). Other areas with increases in expenditure (in 2010 constant dollars) were judicial services with an increase of 44.5 percent, education that showed an increase of 32.8 percent, and employee and other benefits that showed a 33.4 percent increase. The substantial decrease in capital outlays clearly reflects recessionary effects with a decline of 36.1 percent.

## EFFECTS OF DEMOGRAPHIC CHANGE ON FUTURE ECONOMIC CHANGE

Data in Table 5.5 point to the potential shifts in the distribution of income among racial/ethnic groups and on overall income growth at different income levels. The data in this table show that the much more rapid growth in Hispanic and other minority populations and households will be reflected at all income levels. Of all persons at the $200,000 or higher level (values not shown but computed from household data in this table), 80.4 percent were nonHispanic White, 3.2 percent were nonHispanic Black, 8.8 percent were Hispanic, and 7.6 percent were nonHispanic Asian and Other in 2010,

Table 5.4

Net Expenditures* for State Government in Texas by Function in Constant (2010)
and Current (Millions of) Dollars, and Percent Change, 2000–2010

| | 2000 | 2010 | Percent Change | 2000 | 2010 | Percent Change |
|---|---|---|---|---|---|---|
| Function | Constant Dollars | | | Current Dollars | | |
| General Government | | | | | | |
| Executive | $ 1,922.4 | $ 3,211.5 | 67.1 | $ 1,505.1 | $ 3,211.5 | 113.4 |
| Legislative | 123.8 | 131.1 | 5.9 | 96.9 | 131.1 | 35.3 |
| Judicial | 190.4 | 275.2 | 44.5 | 149.1 | 275.2 | 84.6 |
| Total | 2,236.6 | 3,617.9 | 61.8 | 1,751.1 | 3,617.9 | 106.6 |
| Services | | | | | | |
| Health and Human Services | $20,860.7 | $36,300.6 | 74.0 | $16,332.2 | $36,300.6 | 122.3 |
| Public Safety and Corrections | 3,847.5 | 4,704.1 | 22.3 | 3,012.3 | 4,704.1 | 56.2 |
| Transportation | 5,695.9 | 5,972.1 | 4.8 | 4,459.4 | 5,972.1 | 33.9 |
| Natural Resources/ Recreational Services | 1,723.2 | 1,813.3 | 5.2 | 1,349.1 | 1,813.3 | 34.4 |
| Education | 24,401.9 | 32,417.9 | 32.8 | 19,104.7 | 32,417.9 | 69.7 |
| Regulatory Agencies | 250.8 | 332.6 | 32.6 | 196.3 | 332.6 | 69.4 |
| Employee Benefits | 2,505.9 | 3,342.2 | 33.4 | 1,961.9 | 3,342.2 | 70.4 |
| Debt Service | 763.8 | 881.0 | 15.3 | 598.0 | 881.0 | 47.3 |
| Capital Outlay | 885.3 | 565.8 | −36.1 | 693.1 | 565.8 | −18.4 |
| Lottery Winnings Paid | 318.9 | 486.7 | 52.6 | 249.7 | 486.7 | 94.9 |
| Total | $61,253.8 | $86,816.3 | 41.7 | $47,956.7 | $86,816.3 | 81.0 |

*Source*: Texas Comptroller of Public Accounts 2011b, 2012b.
*Data are for Fiscal Years ending August 31 of given year and include funds 1–849, excluding Fund 021 as it is a trust account.

while projections suggest that, by 2050, 50.2 percent of persons with such incomes will be nonHispanic White, 3.4 percent will be nonHispanic Black, 19.8 percent will be Hispanic, and 26.6 percent will be nonHispanic Asian and Other.

It is also clear, however, that in the absence of improved economic resources among nonHispanic Black, Hispanic, and nonHispanic Asian and Other households, future growth in the number of households will be much more extensive at lower income categories than at higher ones. From 2010 to 2050, the total increase in the projected number of households is 127.6 percent but the percentage increase in the number of households is greater than 127.6 percent in all income categories less than $50,000 and is greater than 150 percent in all income categories less than $30,000. It is less than 100 percent in all income categories greater than $100,000 and is only 71.9 percent for households with incomes of $200,000 or more.

Table 5.5

Household Income in Texas by Income Group and Race/Ethnicity of Householder in 2010 and Projected for 2050 Using the Scenario That Assumes 2000–2010 Rates of Net Migration (Percents Computed within Race/Ethnicity Group)

| Household Income | NH* White 2010 | NH* White 2050 | NH Black 2010 | NH Black 2050 | Hispanic 2010 | Hispanic 2050 | NH Asian & Other 2010 | NH Asian & Other 2050 | Total 2010 | Total 2050 |
|---|---|---|---|---|---|---|---|---|---|---|
| Less than $10,000 | 5.5 | 5.4 | 14.1 | 14.4 | 9.5 | 10.4 | 8.3 | 8.5 | 7.8 | 9.2 |
| $10,000 to $14,999 | 4.8 | 5.6 | 8.3 | 9.6 | 7.7 | 8.5 | 4.4 | 4.8 | 6.0 | 7.3 |
| $15,000 to $19,999 | 4.7 | 5.6 | 7.0 | 7.9 | 8.1 | 8.5 | 4.1 | 4.4 | 5.9 | 7.1 |
| $20,000 to $24,999 | 4.7 | 5.4 | 6.2 | 6.7 | 8.1 | 8.1 | 5.1 | 5.3 | 5.9 | 6.8 |
| $25,000 to $29,999 | 4.6 | 5.2 | 6.2 | 6.3 | 6.9 | 6.9 | 4.6 | 4.7 | 5.5 | 6.1 |
| $30,000 to $34,999 | 4.8 | 5.2 | 7.1 | 6.8 | 7.0 | 6.9 | 4.5 | 4.8 | 5.7 | 6.2 |
| $35,000 to $39,999 | 4.7 | 5.0 | 5.5 | 5.3 | 6.1 | 5.9 | 4.1 | 4.3 | 5.2 | 5.4 |
| $40,000 to $44,999 | 4.7 | 4.8 | 5.1 | 4.9 | 5.5 | 5.3 | 4.7 | 4.5 | 5.0 | 5.0 |
| $45,000 to $49,999 | 4.2 | 4.3 | 4.3 | 4.1 | 5.0 | 4.7 | 3.6 | 3.9 | 4.4 | 4.4 |
| $50,000 to $59,999 | 8.0 | 8.1 | 7.9 | 7.4 | 8.5 | 8.2 | 7.0 | 7.0 | 8.1 | 7.9 |
| $60,000 to $74,999 | 10.6 | 10.3 | 8.6 | 8.2 | 9.3 | 8.9 | 9.6 | 9.4 | 9.9 | 9.3 |
| $75,000 to $99,999 | 13.1 | 12.2 | 9.1 | 8.5 | 8.6 | 8.3 | 12.7 | 12.2 | 11.3 | 9.9 |
| $100,000 to $124,999 | 9.1 | 8.1 | 5.1 | 4.7 | 4.7 | 4.5 | 8.9 | 8.5 | 7.3 | 6.0 |
| $125,000 to $149,999 | 5.4 | 4.8 | 2.5 | 2.4 | 2.0 | 1.5 | 6.0 | 5.7 | 4.1 | 3.3 |
| $150,000 to $199,999 | 5.2 | 4.6 | 2.0 | 1.8 | 1.8 | 1.8 | 6.2 | 5.9 | 3.9 | 3.1 |
| $200,000 or more | 5.9 | 5.4 | 1.0 | 1.0 | 1.2 | 1.2 | 6.2 | 6.1 | 4.0 | 3.0 |
| Total Households | 4,803,580 | 5,605,710 | 1,068,108 | 2,163,639 | 2,614,157 | 9,880,494 | 437,088 | 2,655,253 | 8,922,933 | 20,305,096 |

Source: Projections by the authors and 2010 data and rates derived from U.S. Census Bureau 2011d, 2011e.

*NH refers to nonHispanic; values shown are only for the nonHispanic persons in each race category. Hispanic includes Hispanics of all races.

This suggests that, in the absence of change, the number of lower income households will grow more substantially in the future than the number of households with higher incomes.

In Table 5.5 data in the columns for total households show the percentage of households by income levels (in 2010 constant dollars). The data in this table verify the future trend of greater concentration of households at lower income levels. The percentage of households in income categories less than $40,000 will increase from 42 percent of all households in 2010 to 48.1 percent of all households by 2050. The percentage in the $40,000 to $49,999 categories will not change, remaining at 9.4 percent, while the percentage of all households with incomes of $50,000 and above will decrease from 48.6 percent of all households in 2010 to 42.5 percent in 2050. In sum, the data in Tables 5.5 indicate that, although other forms of non-household income are clearly important, in the absence of improvements in Texas minority households' incomes, Texas households overall will become poorer.

Table 5.6 contains data on aggregate household income by race/ethnicity of householder assuming mean household income levels by race/ethnicity in 2010 and projections of households from 2020 to 2050. The increases by race/ethnicity are a function of growth in the number of households in each race/ethnicity group multiplied by the mean income levels. The final column points to the average household income resulting from the aggregation and summation of these household income projections divided by the number of households. The data in the bottom row of this table show that by 2050, Hispanic households will be the largest contributor to the state's aggregate household income base, contributing $467.1 billion to aggregate income, followed by nonHispanic White, nonHispanic Asian and Other and nonHispanic Black households.

The final column shows average income in the state from 2010 to 2050. The net effect of the projected increase in households, in the absence of improved income levels for the fastest growing minority households, is that the average household income in Texas in 2050 will decline from $66,333 in 2010 to $58,574 in 2050. This indicates that the average Texas household will be $7,759 poorer in 2050 than the average household was in 2010 (in 2010 constant dollars). This represents a decrease of 11.7 percent from the 2010 base of $66,333. It further verifies that, in the absence of improvements in the earning capacity of Texas minority households, the average Texas household will be poorer in the future than it is today.

Panel B of Table 5.6 provides data from additional simulations of the impacts of changes in income among racial and ethnic groups. In this table two simulations are provided and compared to the race/ethnicity specific income levels used (but not shown) in the Panel A projections. In one of the two alternative scenarios closure of all minority racial/ethnic groups

Table 5.6

Aggregate Household Income in Texas (in Billions of 2010 Dollars) by Race/Ethnicity and Mean Household Income in Texas in 2010 and Projected to 2050 Using the Projection Scenario That Assumes 2000–2010 Rates of Net Migration for Texas (Panel A) and Assuming Alternative Closures to 2010 NonHispanic White Rates by 2050 (Panel B)

Panel A:

| | Aggregate Household Income (in $Billions) | | | | | Mean Household Income |
|---|---|---|---|---|---|---|
| Year | NH* White | NH Black | Hispanic | NH Asian & Other | Total | |
| 2010 | $ 379.3 | $ 51.1 | $ 126.8 | $ 34.8 | $ 592.0 | $ 66,333 |
| 2020 | 396.6 | 63.3 | 184.8 | 57.0 | 701.7 | 63,492 |
| 2030 | 404.8 | 74.9 | 256.6 | 91.1 | 827.5 | 60,988 |
| 2040 | 413.7 | 87.2 | 348.4 | 139.0 | 988.4 | 59,634 |
| 2050 | 415.5 | 99.3 | 467.1 | 207.3 | 1,189.4 | 58,574 |

Panel B:

| Race/ Ethnicity | Assuming 2010 Income Differentials | | Assuming Closure to Half of Differential Between NH White Income for Minority Households | | Assuming NH White Income for Minority Households | |
|---|---|---|---|---|---|---|
| | Aggregate | Mean | Aggregate | Mean | Aggregate | Mean |
| NH White | $ 415.5 | $ 74,127 | $ 415.50 | $ 74,127 | $ 415.5 | $ 74,127 |
| NH Black | 99.3 | 45,918 | 129.90 | 60,022 | 160.4 | 74,127 |
| Hispanic | 467.1 | 47,280 | 599.80 | 60,704 | 732.4 | 74,127 |
| NH Asian & Other | 207.3 | 78,078 | 207.30 | 78,078 | 207.3 | 78,078 |
| Total | 1,189.4 | 58,574 | 1,352.50 | 66,609 | 1,515.7 | 74,644 |

Source: Projections by the authors and 2010 data and rates derived from U.S. Census Bureau 2011d, 2011e.

*NH refers to nonHispanic; values shown are only for the nonHispanic persons in each race category. Hispanic includes Hispanics of all races.

to one-half the income level of those of nonHispanic Whites in 2010 by 2050 is assumed, and in the second, closure of all groups to the total non-Hispanic White income level in 2010 by 2050 is assumed. Under the half closure scenario, rather than declining by $7,759 from 2010 to 2050, the average income of households will increase by $8,035 to $66,609 compared to the 2010 value without closure. Under this scenario, the average income will increase by $276 from 2010 levels. If total closure were reached, the average income in 2050 will increase to $74,644, a difference of $16,070 and an increase of $8,311 from the mean value in 2010. In addition, when the aggregate income levels are examined, income closure between the racial/ethnic groups will increase aggregate income from the $592.0 billion per year in 2010 to $1.52 trillion in 2050 rather than the $1.19 trillion projected to occur without closure, an annual increase of $326.3 billion. Clearly, incomes of minority populations will substantially increase aggregate incomes.

Values computed from Table 5.7 show the distribution of poverty households by household type in 2010 and projected from 2010 to 2050 under alternative assumptions. The 2010 data in this table show that nonHispanic Black, Hispanic, and nonHispanic Asian and Other households have higher percentages of nonfamily and female households and smaller proportions of family households than nonHispanic White households. Nonfamily and female householder are household types with lower incomes and more limited socioeconomic resources overall than family households.

The alternative scenarios in the three bottom panels of Table 5.7 show the effects of assuming 2010 rates of poverty continuing through 2050, of assuming a partial reduction in the poverty differentials between minority and nonHispanic White households by 2050, and of assuming that all households in 2050 had the poverty rates of nonHispanic Whites in 2050. In the absence of changes in poverty levels among racial/ethnic groups (that is, assuming that current differences continue), the effects of household change will be to increase the overall rate of household poverty by 3.3 percent from 2010 poverty levels (see the increase from 14.4 percent of all households in 2010 to 17.7 percent of all households in 2050 shown in the total column for total households in 2010 and 2050). On the other hand, assuming closure of the difference to one-half of what it was in 2010 will result in a poverty rate of 13.7 (compared to the 14.4 percent level in 2010), and reducing the differential entirely so that all households had the 2010 poverty rates of nonHispanic Whites in 2050 will result in a poverty rate for all households of 9.8 percent. These data show that reducing poverty in those populations that currently have the lowest incomes would substantially reduce the state's total poverty population.

The data in Table 5.8 indicate that depending on how income changes

Table 5.7

Number and Percent of Households in Poverty in Texas by Type and Race/Ethnicity in 2010 and Projected for 2050 Assuming Different Rates of Closure to NonHispanic White Poverty Rates and Using the Projection Scenario That Assumes 2000–2010 Rates of Net Migration for Texas

| Family Type | NH[a] White | | NH Black | | Hispanic | | NH Asian & Other | | Total | |
|---|---|---|---|---|---|---|---|---|---|---|
| | Number | % | Number | % | Number | % | Number | % | Number | % |
| **2010** | | | | | | | | | | |
| Family households | 176,385 | 5.6 | 137,950 | 19.9 | 476,149 | 22.9 | 31,179 | 9.9 | 810,829 | 13.0 |
| Married couple family | 71,688 | 2.8 | 22,411 | 6.7 | 228,020 | 16.4 | 16,784 | 6.7 | 329,781 | 7.3 |
| With related children | 35,694 | 3.5 | 13,924 | 7.8 | 188,793 | 20.0 | 10,354 | 7.0 | 240,177 | 10.5 |
| Other family[b] | 104,697 | 17.1 | 115,539 | 32.1 | 248,129 | 36.1 | 14,395 | 22.6 | 481,048 | 27.9 |
| Male, no spouse | 16,520 | 9.4 | 13,898 | 22.3 | 39,725 | 19.1 | 2,857 | 14.2 | 72,405 | 15.5 |
| With related children | 11,360 | 11.5 | 10,077 | 27.9 | 32,387 | 25.5 | 1,550 | 16.4 | 55,354 | 20.2 |
| Female, no spouse | 88,177 | 20.3 | 101,641 | 34.2 | 208,404 | 43.4 | 11,538 | 26.5 | 408,643 | 32.6 |
| With related children | 73,346 | 27.9 | 89,228 | 42.1 | 188,424 | 52.6 | 9,274 | 33.8 | 360,139 | 41.7 |
| Nonfamily households | 246,320 | 15.7 | 139,845 | 27.5 | 95,377 | 26.6 | 27,908 | 24.5 | 509,450 | 20.0 |
| Total households | 418,544 | 8.7 | 270,597 | 25.3 | 541,258 | 20.7 | 56,743 | 13.0 | 1,287,142 | 14.4 |
| **2050 Assuming (Current 2010) Poverty Rates by Household Type for All Race/Ethnicity Groups** | | | | | | | | | | |
| Family households | 187,558 | 5.3 | 250,018 | 18.3 | 1,677,845 | 21.8 | 183,224 | 9.7 | 2,298,845 | 15.8 |
| Married couple family | 80,183 | 2.8 | 43,649 | 6.6 | 813,836 | 15.3 | 100,632 | 6.6 | 1,038,300 | 10.2 |
| With related children | 33,620 | 3.5 | 24,122 | 7.8 | 644,499 | 20.0 | 57,682 | 7.0 | 759,923 | 14.3 |
| Other family | 107,575 | 16.1 | 206,369 | 29.3 | 864,009 | 33.8 | 82,592 | 21.7 | 1,260,545 | 29.3 |
| Male, no spouse | 16,933 | 9.2 | 26,258 | 21.6 | 140,349 | 18.7 | 16,823 | 14.2 | 200,363 | 17.0 |
| With related children | 10,858 | 11.5 | 17,926 | 27.9 | 113,878 | 25.5 | 8,896 | 16.4 | 151,588 | 23.0 |
| Female, no spouse | 90,642 | 18.8 | 180,111 | 30.9 | 723,660 | 40.1 | 65,769 | 25.0 | 1,060,182 | 33.8 |
| With related children | 71,659 | 27.9 | 157,734 | 42.1 | 656,834 | 52.6 | 52,808 | 33.8 | 939,045 | 46.1 |
| Nonfamily households | 319,857 | 15.7 | 218,888 | 27.5 | 579,070 | 26.6 | 185,495 | 24.5 | 1,303,320 | 22.6 |
| Total households | 507,625 | 9.1 | 468,906 | 21.7 | 2,256,915 | 22.8 | 368,719 | 13.9 | 3,602,165 | 17.7 |

Table 5.7, continued

| Family Type | NH[a] White Number | % | NH Black Number | % | Hispanic Number | % | NH Asian & Other Number | % | Total Number | % |
|---|---|---|---|---|---|---|---|---|---|---|
| **2050 Assuming Closure to Half of NH White Poverty Rates by Household Type for All Race/Ethnicity Groups** | | | | | | | | | | |
| Family households | 187,758 | 5.3 | 201,275 | 14.7 | 1,151,896 | 15.0 | 145,902 | 7.7 | 1,686,831 | 11.6 |
| Married couple family | 80,183 | 2.8 | 31,497 | 4.7 | 486,403 | 9.5 | 73,050 | 4.8 | 671,133 | 6.6 |
| With related children | 33,620 | 3.5 | 17,473 | 5.7 | 378,643 | 11.8 | 43,262 | 5.3 | 472,998 | 8.9 |
| Other family[b] | 107,575 | 16.1 | 169,778 | 24.1 | 665,493 | 26.0 | 72,852 | 19.1 | 1,015,698 | 23.6 |
| Male, no spouse | 16,933 | 9.2 | 18,735 | 15.4 | 106,046 | 14.1 | 13,690 | 11.5 | 155,404 | 13.2 |
| With related children | 10,888 | 11.5 | 12,657 | 19.7 | 82,617 | 18.5 | 7,567 | 14.0 | 113,729 | 17.2 |
| Female, no spouse | 90,642 | 18.8 | 151,043 | 25.9 | 559,447 | 31.0 | 59,162 | 22.5 | 860,294 | 27.5 |
| With related children | 71,669 | 27.9 | 131,132 | 35.0 | 502,615 | 40.3 | 48,199 | 30.9 | 753,615 | 37.0 |
| Nonfamily households | 319,867 | 15.7 | 171,926 | 21.6 | 460,426 | 21.2 | 152,181 | 20.1 | 1,104,400 | 19.1 |
| Total households | 507,625 | 9.1 | 373,201 | 17.2 | 1,612,322 | 16.3 | 298,083 | 11.2 | 2,791,231 | 13.7 |
| **2050 Assuming NH White Poverty Rates by Household Type for All Race/Ethnicity Groups** | | | | | | | | | | |
| Family households | 187,758 | 5.3 | 152,511 | 11.2 | 625,914 | 8.1 | 108,553 | 5.7 | 1,074,736 | 7.4 |
| Married couple family | 80,183 | 2.8 | 19,345 | 2.9 | 158,970 | 3.1 | 45,467 | 3.0 | 303,965 | 3.0 |
| With related children | 33,620 | 3.5 | 10,824 | 3.5 | 112,787 | 3.5 | 28,841 | 3.5 | 186,072 | 3.5 |
| Other family: | 107,575 | 16.1 | 133,166 | 18.9 | 466,944 | 18.3 | 63,086 | 16.5 | 770,771 | 17.9 |
| Male, no spouse | 16,933 | 9.2 | 11,213 | 9.2 | 71,744 | 9.6 | 10,556 | 8.9 | 110,446 | 9.4 |
| With related children | 10,888 | 11.5 | 7,389 | 11.5 | 51,357 | 11.5 | 6,238 | 11.5 | 75,872 | 11.5 |
| Female, no spouse | 90,642 | 18.8 | 121,953 | 21.0 | 395,200 | 21.9 | 52,530 | 20.0 | 660,325 | 21.1 |
| With related children | 71,669 | 27.9 | 104,531 | 27.9 | 348,397 | 27.9 | 43,590 | 27.9 | 568,187 | 27.9 |
| Nonfamily households | 319,867 | 15.7 | 124,965 | 15.7 | 341,782 | 15.7 | 118,868 | 15.7 | 905,482 | 15.7 |
| Total households | 507,625 | 9.1 | 277,476 | 12.8 | 967,696 | 9.8 | 227,421 | 8.6 | 1,980,218 | 9.8 |

*Source*: Projections by the authors and 2010 rates derived from U.S. Census Bureau 2011a, 2011d, 2011f; and Ruggles et al. 2010.

[a]NH refers to nonHispanic; values shown are only for the nonHispanic persons in each race category. Hispanic includes Hispanics of all races.

[b]By sex of the householder. Households without related children not shown.

Table 5.8

State Tax Revenues in Texas (in Billions of 2010 Dollars) by Race/Ethnicity in 2010 and Projections for 2050 Assuming 2011 Tax Rates and Alternative Scenarios of Aggregate Household Income Distribution Using the Population Projection That Assumes 2000–2010 Rates of Net Migration

| Year | Aggregate Household Income (in $Billions) | | | | | Mean Household Tax |
|---|---|---|---|---|---|---|
| | NH* White | NH Black | Hispanic | NH Asian & Other | Total | |
| **2010** | $ 20.6 | $ 3.4 | $ 8.3 | $ 1.9 | $ 34.2 | $ 3,838 |
| **2050** | | | | | | |
| Assuming Current Differentials | 22.9 | 6.8 | 31.1 | 11.3 | 72.2 | 3,556 |
| Assuming Closure to Half | 22.9 | 7.8 | 35.8 | 11.3 | 77.9 | 3,837 |
| Assuming Full Closure | 22.9 | 8.9 | 40.4 | 11.3 | 83.6 | 4,118 |

*Source*: Projections by the authors and 2010 data and rates derived from Texas Comptroller of Public Accounts 2011c; U.S. Census Bureau 2011d, 2011g; Ruggles et al. 2010. *NH refers to nonHispanic; values shown are only for the nonHispanic persons in each race category. Hispanic includes Hispanics of all races.

over time, state tax revenues in Texas could decline or increase substantially. For example, the average tax level in 2010 was approximately $3,838 per household. Because of lower incomes for the most rapidly growing population segments in Texas, the per-household levels will decrease to $3,556 by 2050 if differentials in income levels between racial/ethnic groups continue. However, if complete (full) closure between all groups to the non-Hispanic White level in 2010 occurred by 2050, per-household annual tax revenues will increase to $4,118 in 2050, an annual increase of $280 billion for the state as a whole. The data in this table document that improvement in the incomes of minority Texans could substantially increase state tax revenues as well. Total tax resources will increase from $72.2 billion to $83.6 billion, by $11.4 billion more per year, if there were closure in income levels between nonHispanic Whites and minorities. As more Texas households improve economically, the level of Texas governmental income will also improve.

## EFFECTS OF DEMOGRAPHIC CHANGE ON THE PRIVATE SECTOR

Population change will affect the lives of members of Texas' growing population by impacting their incomes and potential poverty levels; when household incomes increase, private sector expenditures tend to increase. In this section we examine the potential effects of demographic change on the private sector of Texas. Specifically, we examine the effects on consumer expenditures, on assets and net worth, and on housing tenure and the value of housing as a key example of a private sector impacted by demographic change.

The data in Tables 5.9 through 5.11 show projections of consumer expenditures by category through 2050 assuming the number of households by age and race/ethnicity shown and discussed in Chapter 3 and assuming the

Table 5.9

Household Consumer Expenditures in Texas in 2010 (in Millions
of 2010 Dollars), Projections for 2050, and Numeric and
Percent Change for 2010–2050 Using the Population Projection
That Assumes 2000–2010 Rates of Net Migration

| Expenditure Category | All Households | | 2010–2050 Change* | |
|---|---|---|---|---|
| | 2010 | 2050 | Numeric | % |
| Food | $ 54,976.4 | $ 122,446.6 | $ 67,470.2 | 122.7 |
| Alcohol | 3,141.9 | 5,704.2 | 2,562.3 | 81.6 |
| Housing | 147,639.0 | 320,739.5 | 173,100.5 | 117.3 |
| Apparel | 15,965.7 | 37,166.4 | 21,200.7 | 132.8 |
| Transportation | 66,909.7 | 141,211.4 | 74,301.7 | 111.1 |
| Health | 25,274.1 | 52,409.4 | 27,135.3 | 107.4 |
| Entertainment | 20,412.1 | 38,711.4 | 18,299.3 | 89.7 |
| Personal | 5,177.2 | 11,147.1 | 5,969.9 | 115.3 |
| Reading | 749.4 | 1,414.1 | 664.7 | 88.7 |
| Education | 8,598.7 | 17,990.1 | 9,391.4 | 109.2 |
| Tobacco | 2,773.2 | 4,546.8 | 1,773.6 | 64.0 |
| Miscellaneous | 7,050.4 | 13,212.2 | 6,161.8 | 87.4 |
| Cash | 13,249.7 | 26,319.7 | 13,070.0 | 98.6 |
| Insurance | 45,009.7 | 89,413.7 | 44,404.0 | 98.7 |
| Total | 416,927.1 | 882,432.7 | 465,505.6 | 111.7 |

*Source*: Projections by the authors and 2010 data and rates derived from U.S. Census Bureau 2011d, 2011g; Ruggles et al. 2010; U.S. Bureau of Labor Statistics 2011.
*Percents calculated from unrounded values.

Table 5.10

Percent of Consumer Expenditures in Texas by Expenditure Category and Race/Ethnicity in 2010 and Projected for 2050 Using the Population Projection That Assumes 2000–2010 Rates of Net Migration

2010

| Race/Ethnicity | Total | Food | Alcohol | Housing | Apparel | Transportation | Health | Entertainment |
|---|---|---|---|---|---|---|---|---|
| NH* White | 60.6 | 56.2 | 71.4 | 57.6 | 51.3 | 60.6 | 71.2 | 68.9 |
| NH Black | 9.0 | 8.9 | 6.1 | 10.1 | 9.5 | 9.1 | 7.1 | 6.7 |
| Hispanic | 24.7 | 29.4 | 18.5 | 26.5 | 31.2 | 24.9 | 17.5 | 19.7 |
| NH Asian/Other | 5.7 | 5.5 | 4.0 | 5.8 | 8.0 | 5.4 | 4.2 | 4.7 |

| Race/Ethnicity | Personal | Reading | Education | Tobacco | Misc. | Cash | Insurance |
|---|---|---|---|---|---|---|---|
| NH White | 58.0 | 77.8 | 61.1 | 71.7 | 69.6 | 67.3 | 64.1 |
| NH Black | 10.7 | 5.4 | 5.4 | 9.0 | 8.4 | 10.3 | 8.1 |
| Hispanic | 27.0 | 11.8 | 22.6 | 15.5 | 18.1 | 18.9 | 21.4 |
| NH Asian/Other | 4.3 | 5.0 | 10.9 | 3.8 | 3.9 | 3.5 | 6.4 |

2050

| Race/Ethnicity | Total | Food | Alcohol | Housing | Apparel | Transportation | Health | Entertainment |
|---|---|---|---|---|---|---|---|---|
| NH White | 32.3 | 28.5 | 44.2 | 30.0 | 24.1 | 32.0 | 43.6 | 40.5 |
| NH Black | 8.4 | 7.8 | 6.2 | 9.2 | 7.9 | 8.4 | 7.9 | 7.1 |
| Hispanic | 43.3 | 49.0 | 37.1 | 44.8 | 48.9 | 44.1 | 35.3 | 37.8 |
| NH Asian/Other | 16.0 | 14.7 | 12.5 | 16.0 | 19.1 | 15.5 | 13.2 | 14.6 |

| Race/Ethnicity | Personal | Reading | Education | Tobacco | Misc. | Cash | Insurance |
|---|---|---|---|---|---|---|---|
| NH White | 31.0 | 52.1 | 27.9 | 44.3 | 42.5 | 43.0 | 33.7 |
| NH Black | 9.7 | 6.3 | 4.7 | 10.0 | 8.8 | 10.7 | 7.6 |
| Hispanic | 47.3 | 24.5 | 37.9 | 32.5 | 36.3 | 35.3 | 39.4 |
| NH Asian/Other | 12.0 | 17.1 | 29.5 | 13.2 | 12.4 | 11.0 | 19.3 |

Source: Projections by the authors and 2010 data and rates derived from U.S. Census Bureau, 2011d, 2011g; Ruggles et al. 2010; U.S. Bureau of Labor Statistics 2011.
*NH refers to nonHispanic; values shown are only for the nonHispanic persons in each race category. Hispanic includes Hispanics of all races.

Table 5.11

Percent of Net Change in Consumer Expenditures in Texas by Expenditure Category and Race/Ethnicity
Using the Population Projection That Assumes 2000–2010 Rates of Net Migration, 2010–2050

| Race/ Ethnicity | Total | Food | Alcohol | Housing | Apparel | Transportation | Health | Entertainment |
|---|---|---|---|---|---|---|---|---|
| NH* White | 6.3 | 5.2 | 9.6 | 5.9 | 3.1 | 5.1 | 18.0 | 8.1 |
| NH Black | 7.9 | 6.9 | 6.4 | 8.4 | 6.6 | 7.7 | 8.7 | 7.6 |
| Hispanic | 60.4 | 65.4 | 60.8 | 60.7 | 62.6 | 62.0 | 51.9 | 58.5 |
| NH Asian/ Other | 25.4 | 22.5 | 23.2 | 25.0 | 27.7 | 25.2 | 21.4 | 25.8 |
| Total | 100.0 | 100.0 | 100.0 | 100.0 | 100.0 | 100.0 | 100.0 | 100.0 |

| Race/ Ethnicity | Personal | Reading | Education | Tobacco | Misc. | Cash | Insurance |
|---|---|---|---|---|---|---|---|
| NH White | 7.3 | 22.6 | −3.0 | 7.2 | 11.3 | 18.5 | 1.0 |
| NH Black | 8.8 | 7.4 | 3.9 | 11.3 | 9.4 | 11.2 | 7.1 |
| Hispanic | 65.1 | 39.0 | 52.2 | 55.7 | 57.2 | 51.9 | 58.7 |
| NH Asian/ Other | 18.8 | 31.0 | 46.9 | 25.8 | 22.1 | 18.4 | 33.2 |
| Total | 100.0 | 100.0 | 100.0 | 100.0 | 100.0 | 100.0 | 100.0 |

*Source*: Projections by the authors and 2010 data and rates derived from U.S. Census Bureau, 2011d, 2011g; Ruggles et al. 2010; U.S. Bureau of Labor Statistics 2011.
*NH refers to nonHispanic; values shown are only for the nonHispanic persons in each race category. Hispanic includes Hispanics of all races.

per capita average expenditures by age and race/ethnicity of householder and consumer category, evident in the consumer expenditure survey data for 2010 (see sources in Table 5.9). As shown in Table 5.9, the total value of expenditures is projected to more than double from 2010 to 2050 from $416.9 billion to $882.4 billion, an increase of 111.7 percent. This increase, however, is less than the 127.6 percent rate of growth in the total number of households and reflects the fact that the fastest growing segments of Texas population tend to have lower incomes and reduced levels of expenditures compared to nonHispanic White households. Because of the disproportionate (relative to nonHispanic Whites) rates of household growth, the increase in the number of such households can be expected to lead to slower rates of growth in consumer expenditures. These expenditures will increase more slowly than the growth in the total number of households.

The total percent change in expenditures from 2010 to 2050 indicates decreased rates of population growth among nonHispanic White households that accounted for 60.6 percent of consumer expenditures in 2010 (see Table 5.10) but that will increase their expenditures by only 11.2 percent from 2010 to 2050. NonHispanic Black households, which account for

9 percent of expenditures, will increase their expenditures by 94.8 percent from 2010 to 2050; Hispanic expenditures, which accounted for 24.7 percent of all expenditures in 2010, will increase by 265.6 percent from 2010 to 2050; and nonHispanic Asian and Others, which accounted for 5.7 percent of all expenditures in 2010, will increase their expenditures by 490.0 percent.

By 2050, as a result of the differentials in growth among different racial/ethnic groups (see Table 5.10), 43.3 percent of the increase in expenditures will be accounted for by Hispanics, 32.3 percent will be due to non-Hispanic White households, 8.4 percent to nonHispanic Black households, and 16.0 percent to nonHispanic Asian and Other households. Overall (see Table 5.11), 60.4 percent of the net change in consumer expenditures from 2010 to 2050 will be due to Hispanic households, 25.4 percent due to non-Hispanic Asian and Other, 7.9 percent to nonHispanic Black, and 6.3 percent to nonHispanic White households. These data clearly point out that the future of the Texas economy will be increasingly tied to the economic change impacting Texas minority populations.

*Economic Impacts of Change in Household Types*
Tables 5.12 and 5.13 show both how household form affects expenditures and the extent of change expected to result from the change in each form of household over the projection period. The data in Table 5.12 show the levels of expenditures by expenditure category and indicate that the largest total expenditures were by non-family and married-couple households in 2010 and will be so in 2050. At the same time, the analysis indicates (see Table 5.13) that the largest percent growth, reflecting the underlying change in the proportion of households in different types of households, will be in the male- and female-headed households. Consumer expenditures in male- and female-headed households will increase by 126.1 and 123.6 percent, respectively, compared to increases of 100.8 percent for nonfamily households and 112.5 percent for married-couple households. Changes in household form toward households with a smaller number of adults lead to lower overall income levels and expenditures, but it is those households with a single adult that are increasing most rapidly. The net effects of the reduction in the number and proportion of two-adult households is to reduce per household and overall consumer expenditures.

*Impacts of Population Change on Households' Net Worth and Assets*
In this section we examine the effects of demographic change on households' net worth and assets. These data allow us to determine how projected demographic change is likely to impact the future wealth of Texas households.

The data in Panel A of Table 5.14 show the projected change in net worth and assets from 2010 to 2050 due to race/ethnicity related change.

Table 5.12

Consumer Expenditures in Texas by Household Type and Expenditure
Category in 2010 (in Millions of 2010 Dollars) and Projected for 2050 Using the
Population Projection That Assumes 2000–2010 Rates of Net Migration

| Expenditure Category | All Households | Married Couple Families | Male Householder Families | Female Householder Families | Nonfamily Households |
|---|---|---|---|---|---|
| **2010** | | | | | |
| Food | $ 54,976.4 | $ 34,814.0 | $ 2,041.5 | $ 6,126.9 | $11,994.0 |
| Alcohol | 3,141.9 | 1,916.6 | 102.1 | 159.8 | 963.4 |
| Housing | 147,639.0 | 89,672.8 | 6,659.5 | 17,420.2 | 33,886.6 |
| Apparel | 15,965.7 | 9,385.9 | 543.4 | 2,540.0 | 3,496.5 |
| Transportation | 66,909.7 | 43,288.3 | 3,482.1 | 6,741.1 | 13,398.2 |
| Health | 25,274.1 | 17,353.3 | 871.6 | 1,505.8 | 5,543.3 |
| Entertainment | 20,412.1 | 13,456.4 | 714.2 | 1,828.2 | 4,413.3 |
| Personal | 5,177.2 | 3,211.2 | 180.7 | 628.9 | 1,156.3 |
| Reading | 749.4 | 486.7 | 20.1 | 44.7 | 197.8 |
| Education | 8,598.7 | 6,221.4 | 123.2 | 385.0 | 1,869.1 |
| Tobacco | 2,773.2 | 1,391.4 | 189.8 | 228.2 | 963.9 |
| Miscellaneous | 7,050.4 | 4,078.5 | 594.1 | 529.4 | 1,848.3 |
| Cash | 13,249.7 | 8,630.7 | 861.2 | 489.6 | 3,268.2 |
| Insurance | 45,009.7 | 31,700.0 | 2,034.9 | 2,665.6 | 8,609.2 |
| Total | 416,927.1 | 265,607.1 | 18,418.3 | 41,293.7 | 91,607.9 |
| **2050** | | | | | |
| Food | $ 122,446.6 | $ 77,416.0 | $ 4,490.3 | $ 15,176.0 | $25,364.3 |
| Alcohol | 5,704.2 | 3,545.8 | 197.0 | 349.7 | 1,611.8 |
| Housing | 320,739.5 | 197,366.8 | 15,735.3 | 38,039.7 | 69,597.7 |
| Apparel | 37,166.4 | 21,010.1 | 1,007.0 | 7,066.3 | 8,082.9 |
| Transportation | 141,211.4 | 91,398.1 | 8,852.8 | 14,946.8 | 26,013.7 |
| Health | 52,409.4 | 35,696.6 | 2,155.0 | 3,016.2 | 11,541.6 |
| Entertainment | 38,711.4 | 25,679.1 | 1,448.9 | 3,513.0 | 8,070.3 |
| Personal | 11,147.1 | 6,888.3 | 417.9 | 1,365.8 | 2,475.1 |
| Reading | 1,414.1 | 924.2 | 38.5 | 94.0 | 357.4 |
| Education | 17,990.1 | 13,060.2 | 201.5 | 897.8 | 3,830.6 |
| Tobacco | 4,546.8 | 2,314.2 | 300.8 | 318.8 | 1,612.9 |
| Miscellaneous | 13,212.2 | 8,002.5 | 1,136.7 | 995.5 | 3,077.5 |
| Cash | 26,319.7 | 17,465.0 | 1,339.3 | 980.5 | 6,534.9 |
| Insurance | 89,413.7 | 63,780.2 | 4,316.8 | 5,580.4 | 15,736.3 |
| Total | 882,432.7 | 564,547.4 | 41,637.7 | 92,340.5 | 183,907.1 |

*Source*: Projections by the authors and 2010 data and rates derived from U.S. Census Bureau,
2011d, 2011g; Ruggles et al. 2010; U.S. Bureau of Labor Statistics 2011.

Table 5.13

Percent Change in Consumer Expenditures in Texas by Household
Type and Expenditure Category Using the Population Projection That
Assumes 2000–2010 Rates of Net Migration, 2010–2050

| Expenditure Category | All Households | Married Couple Families | Male Householder Families | Female Householder Families | Nonfamily Households |
|---|---|---|---|---|---|
| Food | 122.7 | 122.4 | 119.9 | 147.7 | 111.5 |
| Alcohol | 81.6 | 85.0 | 92.9 | 118.8 | 67.3 |
| Housing | 117.2 | 120.1 | 136.3 | 118.4 | 105.4 |
| Apparel | 132.8 | 123.8 | 85.3 | 178.2 | 131.2 |
| Transportation | 111.0 | 111.1 | 154.2 | 121.7 | 94.2 |
| Health | 107.4 | 105.7 | 147.2 | 100.3 | 108.2 |
| Entertainment | 89.6 | 90.8 | 102.9 | 92.2 | 82.9 |
| Personal | 115.3 | 114.5 | 131.2 | 117.2 | 114.1 |
| Reading | 88.7 | 89.9 | 91.8 | 110.1 | 80.7 |
| Education | 109.2 | 109.9 | 63.6 | 133.2 | 104.9 |
| Tobacco | 64.0 | 66.3 | 58.5 | 39.7 | 67.3 |
| Miscellaneous | 87.4 | 96.2 | 91.3 | 88.0 | 66.5 |
| Cash | 98.6 | 102.4 | 55.5 | 100.3 | 100.0 |
| Insurance | 98.7 | 101.2 | 112.1 | 109.3 | 82.8 |
| Total | 111.7 | 112.5 | 126.1 | 123.6 | 100.8 |

*Source*: Projections by the authors and 2010 data and rates derived from U.S. Census Bureau, 2011d, 2011g; Ruggles et al. 2010; U.S. Bureau of Labor Statistics 2011.

These data indicate that both the net worth of households and their assets will decrease in relative terms. That is, whereas households will increase by 127.6 percent from 2010 to 2050, neither net worth nor any of the forms of assets will increase by that much. In fact, the net worth of households will increase by only 66.6 percent and net worth, excluding home equity, will increase by only 56.9 percent. The average Texas household will have fewer assets and lower net worth in 2050 than in 2010 (in 2010 constant dollars).

One of the reasons for this change is that net worth and assets will increasingly be owned by households that, due to a variety of historical, discriminatory, and other factors, have lower incomes, higher rates of poverty, and hence reduced assets and net worth. Panel A of Table 5.15 shows how extensive the shifts will be among households from different racial/ethnic groups. For example, in 2010, 82.8 percent of total net worth in Texas was in households with a nonHispanic White householder, only 3.3 percent in households with a nonHispanic Black householder, 9.1 percent in households with an Hispanic householder, and 4.8 percent in households with a nonHispanic Asian and Other householder but, by 2050, the percentages

Table 5.14

Race/Ethnicity and Age of Householder Effects on Estimates of Net Worth
and Assets for Households in Texas in 2010 and Projected for 2050 Using the
Population Projection That Assumes 2000–2010 Rates of Net Migration

| Categories of Assets[a] | 2010 | 2050 | Percent[b] Difference |
|---|---|---|---|
| Panel A: Race/Ethnicity Effects | | | |
| Net Worth | $ 2,398,050.9 | $ 3,994,521.1 | 66.6 |
| Interest Earning Assets at Financial Institutions | 178,890.0 | 342,258.2 | 91.3 |
| Regular Checking Accounts | 18,143.7 | 35,586.3 | 96.1 |
| Stocks and Mutual Fund Shares | 2,338,037.2 | 3,542,816.1 | 51.5 |
| Equity in Business or Profession | 1,216,924.7 | 2,354,858.1 | 93.5 |
| Equity in Motor Vehicles | 66,775.9 | 141,171.8 | 111.4 |
| Equity in Own Home | 1,105,354.2 | 2,339,149.3 | 111.6 |
| Rental Property Equity | 3,083,570.9 | 6,414,002.2 | 108.0 |
| U.S. Savings Bonds | 49,294.9 | 98,996.8 | 100.8 |
| IRA or KEOGH Accounts | 727,737.3 | 1,359,825.1 | 86.9 |
| 401K & Thrift Savings Plan | 643,449.3 | 1,238,765.5 | 92.5 |
| Panel B: Age Effects | | | |
| Net Worth | $ 2,688,299.3 | $ 6,838,679.2 | 154.4 |
| Interest Earning Assets at Financial Institutions | 196,928.8 | 496,546.7 | 152.1 |
| Regular Checking Accounts | 20,100.4 | 49,296.6 | 145.3 |
| Stocks and Mutual Fund Shares | 2,505,330.0 | 7,634,173.8 | 204.7 |
| Equity in Business or Profession | 1,325,574.4 | 3,010,295.3 | 127.1 |
| Equity in Motor Vehicles | 70,443.6 | 163,282.6 | 131.8 |
| Equity in Own Home | 1,025,292.5 | 2,576,484.3 | 151.3 |
| Rental Property Equity | 2,942,162.8 | 7,114,605.1 | 141.8 |
| U.S. Savings Bonds | 53,709.7 | 135,080.0 | 151.5 |
| IRA or KEOGH Accounts | 798,014.5 | 1,988,207.8 | 149.1 |
| 401K & Thrift Savings Plan | 756,296.9 | 1,824,003.5 | 141.2 |

Source: Projections by the authors and data and rates derived from U.S. Census Bureau 2008b.
[a]Monetary values in millions of 2010 constant dollars.
[b]Percents computed from unrounded values.

Table 5.15

Projected Proportions of Net Worth and Assets of Households in Texas by Race/Ethnicity (Panel A) and Age (Panel B) of Householder in 2010 and 2050 Using the Population Projection That Assumes 2000–2010 Rates of Net Migration

| Race/Ethnicity and Age | Net Worth | Interest Earning Assets | Regular Checking | Equity in Business/ Profession | Equity in Motor Vehicles | Equity in Own Home | Equity in Rental Property | U.S. Savings Bonds | IRA/ KEOGH | 401K/ Thrift | Stocks/ Mutual Funds |
|---|---|---|---|---|---|---|---|---|---|---|---|
| | | | | | | Categories of Assets | | | | | |
| | | | | Panel A: Race/Ethnicity Effects | | | | | | | |
| | | | | | **2010** | | | | | | |
| NH* White | 82.8 | 73.7 | 70.1 | 69.5 | 63.7 | 63.7 | 65.3 | 66.6 | 71.9 | 71.4 | 87.6 |
| NH Black | 3.3 | 6.0 | 6.3 | 6.9 | 7.8 | 8.3 | 6.7 | 4.9 | 7.8 | 6.4 | 4.1 |
| Hispanic | 9.1 | 13.1 | 18.3 | 19.7 | 22.5 | 21.7 | 22.6 | 26.0 | 15.8 | 16.7 | 4.0 |
| NH Asian/Other | 4.8 | 7.2 | 5.3 | 3.9 | 6.0 | 6.3 | 5.4 | 2.5 | 4.5 | 5.5 | 4.3 |
| | | | | | **2050** | | | | | | |
| NH White | 58.0 | 45.0 | 41.7 | 41.9 | 35.2 | 35.1 | 36.6 | 38.7 | 44.9 | 43.3 | 67.5 |
| NH Black | 4.1 | 6.3 | 6.5 | 7.2 | 7.5 | 7.9 | 6.5 | 5.0 | 8.4 | 6.8 | 5.5 |
| Hispanic | 20.6 | 26.0 | 35.2 | 38.4 | 40.1 | 38.8 | 41.1 | 48.9 | 32.0 | 32.8 | 10.1 |
| NH Asian/Other | 17.3 | 22.7 | 16.6 | 12.5 | 17.2 | 18.2 | 15.7 | 7.4 | 14.7 | 17.1 | 16.9 |

Table 5.15, continued

| Race/Ethnicity and Age | Net Worth | Interest Earning Assets | Regular Checking | Equity in Business/ Profession | Equity in Motor Vehicles | Equity in Own Home | Equity in Rental Property | U.S. Savings Bonds | IRA/ KEOGH | 401K/ Thrift | Stocks/ Mutual Funds |
|---|---|---|---|---|---|---|---|---|---|---|---|
| | | | | | Categories of Assets | | | | | | |
| | | | | | Panel B: Age Effects | | | | | | |
| | | | | | 2010 | | | | | | |
| 15–44 | 18.3 | 22.5 | 9.6 | 36.1 | 33.7 | 19.1 | 26.4 | 26.5 | 23.7 | 25.7 | 9.6 |
| 45–54 | 23.2 | 20.5 | 7.9 | 22.7 | 24.4 | 23.7 | 21.1 | 19.7 | 21.7 | 24.7 | 7.9 |
| 55–64 | 21.9 | 22.1 | 9.8 | 24.1 | 21.1 | 22.8 | 24.9 | 19.0 | 21.5 | 22.4 | 9.8 |
| 65+ | 36.6 | 34.9 | 72.7 | 16.9 | 20.8 | 34.4 | 27.4 | 34.8 | 33.1 | 27.2 | 72.7 |
| | | | | | 2050 | | | | | | |
| 15–44 | 14.7 | 18.1 | 28.2 | 32.2 | 29.4 | 15.5 | 22.1 | 21.3 | 19.3 | 21.6 | 6.5 |
| 45–54 | 17.9 | 16.0 | 14.9 | 19.7 | 20.6 | 18.5 | 17.2 | 15.4 | 17.1 | 20.1 | 5.1 |
| 55–64 | 18.2 | 18.6 | 14.0 | 22.4 | 19.3 | 19.2 | 21.8 | 16.0 | 18.3 | 19.6 | 6.8 |
| 65+ | 49.2 | 47.3 | 42.9 | 25.7 | 30.7 | 46.8 | 38.9 | 47.3 | 45.3 | 38.7 | 81.7 |

*Source:* Projections by the authors and data and rates from U.S. Census Bureau 2008b.

*NH refers to nonHispanic; values shown are only for the nonHispanic persons in each race category. Hispanic includes Hispanics of all races.

for householders from these same racial/ethnic groups will be 58.0, 4.1, 20.6, and 17.3 percent, respectively.

Similarly when assets are examined, the proportion owned by households with a nonHispanic White householder (that exceeded 50 percent in all categories in 2010) will exceed 50 percent in only one category (i.e., stocks and mutual funds) in 2050. By 2050, 55 percent of interest earning assets, 58.3 percent of funds in checking accounts, 58.1 percent of equity in businesses, 64.8 percent of equity in motor vehicles, 64.9 percent of equity in homes, 63.4 percent of equity in rental property, 61.3 percent of equity in savings bonds, 55.1 percent of IRA or KEOGH accounts, and 56.7 percent of 401K and thrift plans will be held by a householder who was nonHispanic Black, Hispanic, or nonHispanic Asian and Other.

The data in Panel B of Tables 5.14 and 5.15 demonstrate the effects of the aging of the Texas population on net worth and assets. As noted above, the Texas population, similar to the United States population as a whole, will age substantially in the coming decades. The data in Panel B of Table 5.14 demonstrate that the aging of the Texas population will increase the value of assets and overall net worth disproportionately relative to the overall increase in the number of households. Whereas racial/ethnic change leads to 2010–2050 decreases in relative assets and net worth that are projected to be less than the 127.6 percent increase in the overall number of households, the aging of the population leads to increases in net worth and assets that are more rapid than the overall increase in the number of households for net worth and for all asset categories (except equity in businesses).

The shift of net worth and asset ownership to older households is evident in the data in Panel B of Table 5.15. For example, whereas 58.5 percent of all net worth was owned by householders 55 years of age or older in 2010, 67.4 percent will be owned by households with a householder 55 years of age or older in 2050. Such increases are evident for all asset categories. The aging of the population increases its overall wealth.

The effects of the aging and of the change in the racial/ethnic composition of the population on net worth and assets are further examined in the data in Table 5.16. The impacts of changes in both variables are examined by comparing the results with the actual race/ethnicity distribution projected for 2050 (from Panel A, Table 5.14) to those made assuming the population total projected for 2050 but with the race/ethnicity distribution of 2010. Similarly, the effects of the changing age distribution are shown in Panel B with the results for the age distribution compared to that with the age distribution assumed to be that of 2010.

The results in the top panel of Table 5.16 clearly show that because of socioeconomic differences among racial/ethnic groups, the projected 2050 values, when compared to ones produced by assuming the continuation of 2010 percentage distributions by race/ethnicity, decrease net worth and

Table 5.16

Race/Ethnicity and Age of Householder Effects on Projections of Net Worth and
Assets for Households in Texas in 2050 by Category Assuming 2010 Distribution
of Households by Race/Ethnicity and Age of Householder and Using the
Population Projection That Assumes 2000–2010 Rates of Net Migration

| Categories of Assets[a] | Assuming 2010 Distribution in 2050 | Assuming 2000–2010 Rates of Net Migration | Percent[b] Difference |
|---|---|---|---|
| Panel A: Race/Ethnicity of Householder Effects | | | |
| Net Worth | $ 5,457,023.3 | $ 3,994,521.1 | −26.8 |
| Interest Earning Assets | 407,083.5 | 342,258.2 | −15.9 |
| Regular Checking Accounts | 41,287.8 | 35,586.3 | −13.8 |
| Stocks and Mutual Fund Shares | 5,320,455.7 | 3,542,816.1 | −33.4 |
| Equity in Business or Profession | 2,769,243.4 | 2,354,858.1 | −15.0 |
| Equity in Motor Vehicles | 151,955.7 | 141,171.8 | −7.1 |
| Equity in Own Home | 2,515,352.7 | 2,339,149.3 | −7.0 |
| Rental Property Equity | 7,016,998.0 | 6,414,002.2 | −8.6 |
| U.S. Savings Bonds | 112,175.8 | 98,996.8 | −11.7 |
| IRA or KEOGH Accounts | 1,656,044.6 | 1,359,825.1 | −17.9 |
| 401K & Thrift Savings Plan | 1,464,238.2 | 1,238,765.5 | −15.4 |
| Panel B: Age of Householder Effects | | | |
| Net Worth | $ 6,117,514.8 | $ 6,838,679.2 | 11.8 |
| Interest Earning Assets | 448,132.6 | 496,546.7 | 10.8 |
| Regular Checking Accounts | 45,740.6 | 49,296.6 | 7.8 |
| Stocks and Mutual Fund Shares | 5,701,148.6 | 7,634,173.8 | 33.9 |
| Equity in Business or Profession | 3,016,487.4 | 3,010,295.3 | −0.2 |
| Equity in Motor Vehicles | 160,302.0 | 163,282.6 | 1.9 |
| Equity in Own Home | 2,333,163.5 | 2,576,484.3 | 10.4 |
| Rental Property Equity | 6,695,208.7 | 7,114,605.1 | 6.3 |
| U.S. Savings Bonds | 122,222.3 | 135,080.0 | 10.5 |
| IRA or KEOGH Accounts | 1,815,967.9 | 1,988,207.8 | 9.5 |
| 401K & Thrift Savings Plan | 1,721,035.0 | 1,824,003.5 | 6.0 |

*Source*: Projections of households by the authors and data and rates from U.S. Census
Bureau 2008b.
[a]Monetary values in millions of 2010 constant dollars.
[b]Percents computed from unrounded values.

asset values compared to those obtained by assuming the less diverse racial/ethnic structure of 2010. On the other hand, the older age distribution projected in 2050 compared to the younger age distribution obtained by assuming the 2010 age structure for the population (shown in Panel B) leads to an increase in overall net worth and assets. In every net worth and asset category in Panel A of Table 5.16, there are decreases in values, while in every category in Panel B, except equity in businesses, there are increases in values. The results in this table show that, given projected socioeconomic differentials by race/ethnicity and by age, growing racial/ethnic diversity will lead to decreases in net worth and asset values and that an increasingly older population will lead to increases in net worth and asset values. The data in this table also indicate that, in the absence of change that increases income among minority households, the negative effects of racial/ethnic change will be larger than the positive effects of the aging of the population. Thus, the total effect of race/ethnicity will be to reduce net worth by $1.46 trillion, while the effects of aging will increase net worth by $721 billion. Overall, then, the net gains due to the aging of the population are substantially exceeded by the decreases resulting from racial/ethnic change (in the absence of factors that reduce socioeconomic differences among racial/ethnic groups).

*Demographic Impacts on Housing*
Population change impacts the level of demand and the forms of housing demanded. Racial/ethnic groups with higher income levels are more likely to live in owner-occupied housing, while those with more limited resources are more likely to live in rental housing. Similarly, age affects both resources for housing, with older persons being more likely to have the resources necessary to own housing and thus being more likely to own housing than persons of younger ages.

Table 5.17 presents data supporting such relationships. In 2010, 71.4 percent of NonHispanic White and 62.1 percent of nonHispanic Asian and Other households lived in owner-occupied housing, compared with 57.5 percent of Hispanic and 44.5 percent of nonHispanic Black households. Median housing values and median gross rent for nonHispanic White households ($150,300 and $871) and nonHispanic Asian and Other households ($186,600 and $873) were higher than those for nonHispanic Black households ($106,100 and $797) or Hispanic households ($93,100 and $728).

Tables 5.18 and 5.19 show projections of the number of households by renter and owner status. The data in Table 5.18 show that the number of units will increase from 8.9 million in 2010 to 20.3 million in 2050, with approximately 12.9 million units being owner households and 7.4 million being renter households by 2050. These figures represent increases of

Table 5.17

Median Owner-Occupied Housing Values, Median Monthly Rents,
Ownership Rates, and Renter Rates in Texas by Race/Ethnicity
of Householder, and Tenure by Age of Householder, 2010

| Housing Characteristic | Race/Ethnicity | | | | |
| --- | --- | --- | --- | --- | --- |
| | NH* White | NH Black | Hispanic | NH Asian & Other | Total |
| Median Housing Values | $150,300 | $106,100 | $93,100 | $186,600 | $128,100 |
| Median Gross Rents | $871 | $797 | $728 | $873 | $801 |
| Tenure | | | | | |
|     Percent Owner | 71.4 | 44.5 | 57.5 | 62.1 | 63.6 |
|     Percent Renter | 28.6 | 55.5 | 42.5 | 37.9 | 36.4 |

| Housing Characteristic | Age Group | | | | |
| --- | --- | --- | --- | --- | --- |
| | 15–59 | 60–64 | 65–74 | 75+ | Total |
| Tenure | | | | | |
|     Percent Owner | 57.6 | 80.3 | 82.4 | 78.8 | 63.6 |
|     Percent Renter | 42.4 | 19.7 | 17.6 | 21.2 | 36.4 |

*Source*: U.S. Census Bureau 2011e.
*NH refers to nonHispanic; values shown are only for the nonHispanic persons in each race category. Hispanic includes Hispanics of all races.

127.6 percent for the total number of households. Such changes clearly reflect the underlying population and tenure characteristics of households.

The total number of nonHispanic White households will increase by 16.7 percent from 2010 to 2050, the number of nonHispanic Black households by 102.6 percent, the number of Hispanic households by 278.0 percent, and the number of nonHispanic Asian and Other households by 507.5 percent. As a result of such differentials in growth, the proportion of all householders who are nonHispanic White will decline from 53.8 percent in 2010 to 27.6 percent in 2050, and the respective values for nonHispanic Black householders will be a decline from 12.0 to 10.7 percent. By contrast, for Hispanic householders the percentages will increase from 29.3 to

Table 5.18

Number of Households in Texas, Percent Change 2010–2050, and
Percent of Households by Race/Ethnicity of Householder and
Housing Tenure in 2010 and Projected to 2050 Using the Population
Projection That Assumes 2000–2010 Rates of Net Migration

| Year | NH* White | NH Black | Hispanic | NH Asian & Other | Total |
|---|---|---|---|---|---|
| Panel A: Number of Households | | | | | |
| **All Households** | | | | | |
| 2010 | 4,803,580 | 1,068,108 | 2,614,157 | 437,088 | 8,922,933 |
| 2050 | 5,605,710 | 2,163,639 | 9,880,494 | 2,655,253 | 20,305,096 |
| **Owner Households** | | | | | |
| 2010 | 3,434,560 | 478,512 | 1,510,983 | 261,379 | 5,685,434 |
| 2050 | 4,086,563 | 1,099,129 | 6,066,623 | 1,678,120 | 12,930,435 |
| **Renter Households** | | | | | |
| 2010 | 1,369,020 | 589,596 | 1,103,174 | 175,709 | 3,237,499 |
| 2050 | 1,519,147 | 1,064,510 | 3,813,871 | 977,133 | 7,374,661 |
| Panel B: Percent Change in Households | | | | | |
| **All Households** | | | | | |
| 2010–2050 | 16.7 | 102.6 | 278.0 | 507.5 | 127.6 |
| **Owner Households** | | | | | |
| 2010–2050 | 19.0 | 129.7 | 301.5 | 542.0 | 127.4 |
| **Renter Households** | | | | | |
| 2010–2050 | 11.0 | 80.5 | 245.7 | 456.1 | 127.8 |

Table 5.18, continued

| Year | NH* White | NH Black | Hispanic | NH Asian & Other | Total |
|------|-----------|----------|----------|------------------|-------|
| Panel C: Race/Ethnicity of Households as a Percent of Households | | | | | |
| **All Households** | | | | | |
| 2010 | 53.8 | 12.0 | 29.3 | 4.9 | 100.0 |
| 2050 | 27.6 | 10.7 | 48.7 | 13.0 | 100.0 |
| **Owner Households** | | | | | |
| 2010 | 60.4 | 8.4 | 26.6 | 4.6 | 100.0 |
| 2050 | 31.6 | 8.5 | 46.9 | 13.0 | 100.0 |
| **Renter Households** | | | | | |
| 2010 | 42.3 | 18.2 | 34.1 | 5.4 | 100.0 |
| 2050 | 20.6 | 14.4 | 51.7 | 13.3 | 100.0 |

*Source*: Projections by the authors and 2010 data and rates derived from U.S. Census Bureau 2011d.
*NH refers to nonHispanic; values shown are only for the nonHispanic persons in each race category. Hispanic includes Hispanics of all races.

48.7 percent, and for nonHispanic Asian and Other householders there is an increase from 4.9 to 13.0 percent.

Of the total net increase of 11,382,163 households from 2010 to 2050 (see Table 5.19), 7.0 percent will be due to the growth in nonHispanic White households, 9.6 percent to growth in the number of nonHispanic Black households, 63.8 percent to the increase in the number of Hispanic households, and 19.6 percent to the increase in the number of Asian and Other households. The shift of the underlying population from nonHispanic White to larger minority, particularly Hispanic, populations is evident in the data on households.

The shift in the age distribution of the population and the differences in the age distributions of owners and renters are clearly reflected in the data in Table 5.20. For example, if one examines the total columns, the younger age structure of renters versus owners is evident. In 2010, 10.2 percent of renters were 65 years of age or older compared to 23 percent of owners; in 2050, 17.9 percent of renters will be 65 years of age or older compared

Table 5.19

Number and Percent of Net Change in Texas Households
by Race/Ethnicity of Householder and Housing
Tenure Using the Population Projection That Assumes
2000–2010 Rates of Net Migration, 2010–2050

| Race/Ethnicity | Number | % |
|---|---|---|
| **Total** | | |
| NH* White | 802,130 | 7.0 |
| NH Black | 1,095,531 | 9.6 |
| Hispanic | 7,266,337 | 63.8 |
| NH Asian & Other | 2,218,165 | 19.6 |
| Total | 11,382,163 | 100.0 |
| **Owner** | | |
| NH White | 652,003 | 9.0 |
| NH Black | 620,617 | 8.6 |
| Hispanic | 4,555,640 | 62.9 |
| NH Asian & Other | 1,416,741 | 19.5 |
| Total | 7,245,001 | 100.0 |
| **Renter** | | |
| NH White | 150,127 | 3.6 |
| NH Black | 474,914 | 11.5 |
| Hispanic | 2,710,697 | 65.5 |
| NH Asian & Other | 801,424 | 19.4 |
| Total | 4,137,162 | 100.0 |

*Source*: Projections by the authors and 2010 data and rates derived
from U.S. Census Bureau 2011d.
*NH refers to nonHispanic; values shown are only for the non-
Hispanic persons in each race category. Hispanic includes Hispanics
of all races.

to 33.2 percent of owners. At the same time these data show that the aging
of the population is evident among both owners and renters with the percentage of elderly householders increasing among both renter and owner
households. What such data indicate is that issues related to the aging, as
well as the diversification, of the population will be important in the future
of Texas housing.

Table 5.20

Percent of Texas Households by Age and Race/Ethnicity of Householder
and Housing Tenure in 2010 and Projected for 2050 Using the Population
Projection That Assumes 2000–2010 Rates of Net Migration

| Age Group | NH* White 2010 | NH* White 2050 | NH Black 2010 | NH Black 2050 | Hispanic 2010 | Hispanic 2050 | NH Asian & Other 2010 | NH Asian & Other 2050 | Total 2010 | Total 2050 |
|---|---|---|---|---|---|---|---|---|---|---|
| **Total** | | | | | | | | | | |
| 15–24 | 4.9 | 3.9 | 6.3 | 4.2 | 6.9 | 5.1 | 6.3 | 4.7 | 5.7 | 4.6 |
| 25–34 | 14.4 | 12.0 | 19.2 | 13.8 | 23.0 | 17.7 | 22.0 | 15.4 | 17.8 | 15.4 |
| 35–44 | 16.5 | 13.7 | 21.7 | 16.6 | 24.8 | 19.7 | 25.7 | 24.5 | 20.0 | 18.4 |
| 45–54 | 21.2 | 14.4 | 22.6 | 17.6 | 20.6 | 19.8 | 21.6 | 21.7 | 21.2 | 18.3 |
| 55–64 | 19.2 | 15.9 | 16.3 | 17.7 | 13.1 | 15.3 | 14.6 | 15.1 | 16.8 | 15.7 |
| 65–74 | 12.6 | 16.5 | 8.3 | 15.8 | 6.8 | 11.7 | 6.7 | 10.7 | 10.1 | 13.3 |
| 75+ | 11.2 | 23.6 | 5.6 | 14.3 | 4.8 | 10.7 | 3.1 | 7.9 | 8.4 | 14.3 |
| **Owner** | | | | | | | | | | |
| 15–24 | 1.1 | 0.8 | 0.8 | 0.5 | 2.2 | 1.5 | 1.2 | 0.9 | 1.4 | 1.1 |
| 25–34 | 9.8 | 8.0 | 9.5 | 6.0 | 16.2 | 11.7 | 13.1 | 8.7 | 11.6 | 9.7 |
| 35–44 | 16.2 | 13.2 | 20.5 | 13.8 | 25.5 | 19.0 | 27.9 | 25.2 | 19.6 | 17.6 |
| 45–54 | 23.2 | 15.4 | 26.3 | 18.1 | 24.4 | 22.1 | 26.6 | 25.3 | 23.9 | 20.0 |
| 55–64 | 22.2 | 18.0 | 21.5 | 20.7 | 16.6 | 18.2 | 19.1 | 18.6 | 20.5 | 18.4 |
| 65–74 | 15.2 | 19.4 | 12.3 | 20.7 | 9.0 | 14.4 | 8.6 | 13.0 | 13.0 | 16.3 |
| 75+ | 12.3 | 25.2 | 9.1 | 20.2 | 6.1 | 13.1 | 3.5 | 8.3 | 10.0 | 16.9 |
| **Renter** | | | | | | | | | | |
| 15–24 | 14.3 | 12.0 | 10.8 | 7.9 | 13.4 | 10.8 | 13.8 | 11.3 | 13.3 | 10.7 |
| 25–34 | 25.9 | 22.7 | 27.1 | 21.8 | 32.3 | 27.3 | 35.2 | 26.9 | 28.8 | 25.5 |
| 35–44 | 17.2 | 15.1 | 22.6 | 19.4 | 24.0 | 20.8 | 22.3 | 23.2 | 20.8 | 19.8 |
| 45–54 | 16.4 | 11.7 | 19.6 | 17.1 | 15.4 | 16.2 | 14.1 | 15.5 | 16.5 | 15.3 |
| 55–64 | 11.7 | 10.2 | 12.0 | 14.7 | 8.3 | 10.5 | 7.9 | 8.9 | 10.4 | 10.8 |
| 65–74 | 6.3 | 8.7 | 5.0 | 10.8 | 3.9 | 7.3 | 3.9 | 6.7 | 5.1 | 8.0 |
| 75+ | 8.2 | 19.6 | 2.9 | 8.3 | 2.8 | 7.1 | 2.8 | 7.5 | 5.1 | 9.9 |

*Source*: Projections by the authors and 2010 data and rates derived from U.S. Census
Bureau 2011d.
*NH refers to nonHispanic; values shown are only for the nonHispanic persons in
each race category. Hispanic includes Hispanics of all races.

Tables 5.21 through 5.23 provide data that allow one to analyze how housing expenditures are likely to change as a result of underlying population change. In these tables the number of households by age, sex, and race/ethnicity of householder are multiplied by average consumer expenditures by age, sex, and race/ethnicity of householder for housing as derived from the consumer expenditure survey.

The data in Table 5.21 indicate that aggregate annual expenditures for housing in Texas will increase from $81.6 billion in 2010 to $181.7 billion in 2050, an increase of $100.1 billion. Approximately $61.4 billion of the $100.1 billion increase from 2010 to 2050 will be due to growth in the number of Hispanic households, approximately $3.9 billion due to growth in nonHispanic White households, $7.5 billion due to growth in nonHispanic Black households, and $27.3 billion due to growth in nonHispanic Asian and Other households. Minority households will clearly dominate growth in total housing expenditures.

The data in Table 5.21 also indicate that total household expenditures will increase rapidly among all racial/ethnic groups and that owner expenditures will generally increase more rapidly than renter expenditures. Computations made using the data in this table indicate that the 2010 to 2050 increase in owner related expenditures for nonHispanic White households will be 7.7 percent compared to 12.2 percent for renter household expenditures. Increases for the same categories will be 105.7 percent and 78.6 percent for nonHispanic Black households, 266.8 and 234.3 percent for Hispanic households, and 512.6 and 444.0 percent for nonHispanic Asian and Other households.

Table 5.21 also presents data showing the percentage of expenditures within owner and renter categories of housing due to each race/ethnicity group for periods from 2010 through 2050. Reflecting differentials in rates of population growth, the data in this table show that the percentage of total expenditures due to nonHispanic White and nonHispanic Black households will decrease among both renter and owner households with the percentage of all nonHispanic White owner households decreasing from 59.4 percent in 2010 to 29.3 percent in 2050 and the percentage of renter households with a nonHispanic White householder decreasing from 41.6 percent to 20.2 percent. The change among nonHispanic Black owners will be from 6.8 percent in 2010 to 6.4 percent in 2050 and among renters from 16.6 to 12.9 percent. On the other hand, the percentage of owners who are Hispanic will increase from 27.0 percent in 2010 to 45.2 percent in 2050 and the equivalent values for renter households will be 35.0 percent and 50.7 percent. NonHispanic Asian and Other households reflect similar patterns of rapid proportional increases to those for Hispanics, with the proportion of owner households increasing from 6.8 to 19.1 percent and the proportion of renters increasing from 6.8 to 16.2 percent. As for other

Table 5.21

Aggregate Annual Expenditures and Percent of Annual Expenditures for Housing in Texas by Race/Ethnicity of the Householder and Housing Tenure in 2010 and Projected to 2050 Using the Population Projection That Assumes 2000–2010 Rates of Net Migration

| Year | NH[a] White | | NH Black | | Hispanic | | NH Asian & Other | | Total |
|---|---|---|---|---|---|---|---|---|---|
| | Expenditures[b] | %[c] | Expenditures | % | Expenditures | % | Expenditures | % | Expenditures |
| **All Households** | | | | | | | | | |
| 2010 | $ 43,583.8 | 53.4 | $ 8,235.4 | 10.1 | $ 24,198.8 | 29.7 | $ 5,577.5 | 6.8 | $ 81,595.5 |
| 2030 | 46,474.3 | 38.5 | 11,979.7 | 9.9 | 47,745.8 | 39.6 | 14,451.0 | 12.0 | 120,650.9 |
| 2050 | 47,439.4 | 26.1 | 15,704.2 | 8.6 | 85,630.2 | 47.1 | 32,873.3 | 18.2 | 181,647.1 |
| **Owner Occupied** | | | | | | | | | |
| 2010 | $ 32,148.9 | 59.4 | $ 3,666.7 | 6.8 | $ 14,580.4 | 27.0 | $ 3,694.2 | 6.8 | $ 54,090.2 |
| 2030 | 34,400.6 | 43.5 | 5,616.4 | 7.1 | 29,340.4 | 37.1 | 9,695.7 | 12.3 | 79,053.1 |
| 2050 | 34,610.6 | 29.3 | 7,543.2 | 6.4 | 53,477.8 | 45.2 | 22,628.9 | 19.1 | 118,260.5 |
| **Renter Occupied** | | | | | | | | | |
| 2010 | $ 11,434.9 | 41.6 | $ 4,568.6 | 16.6 | $ 9,618.4 | 35.0 | $ 1,883.3 | 6.8 | $ 27,505.3 |
| 2030 | 12,073.8 | 29.0 | 6,363.3 | 15.3 | 18,405.4 | 44.2 | 4,755.3 | 11.5 | 41,597.8 |
| 2050 | 12,828.8 | 20.2 | 8,161.1 | 12.9 | 32,152.4 | 50.7 | 10,244.4 | 16.2 | 63,386.6 |

*Source:* Projections by the authors and 2010 data and rates derived from U.S. Census Bureau 2011d; U.S. Bureau of Labor Statistics 2011.
[a]NH refers to nonHispanic; values shown are only for the nonHispanic persons in each race category. Hispanic includes Hispanics of all races.
[b]Monetary values in millions of 2010 constant dollars.
[c]Percents computed from unrounded values.

Table 5.22

Proportion of Annual Expenditures for Housing in Texas by Age of
Householder and Housing Tenure in 2010 and Projected to 2050 Using the
Population Projection That Assumes 2000–2010 Rates of Net Migration

| | Age of Householder | | | | | | |
|------|------|------|------|------|------|------|------|
| Year | 15–24 | 25–34 | 35–44 | 45–54 | 55–64 | 65–74 | 75+ |
| **All Households** | | | | | | | |
| 2010 | 3.8 | 19.0 | 25.0 | 24.3 | 15.3 | 7.7 | 4.9 |
| 2020 | 3.7 | 18.3 | 24.2 | 21.5 | 16.5 | 10.4 | 5.4 |
| 2030 | 3.5 | 18.3 | 23.8 | 21.2 | 14.7 | 11.4 | 7.1 |
| 2040 | 3.4 | 17.6 | 24.7 | 21.2 | 14.5 | 10.3 | 8.3 |
| 2050 | 3.6 | 17.0 | 24.3 | 22.3 | 14.5 | 10.3 | 8.0 |
| **Owner Occupied** | | | | | | | |
| 2010 | 1.0 | 13.3 | 25.4 | 27.8 | 18.1 | 9.5 | 4.9 |
| 2020 | 1.0 | 12.6 | 24.5 | 24.3 | 19.4 | 12.8 | 5.4 |
| 2030 | 1.1 | 12.5 | 24.1 | 24.0 | 17.1 | 14.0 | 7.2 |
| 2040 | 1.0 | 12.0 | 25.0 | 24.0 | 17.0 | 12.6 | 8.4 |
| 2050 | 1.0 | 11.6 | 24.6 | 25.2 | 17.0 | 12.7 | 7.9 |
| **Renter Occupied** | | | | | | | |
| 2010 | 9.3 | 30.3 | 24.2 | 17.5 | 9.7 | 4.1 | 4.9 |
| 2020 | 9.0 | 29.3 | 23.7 | 16.1 | 10.9 | 5.7 | 5.3 |
| 2030 | 8.2 | 29.3 | 23.4 | 15.8 | 9.9 | 6.4 | 7.0 |
| 2040 | 7.8 | 27.9 | 24.3 | 15.9 | 9.9 | 5.9 | 8.3 |
| 2050 | 7.9 | 27.2 | 23.8 | 16.9 | 10.0 | 5.9 | 8.3 |

*Source*: Projections by the authors and 2010 data and rates derived from U.S. Census
Bureau 2011d; U.S. Bureau of Labor Statistics 2011.

factors noted in this work, expenditures for housing will increasingly reflect
the growing and diversifying population segments.

The data in Table 5.22 indicate that housing, like other factors noted
above, will reflect the aging of the population. What is apparent from this
table is that the proportion of annual expenditures for housing of owners
and renters in all ages under 65 will remain stable or decrease over time.
For example, the percentage of expenditures in all age groups through age

64 in 2010 is larger than the percentage in these categories in 2050. On the other hand the percentages of expenditures by persons 65 years of age and older are larger in 2050 than in 2010. The aging of the population will have a marked effect on households and housing.

The changes noted above for housing will also have impacts on the total size of housing expenditures. These changes are examined in Table 5.23. In this table, we demonstrate the effects of the age and race/ethnicity changes projected to occur in the population on housing expenditures. This is accomplished by comparing the values projected and presented in the totals column of Table 5.21, which show the effects of the projected aging and racial/ethnic change in the Texas population, with those obtained (in the upper panel of Table 5.23) by projecting household expenditures in 2050 but assuming that the race/ethnicity of householders in 2050 remained as it was in 2010. It also provides results (in the bottom panel of Table 5.23) showing the effects of age structure on housing expenditures by projecting household expenditures in 2050 but assuming the age of householders in 2050 remained as it was in 2010.

The effects of the aging and diversification of the population on housing expenditures are demonstrated in Table 5.23. In this table, the first column

Table 5.23

Annual Expenditures for Housing in Texas by Tenure in 2050 Assuming Projected Patterns by Race/Ethnicity and Age of Householder and Assuming 2010 Distribution by Race/Ethnicity and Age of Householder and Using the Population Projection That Assumes 2000–2010 Rates of Net Migration

| Housing Tenure | Assuming 2010 Distribution in 2050 | Assuming 2000–2010 Rates of Net Migration | Numerical Difference | Percent Difference |
|---|---|---|---|---|
| **Race/Ethnicity of Householder** | | | | |
| Owner | $ 128,932,460,496 | $ 118,260,539,133 | $ −10,671,921,363 | −8.3 |
| Renter | 62,420,805,013 | 63,386,602,887 | 965,797,874 | 1.5 |
| Total | 191,353,265,509 | 181,647,142,020 | −9,706,123,489 | −6.7 |
| **Age of Householder** | | | | |
| Owner | $ 128,520,159,633 | $ 118,260,539,133 | $ −10,259,620,500 | −8.0 |
| Renter | 64,663,300,665 | 63,386,602,887 | −1,276,697,778 | −2.0 |
| Total | 193,183,460,298 | 181,647,142,020 | −11,536,318,278 | −6.0 |

*Source*: Projections by the authors and 2010 data and rates derived from U.S. Census Bureau 2011d; U.S. Bureau of Labor Statistics 2011.

in the top panel shows the expenditures that will occur if the racial/ethnic composition of the population in 2010 exists in 2050 but the number of households is as projected for 2050. The second column shows the projected expenditures if the 2000 to 2010 racial/ethnic change in households (both growth and diversification) is assumed to continue through 2050. In the second panel, the first column shows the effects of assuming that the 2010 age distribution exists in 2050 but the number of households is as projected in 2050. The second column in this second panel shows the effects of the baseline age assumptions contained in the scenario that assumes 2000 to 2010 patterns of change in age continue to 2050. In other words, the first panel examines the effects of the projected pattern of change in race/ethnicity for both baseline and as projected assuming 2000 to 2010 patterns continue through 2050 and the second panel does the same but for change in age. The aging of the population decreases renter and total housing expenditures.

The results in this table show that assuming that the diversification of the population will continue decreases the aggregate expenditures on owner households by $10.7 billion, or 8.3 percent, while it increases the expenditures of renters by $965.7 million, or 1.5 percent. This is because minority households tend to have lower incomes, and under the second scenario assumed, and shown in the second column of the first panel, total expenditures decrease for owners and increase for renters. The net result of increased diversity is more expenditures for rental housing and less for owner housing, since an older population is one that is likely to already be in permanent housing and less likely to change (thereby not increasing expenditures) for either owner or renter housing.

Overall, then, the results in this chapter show that demographic change has substantial potential to change socioeconomic characteristics. If the projected demographic changes occur (e.g., increased diversity, an older age structure, an increasing diversity of household types) and the socioeconomic differences associated with these demographic statuses do not change, Texas future population will have lower incomes, higher rates of poverty, decreased assets (including lower valued housing), and lower net worth. Texas could clearly benefit from improvements in the socioeconomic characteristics of its most rapidly growing population segments.

## SUMMARY

The data in this chapter demonstrate that demographic trends may have substantial impacts on the socioeconomic characteristics of Texas. We have examined the historical patterns of change in income and poverty, on state tax revenue, and on state expenditures. We have also examined the effects on consumer expenditures, on the net worth and assets of households and on housing in Texas. These have been examined for 2010 through 2050 using projections made by applying age, race/ethnicity, and factor-specific rates to projections of population and households. Although no single analysis can adequately examine all of the economic factors likely to be impacted by demographic change, the analysis presented provides an examination of factors of importance in forming the economic future of Texas. The findings in this chapter suggest:

1.    Texas income levels have increased over the last several decades and the gaps between income levels of the state and those of the nation have narrowed. Despite some closure, household, family, and per capita income levels for Texas are lower than those in the nation as a whole and poverty rates are higher (see Table 5.1 and 5.2). Income is substantially lower and poverty higher for minority households than for nonHispanic White households, with median household incomes for Hispanic and nonHispanic Black households being only 60 to 65 percent of those for nonHispanic White households and per capita incomes being only 40 to 45 percent of those for nonHispanic White households. Poverty rates are roughly two to three times higher for Hispanic and nonHispanic Black households than for nonHispanic White households.

2.    State tax collections have shown steady growth, peaking at $41.4 billion in 2008 before declining during the recession. During the past decade several major areas of expenditures showed substantial increases, with such increases most substantial for health and human services and in the executive branch of state government.

3.    Because the population groups with the highest rates of population growth are those with the lowest socioeconomic resources, future patterns of population growth, in the absence of change that leads to increases in minority incomes, indicate that Texas' overall population will become poorer and less competitive. In the absence of socioeconomic change, the average Texas household income will be more than $7,700 lower in 2050 than it was in 2010 (in 2010 constant dollars). Texas poverty rates will increase from 14.4 to 17.7 percent in the absence of socioeconomic change. If levels of income could be increased so that all race/ethnicity groups had the income levels of nonHispanic Whites in 2010, income levels for 2050 could be increased by more than $8,000 from 2010 levels and by $14,000 more than will occur without such closure (in 2010 constant dollars). Such closure could lead to a reduction in poverty levels from 14.4 percent in 2010 to 9.8 percent in 2050. Similarly, state tax revenues will increase by $11.4 billion per year compared to revenues in the absence of such closure.

4.   Although consumer expenditures are projected to increase by more than 100 percent from 2010 to 2050, because of the disproportionate increase in the number of households with lower incomes, consumer expenditures will not increase proportionally to the growth in the number of households. Therefore consumer markets are projected to increase more slowly than the population, resulting in lower per capita and per household consumer expenditures in the future.

5.   Consumer expenditures will come increasingly from households with an Hispanic or nonHispanic Asian and Other householder, while smaller contributions will come from households with a nonHispanic White or Black householder. Overall, more than 60 percent of the net change in future consumer expenditures will come from consumers who are Hispanic and another 25 percent from consumers who are nonHispanic Asian and Other.

6.   Change in household form will also impact the level and distribution of consumer expenditures. Although the percent increase in expenditures for all forms of households will be less than the total growth in households, so that per household expenditures will decline overall, growth will be largest for households with single adult, male or female, householders.

7.   The reductions in per capita and per household incomes and expenditures will also result in smaller increases in net worth and in assets of all types. Overall the increase in net worth of 66.6 percent will be less than one half the rate of growth in households and, as with other financial resources, ownership of such resources will remain disproportionately in households with a nonHispanic White householder. On the other hand, increases in expenditures will increasingly come from households with Hispanic and nonHispanic Asian and Other householders.

8.   The aging of the population will increasingly lead to net worth and assets being located in households with older householders. In every category of net worth and of assets, the percentage in households with a householder 65 years of age or older will increase more than those for any other age of householder category.

9.   Overall, the average consumer expenditure per household is projected to decrease from 2010 to 2050 due to decreases in income resulting from changes in the demographic characteristics of the population and households. If income for all households were equivalent to those of non-Hispanic White households in 2010, total annual aggregate consumer ex-

penditures will be $111 billion more in 2050 than projected with current income differentials.

10.   Housing will also reflect demographic change, with the overall growth in owner and renter housing units being increasingly due to Hispanic and nonHispanic Asian and Other householders. Both owner and renter households will be increasingly minority; the percentage of owners who are nonHispanic White will be reduced to 31.6 percent in 2050 and the proportion of nonHispanic White renters will be 20.6 percent. Similarly, nonHispanic Black owners will remain at about 8.5 percent, while the percentage of nonHispanic Black renters will decrease to 14.4 percent by 2050. Hispanic households will account for 46.9 percent of owner and 51.7 percent of renter households, and nonHispanic Asian and Other households will account for 13.0 percent of owner and 13.3 percent of renter households in 2050.

11.   Consumer expenditures on housing will follow patterns reflecting the number of units by race/ethnicity and age of householder, with expenditures remaining less than household change and thus resulting in declining per household expenditures over time and with the percentage of such expenditures in all forms of housing coming from minority households increasing over time. By 2050, Hispanic households will account for 45.2 percent of owner and 50.7 percent of renter, nonHispanic White households for 29.3 percent of owner and 20.2 percent of renter, nonHispanic Asian and Other households for 19.1 percent of owner and 16.2 percent of renter, and nonHispanic Black households for 6.4 percent of owner and 12.9 percent of renter expenditures.

The data in this chapter clearly point to substantial economic effects resulting from changing demographic characteristics in Texas. In the absence of change in the economic effects of aging and of racial/ethnic diversification, Texas households in 2050 (in 2010 constant dollars) will be poorer, with less income, higher poverty rates, lower net worth, and fewer assets and will have housing that is of lower value (in 2010 constant dollars) when compared to 2010. Demographic change could result in significant economic change in the Texas economy, with substantial impacts on the economic viability of households and on the state's ability to support state services.

CHAPTER 6

# Public Elementary, Secondary, and Higher Education

Texas has experienced substantial change in education over the past several decades. This change was driven in part by a rapidly growing and changing population but also by numerous other factors. For example, legal issues related to the Hopwood decision (Hopwood v. Texas 21 F.3d 603 [5th cir.1996]), increased funding provided through the Texas Grants Program, the Texas Higher Education Coordinating Board's *Closing the Gaps* program, and an economic downturn that impacted state funding for education have significantly altered the educational environment. Nevertheless, demographic change clearly remains a critical factor for Texas elementary, secondary, and higher education.

This chapter examines the effects of changing demographic characteristics on public elementary, secondary, and higher education in Texas. It uses data on the state's population and education to examine the implications of future population change for educational enrollment, programs, and funding. It analyzes these effects on future enrollment patterns, on enrollment in specialized education programs, on levels of educational attainment, and on the levels of financial need to assess resources required to adequately educate the growing population of children in Texas.

## HISTORICAL PATTERNS OF EDUCATIONAL CHANGE

School enrollment has shown substantial growth, with elementary and secondary enrollments increasing by 50.7 percent from 1990 to 2010 and college and university enrollments increasing by 47.1 percent, an overall 1990 to 2010 change of 49.8 percent in enrollment in all levels of education in Texas. This overall rate of growth roughly mirrors the 48 percent increase in Texas total population (see Table 2.1 and Table 6.1).

Table 6.1

Enrollment and Percent Change in Enrollment of Texas Residents Enrolled
in Elementary and Secondary Schools and Colleges in Texas, 1990–2010[a]

| | | | | Percent Change | | |
|---|---|---|---|---|---|---|
| School Level | 1990 | 2000 | 2010 | 1990–2000 | 2000–2010 | 1990–2010 |
| Elementary and Secondary[b] | 3,606,848 | 4,745,370 | 5,434,352 | 31.6 | 14.5 | 50.7 |
| College and University | 1,199,047 | 1,202,890 | 1,763,448 | 0.3 | 46.6 | 47.1 |
| Total | 4,805,895 | 5,948,260 | 7,197,800 | 23.8 | 21.0 | 49.8 |

*Source*: U.S. Census Bureau 1992, 2002, 2011a.
[a]Data are self-reported enrollment as presented in the decennial censuses for the census years indicated and for the annual year of 2010. The enrollment so reported includes enrollment in any type of institution or form of school (private, public, home school, etc.) and any level of involvement (post-graduate, part-time, etc.).
[b]Includes persons in preprimary education and related programs.

Texas elementary and secondary and higher education populations also reflect the substantial change in the racial/ethnic characteristics of the total population of Texas. In 1990 (see Table 6.2), 50.2 percent of all elementary and secondary students in Texas public schools were nonHispanic White, 14.5 percent were nonHispanic Black, 33.2 percent were Hispanic, and 2.1 percent were members of Asian and Other racial/ethnic groups. By 2010, 31.9 percent were nonHispanic White, 13.0 percent were non-Hispanic Black, 49.5 percent were Hispanic, and 5.6 percent were members of Asian and Other racial/ethnic groups. Recent data from the Texas Education Agency (not shown here) indicate that by the Fall of 2011, a majority of all students in Texas public elementary and secondary schools were Hispanic.

Rapid change has also occurred in the racial/ethnic composition of student populations in Texas colleges and universities, but change is less than that for the public schools because higher dropout rates in high school and lower rates of college attendance decrease the number of students who matriculate to colleges and universities. In 1990 (see Table 6.2), 69.7 percent of those enrolled in college were nonHispanic White, 9.0 percent were nonHispanic Black, 17.8 percent were Hispanic, and 3.5 percent were non-Hispanic Asian and Other. In 2010, 46.2 percent of those in public colleges

Table 6.2

Enrollments Percent and Percent Change in Enrollment by Race/Ethnicity
for Texas' Public Community Colleges and Universities, Public Elementary
and Secondary Schools, and Selected Education Programs, 1990–2010

| Year/Time Period | NH[a] White % | NH Black % | Hispanic % | NH Asian & Other % | Total Enrolled |
|---|---|---|---|---|---|
| **Total Public Colleges and Universities** | | | | | |
| 1990 | 69.7 | 9.0 | 17.8 | 3.5 | 768,836 |
| 2000 | 58.1 | 10.9 | 25.4 | 5.6 | 835,153 |
| 2010 | 46.2 | 15.7 | 31.9 | 6.2 | 1,276,328 |
| % Change 1990–2000 | −9.5 | 30.9 | 55.5 | 75.0 | 8.6 |
| % Change 2000–2010 | 21.6 | 119.8 | 91.6 | 69.9 | 52.8 |
| **Total Elementary and Secondary** | | | | | |
| 1990 | 50.2 | 14.5 | 33.2 | 2.1 | 3,254,331 |
| 2000 | 43.1 | 14.4 | 39.6 | 2.9 | 4,000,658 |
| 2010 | 31.9 | 13.0 | 49.5 | 5.6 | 4,847,844 |
| % Change 1990–2000 | 5.9 | 22.4 | 46.3 | 63.6 | 22.9 |
| % Change 2000–2010 | −10.4 | 9.7 | 51.6 | 135.8 | 21.2 |
| **Bilingual/ESL** | | | | | |
| 2000 | 1.3 | 0.5 | 93.6 | 4.6 | 495,515 |
| 2010 | 1.5 | 1.1 | 89.6 | 7.9 | 779,771 |
| % Change 2000–2010 | 77.1 | 253.6 | 50.5 | 171.7 | 57.4 |
| **Gifted and Talented** | | | | | |
| 2000 | 59.2 | 10.0 | 25.9 | 4.9 | 334,901 |
| 2010 | 46.9 | 8.1 | 36.7 | 8.3 | 367,924 |
| % Change 2000–2010 | −13.1 | −10.8 | 55.9 | 87.1 | 9.9 |
| **Special Education** | | | | | |
| 2000 | 45.2 | 17.7 | 36.1 | 1.0 | 488,074 |
| 2010 | 35.1 | 17.9 | 44.8 | 2.2 | 445,327 |
| % Change 2000–2010 | −29.2 | −7.7 | 13.4 | 99.1 | −8.8 |
| **Career and Technology Education** | | | | | |
| 2000 | 46.7 | 15.0 | 35.6 | 2.7 | 740,817 |
| 2010[b] | 35.7 | 11.0 | 48.7 | 4.6 | 1,027,435 |
| % Change 2000–2010 | 6.1 | 1.4 | 89.6 | 140.3 | 38.7 |

*Source*: Texas Education Agency 2001c, 2011d, 2011e, 2012b; Texas Higher Education Coordinating Board 2001b, 2011c.
[a]NH refers to nonHispanic; values for categories labeled NH are only for the nonHispanic persons in each race category. Hispanic includes Hispanics of all races.
[b]Enrollment calculated from percent distribution.
*Note*: Enrollment data based upon 1989–90, 1999–2000, and 2009–10 school years.

and universities were nonHispanic White, 15.7 percent were nonHispanic Black, 31.9 percent were Hispanic, and 6.2 percent were nonHispanic Asian and Others.

Tables 6.3 and 6.4 show that wide disparities in educational attainment remain despite some progress. Table 6.3 shows the levels of education as recorded in the 1990 and 2000 censuses and the 2010 American Community Survey. In 2010, only 11.6 percent of Hispanics aged 25 or older had a bachelor's degree or higher level of education, compared with 46.0 percent of nonHispanic Asian and Other, 34.1 percent of nonHispanic White, and 19.7 percent of nonHispanic Black. Conversely, 40.4 percent of Hispanics had less than a high school level of education in 2010.

There are signs of improvement in levels of education for Texas minority students. For example, the high school and higher level of educational completion rate for Hispanics in 2010 was 59.6 percent, which reflects an increase from 44.6 percent in 1990 and 49.3 percent in 2000. Similarly the

Table 6.3

Percent of Population 25 Years of Age and Older in Texas Who
Are High School Graduates and Higher or College Graduates
and Higher by Race/Ethnicity, 1990, 2000 and 2010

| Educational Attainment Level (Percent) | NH* White | NH Black | Hispanic | NH Asian & Other | Total |
|---|---|---|---|---|---|
| **1990** | | | | | |
| High School Graduates and Higher | 81.5 | 66.2 | 44.6 | 79.1 | 72.1 |
| College Graduates and Higher | 25.2 | 12.0 | 7.3 | 41.3 | 20.3 |
| **2000** | | | | | |
| High School Graduates and Higher | 87.2 | 75.8 | 49.3 | 80.7 | 75.7 |
| College Graduates and Higher | 30.0 | 15.3 | 8.9 | 47.8 | 23.2 |
| **2010** | | | | | |
| High School Graduates and Higher | 92.0 | 86.4 | 59.6 | 87.1 | 80.7 |
| College Graduates and Higher | 34.1 | 19.7 | 11.6 | 46.0 | 25.9 |

*Source*: U.S. Census Bureau 1992, 2002, 2011a.
*NH refers to nonHispanic; values for categories labeled NH are only for the non-Hispanic persons in each race category. Hispanic includes Hispanics of all races.

Table 6.4

Public Community College and University Enrollment Rates (Per 100
Persons Ages 18–35) in Texas by Race/Ethnicity, 2000 and 2010

| Year | NH* White | NH Black | Hispanic | NH Asian & Other | Total |
|------|-----------|----------|----------|------------------|-------|
| **Community College** | | | | | |
| 2000 | 6.5 | 5.2 | 4.8 | 6.8 | 5.7 |
| 2010 | 11.9 | 12.2 | 9.3 | 20.8 | 11.4 |
| **Public University** | | | | | |
| 2000 | 7.5 | 4.7 | 3.3 | 10.3 | 5.7 |
| 2010 | 10.4 | 8.4 | 5.3 | 24.2 | 8.9 |

*Source*: U.S. Census Bureau 2011c, 2002; Texas Higher Education Coordinating Board
2001b, 2002a, 2011c.
*NH refers to nonHispanic; values for categories labeled NH are only for the non-
Hispanic persons in each race category. Hispanic includes Hispanics of all races.
*Note*: Public university includes public universities and public health universities.

percentage of nonHispanic Black persons with a high school degree or
higher increased from 66.2 percent in 1990 to 75.8 percent in 2000 and to
86.4 in 2010. These percentages were larger than those for the other racial/
ethnic groups and indicate that Hispanic and nonHispanic Black students
are experiencing higher rates of success at the high school level and above
than was true in past decades. At the same time, all racial/ethnic groups
increased their rates of completion at this education level, and the high
school and higher completion rates for all other groups remain more than
20 percent higher than the completion rates for Hispanics. In addition, if
one examines closure rates, the results are clearly mixed. For example, the
gap at the high school and higher level of education between nonHispanic
White and Hispanics decreased from 36.9 percent in 1990 to 32.4 percent
in 2010, but, although more Hispanics are enrolled in college, the college
and higher gap increased from 17.9 percent in 1990 to 22.5 percent in 2010.

Lower rates of educational involvement at the college level (among
persons 18 to 35 years of age) are reflected in college enrollment rates
for 2010 (Table 6.4). In 2010, only 9.3 percent of Hispanic, compared to
12.2 percent of nonHispanic Black, 11.9 percent of nonHispanic White,
and 20.8 percent of nonHispanic Asian and Other persons 18 to 35 years

Table 6.5

Educational Attainment for the Population Age 25 and Older in Texas in 2010

| Race/Ethnicity | Population Age 25 and Older | Less than High School | High School Diploma | Some College or Associates Degree | Bachelor Degree or More |
|---|---|---|---|---|---|
| NH* White | 8,099,053 | 8.0 | 25.3 | 32.6 | 34.1 |
| NH Black | 1,762,154 | 13.7 | 30.4 | 36.3 | 19.6 |
| Hispanic | 5,063,779 | 40.4 | 25.8 | 22.2 | 11.6 |
| NH Asian & Other | 847,136 | 12.9 | 17.3 | 23.8 | 46.0 |
| Total | 15,772,122 | 19.3 | 25.6 | 29.2 | 25.9 |

*Source*: U.S. Census Bureau 2011a.
*NH refers to nonHispanic; values for categories labeled NH are only for the nonHispanic persons in each race category. Hispanic includes Hispanics of all races.

of age were enrolled in community college. Similarly, university enrollment rates were 24.2 percent for nonHispanic Asian and Other, 10.4 percent for nonHispanic White, 8.4 percent for nonHispanic Black, and 5.3 percent for Hispanic persons 18 to 35 years of age. Given the importance of a college education for economic success in the United States, increasing college enrollment rates in Texas is essential.

The data in Table 6.5 indicate that despite the progress noted above, the percentage of persons 25 years of age or older with low levels of education is high, particularly among minority populations. Whereas only 8.0 percent of adult nonHispanic White persons 25 years of age or older had less than a high school level of education, 12.9 percent of nonHispanic Asian and Other, 13.7 percent of nonHispanic Black, and 40.4 percent of Hispanics 25 years of age or older had less than a high school level of education. Substantial educational disparities remain evident in the Texas population.

Funding for education in Texas is a function of the funds appropriated (Table 6.6). Despite the fact that the increase in enrollment in Texas involves persons with high levels of need for expanded educational services and despite the 21.0 percent increase in enrollment in all levels of education, the 14.5 percent increase in enrollment in elementary and secondary education, and the 46.6 percent increase in college enrollment from 2000 to 2010 (see Table 6.1), expenditures for elementary and secondary education increased by 24.8 percent, by only 3.0 percent per student. State expenditures for higher education increased by 10.0 percent and per student expenditures decreased by 28.1 percent. Given the specialized educational needs

Table 6.6

Total and Per Student General Revenue Expenditures (in 2010 Dollars) for Texas
Public Elementary and Secondary Schools, Selected Education Programs, and Public
Colleges and Universities, and Percent Change in Expenditures, 2000 and 2010

| | 2000 | | 2010 | | Percent[a] Change 2000–2010 | |
|---|---|---|---|---|---|---|
| Program | Total[b] | Per Student | Total[b] | Per Student | Total | Per Student |
| Elementary and Secondary | $ 29,237.5 | $ 7,308 | $ 36,491.1 | $ 7,527 | 24.8 | 3.0 |
| Bilingual/ESL | 748.0 | 1,509 | 1,295.7 | 1,662 | 73.2 | 10.1 |
| Gifted and Talented | 311.4 | 930 | 418.0 | 1,136 | 34.2 | 22.2 |
| Special Education | 2,202.6 | 4,513 | 4,800.2 | 10,779 | 117.9 | 138.8 |
| Career and Technology Education[c] | 717.5 | 969 | 1,009.2 | 982 | 40.7 | 1.4 |
| Public Colleges and Public Universities | 3,406.9 | 4,079 | 3,746.0 | 2,935 | 10.0 | −28.1 |

*Source*: Texas Education Agency 2001a, 2001e, 2011a, 2012b; Texas Higher Education Coordinating
Board 2001a, 2001c, 2011a, 2011c.
*Note*: Enrollment data based upon 1999–2000 and 2009–2010 school years.
[a]Percents computed from unrounded values.
[b]In millions of 2010 constant dollars.
[c]Enrollment calculated from percent distribution.

of the Texas school population and the costs of programs to address such
needs, it is apparent that levels of expenditures have not kept pace with the
needs of the state's school-age population.

## PROJECTIONS OF ENROLLMENT IN PUBLIC
## EDUCATIONAL INSTITUTIONS

The projections of school enrollment discussed here were completed by
applying 2010 age, sex, and race/ethnicity specific enrollment rates by educational level to the projected population (under the 1.0, 2000–2010 rates
of migration scenario) by age, sex, and race/ethnicity. These projections
assume constant (2010) enrollment rates by age, sex, and race/ethnicity.
Although it would be desirable to trend such enrollment rates over time
to take into account projected future patterns of change, differentials
and sometimes erratic rates of growth over time and among racial/ethnic
groups make it problematic to do so. As a result, enrollment rates from

2010 are assumed for all projected years in producing the results shown in Tables 6.7 through 6.10.

Changes similar to those in the population are projected to occur in the elementary and secondary and college and university populations. However, because such populations are younger and minority population growth has been greater at younger ages, the diversification of the school population is more extensive in elementary and secondary school populations than in the total population. From 2010 to 2050 (see second panels of Tables 6.7–6.10), the Texas elementary and secondary school population is projected to grow from 4,847,844 in 2010 to 9,366,443 by 2050, increasing by 4,518,599 or by 93.2 percent. By 2050, the state's elementary and secondary student population will be 15.4 percent nonHispanic White, 8.5 percent nonHispanic Black, 64.2 percent Hispanic, and 11.9 percent nonHispanic Asian and Other, compared to 31.9 percent nonHispanic White, 13.0 percent nonHispanic Black, 49.5 percent Hispanic, and 5.6 percent nonHispanic Asian and Other in 2010 (see Table 6.9).

The projected growth in public college and university enrollment (see bottom panel of Tables 6.7–6.10) will be from 1,276,327 in 2010 to 2,384,969 in 2050, an increase of 1,108,642 or 86.9 percent. By 2050, public college and university enrollment will consist of 22.3 percent nonHispanic White, 12.5 percent nonHispanic Black, 50.1 percent Hispanic, and 15.1 percent nonHispanic Asian and Other students. These values compare to 46.2 percent nonHispanic White, 15.7 percent nonHispanic Black, 31.9 percent Hispanic, and 6.2 percent nonHispanic Asian and Other in 2010. The smaller percentage of Hispanics in college and universities than in the population as a whole, and in elementary and secondary schools, reflects the fact that this population had lower rates of enrollment in higher education (and higher pre-college dropout rates) than the population overall.

All of the projected increase in elementary and secondary school enrollment between 2010 and 2050 will be accounted for by minority students. NonHispanic White students are projected to decrease by 101,495, while Hispanic students will account for 80.0 percent of the increase, a net increase of 3,613,993 Hispanic students (Table 6.10).

Similarly, nonHispanic White public college and university enrollment will decrease by 56,789 (accounting for –5.1 percent of net enrollment growth). NonHispanic Black enrollment will increase by 97,416 (accounting for 8.8 percent of net enrollment growth). Hispanic enrollment will increase by 787,428 and account for 71.0 percent of the net growth in enrollment, and nonHispanic Asian and Other enrollment will increase by 280,587, accounting for 25.3 percent of net growth.

For all educational levels combined, the increase in enrollment will be 5,627,241. NonHispanic White enrollment will decline by 158,284 (accounting for –2.8 percent of the net growth), nonHispanic Black enrollment

Table 6.7

Total Public Education (All Levels), Public Elementary and Secondary School,
Public Community College, Public University, and Total Public College and
University Enrollment in Texas by Race/Ethnicity in 2010 and Projected to 2050
Using the Projections That Assume 2000–2010 Rates of Net Migration for Texas

| Year | NH[a] White | NH Black | Hispanic | NH Asian & Other | Total |
|------|-------------|----------|----------|------------------|-------|
| **Total Public Education (All Levels)[b]** | | | | | |
| 2010 | 2,137,393 | 832,202 | 2,805,785 | 348,791 | 6,124,171 |
| 2020 | 2,109,148 | 874,294 | 3,490,796 | 533,046 | 7,007,284 |
| 2030 | 2,128,376 | 955,194 | 4,428,574 | 682,196 | 8,194,340 |
| 2040 | 2,037,804 | 1,028,997 | 5,778,539 | 973,986 | 9,819,326 |
| 2050 | 1,979,109 | 1,095,342 | 7,207,206 | 1,469,755 | 11,751,412 |
| **Public Elementary and Secondary Schools** | | | | | |
| 2010 | 1,547,693 | 632,401 | 2,398,684 | 269,066 | 4,847,844 |
| 2020 | 1,548,792 | 646,756 | 2,917,449 | 406,755 | 5,519,752 |
| 2030 | 1,577,470 | 706,263 | 3,715,984 | 480,533 | 6,480,250 |
| 2040 | 1,479,111 | 754,173 | 4,865,439 | 726,452 | 7,825,175 |
| 2050 | 1,446,198 | 798,125 | 6,012,677 | 1,109,443 | 9,366,443 |
| **Public Community Colleges** | | | | | |
| 2010 | 314,976 | 130,786 | 263,600 | 37,261 | 746,623 |
| 2020 | 299,721 | 149,167 | 370,868 | 58,999 | 878,755 |
| 2030 | 296,231 | 163,939 | 459,618 | 92,693 | 1,012,481 |
| 2040 | 297,987 | 181,123 | 590,855 | 117,643 | 1,187,608 |
| 2050 | 285,152 | 196,248 | 771,788 | 170,627 | 1,423,815 |
| **Public Universities[b]** | | | | | |
| 2010 | 274,724 | 69,015 | 143,501 | 42,464 | 529,704 |
| 2020 | 260,635 | 78,371 | 202,479 | 67,292 | 608,777 |
| 2030 | 254,675 | 84,992 | 252,972 | 108,970 | 701,609 |
| 2040 | 260,706 | 93,701 | 322,245 | 129,891 | 806,543 |
| 2050 | 247,759 | 100,969 | 422,741 | 189,685 | 961,154 |
| **Total Public Colleges and Universities[b]** | | | | | |
| 2010 | 589,700 | 199,801 | 407,101 | 79,725 | 1,276,327 |
| 2020 | 560,356 | 227,538 | 573,347 | 126,291 | 1,487,532 |
| 2030 | 550,906 | 248,931 | 712,590 | 201,663 | 1,714,090 |
| 2040 | 558,693 | 274,824 | 913,100 | 247,534 | 1,994,151 |
| 2050 | 532,911 | 297,217 | 1,194,529 | 360,312 | 2,384,969 |

*Source*: Projections by the authors and 2010 data and rates derived from Texas Education Agency
2001e; Texas Higher Education Coordinating Board 2011c.
[a]NH refers to nonHispanic; values for categories labeled NH are only for the nonHispanic persons
in each race category. Hispanic includes Hispanics of all races.
[b]Excludes public health related educational institutions.

Table 6.8

Percent Change in Projected Total Public Education (All Levels), Public Elementary and Secondary School, Public Community College, Public University, and Total Public College and University Enrollment in Texas by Race/Ethnicity in 2010 and Projected to 2050 Using the Projections That Assume 2000–2010 Rates of Net Migration for Texas

| Time Period | NH[a] White | NH Black | Hispanic | NH Asian & Other | Total |
|---|---|---|---|---|---|
| **Total Public Education (All Levels)[b]** | | | | | |
| 2010–2020 | −1.3 | 5.1 | 24.4 | 52.8 | 14.4 |
| 2020–2030 | 0.9 | 9.3 | 26.9 | 28.0 | 16.9 |
| 2030–2040 | −4.3 | 7.7 | 30.5 | 42.8 | 19.8 |
| 2040–2050 | −2.9 | 6.4 | 24.7 | 50.9 | 19.7 |
| 2010–2050 | −7.4 | 31.6 | 156.9 | 321.4 | 91.9 |
| **Public Elementary and Secondary Schools** | | | | | |
| 2010–2020 | 0.1 | 2.3 | 21.6 | 51.2 | 13.9 |
| 2020–2030 | 1.9 | 9.2 | 27.4 | 18.1 | 17.4 |
| 2030–2040 | −6.2 | 6.8 | 30.9 | 51.2 | 20.8 |
| 2040–2050 | −2.2 | 5.8 | 23.6 | 52.7 | 19.7 |
| 2010–2050 | −6.6 | 26.2 | 150.7 | 312.3 | 93.2 |
| **Public Community Colleges** | | | | | |
| 2010–2020 | −4.8 | 14.1 | 40.7 | 58.3 | 17.7 |
| 2020–2030 | −1.2 | 9.9 | 23.9 | 57.1 | 15.2 |
| 2030–2040 | 0.6 | 10.5 | 28.6 | 26.9 | 17.3 |
| 2040–2050 | −4.3 | 8.4 | 30.6 | 45.0 | 19.9 |
| 2010–2050 | −9.5 | 50.1 | 192.8 | 357.9 | 90.7 |
| **Public Universities[b]** | | | | | |
| 2010–2020 | −5.1 | 13.6 | 41.1 | 58.5 | 14.9 |
| 2020–2030 | −2.3 | 8.4 | 24.9 | 61.9 | 15.2 |
| 2030–2040 | 2.4 | 10.2 | 27.4 | 19.2 | 15.0 |
| 2040–2050 | −5.0 | 7.8 | 31.2 | 46.0 | 19.2 |
| 2010–2050 | −9.8 | 46.3 | 194.6 | 346.7 | 81.5 |
| **Total Public Colleges and Universities[b]** | | | | | |
| 2010–2020 | −5.0 | 13.9 | 40.8 | 58.4 | 16.5 |
| 2020–2030 | −1.7 | 9.4 | 24.3 | 59.7 | 15.2 |
| 2030–2040 | 1.4 | 10.4 | 28.1 | 22.7 | 16.3 |
| 2040–2050 | −4.6 | 8.1 | 30.8 | 45.6 | 19.6 |
| 2010–2050 | −9.6 | 48.8 | 193.4 | 351.9 | 86.9 |

*Source*: Projections by the authors and 2010 data and rates derived from Texas Education Agency 2011c, 2011d, 2011e; Texas Higher Education Coordinating Board 2011c.

[a]NH refers to nonHispanic; values for categories labeled NH are only for the nonHispanic persons in each race category. Hispanic includes Hispanics of all races.

[b]Excludes public health related educational institutions.

*Note*: Enrollment data based on 2009–10 school year.

Table 6.9

Percent of Total Public Education (All Levels), Public Elementary and Secondary
School, Public Community College, Public University, and Total Public College and
University Enrollment in Texas by Race/Ethnicity in 2010 and Projected to 2050
Using the Projections That Assume 2000–2010 Rates of Net Migration for Texas

| Year | NH[a] White | NH Black | Hispanic | NH Asian & Other |
|---|---|---|---|---|
| **Total Public Education (All Levels)[b]** | | | | |
| 2010 | 34.9 | 13.6 | 45.8 | 5.7 |
| 2020 | 30.1 | 12.5 | 49.8 | 7.6 |
| 2030 | 26.0 | 11.7 | 54.0 | 8.3 |
| 2040 | 20.8 | 10.5 | 58.8 | 9.9 |
| 2050 | 16.8 | 9.3 | 61.3 | 12.6 |
| **Public Elementary and Secondary Schools** | | | | |
| 2010 | 31.9 | 13.0 | 49.5 | 5.6 |
| 2020 | 28.1 | 11.7 | 52.9 | 7.3 |
| 2030 | 24.3 | 10.9 | 57.3 | 7.5 |
| 2040 | 18.9 | 9.6 | 62.2 | 9.3 |
| 2050 | 15.4 | 8.5 | 64.2 | 11.9 |
| **Public Community Colleges** | | | | |
| 2010 | 42.2 | 17.5 | 35.3 | 5.0 |
| 2020 | 34.1 | 17.0 | 42.2 | 6.7 |
| 2030 | 29.3 | 16.2 | 45.4 | 9.1 |
| 2040 | 25.1 | 15.3 | 49.8 | 9.8 |
| 2050 | 20.0 | 13.8 | 54.2 | 12.0 |
| **Public Universities[b]** | | | | |
| 2010 | 51.9 | 13.0 | 27.1 | 8.0 |
| 2020 | 42.8 | 12.9 | 33.3 | 11.0 |
| 2030 | 36.3 | 12.1 | 36.1 | 15.5 |
| 2040 | 32.3 | 11.6 | 40.0 | 16.1 |
| 2050 | 25.8 | 10.5 | 44.0 | 19.7 |
| **Total Public Colleges and Universities[b]** | | | | |
| 2010 | 46.2 | 15.7 | 31.9 | 6.2 |
| 2020 | 37.7 | 15.3 | 38.5 | 8.5 |
| 2030 | 32.1 | 14.5 | 41.6 | 11.8 |
| 2040 | 28.0 | 13.8 | 45.8 | 12.4 |
| 2050 | 22.3 | 12.5 | 50.1 | 15.1 |

*Source*: Projections by the authors and 2010 data and rates derived from Texas Education Agency
2011c, 2011d, 2011e; Texas Higher Education Coordinating Board 2011c.
[a]NH refers to nonHispanic; values for categories labeled NH are only for the nonHispanic persons
in each race category. Hispanic includes Hispanics of all races.
[b]Excludes public health related educational institutions.
*Note*: Enrollment data based on 2009–10 school years.

Table 6.10

Number and Percent of Net Change in Projected Total Public
Education (All Levels), Public Elementary and Secondary
School, Public Community College, Public University, and
Total Public College and University Enrollment in Texas Due to
Each Race/Ethnicity Group Using the Projections That Assume
2000–2010 Rates of Net Migration for Texas, 2010–2050

| Race/Ethnicity | Number | Percent |
|---|---|---|
| **Total Public Education (All Levels)[b]** | | |
| NH[a] White | −158,284 | −2.8 |
| NH Black | 263,140 | 4.7 |
| Hispanic | 4,401,421 | 78.2 |
| NH Asian & Other | 1,120,964 | 19.9 |
| Total | 5,627,241 | 100.0 |
| **Public Elementary and Secondary Schools** | | |
| NH White | −101,495 | −2.2 |
| NH Black | 165,724 | 3.7 |
| Hispanic | 3,613,993 | 80.0 |
| NH Asian & Other | 840,377 | 18.5 |
| Total | 4,518,599 | 100.0 |
| **Public Community Colleges** | | |
| NH White | −29,824 | −4.4 |
| NH Black | 65,462 | 9.7 |
| Hispanic | 508,188 | 75.0 |
| NH Asian & Other | 133,366 | 19.7 |
| Total | 677,192 | 100.0 |
| **Public Universities[b]** | | |
| NH White | −26,965 | −6.2 |
| NH Black | 31,954 | 7.4 |
| Hispanic | 279,240 | 64.7 |
| NH Asian & Other | 147,221 | 34.1 |
| Total | 431,450 | 100.0 |
| **Total Public Colleges and Universities[b]** | | |
| NH White | −56,789 | −5.1 |
| NH Black | 97,416 | 8.8 |
| Hispanic | 787,428 | 71.0 |
| NH Asian & Other | 280,587 | 25.3 |
| Total | 1,108,642 | 100.0 |

*Source*: Projections by the authors and 2010 data and rates derived from Texas
Education Agency 2011c, 2011d, 2011e; Texas Higher Education Coordinating
Board 2011c.
[a]NH refers to nonHispanic; values for categories labeled NH are only for the non-
Hispanic persons in each race category. Hispanic includes Hispanics of all races.
[b]Excludes public health related educational institutions.

will increase by 263,140 (accounting for 4.7 percent of net growth), Hispanic enrollment will increase by 4,401,421 (accounting for 78.2 percent of the net growth), and nonHispanic Asian and Other enrollment will increase by 1,120,964 (accounting for 19.9 percent of the net growth).

It is evident that growth in school enrollment will be substantial and will increasingly involve growth in minority populations. Unfortunately, the increase in enrollment is less than would be expected because of substantial numbers of dropouts from secondary school and lower rates of enrollment in higher education.

## PROJECTED INCREASES IN SPECIALIZED EDUCATION PROGRAMS

Increases in school enrollment in Texas are likely to be especially large in programs intended to provide specific types of assistance to the state's fastest growing population segments. Tables 6.11 and 6.12 show 2010 and projected 2050 enrollment in several specialized programs. The data show substantial increases in the enrollment in such programs among Hispanics and nonHispanic Asians and Others. For example, the number of Hispanics in economically disadvantaged programs is projected to increase from 1,866,376 in 2010 to 4,664,027 in 2050, and the number in bilingual/ESL programs is projected to increase from 698,450 in 2010 to 1,717,327 in 2050. Large (relative to the population) percent increases will also occur for nonHispanic Asians and Others, with this group showing percent increases larger than the total percent change for enrollment in all programs. The number of nonHispanic Black children in such programs will increase by 31 percent to more than 33 percent of all children in such programs while the number of nonHispanic White children either declines or grows relatively slowly (the single exception being the 25.5 percent increase in special education enrollment among nonHispanic White children).

Overall the change in enrollment in these programs largely reflects the increase in the Hispanic and Asian and Other populations most likely to be involved in such programs. Whereas the total enrollment in elementary and secondary education is projected to increase by 93.2 percent from 2010 to 2050, only the number enrolled in gifted and talented and special education will increase more slowly than this overall level of enrollment. At the same time, the differentials in levels of growth among minority racial/ethnic groups is apparent, with the rapidly growing population of Hispanic children making up more than 50 percent of all children in all programs by 2050. These data show that growth in such programs is likely to be substantial, impacting program and related personnel needs and costs in these areas.

Table 6.11

Enrollment in Selected Public Elementary and Secondary School Programs in Texas by Race/
Ethnicity in 2010 and Projected for 2050 and Percent Change in Enrollment, 2010–2050,
Using the Population Projections That Assume 2000–2010 Rates of Net Migration

| Program | NH[a] White | NH Black | Hispanic | NH Asian & Other | Total |
|---|---|---|---|---|---|
| **2010** | | | | | |
| Bilingual/ESL | 11,388 | 8,549 | 698,450 | 61,384 | 779,771 |
| Economically Disadvantaged | 443,933 | 475,994 | 1,866,376 | 66,874 | 2,853,177 |
| Gifted and Talented | 172,440 | 29,791 | 135,007 | 30,686 | 367,924 |
| Immigrants | 5,178 | 3,789 | 57,232 | 14,233 | 80,432 |
| Limited English Proficiency (LEP) | 11,878 | 9,071 | 750,864 | 45,261 | 817,074 |
| Special Education | 156,066 | 79,828 | 199,683 | 9,750 | 445,327 |
| Title I | 699,903 | 463,243 | 1,889,165 | 74,008 | 3,126,319 |
| Career and Technology Education[b] | 366,794 | 113,018 | 500,361 | 47,262 | 1,027,435 |
| **2050** | | | | | |
| Bilingual/ESL | 11,292 | 11,231 | 1,717,327 | 236,646 | 1,976,496 |
| Economically Disadvantaged | 430,846 | 629,240 | 4,664,027 | 273,345 | 5,997,458 |
| Gifted and Talented | 162,060 | 39,576 | 339,995 | 131,301 | 672,932 |
| Immigrants | 5,037 | 5,003 | 143,335 | 57,965 | 211,340 |
| Limited English Proficiency (LEP) | 11,894 | 11,937 | 1,852,422 | 178,226 | 2,054,479 |
| Special Education | 195,931 | 105,863 | 503,852 | 39,113 | 844,759 |
| Title I | 681,195 | 611,433 | 4,703,690 | 296,846 | 6,293,164 |
| Career and Technology Education[b] | 363,934 | 150,745 | 1,321,913 | 212,911 | 2,049,503 |
| **Percent Change 2010–2050** | | | | | |
| Bilingual/ESL | −0.8 | 31.4 | 145.9 | 285.5 | 153.5 |
| Economically Disadvantaged | −2.9 | 32.2 | 149.9 | 308.7 | 110.2 |
| Gifted and Talented | −6.0 | 32.8 | 151.8 | 327.9 | 82.9 |
| Immigrants | −2.7 | 32.0 | 150.4 | 307.3 | 162.8 |
| Limited English Proficiency (LEP) | 0.1 | 31.6 | 146.7 | 293.8 | 151.4 |
| Special Education | 25.5 | 32.6 | 152.3 | 301.2 | 89.7 |
| Title I | −2.7 | 32.0 | 149.0 | 301.1 | 101.3 |
| Career and Technology Education[b] | −0.8 | 33.4 | 164.2 | 350.5 | 99.5 |

*Source*: Projections by the authors and 2010 data and rates derived from Texas Education Agency
2012b, 2011c, 2011d, 2011e.
[a]NH refers to nonHispanic; values for categories labeled NH are only for the nonHispanic persons in
each race category. Hispanic includes Hispanics of all races.
[b]Beginning with the 2005–06 school year, data reflect students in Grades 9–12 only who are participating in career and technical education programs. Students taking career and technical courses as
electives are excluded. Enrollment calculated from percent distribution.

Table 6.12

Percent of Enrollment in Selected Public Elementary and Secondary School
Programs in Texas by Race/Ethnicity in 2010 and Projected for 2050 Using
the Population Projection That Assumes 2000–2010 Rates of Net Migration

| Program | NH[a] White | NH Black | Hispanic | NH Asian & Other |
|---|---|---|---|---|
| **2010** | | | | |
| Bilingual/ESL | 1.5 | 1.1 | 89.6 | 7.8 |
| Economically Disadvantaged | 15.6 | 16.7 | 65.4 | 2.3 |
| Gifted and Talented | 46.9 | 8.1 | 36.7 | 8.3 |
| Immigrants | 6.4 | 4.7 | 71.2 | 17.7 |
| Limited English Proficiency (LEP) | 1.5 | 1.1 | 91.9 | 5.5 |
| Special Education | 35.0 | 17.9 | 44.8 | 2.3 |
| Title I | 22.4 | 14.8 | 60.4 | 2.4 |
| Career and Technology Education[b] | 35.7 | 11.0 | 48.7 | 4.6 |
| **2050** | | | | |
| Bilingual/ESL | 0.6 | 0.6 | 86.9 | 11.9 |
| Economically Disadvantaged | 7.2 | 10.5 | 77.8 | 4.5 |
| Gifted and Talented | 24.1 | 5.9 | 50.5 | 19.5 |
| Immigrants | 2.4 | 2.4 | 67.8 | 27.4 |
| Limited English Proficiency (LEP) | 0.6 | 0.6 | 90.2 | 8.6 |
| Special Education | 23.2 | 12.5 | 59.6 | 4.7 |
| Title I | 10.8 | 9.7 | 74.7 | 4.8 |
| Career and Technology Education[b] | 17.8 | 7.4 | 64.5 | 10.3 |

Source: Projections by the authors and 2010 data and rates derived from Texas Education Agency 2012b, 2011c, 2011d, 2011e.
[a]NH refers to nonHispanic; values for categories labeled NH are only for the non-Hispanic persons in each race category. Hispanic includes Hispanics of all races.
[b]Beginning with the 2005–06 school year, data reflect students in Grades 9–12 only who are participating in career and technical education programs. Students taking career and technical courses as electives are excluded.

## PUBLIC EXPENDITURES FOR EDUCATION

The data in Table 6.13 show projections of total state expenditures for public elementary and secondary schools, public community colleges, and public universities, as well as for selected specialized programs. These data indicate that expenditures will need to increase substantially with increases

Table 6.13

Education Expenditures (in Millions of 2010 Dollars) for Total Public
Elementary and Secondary Schools and Selected Elementary and Secondary
Education Programs in Texas in 2010 and Projected to 2050 Using the
Population Projections That Assume 2000–2010 Rates of Net Migration

| Year | Total Public Elementary and Secondary | Total Community Colleges | Total Public Universities | Total Public Colleges and Universities |
|---|---|---|---|---|
| 2010 | $ 36,491.1 | $ 1,202.3 | $ 2,543.7 | $ 3,746.0 |
| 2020 | 41,548.7 | 1,415.1 | 2,923.4 | 4,338.5 |
| 2030 | 48,778.7 | 1,630.4 | 3,369.2 | 4,999.6 |
| 2040 | 58,902.3 | 1,912.4 | 3,873.1 | 5,785.5 |
| 2050 | 70,503.9 | 2,292.8 | 4,615.6 | 6,908.4 |

Selected Elementary and Secondary Programs

| Year | Bilingual/ESL | Gifted & Talented | Special Education | Career and Technology Education |
|---|---|---|---|---|
| 2010 | $ 1,295.7 | $ 418.0 | $ 4,800.2 | $ 1,009.2 |
| 2020 | 1,456.1 | 480.1 | 5,511.5 | 1,204.0 |
| 2030 | 1,727.2 | 556.4 | 6,399.2 | 1,351.4 |
| 2040 | 2,064.2 | 672.2 | 7,708.6 | 1,643.6 |
| 2050 | 2,460.6 | 803.5 | 9,218.3 | 1,974.3 |

*Source*: Projections by the authors and 2010 data and rates derived from Texas Education Agency 2011a, 2012b, 2011c, 2011d, 2011e; Texas Higher Education Coordinating Board 2011a, 2011b.

equivalent to the increases in enrollment in these programs. Expenditures for bilingual programs will increase by more than $1.1 billion, expenditures for gifted and talented programs by more than $385 million, expenditures for special education programs by more than $4.4 billion, and expenditures for career and technology education by more than $965 million from 2010 to 2050.

Table 6.13 also provides projections of total expenditures for public elementary and secondary schools, and for public community colleges and public universities, computed by multiplying 2010 expenditures per student by the projected number of students in each year. It is critical to understand that these 2010 expenditures occurred under conditions of budget austerity and do not necessarily indicate the actual costs of providing the educational programs at each educational level. Additionally, these costs are in 2010 constant dollars and do not show any adjustments for potential inflation over time.

These data show that elementary and secondary expenditures will increase by more than $34 billion from 2010 to 2050, community college expenditures by nearly $1.1 billion, and public university costs by nearly $2.1 billion. Combined costs for public colleges and universities are projected to increase from $3.7 billion to more than $6.9 billion from 2010 to 2050 (an increase of $3.2 billion in 2010 constant dollars). Clearly, the demands on the Texas budget will be increased by the state's growing and diversifying school population.

## PROJECTIONS OF UNMET FINANCIAL NEED

One of the critical issues related to growing college enrollment is the costs of college attendance, those borne by the public and those borne by parents and other guardians and by the students themselves. Of particular concern are those costs of attendance at a college that cannot be met through the resources of the students or their families but rather must be met by federal (e.g., Pell) grants or state (e.g., Texas) grants, student employment, student or student's family's loans, or other sources. Those costs of attendance that cannot be paid by students or students' families (i.e., the expected family contribution) are referred to as unmet need.

Tables 6.14 through 6.19 present data showing projections of students who will have unmet financial needs given the rates of need by race/ethnicity of students in 2010 and the projected number of students. The data in these tables show that the number of persons with unmet financial need will increase substantially over the 40-year period covered by these projections. The number of students in community colleges with unmet need, and hence requiring financial assistance of some kind to attend college, is projected to nearly double, as is the number of students in universities requiring assistance over the same period. The number of community college students needing financial assistance will increase from 366,894 to 781,177, by 414,283 or 112.9 percent from 2010 to 2050. The number of university students needing assistance will increase from 319,673 to 619,391, by 299,718 or 93.8 percent (see Tables 6.14 and 6.15). The total number of persons with unmet financial need for all of higher education will increase from 686,567 in 2010 to 1,400,568 in 2050, an increase of 714,001 or 104.0 percent.

Table 6.14

Number of Students with Financial Need Unmet by Household
Resources Enrolled at Public Colleges and Universities in Texas by
Race/Ethnicity in 2010 and Projected to 2050 Using the Population
Projection That Assumes 2000–2010 Rates of Net Migration

| Year | NH* White | NH Black | Hispanic | NH Asian & Other | Total |
|------|-----------|----------|----------|------------------|-------|
| **Public Community College** | | | | | |
| 2010 | 111,871 | 70,629 | 163,781 | 20,613 | 366,894 |
| 2020 | 106,452 | 80,555 | 230,428 | 32,639 | 450,074 |
| 2030 | 105,212 | 88,532 | 285,570 | 51,279 | 530,593 |
| 2040 | 105,836 | 97,812 | 367,110 | 65,081 | 635,839 |
| 2050 | 101,277 | 105,980 | 479,527 | 94,393 | 781,177 |
| **Public Universities** | | | | | |
| 2010 | 134,003 | 63,311 | 92,472 | 29,887 | 319,673 |
| 2020 | 127,130 | 71,894 | 130,477 | 47,361 | 376,862 |
| 2030 | 124,223 | 77,967 | 163,015 | 76,695 | 441,900 |
| 2040 | 127,165 | 85,957 | 207,655 | 91,420 | 512,197 |
| 2050 | 120,849 | 92,624 | 272,414 | 133,504 | 619,391 |
| **Total Public Colleges and Universities** | | | | | |
| 2010 | 245,874 | 133,940 | 256,253 | 50,500 | 686,567 |
| 2020 | 233,582 | 152,449 | 360,905 | 80,000 | 826,936 |
| 2030 | 229,435 | 166,499 | 448,585 | 127,974 | 972,493 |
| 2040 | 233,001 | 183,769 | 574,765 | 156,501 | 1,148,036 |
| 2050 | 222,126 | 198,604 | 751,941 | 227,897 | 1,400,568 |

*Source*: Projections by the authors and 2010 data and rates derived from Texas Higher
Education Coordinating Board 2010.
*NH refers to nonHispanic; values for categories labeled NH are only for the non-
Hispanic persons in each race category. Hispanic includes Hispanics of all races.

Those in need will increasingly be Hispanic and Asian and Other students. Of the total 686,567 students with unmet need in 2010, 35.8 percent were nonHispanic White, 19.5 percent were nonHispanic Black,
37.3 percent were Hispanic, and 7.4 percent were nonHispanic Asian and
Other. By 2050, of the 1,400,568 needing assistance, 15.9 percent will be

Table 6.15

Percent Change in Projected Number of Students with Financial
Need Unmet by Household Resources Enrolled at Public Colleges and
Universities in Texas in 2010 and Projected to 2050 Using the Population
Projection That Assumes 2000–2010 Rates of Net Migration

| Time Period | NH* White | NH Black | Hispanic | NH Asian & Other | Total |
|---|---|---|---|---|---|
| **Public Community Colleges** | | | | | |
| 2010–2020 | −4.8 | 14.1 | 40.7 | 58.3 | 22.7 |
| 2020–2030 | −1.2 | 9.9 | 23.9 | 57.1 | 17.9 |
| 2030–2040 | 0.6 | 10.5 | 28.6 | 26.9 | 19.8 |
| 2040–2050 | −4.3 | 8.4 | 30.6 | 45.0 | 22.9 |
| 2010–2050 | −9.5 | 50.1 | 192.8 | 357.9 | 112.9 |
| **Public Universities** | | | | | |
| 2010–2020 | −5.1 | 13.6 | 41.1 | 58.5 | 17.9 |
| 2020–2030 | −2.3 | 8.4 | 24.9 | 61.9 | 17.3 |
| 2030–2040 | 2.4 | 10.2 | 27.4 | 19.2 | 15.9 |
| 2040–2050 | −5.0 | 7.8 | 31.2 | 46.0 | 20.9 |
| 2010–2050 | −9.8 | 46.3 | 194.6 | 346.7 | 93.8 |
| **Total Public Colleges and Universities** | | | | | |
| 2010–2020 | −5.0 | 13.8 | 40.8 | 58.4 | 20.4 |
| 2020–2030 | −1.8 | 9.2 | 24.3 | 60.0 | 17.6 |
| 2030–2040 | 1.6 | 10.4 | 28.1 | 22.3 | 18.1 |
| 2040–2050 | −4.7 | 8.1 | 30.8 | 45.6 | 22.0 |
| 2010–2050 | −9.7 | 48.3 | 193.4 | 351.3 | 104.0 |

*Source*: Projections by the authors and 2010 data and rates derived from Texas Higher
Education Coordinating Board 2010.
*NH refers to nonHispanic; values for categories labeled NH are only for the non-
Hispanic persons in each race category. Hispanic includes Hispanics of all races.

nonHispanic White, 14.2 percent nonHispanic Black, 53.6 percent Hispanic, and 16.3 percent nonHispanic Asian and Other (see Table 6.16).
This change reflects the fact that the number of nonHispanic White students in need is projected to decrease by 9.7 percent, while the number of
nonHispanic Black students is projected to increase by 48.3 percent, the

Table 6.16

Percent of Students with Financial Need Unmet by Household
Resources Enrolled at Public Colleges and Universities by Race/
Ethnicity in Texas in 2010 and Projected to 2050 Using the Population
Projection That Assumes 2000–2010 Rates of Net Migration

| Year | NH* White | NH Black | Hispanic | NH Asian & Other | Total |
|------|-----------|----------|----------|------------------|-------|
| **Public Community Colleges** | | | | | |
| 2010 | 30.5 | 19.3 | 44.6 | 5.6 | 100.0 |
| 2020 | 23.7 | 17.9 | 51.1 | 7.3 | 100.0 |
| 2030 | 19.8 | 16.7 | 53.8 | 9.7 | 100.0 |
| 2040 | 16.6 | 15.4 | 57.8 | 10.2 | 100.0 |
| 2050 | 13.0 | 13.6 | 61.3 | 12.1 | 100.0 |
| **Public Universities** | | | | | |
| 2010 | 42.0 | 19.8 | 28.9 | 9.3 | 100.0 |
| 2020 | 33.7 | 19.1 | 34.6 | 12.6 | 100.0 |
| 2030 | 28.1 | 17.6 | 36.9 | 17.4 | 100.0 |
| 2040 | 24.8 | 16.8 | 40.6 | 17.8 | 100.0 |
| 2050 | 19.5 | 15.0 | 43.9 | 21.6 | 100.0 |
| **Total Public Colleges and Universities** | | | | | |
| 2010 | 35.8 | 19.5 | 37.3 | 7.4 | 100.0 |
| 2020 | 28.2 | 18.4 | 43.7 | 9.7 | 100.0 |
| 2030 | 23.6 | 17.1 | 46.1 | 13.2 | 100.0 |
| 2040 | 20.3 | 16.0 | 50.1 | 13.6 | 100.0 |
| 2050 | 15.9 | 14.2 | 53.6 | 16.3 | 100.0 |

*Source*: Projections by the authors and 2010 data and rates derived from Texas Higher
Education Coordinating Board 2010.
*NH refers to nonHispanic; values for categories labeled NH are only for the non-
Hispanic persons in each race category. Hispanic includes Hispanics of all races.

number of Hispanic students to increase by 193.4 percent, and the number
of nonHispanic Asian and Other students to increase by 351.3 percent
(Table 6.15).

The extent of unmet need and its role in creating increased levels of debt
can be ascertained by examining the percentage of students with unmet
need exceeding the $10,000 level. We estimated that in 2000 (Murdock et al.

Table 6.17

Number and Percent of Students with Financial Need (in 2010 Dollars) Unmet by Household Resources in Public Colleges and Universities by Need Category within Race/Ethnicity Groups in Texas in 2010 and Projected for 2050 Using the Population Projection That Assumes 2000–2010 Rates of Net Migration

| Need Category | NH*White | NH Black | Hispanic | NH Asian & Other | Total |
|---|---|---|---|---|---|
| **2010** | | **Public Community Colleges** | | | |
| $ ≥20,000 | 2.8 | 2.1 | 6.6 | 2.0 | 4.3 |
| 15,000–19,999 | 19.0 | 27.6 | 19.8 | 20.5 | 21.1 |
| 10,000–14,999 | 40.7 | 41.8 | 41.0 | 40.0 | 41.0 |
| <10,000 | 37.5 | 28.5 | 32.6 | 37.5 | 33.6 |
| Total | 111,871 | 70,629 | 163,781 | 20,613 | 366,894 |
| | | **Public Universities** | | | |
| $ ≥20,000 | 24.4 | 42.0 | 29.1 | 38.1 | 30.5 |
| 15,000–19,999 | 27.1 | 26.2 | 32.4 | 24.0 | 28.2 |
| 10,000–14,999 | 19.1 | 14.2 | 17.7 | 17.9 | 17.6 |
| <10,000 | 29.4 | 17.6 | 20.8 | 20.0 | 23.7 |
| Total | 134,003 | 63,311 | 92,472 | 29,887 | 319,673 |
| | | **Total Public Colleges and Universities** | | | |
| $ ≥20,000 | 14.6 | 21.0 | 14.7 | 23.4 | 16.5 |
| 15,000–19,999 | 23.5 | 26.9 | 24.3 | 22.6 | 24.4 |
| 10,000–14,999 | 28.9 | 28.8 | 32.6 | 26.9 | 30.1 |
| <10,000 | 33.0 | 23.3 | 28.4 | 27.1 | 29.0 |
| Total | 245,874 | 133,940 | 256,253 | 50,500 | 686,567 |
| **2050** | | **Public Community Colleges** | | | |
| $ ≥20,000 | 2.8 | 2.2 | 6.6 | 2.0 | 5.0 |
| 15,000–19,999 | 19.1 | 27.5 | 19.8 | 20.4 | 20.8 |
| 10,000–14,999 | 40.4 | 41.8 | 40.9 | 40.2 | 40.9 |
| <10,000 | 37.7 | 28.5 | 32.7 | 37.4 | 33.3 |
| Total | 101,277 | 105,980 | 479,527 | 94,393 | 781,177 |
| | | **Public Universities** | | | |
| $ ≥20,000 | 24.4 | 41.9 | 29.0 | 38.1 | 32.0 |
| 15,000–19,999 | 27.1 | 26.2 | 32.5 | 24.0 | 28.6 |
| 10,000–14,999 | 19.1 | 14.3 | 17.7 | 17.9 | 17.5 |
| <10,000 | 29.4 | 17.6 | 20.8 | 20.0 | 21.9 |
| Total | 120,849 | 92,624 | 272,414 | 133,504 | 619,391 |
| | | **Total Public Colleges and Universities** | | | |
| $ ≥20,000 | 14.6 | 20.8 | 14.7 | 23.2 | 16.9 |
| 15,000–19,999 | 23.5 | 26.9 | 24.4 | 22.5 | 24.3 |
| 10,000–14,999 | 28.7 | 29.0 | 32.5 | 27.1 | 30.6 |
| <10,000 | 33.2 | 23.3 | 28.4 | 27.2 | 28.2 |
| Total | 222,126 | 198,604 | 751,941 | 227,897 | 1,400,568 |

*Source*: Projections by the authors and 2010 data and rates derived from Texas Higher Education Coordinating Board 2010.
*NH refers to nonHispanic; values for categories labeled NH are only for the nonHispanic persons in each race category. Hispanic includes Hispanics of all races.

Table 6.18

Percent of Students with Financial Need (in 2010 Dollars) Unmet by Household Resources in Public Colleges and Universities by Race/Ethnicity within Need Category in Texas in 2010 and Projected to 2050 Using the Population Projection That Assumes 2000–2010 Rates of Net Migration

| Need Category | NH* White | NH Black | Hispanic | NH Asian & Other | Total Number |
|---|---|---|---|---|---|
| **2010** | | **Public Community Colleges** | | | |
| $ ≥20,000 | 19.7 | 9.6 | 68.1 | 2.6 | 100.0 |
| 15,000–19,999 | 27.6 | 25.2 | 41.7 | 5.5 | 100.0 |
| 10,000–14,999 | 30.2 | 19.6 | 44.7 | 5.5 | 100.0 |
| <10,000 | 34.0 | 16.3 | 43.4 | 6.3 | 100.0 |
| Total | 30.5 | 19.3 | 44.6 | 5.6 | 100.0 |
| | | **Public Universities** | | | |
| $ ≥20,000 | 33.6 | 27.2 | 27.5 | 11.7 | 100.0 |
| 15,000–19,999 | 40.3 | 18.4 | 33.3 | 8.0 | 100.0 |
| 10,000–14,999 | 45.4 | 16.0 | 29.1 | 9.5 | 100.0 |
| <10,000 | 52.0 | 14.7 | 25.4 | 7.9 | 100.0 |
| Total | 42.0 | 19.8 | 28.9 | 9.3 | 100.0 |
| | | **Total Public College and Universities** | | | |
| $ ≥20,000 | 31.6 | 24.8 | 33.2 | 10.4 | 100.0 |
| 15,000–19,999 | 34.5 | 21.5 | 37.2 | 6.8 | 100.0 |
| 10,000–14,999 | 34.4 | 18.6 | 40.4 | 6.6 | 100.0 |
| <10,000 | 40.9 | 15.7 | 36.5 | 6.9 | 100.0 |
| Total | 35.8 | 19.5 | 37.3 | 7.4 | 100.0 |
| **2050** | | **Public Community Colleges** | | | |
| $ ≥20,000 | 7.4 | 6.1 | 81.6 | 4.9 | 100.0 |
| 15,000–19,999 | 11.9 | 17.9 | 58.3 | 11.9 | 100.0 |
| 10,000–14,999 | 12.8 | 13.8 | 61.5 | 11.9 | 100.0 |
| <10,000 | 14.7 | 11.6 | 60.2 | 13.5 | 100.0 |
| Total | 13.0 | 13.6 | 61.3 | 12.1 | 100.0 |
| | | **Public Universities** | | | |
| $ ≥20,000 | 14.9 | 19.6 | 39.8 | 25.7 | 100.0 |
| 15,000–19,999 | 18.5 | 13.7 | 49.8 | 18.0 | 100.0 |
| 10,000–14,999 | 21.3 | 12.2 | 44.5 | 22.0 | 100.0 |
| <10,000 | 26.3 | 12.0 | 41.9 | 19.8 | 100.0 |
| Total | 19.5 | 15.0 | 43.9 | 21.6 | 100.0 |
| | | **Total Public College and Universities** | | | |
| $ ≥20,000 | 13.7 | 17.4 | 46.6 | 22.3 | 100.0 |
| 15,000–19,999 | 15.3 | 15.7 | 53.9 | 15.1 | 100.0 |
| 10,000–14,999 | 15.0 | 13.4 | 57.2 | 14.4 | 100.0 |
| <10,000 | 18.6 | 11.7 | 53.9 | 15.8 | 100.0 |
| Total | 15.9 | 14.2 | 53.6 | 16.3 | 100.0 |

*Source*: Projections by the authors and 2010 data and rates derived from Texas Higher Education Coordinating Board 2010.
*NH refers to nonHispanic; values for categories labeled NH are only for the nonHispanic persons in each race category. Hispanic includes Hispanics of all races.

2003), 16.2 percent of nonHispanic White students with unmet need had $10,000 or more such need, as did 29.3 percent of nonHispanic Black, 25.4 percent of Hispanic, 31.8 percent of Asian and Other, and 21.5 percent of all students. As of 2010, 67.0 percent of nonHispanic White, 76.7 percent of nonHispanic Black, 71.6 percent of Hispanic, 72.9 percent of nonHispanic Asian and Other students, and 71.0 percent of the total number of students in need had levels of need of $10,000 or more. The percentage of all students with an excess of $10,000 in unmet need more than tripled in a single decade, from 21.5 percent in 2000 to 71.0 percent in 2010.

The data in Table 6.18 show that students with unmet need will increasingly be from population segments that generally have more limited economic resources, particularly from Hispanic populations. For example, of all students (in both community colleges and public universities) with $20,000 or more unmet need in 2010, 31.6 percent were nonHispanic White, 24.8 percent nonHispanic Black, 33.2 percent Hispanic, and 10.4 percent nonHispanic Asian and Other, while by 2050 the student population with more than $20,000 in unmet need will be 13.7 percent nonHispanic White, 17.4 percent nonHispanic Black, 46.6 percent Hispanic, and 22.3 percent nonHispanic Asian and Other.

Table 6.19 shows the amount of financial assistance in 2010 and that projected to be needed in the future from all non-household sources (including federal, institutional, loan, etc.) and from the State of Texas (through a variety of state sources, see Table 5 in the Texas Higher Education Coordinating Board: Financial Aid Report for FY 2010 for a listing of these sources). These data exclude aid to international students and students in health related institutions. Both the level of financial assistance required overall and that provided by the state are fixed per capita amounts within need levels and are reported here in 2010 constant dollars.

The data in Table 6.19 show both the level of expenditures required to cover the total level of unmet need and that provided by the state in 2010. The data for 2010 show the federal and state response to growing costs of attendance. By 2010 the state's level of assistance to students represented only 7.1 percent of the total unmet need of nearly $7.4 billion. By 2050, the total expenditures required to cover unmet need will be nearly $20.0 billion and if the state continues to provide the same level of support per student, it will need to provide more than $1.4 billion in aid (versus $523 million in 2010). These are projected increases of more than $12.6 billion from 2010 to 2050 for all expenditures and an increase of nearly $913 million in state expenditures. These data show that the state's students will increasingly need to rely on federal grant and loan programs to meet costs for attending college. This level of state increase in need may result in a decrease in attendance among students with limited resources and may reduce the skill levels and competitiveness of Texas workers.

Table 6.19

Students Receiving Financial Aid and Total and State Financial
Assistance Expenditures (in Millions of 2010 Constant Dollars) for
Higher Education Students Receiving Aid in Texas in 2010 by Family
Contribution Level and Projected for 2050 Using the Population
Projection That Assumes 2000–2010 Rates of Net Migration

| Expected Family Contribution | Students | | All Expenditures | | State Expenditures | |
|---|---|---|---|---|---|---|
| | Number | % | Number | % | Number | % |
| **2010** | | | | | | |
| None | 420,630 | 45.9 | $ 3,316.6 | 45.0 | $ 255.8 | 48.9 |
| $ 1–2,000 | 116,509 | 12.7 | 979.2 | 13.3 | 89.5 | 17.1 |
| 2,001–5,000 | 112,430 | 12.3 | 862.0 | 11.7 | 74.6 | 14.3 |
| 5,001–10,000 | 101,161 | 11.1 | 772.9 | 10.5 | 45.1 | 8.5 |
| 10,000+ | 165,029 | 18.0 | 1,434.2 | 19.5 | 58.5 | 11.2 |
| Total | 915,759 | 100.0 | 7,364.9 | 100.0 | 523.6 | 100.0 |
| Average Per Student* | | | $8,042 | | $572 | |
| **2050** | | | | | | |
| None | 1,187,822 | 48.9 | $ 9,603.3 | 48.0 | $ 735.5 | 51.2 |
| $ 1–2,000 | 322,368 | 13.3 | 2,778.2 | 13.9 | 252.0 | 17.5 |
| 2,001–5,000 | 295,367 | 12.1 | 2,322.1 | 11.6 | 199.6 | 13.9 |
| 5,001–10,000 | 251,954 | 10.3 | 1,973.8 | 9.9 | 114.3 | 8.0 |
| 10,000+ | 373,564 | 15.4 | 3,328.7 | 16.6 | 134.9 | 9.4 |
| Total | 2,431,075 | 100.0 | 20,006.1 | 100.0 | 1,436.3 | 100.0 |
| Average Per Student* | | | $8,229 | | $591 | |

*Source*: Projections by the authors and 2010 data and rates derived from Texas Higher Education Coordinating Board 2010.
Note: Estimates and projections include Texas resident students receiving financial aid at public and non-profit institutions of higher learning in Texas. Students attending health related institutions are not included in these estimates or projections.
*In 2010 constant dollars.

## SUMMARY

1.  Texas public school and public college and university enrollment has increased substantially. Elementary and secondary enrollment increased from 3.6 million in 1990, to 4.7 million in 2000, and to 5.4 million in 2010, an increase from 1990 to 2010 of 50.7 percent. Public community college and university enrollment increased from 1,199,047 in 1990, to 1,202,890 in 2000, and to 1,763,448 in 2010, an increase of 47.1 percent from 1990 to 2010. By 2050, public elementary and secondary school enrollment is projected to be 9,366,444, and public college and university enrollment is projected to be 2,384,968, an increase of 93.2 percent for public elementary and secondary schools and 86.9 percent for public colleges and universities.

2.  Texas school populations have become increasingly diverse. In 1990, 50.2 percent of Texas elementary and secondary school students were nonHispanic White, 14.5 percent nonHispanic Black, 33.2 percent Hispanic, and 2.1 percent nonHispanic Asian and Other. By 2010, these values were 31.9 percent, 13.0 percent, 49.5 percent, and 5.6 percent. By 2050, projections indicate that 15.4 percent of public elementary and secondary enrollment will be nonHispanic White, 8.5 percent will be nonHispanic Black, 64.2 percent will be Hispanic, and 11.9 percent will be nonHispanic Asian and Other. Among public colleges and universities, the percentage of those enrolled in 1990 who were nonHispanic White was 69.7 percent, 9.0 percent were nonHispanic Black, 17.8 percent were Hispanic, and 3.5 percent were nonHispanic Asian and Other. In 2010, the respective proportions were 46.2 percent, 15.7 percent, 31.9 percent, and 6.2 percent. By 2050, these proportions will be 22.3 percent, 12.5 percent, 50.1 percent, and 15.1 percent. Texas schools, like its population, will become increasingly diverse.

3.  Texas general revenue expenditures for elementary and secondary school enrollment increased by 24.8 percent from 2000 to 2010, exceeding the 21.2 percent increase in enrollment. This was due, in part, to increases in costs for specialized programs (such as bilingual/ESL, economically disadvantaged, gifted and talented, etc.), with growth in enrollment that exceeded 34 percent in all such programs. Even with the inclusion of increases for such special programs, the net increase in expenditures per student was only 3.0 percent from 2000 to 2010, far below the level necessary to make up for inflation and to meet student needs. Public college and university enrollment increased by 52.8 percent from 2000 to 2010 while general revenue expenditures increased by only 10.0 percent, resulting in a reduction in per student expenditures of more than 28 percent.

4. Given the state's patterns of population growth, growth in rates of college and university completion among minority students is essential to maintain a competitive workforce. However, the overall rates of increase in the number of students with financial need unmet by family resources are exceeding the rates of increase in the total number of students. For example, for the total 2010 to 2050 projection period, the increase in the number of students with unmet need is expected to be 104.0 percent compared to projected overall enrollment growth of 86.9 percent. Growth in the number of students in need is projected to exceed 193 percent for Hispanic students and be more than 351 percent for nonHispanic Asian and Other students. Overall total expenditures for student financial assistance from all sources will increase from roughly $7.4 billion in 2010 to more than $20.0 billion in 2050, and state expenditures on financial need, under the assumption that expenditures will remain at the 2010 level (7.1 percent of the unmet need), will increase from $523 million in 2010 to $1.4 billion in 2050. With increasing numbers of students and increasing levels of unmet need, Texas may need to consider substantially increasing its level of assistance to students to ensure that there is a competitive workforce in the future.

The data in this chapter indicate both the challenges and opportunities facing the state because of its growing school population. If Texas fails to adequately educate its growing population of minority students, the state will have a less well educated and a poorer population than it has today. However, if it can successfully educate this population, it could have a younger and more competitive workforce than the nation as a whole. The challenge is providing the resources necessary to ensure that Texas students and workers are competitive in the increasingly international workforce of the future.

CHAPTER 7

# Health, Human, and Correctional Services in Texas

Critical to the creation of a productive population and workforce necessary to forge a prosperous future are a variety of health and human services and the rehabilitation of Texans who become incarcerated. In this chapter, we examine health services provided largely by the private sector, publicly provided human services that address needs for basic income, health care, and other assistance, and the size and costs of future correctional programs in Texas.

## HEALTH AND HEALTH CARE IN TEXAS

### Health Related Incidences and Disabling Conditions

Health care facility and personnel requirements in Texas will grow substantially in the future as a result of the increase in the state's population. However, because of the aging of the population, the population needing health services will increase faster than the total population. Texas' population is projected to increase by more than 30.1 million people from 2010 to 2050, an increase of 119.5 percent to a total population of 55.2 million people. As the data in Table 7.1 indicate, the number of incidences of disease and disorders in Texas will increase even more rapidly, with the number of incidences increasing by 84.3 million incidences, or by 136.8 percent, from 2010 to 2050.

As with other factors tied to population change, the most rapid growth in health incidences will occur among the Hispanic, nonHispanic Asian and Other, and nonHispanic Black populations. Whereas the number of incidences involving nonHispanic White population members will increase by 18.3 percent from 2010 to 2050, the number of incidences involving nonHispanic Black population members will increase by 123.9 percent,

Table 7.1

Projections of Incidences of Diseases/Disorders and Percent
Change in Incidences of Diseases/Disorders in Texas by Race/
Ethnicity from 2010 to 2050 Using the Population Projection That
Assumes 2000–2010 Rates of Net Migration, 2010–2050

| Year | NH* White | NH Black | Hispanic | NH Asian & Other | Total |
|---|---|---|---|---|---|
| **Number of Incidences** | | | | | |
| 2010 | 34,400,777 | 7,595,342 | 17,072,316 | 2,592,134 | 61,660,569 |
| 2020 | 37,891,233 | 9,970,823 | 25,851,970 | 4,393,091 | 78,107,117 |
| 2030 | 40,207,165 | 12,437,276 | 37,560,027 | 7,255,396 | 97,459,864 |
| 2040 | 41,072,929 | 14,796,133 | 52,332,506 | 11,200,174 | 119,401,742 |
| 2050 | 40,713,269 | 17,009,228 | 71,280,514 | 17,007,539 | 146,010,550 |
| **Percent Change in Incidences** | | | | | |
| 2010–2020 | 10.1 | 31.3 | 51.4 | 69.5 | 26.7 |
| 2020–2030 | 6.1 | 24.7 | 45.3 | 65.2 | 24.8 |
| 2030–2040 | 2.2 | 19.0 | 39.3 | 54.4 | 22.5 |
| 2040–2050 | −0.9 | 15.0 | 36.2 | 51.9 | 22.3 |
| 2010–2050 | 18.3 | 123.9 | 317.5 | 556.1 | 136.8 |

*Source*: Projections by the authors and 2010 data and rates derived from National
Center for Health Statistics 2012c.
*NH refers to nonHispanic; values shown are only for the nonHispanic persons in
each race category. Hispanic includes Hispanics of all races.

those involving Hispanics will increase by 317.5 percent, and those involving nonHispanic Asian and Other persons will increase by 556.1 percent.

By 2050, 28.1 percent of all incidences will involve nonHispanic White,
12.0 percent nonHispanic Black, 47.9 percent Hispanic, and 12.0 per-
cent nonHispanic Asian and Other, compared to 55.5 percent, 12.8 per-
cent, 27.3 percent, and 4.4 percent in these groups, respectively, in 2010
(Table 7.2). As might be expected, the overall age differentials between
racial/ethnic groups are reflected in the percentages of those having incidences of different types of diseases and disorders. Those incidences of diseases disproportionately impacting older persons show higher prevalence
among nonHispanic Whites and lower prevalence among persons from all
other racial and ethnic groups.

For example, whereas nonHispanic Whites will account for 28.1 percent of all incidences, they will account for 35.1 percent of most coronary incidences, 43.4 percent of emphysema cases, 47.9 percent of cancer incidences, and 49.9 percent of all incidences involving hearing difficulties by 2050. NonHispanic Black residents will account for 12 percent of all

Table 7.2

Projected Percent of the Prevalence of Selected Diseases/Disorders in Texas by Race/Ethnicity and Type of Diseases/Disorders for Adults (18 Years of Age and Older) for 2010 and 2050 Using the Population Projection That Assumes 2000–2010 Rates of Net Migration

| Disease/Disorder | NH* White | | NH Black | | Hispanic | | NH Asian & Other | |
|---|---|---|---|---|---|---|---|---|
| | 2010 | 2050 | 2010 | 2050 | 2010 | 2050 | 2010 | 2050 |
| High Blood Pressure | 54.2 | 26.7 | 15.0 | 14.0 | 26.4 | 47.0 | 4.4 | 12.3 |
| Coronary Heart Disease | 63.1 | 35.1 | 10.3 | 10.2 | 21.7 | 40.4 | 4.9 | 14.3 |
| Angina Pectoris | 65.6 | 35.6 | 7.9 | 8.2 | 21.4 | 41.4 | 5.1 | 14.8 |
| Heart Attack | 65.6 | 37.0 | 10.1 | 10.2 | 19.6 | 38.0 | 4.7 | 14.8 |
| Other Heart Condition/Disease | 67.7 | 39.6 | 10.4 | 11.3 | 18.1 | 36.9 | 3.8 | 12.2 |
| Stroke | 55.5 | 28.7 | 15.4 | 15.0 | 25.0 | 44.9 | 4.1 | 11.4 |
| Emphysema | 73.0 | 43.4 | 7.2 | 9.7 | 15.5 | 32.5 | 4.3 | 14.4 |
| Asthma | 51.9 | 25.7 | 14.3 | 12.6 | 28.5 | 48.1 | 5.3 | 13.6 |
| Asthma Attack Past Year | 51.2 | 23.6 | 13.3 | 11.0 | 29.0 | 49.3 | 6.5 | 16.1 |
| Ulcer | 58.3 | 29.0 | 10.6 | 10.6 | 26.2 | 46.7 | 4.9 | 13.7 |
| Ulcer Past Year | 46.3 | 19.0 | 11.4 | 9.7 | 37.4 | 57.6 | 4.9 | 13.7 |
| Cancer | 75.6 | 47.9 | 7.2 | 9.8 | 14.7 | 32.9 | 2.5 | 9.4 |
| Diabetes | 45.3 | 19.4 | 13.9 | 12.0 | 35.8 | 56.6 | 5.0 | 12.0 |
| Hay Fever Past Year | 62.3 | 31.6 | 10.4 | 10.1 | 21.6 | 41.9 | 5.7 | 16.4 |
| Sinusitis Past Year | 57.8 | 29.2 | 13.4 | 13.4 | 24.4 | 44.8 | 4.4 | 12.6 |
| Chronic Bronchitis Past Year | 61.2 | 33.2 | 11.4 | 11.5 | 23.7 | 44.5 | 3.7 | 10.8 |
| Weak/Failing Kidneys Past Year | 47.4 | 22.5 | 16.4 | 16.4 | 33.9 | 54.6 | 2.3 | 6.5 |
| Liver Condition Past Year | 45.2 | 17.7 | 10.1 | 8.5 | 39.4 | 61.4 | 5.3 | 12.4 |
| Pregnancy related | 32.6 | 13.7 | 11.6 | 8.4 | 50.7 | 68.2 | 5.1 | 9.7 |
| Ever Worn Hearing Aid | 75.9 | 49.9 | 5.2 | 5.7 | 16.6 | 35.7 | 2.3 | 8.7 |
| Vision Impairment | 51.6 | 24.7 | 14.7 | 13.6 | 29.9 | 51.5 | 3.8 | 10.2 |
| Blindness | 51.4 | 26.8 | 23.1 | 18.6 | 18.1 | 30.5 | 7.4 | 24.1 |
| Lost All Teeth | 61.3 | 32.2 | 12.0 | 13.3 | 23.4 | 44.5 | 3.3 | 10.0 |
| Sad Past Month | 41.2 | 17.2 | 13.9 | 10.1 | 41.1 | 63.8 | 3.8 | 8.9 |
| Nervous Past Month | 50.5 | 22.1 | 9.2 | 7.9 | 37.1 | 62.1 | 3.2 | 7.9 |
| Restless Past Month | 51.0 | 24.3 | 14.1 | 12.0 | 30.7 | 52.7 | 4.2 | 11.0 |
| Hopeless Past Month | 41.9 | 16.6 | 11.9 | 8.4 | 42.2 | 65.9 | 4.0 | 9.1 |
| Everything an Effort Past Month | 43.1 | 20.1 | 18.0 | 14.0 | 33.9 | 53.6 | 5.0 | 12.3 |
| Worthlessness Past Month | 46.3 | 19.9 | 12.8 | 10.1 | 37.5 | 61.6 | 3.4 | 8.4 |
| Total | 55.5 | 28.1 | 12.8 | 12.0 | 27.3 | 47.9 | 4.4 | 12.0 |

*Source*: Projections by the authors and 2010 data and rates derived from National Center for Health Statistics 2012c.

*NH refers to nonHispanic; values shown are only for the nonHispanic persons in each race category. Hispanic includes Hispanics of all races.

incidences but 14 percent of all incidences involving high blood pressure, 15 percent of all stroke incidences, 16.4 percent of kidney related incidences, and 18.6 percent of incidences related to blindness by 2050.

While accounting for 47.9 percent of all incidences by 2050, Hispanics will account for 49.3 percent of those having asthma attacks in the past year, 57.6 percent of those having ulcer attacks, 56.6 percent of diabetes incidences, 54.6 percent of kidney problems, 61.4 percent of liver conditions, and 68.2 percent of pregnancy related incidences in 2050. Prevalence among the nonHispanic Asians and Others will exceed its 12 percent of all incidences for asthma and other respiratory diseases, heart, ulcer, and liver related diseases and will be double their population's proportion of all incidences of blindness.

Particularly evident are the effects that populations with more limited socioeconomic resources (which may result in more limited access to medical resources and less access to information on the long-term effects of inadequate treatment) may have on the incidence of disabling conditions (see Table 7.3). The data on persons with disabilities show that whereas the population of the state is projected to increase by 119.5 percent from 2010 to 2050 and the number of incidences of diseases and disorders to increase by 136.8 percent, the prevalence of conditions associated with disabilities will increase by 198.8 percent, with increases of 46.1 percent for nonHispanic White, 183.3 percent for nonHispanic Black, 462.7 percent for Hispanic, and 787.5 percent for nonHispanic Asians and Other persons. This suggests that the state's changing demographics will result not only in more people who will be seeking services at Texas health care facilities in the future, but that there will also be larger numbers and proportions with serious debilitating conditions.

*Health Care Personnel*
The number of Texas health care personnel has increased but substantial additional growth in this workforce will be necessary. Texas had 284,156 health care personnel of various types in 2010 (Table 7.4, Panel A). This represented an increase of roughly 90,000 professionals, or 46.3 percent, from 2000 to 2010 (see Murdock et al. 2003: 108). The number of physicians increased by more than 21,000, and the number of registered nurses increased by more than 45,000. However, by 2050 assuming 2010 population to physician ratios by race/ethnicity apply to the future population, 107,876 physicians will be required, an increase of 101.8 percent. Under current ratios, the total number of all health care workers will increase by 315,880 by 2050, by 111.2 percent from 2010 to 2050.

Panel B of Table 7.4 shows what the race/ethnicity distribution of health professionals in 2010 would be if it reflected the overall population by race/ethnicity in 2010. If the population of health professionals reflected

Table 7.3

Projections of the Prevalence of Conditions Associated with Disabilities
and Percent Change in Prevalence of Conditions Associated with
Disabilities in Texas by Race/Ethnicity from 2010 to 2050 Using the
Population Projection That Assumes 2000–2010 Rates of Net Migration

| Year | NH* White | NH Black | Hispanic | NH Asian & Other | Total |
|------|-----------|----------|----------|------------------|-------|
| **Number of Incidences** | | | | | |
| 2010 | 2,540,162 | 603,721 | 1,107,393 | 178,505 | 4,429,781 |
| 2020 | 3,022,918 | 849,940 | 1,809,414 | 334,431 | 6,016,703 |
| 2030 | 3,491,401 | 1,148,456 | 2,896,541 | 600,144 | 8,136,542 |
| 2040 | 3,737,476 | 1,453,117 | 4,370,046 | 997,082 | 10,557,721 |
| 2050 | 3,711,228 | 1,710,472 | 6,230,801 | 1,584,249 | 13,236,750 |
| **Percent Change in Incidences** | | | | | |
| 2010–2020 | 19.0 | 40.8 | 63.4 | 87.4 | 35.8 |
| 2020–2030 | 15.5 | 35.1 | 60.1 | 79.5 | 35.2 |
| 2030–2040 | 7.0 | 26.5 | 50.9 | 66.1 | 29.8 |
| 2040–2050 | −0.7 | 17.7 | 42.6 | 58.9 | 25.4 |
| 2010–2050 | 46.1 | 183.3 | 462.7 | 787.5 | 198.8 |

*Source*: Projections by the authors and 2010 data and rates derived from National
Center for Health Statistics 2012c.
*NH refers to nonHispanic; values shown are only for the nonHispanic persons in
each race category. Hispanic includes Hispanics of all races.

the racial and ethnic characteristics of the Texas workforce age population in 2010 (compare data in Panel A to that in Panel B), the number of
nonHispanic Black health care professionals would need to increase by
33.1 percent, the number of Hispanic health professionals would need to
increase by 228.9 percent, the number of nonHispanic Asian and Other
professionals would need to decrease by 55.2 percent, and the number of
nonHispanic White professionals would need to decrease by 32.8 percent.

The data in Panel C of Table 7.4 show how extensive projected change
in the numbers of health care workers by type in 2050 will have to be if
the number of workers by race/ethnicity is to reflect the race/ethnicity
composition of the population of workforce age in 2050. By 2050, of the
600,036 projected health care workers, only 21.8 percent (130,808) will be
nonHispanic White, 9.4 percent will be nonHispanic Black, 55.6 percent

Table 7.4

Health Care Personnel in Texas by Specialty and Race/Ethnicity in 2010 (Actual) and
Simulated to Reflect 2010 and Projected 2050 Population Distribution by Race/Ethnicity
Using the Population Projection That Assumes 2000–2010 Rates of Net Migration

| Health Personnel | NH* White | NH Black | Hispanic | NH Asian & Other | Total |
|---|---|---|---|---|---|
| **Panel A: 2010 Actual** | | | | | |
| Physicians | 38,711 | 2,316 | 6,535 | 5,893 | 53,455 |
| Dentists | 16,889 | 964 | 2,511 | 3,739 | 24,103 |
| Optometrists | 1,924 | 103 | 300 | 750 | 3,077 |
| Pharmacists | 11,456 | 2,896 | 1,882 | 4,194 | 20,428 |
| Registered Nurses | 116,391 | 18,137 | 21,124 | 20,846 | 176,498 |
| Veterinarians | 5,521 | 58 | 84 | 65 | 5,728 |
| Podiatrists | 690 | 71 | 48 | 58 | 867 |
| Total | 191,582 | 24,545 | 32,484 | 35,545 | 284,156 |
| **Projected to Reflect Population's Race/Ethnicity Distribution** | | | | | |
| **Panel B: 2010 Distribution** | | | | | |
| Physicians | 24,216 | 6,147 | 20,099 | 2,993 | 53,455 |
| Dentists | 10,918 | 2,772 | 9,063 | 1,350 | 24,103 |
| Optometrists | 1,394 | 354 | 1,157 | 172 | 3,077 |
| Pharmacists | 9,254 | 2,349 | 7,681 | 1,144 | 20,428 |
| Registered Nurses | 79,954 | 20,297 | 66,363 | 9,884 | 176,498 |
| Veterinarians | 2,594 | 659 | 2,154 | 321 | 5,728 |
| Podiatrists | 392 | 100 | 326 | 49 | 867 |
| Total | 128,722 | 32,678 | 106,843 | 15,913 | 284,156 |
| **Panel C: 2050 Distribution** | | | | | |
| Physicians | 23,517 | 10,140 | 59,979 | 14,240 | 107,876 |
| Dentists | 11,487 | 4,953 | 29,296 | 6,955 | 52,691 |
| Optometrists | 1,741 | 751 | 4,441 | 1,054 | 7,987 |
| Pharmacists | 11,129 | 4,799 | 28,385 | 6,739 | 51,052 |
| Registered Nurses | 81,105 | 34,972 | 206,855 | 49,109 | 372,041 |
| Veterinarians | 1,514 | 653 | 3,862 | 917 | 6,946 |
| Podiatrists | 315 | 136 | 802 | 190 | 1,443 |
| Total | 130,808 | 56,404 | 333,620 | 79,204 | 600,036 |

*Source*: Projections by the authors and 2010 data and rates derived Texas Department of State
Health Services 2012b.
*NH refers to nonHispanic; values shown are only for the nonHispanic persons in each race
category. Hispanic includes Hispanics of all races.

will be Hispanic, and 13.2 percent will be nonHispanic Asian and Other, compared to 67.4 percent who were nonHispanic White, 8.7 percent who were nonHispanic Black, 11.4 percent who were Hispanic, and 12.5 percent who were nonHispanic Asian and Other in 2010. Clearly such a change in the racial/ethnic composition of the health workforce is not necessary to deliver effective treatment, since health care professionals use their skills to treat persons of any race/ethnicity, but such projections make apparent that to achieve a medical services workforce that is representative of the population will require substantial efforts to increase the number of Hispanic and nonHispanic Black health care professionals.

The data in Table 7.5 and 7.6 show that enrollment in health related institutions in Texas is expected to nearly double by 2050, and that the race/ethnicity of graduates will substantially diversify from 2010 to 2050, assuming 2010 age and race/ethnicity specific rates of enrollment in such programs. Health-related institutions will enroll only about 6.3 percent of the total number in the healthcare workforce in 2050 as they did in 2010, suggesting that replacement of the workforce from the Texas population will require 16 years, approximately a generational length of time. The rate of growth projected, of 105.7 percent, will not keep pace with the 119.5 percent rate of growth of the population. As a result, Texas will require a net inmigration of health care professionals if the needs of its expanding population are to be met. This could both represent an opportunity for inmigration for Texas but also a loss of opportunity for native Texans to obtain good jobs in the state.

The ability to meet more of the state's medical needs with Texans is obvious when one examines the projections in Tables 7.6, which show that if minority Texans could become involved in health care professions at the same rate as nonHispanic White Texans, health institutions could produce 50,638 health care professionals by 2050, rather than the 37,653 health care professionals expected under current rates of participation. This will represent an increase of 34.5 percent. As with other factors examined in this work, growth will require increased participation of minority population members, with projected increases of 37.2 percent for nonHispanic Black and 113.9 percent for Hispanic persons.

Table 7.7 shows data on projected physician contacts and related costs, days of hospital care and associated costs, and the number of nursing home residents and associated costs (all costs in 2010 dollars). These projections were made using race/ethnicity specific rates obtained from federal agencies reporting data for these groups (see sources on Table 7.7). The number of physician visits was computed by multiplying the average number of physician visits per population unit for persons of a given age by the number of persons of that age as projected for each time period. Costs were obtained by multiplying the number of visits by the average costs per visit

Table 7.5

Enrollment of Texas Residents in Texas Health Related Institutions
by Race/Ethnicity in 2010 and Numeric and Percent Change in
Projected Enrollment to 2050 Using the Population Projection
That Assumes 2000–2010 Rates of Net Migration

| Year | NH* White | NH Black | Hispanic | NH Asian & Other | Total |
|------|-----------|----------|----------|------------------|-------|
| **Health Related Institutions** | | | | | |
| 2010 | 10,209 | 1,510 | 3,322 | 3,263 | 18,304 |
| 2020 | 10,027 | 1,803 | 4,830 | 5,100 | 21,760 |
| 2030 | 9,503 | 2,012 | 6,423 | 8,482 | 26,420 |
| 2040 | 10,086 | 2,226 | 7,935 | 10,545 | 30,792 |
| 2050 | 9,787 | 2,446 | 10,597 | 14,823 | 37,653 |
| **Numeric Change** | | | | | |
| 2010–2020 | −182 | 293 | 1,508 | 1,837 | 3,456 |
| 2020–2030 | −524 | 209 | 1,593 | 3,382 | 4,660 |
| 2030–2040 | 583 | 214 | 1,512 | 2,063 | 4,372 |
| 2040–2050 | −299 | 220 | 2,662 | 4,278 | 6,861 |
| 2010–2050 | −422 | 936 | 7,275 | 11,560 | 19,349 |
| **Percent Change** | | | | | |
| 2010–2020 | −1.8 | 19.4 | 45.4 | 56.3 | 18.9 |
| 2020–2030 | −5.2 | 11.6 | 33.0 | 66.3 | 21.4 |
| 2030–2040 | 6.1 | 10.6 | 23.5 | 24.3 | 16.5 |
| 2040–2050 | −3.0 | 9.9 | 33.5 | 40.6 | 22.3 |
| 2010–2050 | −4.1 | 62.0 | 219.0 | 354.3 | 105.7 |

*Source*: Projections by the authors and 2010 data and rates derived from Texas Higher
Education Coordinating Board 2011c.
*NH refers to nonHispanic; values shown are only for the nonHispanic persons in
each race category. Hispanic includes Hispanics of all races.

for persons of that age. A similar methodology was used to determine the
number of hospital days of care and costs. Average costs per day of care
by age of patient were then used to project total costs. To obtain nursing home enrollment by age, the percentage of persons in each age group
in nursing homes was multiplied by the population in that age group. To
project costs, the average monthly costs were multiplied by the number

Table 7.6

Projected Enrollment of Texas Residents in Texas Health Related Institutions
by Race/Ethnicity in 2050 Using Alternative Enrollment Rate Assumptions

| Race/Ethnicity | Assuming 2010 Enrollment Differentials | Assuming NH* White Enrollment Rates for Minority Groups |
|---|---|---|
| NH* White | 9,787 | 9,787 |
| NH Black | 2,446 | 3,357 |
| Hispanic | 10,597 | 22,671 |
| NH Asian & Other | 14,823 | 14,823 |
| Total | 37,653 | 50,638 |

*Source*: Projections by the authors and data and rates derived from Texas Higher Education Coordinating Board 2011c.
*NH refers to nonHispanic; values shown are only for the nonHispanic persons in each race category. Hispanic includes Hispanics of all races.

of persons projected to be in nursing homes. As with other projections, one cannot take into account other factors (e.g., inflation rates, change in medical practice patterns, etc.) likely to have an impact on actual future costs. All costs are presented in 2010 constant dollars. Our intention is to simulate the magnitude of the effects of population change on health care services and costs in the coming years.

The data in Panel A of Table 7.7 show that, if the projections in population under the 1.0 scenario occur, the increase in the size and the aging of the population will result in a substantial increase in the number of physician contacts and associated costs. Although the population under this scenario is projected to increase by 119.5 percent, the number of households by 127.6 percent, and the total number of incidences of disease and disorders by 136.8 percent, the number of physician contacts will increase by more than 143.9 percent and costs by 148.6 percent. The number of hospital days will increase by 173.7 percent and associated costs by 176.3 percent, and the number of nursing home residents will increase by 324.7 percent and costs by the same 324.7 percent (since costs for nursing homes are projected by assuming a constant cost per resident per day, rather than the variable costs by age associated with physician visits and hospital care).

That the increase in contacts and costs is strongly impacted by the aging of the population is evident in the fact that for physician costs, of the total increase in contacts of 92,030,469 from 2010 to 2050 (as shown in Panel A of Table 7.7), 41,456,512 of the increased number of contacts will be due to

Table 7.7

Physician Contacts, Days of Hospital Care, and Number of Nursing
Home Residents in Texas by Age of Patient and Associated Costs for
2010 (in Thousands of 2010 Dollars) and Projected for 2050 Using the
Population Projection That Assumes 2000–2010 Rates of Net Migration

| Age of Patient | Number | Costs (in thousands) |
|---|---|---|
| Panel A: Physician Contacts and Total Costs | | |
| **2010** | | |
| <18 | 11,436,718 | $ 1,700,928 |
| 18–54 | 26,366,787 | 5,540,646 |
| 55–64 | 10,250,911 | 2,361,205 |
| 65–74 | 8,592,397 | 1,983,703 |
| 75+ | 7,306,078 | 1,649,922 |
| Total | 63,952,891 | 13,236,404 |
| **2050** | | |
| <18 | 22,065,761 | $ 3,281,735 |
| 18–54 | 54,167,902 | 11,373,952 |
| 55–64 | 22,394,710 | 5,158,420 |
| 65–74 | 26,846,530 | 6,197,986 |
| 75+ | 30,508,457 | 6,889,684 |
| Total | 155,983,360 | 32,901,777 |
| Panel B: Hospital Days and Associated Costs | | |
| **2010** | | |
| <18 | 1,017,380 | $ 1,474,016 |
| 18–44 | 3,037,894 | 6,078,908 |
| 45–64 | 5,645,161 | 14,152,492 |
| 65+ | 2,860,220 | 6,426,277 |
| Total | 12,560,655 | 28,131,693 |
| **2050** | | |
| <18 | 1,962,618 | $ 2,843,509 |
| 18–44 | 6,294,833 | 12,596,130 |
| 45–64 | 13,834,182 | 34,682,474 |
| 65+ | 12,281,087 | 27,592,866 |
| Total | 34,372,720 | 77,714,979 |

Table 7.7, continued

| Age of Patient | Number | Costs (in thousands) |
|---|---|---|
| | Panel C: Nursing Home Residents and Monthly Costs | |
| | **2010** | |
| 0–64 | 10,021 | $ 31,716 |
| 65–74 | 8,199 | 25,950 |
| 75–84 | 24,597 | 77,850 |
| 85+ | 48,282 | 152,813 |
| Total | 91,099 | 288,329 |
| | **2050** | |
| 0–64 | 20,191 | $ 63,905 |
| 65–74 | 25,622 | 81,094 |
| 75–84 | 94,147 | 297,975 |
| 85+ | 246,958 | 781,622 |
| Total | 386,918 | 1,224,596 |

*Source*: Projections by the authors and 2010 data and rates derived from National Center for Health Statistics 2011, 2012a, 2012b; C. Caffrey et al. 2012.

populations 65 years of age or older. This population will be 20.9 percent of the state's total population in 2050 but will account for 45 percent of the increase in contacts. Similarly, of the cost increases of $19.7 billion from 2010 to 2050, nearly $9.5 billion or 48.1 percent of the total increase will be costs associated with persons 65 years of age or older. These increases in contacts and costs are likely to substantially impact public and private health care budgets and health care insurance in the coming decades.

The data in Panel B of Table 7.7 for hospital days and costs show similar patterns to those for the number of physician contacts and related costs. However, because of the fact that elderly patients impact hospital use more than they impact total visits and there are higher costs associated with hospital care, the effects are even larger. The number of days of care will increase by 173.7 percent and the total associated costs will increase by 176.3 percent from 2010 to 2050. Of the 21.8 million increase in hospital days of care from 2010 to 2050, 9.4 million or 43.2 percent will be due to persons 65 years of age or older; of the total increase in costs of $49.6 billion, $21.2 billion or 42.7 percent will be due to persons in this age group.

The most dramatic increases in costs associated with an aging population are those related to nursing homes. Because of the extensive levels of care involved, the costs of such care per resident are extensive, and because of the aging of the Texas population, the number needing such care will increase substantially. As shown in Panel C of Table 7.7, the number of persons in nursing homes (under the 1.0 scenario) is projected to increase by 295,819 from 2010 to 2050, an increase of 324.7 percent. The associated costs will increase from $288.3 million in 2010 to $1.2 billion in 2050, also by 324.7 percent.

Overall, the data in Table 7.7 show that the increase in personnel, hospital space, and nursing home beds required to meet future health care needs in Texas will be extensive and costly. Planning for these needs is clearly essential for those involved in elder care in both the public and private sectors.

### Public Health Care Assistance Programs

The data in Tables 7.8 and 7.9 show Medicaid and CHIP (Children's Health Insurance Program) enrollments and costs from 2005 to 2010. The overall rate of the state's population growth from 2000 to 2010 is 20.6 percent; it is reflected in the 20.7 percent growth in Medicaid, while the growth in CHIP participants (76.1 percent) reflects both an increase in the state's participation in the program and population growth (Texas Health and Human Services Commission 2013b, 2013c). Similarly, reflective of the economic characteristics of Texas' more diverse population, the increase in the number of participants in these programs in Texas is greater than the 18.7 percent growth in the number of participants in Medicaid and the 26.9 percent growth in the number of CHIP participants in the nation.

These differences in enrollment are reflected in the relative increase in costs (Table 7.9). The 2005–2010 increase in Medicaid costs in Texas was 37.5 percent, compared to 35.5 percent in the nation, and the 146.8 percent increase in CHIP expenditures in Texas far exceeded the 42.8 percent increase in the United States as a whole. Although over 70 percent of the costs for such programs in Texas will be paid by the Federal government, when the 160.3 percent increase in CHIP costs expected to be paid by Texas is considered, it is clear that such programs are likely to become of increasing concern to Texas decision makers in the coming years.

The data in Tables 7.10 and 7.11 show projections of change in the number of recipients from 2010 to 2050 assuming 2010 eligibility criteria and enrollment rates by age, sex, and race/ethnicity continue. These data show that the 106.9 percent increase in the number of CHIP recipients from 2010 to 2050 will be less than, while the 125.3 percent increase in Medicaid recipients will exceed, the projected 119.5 percent increase in the total population from 2010 to 2050. Both Medicaid and CHIP recipient populations are more racially and ethnically diverse than the total population.

Table 7.8

Enrollment and Change in Enrollment in Medicaid Programs
and in the Children's Health Insurance Program (CHIP)
in Texas and the United States, 2005–2010

| Program | 2005 | 2010 | Change 2005–2010 | |
| --- | --- | --- | --- | --- |
| | | | Numeric | Percent |
| **Texas** | | | | |
| Medicaid Programs | | | | |
| Aged | 235,806 | 239,813 | 4,006 | 1.7 |
| Children's Medicaid | 1,953,270 | 2,410,693 | 457,423 | 23.4 |
| Disabled and Blind | 359,833 | 486,523 | 126,690 | 35.2 |
| TANF Adults | 63,646 | 54,779 | −8,867 | −13.9 |
| Pregnant Women | 120,987 | 129,541 | 8,554 | 7.1 |
| Medically Needy | 49,398 | 37,119 | −12,279 | −24.9 |
| Total Medicaid | 2,782,940 | 3,358,467 | 575,527 | 20.7 |
| CHIP | 326,473 | 574,902 | 248,429 | 76.1 |
| **United States** | | | | |
| Total Medicaid | 42,442,433 | 50,398,467 | 7,956,034 | 18.7 |
| CHIP | 4,043,863 | 5,132,082 | 1,088,219 | 26.9 |

*Source*: Estimates derived from Health Management Associates 2012a, 2012b. Program specific enrollment estimates from Texas Health and Human Services Commission 2013b.

Reflecting the reduced wealth of Texas minority populations, CHIP recipients were 78.8 percent minority and Medicaid recipients were 78 percent minority in 2010, and both programs become roughly 90 percent minority by 2050. Of the total net increase in the number of recipients from 2010 to 2050, all of the increase in the number of CHIP recipients will be due to minority populations and 99.3 percent of the net increase in the number of Medicaid recipients will be due to minority populations. Such demographics make it clear that the growth in minority populations, in the absence of increases in their socioeconomic resources, is likely to increase the number of persons in Texas needing assistance to obtain health care services.

The data on projected total and state costs (see Table 7.12) were obtained by multiplying per capita rates by the number of recipients so that the percent change in costs is identical to the change for the increases in

Table 7.9

Federal and Texas Expenditures for Medicaid and CHIP (in Millions of 2010 Dollars), and Per Recipient Costs in Texas, 2005–2010

| Area | 2005 | 2006 | 2007 | 2008 | 2009 | 2010 | Percent Change 2005–2010 |
|---|---|---|---|---|---|---|---|
| **Medicaid** | | | | | | | |
| United States | $ 194,812.5 | $ 187,352.7 | $ 192,001.3 | $ 195,613.0 | $ 247,024.4 | $ 263,998.5 | 35.5 |
| Texas total | 19,780.6 | 19,590.4 | 21,652.1 | 21,732.8 | 24,096.1 | 27,199.6 | 37.5 |
| Federal costs | 12,070.9 | 11,925.4 | 13,187.7 | 13,191.8 | 16,447.8 | 19,088.4 | 58.1 |
| Texas state costs | 7,709.7 | 7,665.0 | 8,464.4 | 8,541.0 | 7,648.3 | 8,111.2 | 5.2 |
| per recipient | 2,770.3 | 2,736.8 | 2,954.5 | 2,962.9 | 2,467.4 | 2,415.3 | –12.8 |
| **CHIP** | | | | | | | |
| United States | $ 5,890.3 | $ 6,443.0 | $ 6,847.9 | $ 7,555.7 | $ 8,011.1 | $ 8,411.1 | 42.8 |
| Texas total | 442.4 | 402.0 | 558.9 | 1,001.4 | 997.6 | 1,091.7 | 146.8 |
| Federal costs | 321.3 | 291.3 | 405.5 | 724.9 | 713.8 | 776.3 | 141.6 |
| Texas state costs | 121.1 | 110.7 | 153.4 | 276.5 | 283.8 | 315.4 | 160.3 |
| per recipient | 371.1 | 377.5 | 469.7 | 498.5 | 520.8 | 548.6 | 47.8 |

*Source:* Centers for Medicare and Medicaid Services (CMS) 2013; Health Management Associates 2012a, 2012b.
*Note:* Consumer Price Index Research Series Using Current Methods (CPI-U-RS, 1977 = 100). Enrollment data for June of each year. Expenditures for FY. Medicaid includes disproportionate share hospital (DSH) payments.

Table 7.10

CHIP Recipients in Texas, Percent Change in Projected
Recipients, Percent of Recipients by Race/Ethnicity, and Net
Change in Recipients, Using the Population Projection That
Assumes 2000–2010 Rates of Net Migration, 2010–2050

| Year/Period | NH* White | NH Black | Hispanic | NH Asian & Other | Total |
|---|---|---|---|---|---|
| **Panel A: CHIP Recipients** | | | | | |
| 2010 | 121,959 | 72,463 | 352,025 | 28,455 | 574,902 |
| 2020 | 123,241 | 77,828 | 431,811 | 42,199 | 675,079 |
| 2030 | 123,836 | 84,859 | 543,429 | 50,350 | 802,474 |
| 2040 | 116,799 | 90,636 | 704,971 | 75,353 | 987,759 |
| 2050 | 114,209 | 95,904 | 866,631 | 112,723 | 1,189,467 |
| **Panel B: Percent Change in Projected CHIP Recipients** | | | | | |
| 2010–2020 | 1.1 | 7.4 | 22.7 | 48.3 | 17.4 |
| 2020–2030 | 0.5 | 9.0 | 25.8 | 19.3 | 18.9 |
| 2030–2040 | −5.7 | 6.8 | 29.7 | 49.7 | 23.1 |
| 2040–2050 | −2.2 | 5.8 | 22.9 | 49.6 | 20.4 |
| 2010–2050 | −6.4 | 32.3 | 146.2 | 296.1 | 106.9 |
| **Panel C: Percent of CHIP Recipients by Race/Ethnicity** | | | | | |
| 2010 | 21.2 | 12.6 | 61.2 | 5.0 | 100.0 |
| 2020 | 18.3 | 11.5 | 64.0 | 6.2 | 100.0 |
| 2030 | 15.4 | 10.6 | 67.7 | 6.3 | 100.0 |
| 2040 | 11.8 | 9.2 | 71.4 | 7.6 | 100.0 |
| 2050 | 9.6 | 8.1 | 72.9 | 9.4 | 100.0 |

**Panel D: Number and Percent of Net Change in CHIP Recipients, 2010–2050**

| Race/Ethnicity | Number | Percent |
|---|---|---|
| NH White | −7,750 | −1.3 |
| NH Black | 23,441 | 3.8 |
| Hispanic | 514,606 | 83.7 |
| NH Asian & Other | 84,268 | 13.8 |
| Total | 614,565 | 100.0 |

*Source*: Projections by the authors and 2010 data and rates derived from Health Management Associates 2012a; Texas Health and Human Services Commission 2013a.
*NH refers to nonHispanic; values shown are only for the nonHispanic persons in each race category. Hispanic includes Hispanics of all races.

Table 7.11

Medicaid Recipients in Texas, Percent Change in Recipients,
Percent of Recipients by Race/Ethnicity, and Net Change in
Recipients, Using the Population Projection That Assumes
2000–2010 Rates of Net Migration, 2010–2050

| Year/Period | NH* White | NH Black | Hispanic | NH Asian & Other | Total |
|---|---|---|---|---|---|
| **Panel A: Medicaid Recipients** | | | | | |
| 2010 | 738,484 | 599,318 | 1,942,833 | 77,832 | 3,358,467 |
| 2020 | 774,207 | 685,199 | 2,485,323 | 126,469 | 4,071,198 |
| 2030 | 796,516 | 779,897 | 3,263,488 | 191,214 | 5,031,115 |
| 2040 | 780,817 | 864,706 | 4,256,531 | 303,616 | 6,205,670 |
| 2050 | 766,659 | 943,901 | 5,386,378 | 468,110 | 7,565,048 |
| **Panel B: Percent Change in Projected Medicaid Recipients** | | | | | |
| 2010–2020 | 4.8 | 14.3 | 27.9 | 62.5 | 21.2 |
| 2020–2030 | 2.9 | 13.8 | 31.3 | 51.2 | 23.6 |
| 2030–2040 | −2.0 | 10.9 | 30.4 | 58.8 | 23.3 |
| 2040–2050 | −1.8 | 9.2 | 26.5 | 54.2 | 21.9 |
| 2010–2050 | 3.8 | 57.5 | 177.2 | 501.4 | 125.3 |
| **Panel C: Percent of Medicaid Recipients by Race/Ethnicity** | | | | | |
| 2010 | 22.0 | 17.8 | 57.8 | 2.4 | 100.0 |
| 2020 | 19.0 | 16.8 | 61.0 | 3.2 | 100.0 |
| 2030 | 15.8 | 15.5 | 64.9 | 3.8 | 100.0 |
| 2040 | 12.6 | 13.9 | 68.6 | 4.9 | 100.0 |
| 2050 | 10.1 | 12.5 | 71.2 | 6.2 | 100.0 |

**Panel D: Number and Percent of Net Change in Medicaid Recipients, 2010–2050**

| Race/Ethnicity | Number | Percent |
|---|---|---|
| NH White | 28,175 | 0.7 |
| NH Black | 344,583 | 8.2 |
| Hispanic | 3,443,545 | 81.9 |
| NH Asian & Other | 390,278 | 9.2 |
| Total | 4,206,581 | 100.0 |

*Source*: Projections by the authors and 2010 data and rates derived from Health Management Associates 2012b; Texas Health and Human Services Commission 2013b.
*NH refers to nonHispanic; values shown are only for the nonHispanic persons in each race category. Hispanic includes Hispanics of all races.

Table 7.12

Total Costs and State Costs (in Thousands of 2010 Constant Dollars) for Children's Health Insurance Program (CHIP) and Medicaid in Texas by Race/Ethnicity of Recipients in 2010 and Projected to 2050 Using the Population Projection That Assumes 2000–2010 Rates of Net Migration

| Year | NH[a] White | NH Black | Hispanic | NH Asian & Other | Total[b] |
|------|-----------|----------|----------|------------------|----------|
| | | | Panel A: CHIP | | |
| | | | **Total costs** | | |
| 2010 | $ 231,593.5 | $ 137,603.3 | $ 668,476.4 | $ 54,034.5 | $ 1,091,707.7 |
| 2030 | 235,157.9 | 161,142.6 | 1,031,942.2 | 95,611.9 | 1,523,854.6 |
| 2050 | 216,876.7 | 182,116.5 | 1,645,685.3 | 214,054.9 | 2,258,733.3 |
| | | | **State costs** | | |
| 2010 | 66,906.4 | 39,753.0 | 193,120.0 | 15,610.3 | 315,389.7 |
| 2030 | 67,936.1 | 46,553.4 | 298,123.7 | 27,621.9 | 440,235.1 |
| 2050 | 62,654.8 | 52,612.7 | 475,431.5 | 61,839.5 | 652,538.5 |
| | | | Panel B: Medicaid | | |
| | | | **Total costs** | | |
| 2010 | $ 5,980,855.3 | $ 4,853,773.7 | $ 15,734,671.3 | $ 630,348.0 | $ 27,199,648.3 |
| 2030 | 6,450,846.5 | 6,316,252.1 | 26,430,429.7 | 1,548,609.4 | 40,746,137.6 |
| 2050 | 6,209,039.8 | 7,644,492.3 | 43,623,351.7 | 3,791,142.6 | 61,268,026.4 |
| | | | **State costs** | | |
| 2010 | 1,783,556.0 | 1,447,448.1 | 4,692,250.0 | 187,976.6 | 8,111,230.7 |
| 2030 | 1,923,712.5 | 1,883,575.0 | 7,881,841.4 | 461,812.2 | 12,150,941.0 |
| 2050 | 1,851,603.1 | 2,279,670.7 | 13,008,957.6 | 1,130,560.0 | 18,270,791.3 |

*Source*: Projections by the authors and 2010 data and rates derived from Centers for Medicare and Medicaid Services 2013; Health Management Associates 2012a, 2012b; Texas Health and Human Services Commission 2013b.
[a]NH refers to nonHispanic; values shown are only for the nonHispanic persons in each race category. Hispanic includes Hispanics of all races.
[b]Total costs computed from unrounded values.

enrollment. However, an examination of the projected costs suggests significant increases. Total costs for CHIP will increase from $1.1 billion in 2010 to nearly $2.3 billion in 2050, with the related state costs increasing from $315 million to $652 million. Total costs for Medicaid will increase from $27.2 billion in 2010 to $61.3 billion in 2050, with state costs increasing from $8.1 billion to $18.3 billion.

### Medically Uninsured

Costs for medical treatment and hospitalization may be substantial. As a result, whether one is insured or uninsured can be the difference between the accumulation of major debt, with negative consequences for the patients and their households. Similarly, those who lack insurance but need critical care will also impact the state's private and public sector costs. Likely levels of uninsured persons in Texas without the provisions of the Affordable Care Act (ACA) in place are shown in Table 7.13 and likely levels with ACA are shown in Table 7.14. Although the ACA is now federal law, we provide projections both with and without ACA because the time necessary to implement ACA will likely result in the number of uninsured individuals being somewhere between pre-ACA and ACA levels for the period of implementation. Thus both pre- and post-ACA implementation levels are shown here.

The data in Table 7.13 show that the rate of growth in the number of uninsured persons will increase by 145.9 percent between 2010 and 2050, compared to an increase of 119.5 percent for the population for the same periods, with the pre-ACA patterns of use in place. This disparity in growth rates is due to the fact that the Texas population, like the entire United States population, is aging and that its most rapidly growing population segments are more likely to be uninsured. As a result, in the absence of the implementation of the ACA, the number of persons who will be medically uninsured is projected to increase by nearly 8.8 million, from 6.0 million in 2010 to 14.8 million in 2050. Of this increase, 7.3 million will be Hispanic, nearly 1.2 million will be nonHispanic Asian and Other, and roughly 397,000 will be nonHispanic Black; the number of uninsured nonHispanic White persons will decline by nearly 145,000.

In comparison, under the ACA, the number of uninsured persons in Texas will decrease substantially (Cline and Murdock 2012). The number of uninsured in 2050 will be 7,852,252 with the ACA fully implemented (Table 7.14) compared to 14,763,862 million who will be uninsured under the current health care system (Table 7.13). Data in Table 7.14 compared to data in Table 7.13 show that the number of uninsured in Texas will decrease by 6,911,610 by 2050 as a result of the implementation of the ACA. Significantly, roughly 3.6 million of this change will occur before 2020, indicating that the provisions of the act will have substantial near-term effects on the

Table 7.13

Medically Uninsured in Texas by Race/Ethnicity in 2010 and Projected to
2050 Using the Population Projection That Assumes 2000–2010 Rates of Net
Migration and Without Implementation of the Affordable Care Act

| | | | Race/Ethnicity | | |
|---|---|---|---|---|---|
| Year | NH* White | NH Black | Hispanic | NH Asian & Other | Total |
| **Number of Uninsured** | | | | | |
| 2010 | 1,596,974 | 646,579 | 3,473,382 | 285,880 | 6,002,815 |
| 2020 | 1,564,571 | 757,952 | 4,780,916 | 442,093 | 7,545,532 |
| 2030 | 1,498,261 | 849,594 | 6,396,906 | 682,238 | 9,426,999 |
| 2040 | 1,481,862 | 948,574 | 8,346,828 | 997,322 | 11,774,586 |
| 2050 | 1,452,387 | 1,043,211 | 10,817,519 | 1,450,745 | 14,763,862 |
| **Numeric Change** | | | | | |
| 2010–2020 | −32,403 | 111,373 | 1,307,534 | 156,213 | 1,542,717 |
| 2020–2030 | −66,310 | 91,642 | 1,615,990 | 240,145 | 1,881,467 |
| 2030–2040 | −16,399 | 98,980 | 1,949,922 | 315,084 | 2,347,587 |
| 2040–2050 | −29,475 | 94,637 | 2,470,691 | 453,423 | 2,989,276 |
| 2010–2050 | −144,587 | 396,632 | 7,344,137 | 1,164,865 | 8,761,047 |
| **Percent Change** | | | | | |
| 2010–2020 | −2.0 | 17.2 | 37.6 | 54.6 | 25.7 |
| 2020–2030 | −4.2 | 12.1 | 33.8 | 54.3 | 24.9 |
| 2030–2040 | −1.1 | 11.7 | 30.5 | 46.2 | 24.9 |
| 2040–2050 | −2.0 | 10.0 | 29.6 | 45.5 | 25.4 |
| 2010–2050 | −9.1 | 61.3 | 211.4 | 407.5 | 145.9 |
| **Percent of the Uninsured** | | | | | |
| 2010 | 26.6 | 10.8 | 57.9 | 4.7 | 100.0 |
| 2020 | 20.7 | 10.0 | 63.4 | 5.9 | 100.0 |
| 2030 | 15.9 | 9.0 | 67.9 | 7.2 | 100.0 |
| 2040 | 12.6 | 8.1 | 70.9 | 8.4 | 100.0 |
| 2050 | 9.8 | 7.1 | 73.3 | 9.8 | 100.0 |
| **Percent Uninsured** | | | | | |
| 2010 | 14.0 | 22.4 | 36.7 | 20.4 | 23.9 |
| 2020 | 13.1 | 21.8 | 36.8 | 20.4 | 24.7 |
| 2030 | 12.3 | 20.8 | 36.1 | 20.7 | 25.3 |
| 2040 | 12.2 | 20.4 | 35.5 | 20.1 | 26.0 |
| 2050 | 12.1 | 20.1 | 35.2 | 19.9 | 26.7 |

*Source*: Projections by the authors and 2010 data and rates of uninsured derived from Ruggles
et al. 2010; U.S. Census Bureau 2012d.
*NH refers to nonHispanic; values shown are only for the nonHispanic persons in each race
category. Hispanic includes Hispanics of all races.

Table 7.14

Medically Uninsured in Texas by Race/Ethnicity in 2010 and Projected to
2050 Using the Population Projection That Assumes 2000–2010 Rates of Net
Migration and Assuming Full Implementation of the Affordable Care Act

| Year | Race/Ethnicity | | | | |
| | NH* White | NH Black | Hispanic | NH Asian & Other | Total |
| --- | --- | --- | --- | --- | --- |
| **Number of Uninsured** | | | | | |
| 2010 | 1,596,974 | 646,579 | 3,473,382 | 285,880 | 6,002,815 |
| 2020 | 848,904 | 339,479 | 2,428,146 | 307,663 | 3,924,192 |
| 2030 | 823,241 | 382,880 | 3,268,583 | 475,347 | 4,950,051 |
| 2040 | 814,956 | 428,973 | 4,271,353 | 701,836 | 6,217,118 |
| 2050 | 799,950 | 473,576 | 5,564,351 | 1,014,375 | 7,852,252 |
| **Numeric Change** | | | | | |
| 2010–2020 | −748,070 | −307,100 | −1,045,236 | 21,783 | −2,078,623 |
| 2020–2030 | −25,663 | 43,401 | 840,437 | 167,684 | 1,025,859 |
| 2030–2040 | −8,285 | 46,093 | 1,002,770 | 226,489 | 1,267,067 |
| 2040–2050 | −15,006 | 44,603 | 1,292,998 | 312,539 | 1,635,134 |
| 2010–2050 | −797,024 | −173,003 | 2,090,969 | 728,495 | 1,849,437 |
| **Percent Change** | | | | | |
| 2010–2020 | −46.8 | −47.5 | −30.1 | 7.6 | −34.6 |
| 2020–2030 | −3.0 | 12.8 | 34.6 | 54.5 | 26.1 |
| 2030–2040 | −1.0 | 12.0 | 30.7 | 47.6 | 25.6 |
| 2040–2050 | −1.8 | 10.4 | 30.3 | 44.5 | 26.3 |
| 2010–2050 | −49.9 | −26.8 | 60.2 | 254.8 | 30.8 |
| **Percent of the Uninsured** | | | | | |
| 2010 | 26.6 | 10.8 | 57.9 | 4.7 | 100.0 |
| 2020 | 21.6 | 8.7 | 61.9 | 7.8 | 100.0 |
| 2030 | 16.6 | 7.7 | 66.0 | 9.7 | 100.0 |
| 2040 | 13.1 | 6.9 | 68.7 | 11.3 | 100.0 |
| 2050 | 10.2 | 6.0 | 70.9 | 12.9 | 100.0 |
| **Percent Uninsured** | | | | | |
| 2010 | 14.0 | 22.4 | 36.7 | 20.4 | 23.9 |
| 2020 | 7.1 | 9.8 | 18.7 | 14.2 | 12.8 |
| 2030 | 6.7 | 9.4 | 18.5 | 14.5 | 13.3 |
| 2040 | 6.7 | 9.2 | 18.2 | 14.2 | 13.7 |
| 2050 | 6.7 | 9.1 | 18.1 | 13.9 | 14.2 |

*Source*: Projections by the authors and 2010 data and rates of uninsured derived from Ruggles
et al.2010; U.S. Census Bureau 2012d.
*NH refers to nonHispanic; values shown are only for the nonHispanic persons in each race
category. Hispanic includes Hispanics of all races.

number of uninsured. Whatever other factors may need to be considered in the evaluation or implementation of ACA at the state level, it is evident that millions of Texans who would not otherwise have had health insurance are likely to have such insurance under provisions of the Affordable Care Act.

## TANF AND SNAP IN TEXAS

Because of the rapid growth in younger and more diverse populations in Texas, the number of persons in the Temporary Assistance to Needy Families (TANF) and in the Supplemental Nutrition Assistance Program (SNAP) is projected to increase substantially. The recent and projected growth in these programs is shown in Tables 7.15 through 7.19.

The data in Tables 7.15 and 7.16 show 2005–2010 patterns of enrollment change and expenditure increases. Because of changes in enforcement and eligibility, enrollment in TANF decreased both in Texas and in the United States as a whole during the period from 2005 to 2010. The number of persons in TANF in Texas decreased by 42 percent, while there was a decrease of 3.2 percent in the nation. On the other hand, both the nation and Texas showed rapid growth in enrollment in SNAP, with the number of persons using SNAP increasing to 40.3 million in the United States, an increase of 56.7 percent from 2005 to 2010, while the number of persons receiving SNAP increased to more than 3.6 million in Texas in 2010, an increase of 45.4 percent from 2005 to 2010. Clearly these programs, which have substantial impacts on access to financial assistance and improved nutrition, have shown growth far exceeding population growth. Again change in rules for the receipt of such benefits, enforcement changes, and population growth and diversification has led to substantial increases in program use.

The data in Table 7.16 reflect the patterns of use noted above. Whereas national and Texas costs for TANF decreased from 2005 to 2010 (by 4.0 percent and 14.7 percent, respectively), those for SNAP increased (by 96.8 percent for the nation and 81.6 percent for Texas). As shown in this table, only part of the costs for these services are borne by the state, however, with Texas paying for $247.1 of the total $801.3 million in TANF costs and $501.2 million of the total $5.9 billion for SNAP costs from 2005 to 2010. The growing Texas population and its relatively high levels of poverty and large number of families with low incomes are increasing the number of persons dependent on assistance from the state and nation.

The data in Tables 7.17 and 7.18 show that the number of persons receiving benefits through TANF and SNAP will increase substantially in the coming years. The total number of persons enrolled in TANF is projected to increase by 126,499 or by 108.4 percent from 2010 to 2050, with the number of nonHispanic Whites decreasing by 7.6 percent, while the number

Table 7.15

Number and Percent Change in Enrollment for Temporary Assistance for Needy Families (TANF) and Supplemental Nutrition Assistance Program (SNAP) in the United States and Texas, 2005–2010

| Area | 2005 | 2006 | 2007 | 2008 | 2009 | 2010 | Percent Change 2005–2010 |
|---|---|---|---|---|---|---|---|
| **Temporary Assistance for Needy Families (TANF)** | | | | | | | |
| United States | 4,548,503 | 4,148,498 | 3,896,830 | 3,795,007 | 4,154,366 | 4,402,921 | –3.2 |
| Texas | 201,365 | 153,016 | 132,841 | 115,057 | 107,836 | 116,740 | –42.0 |
| **Supplemental Nutrition Assistance Program (SNAP)** | | | | | | | |
| United States | 25,717,830 | 26,548,833 | 26,316,045 | 28,222,630 | 33,489,975 | 40,301,878 | 56.7 |
| Texas | 2,441,975 | 2,622,548 | 2,422,198 | 2,532,047 | 3,003,156 | 3,551,581 | 45.4 |

*Source:* U.S. Department of Health and Human Services 2013a; U.S. Department of Agriculture 2013.
*Note:* TANF average monthly participation for each calendar year shown. SNAP average monthly participation for each fiscal year shown.

Table 7.16

Federal and Texas Expenditures for Temporary Assistance for Needy Families (TANF) and Supplemental Nutrition Assistance Program (SNAP) (in Millions of 2010 Dollars), and Per Recipient Costs in Texas, 2005–2010

| Area | 2005 | 2006 | 2007 | 2008 | 2009 | 2010 | Percent Change 2005–2010 |
|---|---|---|---|---|---|---|---|
| **Temporary Assistance for Needy Families (TANF)** | | | | | | | |
| United States | $ 15,818.6 | $ 14,674.6 | $ 14,339.9 | $ 14,657.0 | $ 15,429.1 | $ 15,178.6 | -4.0 |
| Texas total | 939.8 | 782.4 | 824.0 | 832.3 | 814.6 | 801.3 | -14.7 |
| Federal costs | 537.9 | 532.0 | 493.4 | 577.7 | 563.4 | 554.2 | 3.0 |
| Texas state costs | 401.9 | 250.4 | 330.7 | 254.6 | 251.2 | 247.1 | -38.5 |
| per recipient | 1,995.9 | 2,636.3 | 2,489.1 | 2,213.0 | 2,329.5 | 2,116.9 | 6.1 |
| **Supplemental Nutrition Assistance Program (SNAP)** | | | | | | | |
| United States | $ 34,702.8 | $ 35,581.1 | $ 34,901.8 | $ 38,116.3 | $ 54,511.2 | $ 68,306.9 | 96.8 |
| Texas total | 3,275.0 | 3,549.6 | 3,165.5 | 3,450.8 | 4,881.3 | 5,948.6 | 81.6 |
| Federal costs | 2,970.0 | 3,178.6 | 2,858.3 | 3,107.0 | 4,471.7 | 5,447.4 | 83.4 |
| Texas state costs | 304.9 | 371.0 | 307.2 | 343.8 | 409.5 | 501.2 | 64.3 |
| per recipient | 124.9 | 141.5 | 126.8 | 135.8 | 136.4 | 141.1 | 13.0 |

*Source:* U.S. Department of Health and Human Services 2013a, 2013b; U.S. Department of Agriculture 2013.
*Note:* 2010 estimate using 2009 data.

## Table 7.17

Temporary Assistance for Needy Families (TANF) Enrollment in Texas, Percent Change in Projected Enrollment, Percent of Enrollment by Race/ Ethnicity, and Net Change in Enrollment 2010–2050, Using the Population Projection That Assumes 2000–2010 Rates of Net Migration

| Year/Period | NH* White | NH Black | Hispanic | NH Asian & Other | Total |
|---|---|---|---|---|---|
| **Panel A: TANF Enrollment** | | | | | |
| 2010 | 14,593 | 28,529 | 71,818 | 1,800 | 116,740 |
| 2020 | 14,681 | 31,540 | 89,569 | 2,533 | 138,323 |
| 2030 | 14,385 | 34,499 | 115,165 | 3,287 | 167,336 |
| 2040 | 13,791 | 37,201 | 147,356 | 4,942 | 203,290 |
| 2050 | 13,483 | 39,732 | 182,884 | 7,140 | 243,239 |
| **Panel B: Percent Change in Projected TANF Enrollment** | | | | | |
| 2010–2020 | 0.6 | 10.6 | 24.7 | 40.7 | 18.5 |
| 2020–2030 | −2.0 | 9.4 | 28.6 | 29.8 | 21.0 |
| 2030–2040 | −4.1 | 7.8 | 28.0 | 50.3 | 21.5 |
| 2040–2050 | −2.2 | 6.8 | 24.1 | 44.5 | 19.7 |
| 2010–2050 | −7.6 | 39.3 | 154.6 | 296.7 | 108.4 |
| **Panel C: Percent Change of TANF Enrollment by Race/Ethnicity** | | | | | |
| 2010 | 12.5 | 24.4 | 61.5 | 1.6 | 100.0 |
| 2020 | 10.6 | 22.8 | 64.8 | 1.8 | 100.0 |
| 2030 | 8.6 | 20.6 | 68.8 | 2.0 | 100.0 |
| 2040 | 6.8 | 18.3 | 72.5 | 2.4 | 100.0 |
| 2050 | 5.5 | 16.3 | 75.2 | 3.0 | 100.0 |

**Panel D: Number and Percent of Net Change in TANF Enrollment, 2010–2050**

| | Number | Percent |
|---|---|---|
| NH White | −1,110 | −0.9 |
| NH Black | 11,203 | 8.9 |
| Hispanic | 111,066 | 87.8 |
| NH Asian & Other | 5,340 | 4.2 |
| Total | 126,499 | 100.0 |

*Source*: Projections by the authors and 2010 data and rates derived from Texas Health and Human Services Commission 2013b; U.S. Department of Health and Human Services 2013a.
*NH refers to nonHispanic; values shown are only for the nonHispanic persons in each race category. Hispanic includes Hispanics of all races.

Table 7.18

Supplemental Nutrition Assistance Program (SNAP) Recipients in Texas,
Percent Change in Projected Recipients, Percent of Recipients by Race/
Ethnicity, and Net Change in Recipients to 2050 Using the Population
Projection That Assumes 2000–2010 Rates of Net Migration

| Year/Period | NH* White | NH Black | Hispanic | NH Asian & Other | Total |
|---|---|---|---|---|---|
| **Panel A: SNAP Recipients** | | | | | |
| 2010 | 731,625 | 681,904 | 1,885,889 | 252,166 | 3,551,584 |
| 2020 | 747,017 | 785,407 | 2,503,116 | 368,397 | 4,403,937 |
| 2030 | 738,048 | 892,330 | 3,364,497 | 528,566 | 5,523,441 |
| 2040 | 720,609 | 988,385 | 4,397,105 | 791,556 | 6,897,655 |
| 2050 | 707,385 | 1,080,378 | 5,649,906 | 1,145,942 | 8,583,611 |
| **Panel B: Percent Change In Projected SNAP Recipients** | | | | | |
| 2010–2020 | 2.1 | 15.2 | 32.7 | 46.1 | 24.0 |
| 2020–2030 | −1.2 | 13.6 | 34.4 | 43.5 | 25.4 |
| 2030–2040 | −2.4 | 10.8 | 30.7 | 49.8 | 24.9 |
| 2040–2050 | −1.8 | 9.3 | 28.5 | 44.8 | 24.4 |
| 2010–2050 | −3.3 | 58.4 | 199.6 | 354.4 | 141.7 |
| **Panel C: Percent of SNAP Recipients by Race/Ethnicity** | | | | | |
| 2010 | 20.6 | 19.2 | 53.1 | 7.1 | 100.0 |
| 2020 | 17.0 | 17.8 | 56.8 | 8.4 | 100.0 |
| 2030 | 13.4 | 16.2 | 60.9 | 9.5 | 100.0 |
| 2040 | 10.4 | 14.3 | 63.7 | 11.6 | 100.0 |
| 2050 | 8.2 | 12.6 | 65.8 | 13.4 | 100.0 |

**Panel D. Number and Percent of Net Change in SNAP Recipients, 2010–2050**

| | Number | Percent |
|---|---|---|
| NH White | −24,240 | −0.5 |
| NH Black | 398,474 | 7.9 |
| Hispanic | 3,764,017 | 74.8 |
| NH Asian & Other | 893,776 | 17.8 |
| Total | 5,032,027 | 100.0 |

*Source*: Projections by the authors and 2010 data and rates derived from U.S. Department of Agriculture 2013; Texas Health and Human Services Commission 2013d.
*NH refers to nonHispanic; values shown are only for the nonHispanic persons in each race category. Hispanic includes Hispanics of all races.

of nonHispanic Black persons enrolled will increase by 39.3 percent, the number of Hispanics will increase by 154.6 percent, and the number of nonHispanic Asian and Others will increase by 296.7 percent from 2010 to 2050. Of the overall increase in enrollment in TANF, 87.8 percent will be due to enrollment increases in the number of Hispanic participants, with a decline occurring among nonHispanic White (of 0.9 percent) and increases of only 4.2 percent in nonHispanic Asian and Other and 8.9 percent in nonHispanic Black participants. In 2050, 5.5 percent of TANF recipients will be nonHispanic White, 16.3 percent will be nonHispanic Black, 75.2 percent will be Hispanic, and 3.0 percent will be nonHispanic Asian and Other.

The change in enrollment in SNAP shows similar patterns, but because it is a program relating to nutrition, it has larger impacts on those minority population groups with larger proportions of children. As a result, the total number of recipients increases by 5,032,027 or 141.7 percent between 2010 and 2050 (compared to 108.4 percent for TANF). The number of nonHispanic White participants declines by 3.3 percent while the number of nonHispanic Black participants is projected to increase by 58.4 percent, the number of Hispanic participants to increase by 199.6 percent, and the number of nonHispanic Asian and Other participants to increase by 354.4 percent. As for TANF, the net change in SNAP will include a 0.5 percent decline in the net number of nonHispanic White recipients, a 7.9 percent net increase in the number of nonHispanic Black recipients, a 74.8 percent net increase in the number of Hispanic recipients, and a 17.8 percent net increase in the number of nonHispanic Asian and Other recipients. As a result, of those receiving benefits in 2050, 8.2 percent will be nonHispanic White, 12.6 percent will be nonHispanic Black, 65.8 percent will be Hispanic, and 13.4 percent will be nonHispanic Asian and Other.

Table 7.19 shows the projected increase in costs for providing TANF and SNAP services to Texans in the coming years. Because these costs are obtained by multiplying per capita participant costs by the number of participants, the overall percent increases in total and state costs are equal to the percent increases in the number of participants (of 108.4 percent for TANF and 141.7 percent for SNAP). The data show total costs for TANF increasing from $801.3 million in 2010 to nearly $1.7 billion in 2050, and Texas' costs increasing from $247.1 to $514.9 million from 2010 to 2050. Total costs for providing SNAP services will increase from $5.9 to nearly $14.4 billion, with Texas' costs projected to increase from $501.1 million in 2010 to $1.2 billion in 2050. The numerical increase in costs shows the total costs for Texans on TANF increasing by $868.3 million from 2010 to 2050, with the portion of such costs paid for by the state increasing by $267.8 million. The cost increases are larger for SNAP, with a total increase in costs of $8.4 billion from 2010 to 2050 and with state costs increasing by

Table 7.19

Total Costs and State Costs (in Thousands of 2010 Constant Dollars) for Temporary
Assistance for Needy Families (TANF) and Supplemental Nutrition Assistance Program
(SNAP) in Texas by Race/Ethnicity of Recipient in 2010 and Projected Enrollment to
2050 Using the Population Projection That Assumes 2000–2010 Rates of Net Migration

| Year | NH[a] White | NH Black | Hispanic | NH Asian & Other | Total[b] |
|---|---|---|---|---|---|
| **Panel A: TANF** | | | | | |
| **Total costs** | | | | | |
| 2010 | $ 100,166.4 | $ 195,823.1 | $ 492,958.8 | $ 12,355.2 | $ 801,303.4 |
| 2020 | 100,770.4 | 216,490.6 | 614,801.6 | 17,386.5 | 949,449.1 |
| 2030 | 98,738.6 | 236,801.1 | 790,492.6 | 22,562.0 | 1,148,594.3 |
| 2040 | 94,661.4 | 255,347.7 | 1,011,451.6 | 33,921.9 | 1,395,382.6 |
| 2050 | 92,547.3 | 272,720.4 | 1,255,315.8 | 49,009.0 | 1,669,592.5 |
| **State costs** | | | | | |
| 2010 | $ 30,893.4 | $ 60,395.9 | $ 152,038.7 | $ 3,810.6 | $ 247,138.6 |
| 2020 | 31,079.7 | 66,770.2 | 189,617.6 | 5,362.4 | 292,829.8 |
| 2030 | 30,453.0 | 73,034.4 | 243,804.3 | 6,958.6 | 354,250.3 |
| 2040 | 29,195.5 | 78,754.5 | 311,952.7 | 10,462.2 | 430,364.9 |
| 2050 | 28,543.5 | 84,112.6 | 387,165.4 | 15,115.4 | 514,937.0 |
| **Panel B: SNAP** | | | | | |
| **Total costs** | | | | | |
| 2010 | $ 1,224,740.3 | $ 1,141,507.3 | $ 3,156,978.2 | $ 422,125.9 | $ 5,945,351.6 |
| 2020 | 1,250,506.5 | 1,314,771.3 | 4,190,216.2 | 616,696.6 | 7,372,190.5 |
| 2030 | 1,235,492.4 | 1,493,760.4 | 5,632,168.0 | 884,819.5 | 9,246,240.2 |
| 2040 | 1,206,299.5 | 1,654,556.5 | 7,360,753.8 | 1,325,064.7 | 11,546,674.5 |
| 2050 | 1,184,162.5 | 1,808,552.8 | 9,457,942.6 | 1,918,306.9 | 14,368,964.8 |
| **State costs** | | | | | |
| 2010 | $ 103,239.6 | $ 96,223.5 | $ 266,117.8 | $ 35,583.1 | $ 501,164.0 |
| 2020 | 105,411.6 | 110,828.8 | 353,214.7 | 51,984.5 | 621,439.6 |
| 2030 | 104,146.0 | 125,916.7 | 474,764.2 | 74,585.9 | 779,412.8 |
| 2040 | 101,685.1 | 139,471.0 | 620,475.5 | 111,696.5 | 973,328.1 |
| 2050 | 99,819.1 | 152,452.1 | 797,258.2 | 161,703.9 | 1,211,233.3 |

*Source*: Projections by the authors and 2010 data and rates derived from U.S. Department of
Health and Human Services 2013a; Texas Health and Human Services Commission 2013d; U.S.
Department of Agriculture 2013.
[a]NH refers to nonHispanic; values shown are only for the nonHispanic persons in each race
category. Hispanic includes Hispanics of all races.
[b]Total costs computed from unrounded values.

$710.1 million. In the absence of change in the socioeconomic characteristics of the most rapidly growing Texas population segments, the costs for the provision of these basic services will increase substantially.

## CORRECTIONAL SERVICES: YOUTH AND ADULT

Tables 7.20 through 7.25 provide data that allow the characteristics of adult prison and juvenile offenders to be examined for recent periods and to be projected for the future. When compared to earlier decades, the growth in such services has decreased substantially. For example, in the predecessor to this work (Murdock et al. 2003), the number of juvenile offenders was shown to have increased substantially, with an increase of 16.0 percent from 1989 to 1999 at the national level and 80.9 percent for Texas. The number of adult offenders increased by 76.5 percent from 1990 to 2000 at the national level and by 198.6 percent in Texas.

The number of juvenile offenders in the nation declined by 28.2 percent from 2000 to 2010, while the number of juvenile offenders in Texas increased by 27.8 percent (Table 7.20). The number of adult offenders increased by 15.8 percent in Texas and by 15.3 percent nationally. These substantial reductions in growth rates (compared to the 1989–1999 change) are a result of changes in procedures and policies for handling offenders and are related to rates of incarceration as well as changes in the rates of growth in prison age populations.

The aging of the incarcerated populations is evident in Table 7.21. In the juvenile offender population, the percentage of offenders in all ages 15 and under is less, and the percentage of offenders in all ages 16 and older is greater, in 2010 than in 2000. Similarly in the adult offender population, the percentage in age groups less than 40 is greater in 2000 than in 2010 and the percentage in age groups 40 and over is greater in 2010 than in 2000. Offender populations are aging.

The data in Table 7.22 show differences in the relative percentage of crimes in different offense types between 2000 and 2010. The percentage of crimes that were violent crimes increased from 49.0 percent in 2000 to 51.2 percent in 2010 while the percentage of crimes that were property crimes decreased from 21.0 to 16.6 percent. The percentage of offenses that involved drug offenses also declined from 19.9 to 17.8 percent while the percentage in the other and unclassified offense category increased from 10.1 percent of all offenses in 2000 to 14.4 percent in 2010, with the largest increase in this category being in sex offenses. Through 2010, it is evident that serious violent, drug, and property crimes continued to dominate Texas offenses.

The projections relating to juvenile and adult prisoners in Tables 7.23 and 7.24 show substantial increases in the number of offenders from 2010

Table 7.20

Number and Percent Change in Persons in Juvenile Facilities
in Texas, Adults in State Prisons in Texas, and Juveniles and
Adults in Prisons in the United States, 2000–2010

| Area | Year | | Percent Change 2000–2010 |
|---|---|---|---|
| | 2000 | 2010 | |
| **Juvenile Offenders** | | | |
| Texas | 7,808 | 9,979 | 27.8 |
| United States | 110,284 | 79,166 | −28.2 |
| **Adult Offenders** | | | |
| Texas | 133,680 | 154,795 | 15.8 |
| United States* | 1,316,333 | 1,518,104 | 15.3 |

*Source*: Texas Juvenile Probation Commission 2001, 2011; Sickmund 2002; Glaze
2010; Texas Department of Criminal Justice 2001, 2011.
*Includes prisoners held in state or federal correctional facilities or privately operated
facilities.

to 2050 but, due to an aging population and changes in incarceration policies, the growth in the number of juvenile offenders will be less than the
overall growth in populations. The projected 87.9 percent increase in the
number of juvenile offenders from 9,979 in 2010 to 18,753 in 2050 (see
Table 7.23) is less than the 119.5 percent increase in the total population
of Texas.

What is apparent in Table 7.23 is that juvenile offenders are projected
to be increasingly minority population members, particularly Hispanic
youth. In 2010, 20.0 percent of such offenders were nonHispanic White,
33.3 percent were nonHispanic Black, 45.9 percent were Hispanic, and
0.8 percent were nonHispanic Asian and Other. By 2050 only 9.9 percent
are projected to be nonHispanic White, so that the proportion of such
youth will decrease by 10.1 percent from 20.0 to 9.9 percent. Similarly, the
percentage who will be nonHispanic Black will decrease from 33.3 percent
in 2010 to 23.5 percent in 2050. On the other hand, the percentage of youth
offenders who are Hispanic will increase from 45.9 percent of all youth
offenders in 2010 to 64.7 percent by 2050. The similar figures for non-
Hispanic Asian and Others will be from 0.8 percent of all youth offenders

Table 7.21

Percent of Juvenile and Adult Offenders in Texas by
Selected Demographic Characteristics, 2000–2010

| Characteristic | 2000 | 2010 |
|---|---|---|
| Panel A: Juvenile Offenders | | |
| *Age at Commitment to Texas Juvenile Justice Department Facilities* | | |
| <12 | 1.2 | 0.9 |
| 13 | 4.8 | 2.3 |
| 14 | 13.6 | 9.7 |
| 15 | 25.9 | 22.2 |
| 16 | 39.7 | 41.7 |
| 17 | 14.4 | 22.3 |
| 18+ | 0.4 | 0.9 |
| Total Number | 2,558 | 1,056 |
| *Persons Admitted to Texas Juvenile Justice Department Facilities by Race/Ethnicity*[a] | | |
| NH* White | 25.2 | 20.6 |
| NH Black | 33.6 | 34.3 |
| Hispanic | 40.2 | 44.4 |
| NH Asian & Other | 1.0 | 0.7 |
| Total Number | 2,558 | 1,056 |
| Panel B: Adult Offenders | | |
| *Age of Inmates On-Hand*[b] | | |
| 15–24 | 15.4 | 13.4 |
| 25–29 | 16.9 | 15.8 |
| 30–39 | 34.8 | 28.9 |
| 40–49 | 23.8 | 24.9 |
| 50–59 | 7.1 | 13.0 |
| 60+ | 2.0 | 4.0 |
| Total Number | 133,680 | 154,795 |
| *Inmates On-Hand by Race/Ethnicity*[b,c] | | |
| White | 30.8 | 31.0 |
| Black | 43.3 | 36.2 |
| Hispanic | 25.5 | 32.3 |
| Other | 0.4 | 0.5 |
| Total Number | 133,680 | 154,795 |

*Source*: Texas Juvenile Probation Commission 2001, 2011; Texas Department of Criminal Justice 2001, 2011.

*NH refers to nonHispanic; values shown are only for the nonHispanic persons in each race category. Hispanic includes Hispanics of all races.

[a]Data do not include recommitants, revocation, or reclassifications. Data do include VCP (violator of CINS probation) admissions or offenders temporarily on Bench Warrant.

[b]On-hand counts are one-day counts as of August 31 for all years.

[c]Race and ethnicity are as identified by Texas Department of Criminal Justice.

## Table 7.22

Percent of Inmates On-Hand in Adult Correctional
Facilitates in Texas by Offense Category, 2000–2010

| Offense | 2000 | 2010 |
|---|---|---|
| **Violent** | | |
| Homicide | 10.4 | 10.5 |
| Kidnapping | 0.8 | 0.9 |
| Sexual Assault | 11.2 | 12.6 |
| Robbery | 16.8 | 14.7 |
| Assault | 9.8 | 12.5 |
| Total Violent | 49.0 | 51.2 |
| **Property** | | |
| Arson | 0.5 | 0.5 |
| Burglary | 14.5 | 9.9 |
| Larceny | 2.7 | 3.5 |
| Stolen Vehicle | 1.6 | 0.9 |
| Forgery | 1.3 | 1.0 |
| Fraud | 0.4 | 0.8 |
| Total Property | 21.0 | 16.6 |
| Total Drugs | 19.9 | 17.8 |
| **Other and Unclassified Offenses** | | |
| Sex Offense | 2.5 | 4.8 |
| Escape | 0.5 | 1.3 |
| Weapons | 1.2 | 1.8 |
| Traffic/DWI | 4.4 | 4.3 |
| Public Order Crime | 0.6 | 1.4 |
| All Other | 0.4 | 0.8 |
| Unknown | 0.5 | — |
| Total Other and Unclassified | 10.1 | 14.4 |
| Total Number of Inmates | 133,680 | 154,795 |

Source: Texas Department of Criminal Justice 2001, 2011.
Note: All counts are one-day counts as of August 31 for all years.

Table 7.23

Texas Juvenile Justice Department (TJJD) Population in Texas in 2010 and
Projected Through 2050, Percent Change in Projected Population, Percent
of Population by Race/Ethnicity, and Net Change in Population Using the
Population Projection That Assumes 2000–2010 Rates of Net Migration

| Year/Period | NH* White | NH Black | Hispanic | NH Asian & Other | Total |
|---|---|---|---|---|---|
| **Panel A: TJJD Population** | | | | | |
| 2010 | 1,999 | 3,326 | 4,577 | 77 | 9,979 |
| 2020 | 1,930 | 3,566 | 6,175 | 137 | 11,808 |
| 2030 | 2,071 | 3,869 | 7,105 | 152 | 13,197 |
| 2040 | 1,930 | 4,178 | 9,698 | 217 | 16,023 |
| 2050 | 1,848 | 4,414 | 12,144 | 347 | 18,753 |
| **Panel B: Percent Change in Projected TJJD Population** | | | | | |
| 2010–2020 | −3.5 | 7.2 | 34.9 | 77.9 | 18.3 |
| 2020–2030 | 7.3 | 8.5 | 15.1 | 10.9 | 11.8 |
| 2030–2040 | −6.8 | 8.0 | 36.5 | 42.8 | 21.4 |
| 2040–2050 | −4.2 | 5.6 | 25.2 | 59.9 | 17.0 |
| 2010–2050 | −7.6 | 32.7 | 165.3 | 350.6 | 87.9 |
| **Panel C: Percent of TJJD Population by Race/Ethnicity** | | | | | |
| 2010 | 20.0 | 33.3 | 45.9 | 0.8 | 100.0 |
| 2020 | 16.3 | 30.2 | 52.3 | 1.2 | 100.0 |
| 2030 | 15.7 | 29.3 | 53.8 | 1.2 | 100.0 |
| 2040 | 12.0 | 26.1 | 60.5 | 1.4 | 100.0 |
| 2050 | 9.9 | 23.5 | 64.7 | 1.9 | 100.0 |

**Panel D: Number and Percent of Net Change in TJJD Population 2010–2050**

| | Number | Percent |
|---|---|---|
| NH White | −151 | −1.7 |
| NH Black | 1,088 | 12.4 |
| Hispanic | 7,567 | 86.2 |
| NH Asian & Other | 270 | 3.1 |
| Total | 8,774 | 100.0 |

*Source*: Projections by the authors and 2010 data and rates derived from Texas Juvenile Probation Commission 2001, 2011.
*NH refers to nonHispanic; values shown are only for the nonHispanic persons in
each race category. Hispanic includes Hispanics of all races.

Table 7.24

Prison Population in Texas in 2010 and Projected Through 2050, Percent
Change in Projected Prison Population, Percent of Population by Race/
Ethnicity, and Net Change in Population Using the Population Projection
That Assumes 2000–2010 Rates of Net Migration, 2010–2050

| Year/Period | NH* White | NH Black | Hispanic | NH Asian & Other | Total |
|---|---|---|---|---|---|
| **Panel A: Texas Prison Population** | | | | | |
| 2010 | 48,027 | 56,057 | 49,935 | 776 | 154,795 |
| 2020 | 46,501 | 65,999 | 70,337 | 1,216 | 184,053 |
| 2030 | 45,246 | 75,748 | 96,036 | 1,934 | 218,964 |
| 2040 | 45,124 | 85,490 | 126,456 | 2,827 | 259,897 |
| 2050 | 44,425 | 94,581 | 165,777 | 4,077 | 308,860 |
| **Panel B: Percent Change in Projected Texas Prison Population** | | | | | |
| 2010–2020 | −3.2 | 17.7 | 40.9 | 56.7 | 18.9 |
| 2020–2030 | −2.7 | 14.8 | 36.5 | 59.0 | 19.0 |
| 2030–2040 | −0.3 | 12.9 | 31.7 | 46.2 | 18.7 |
| 2040–2050 | −1.5 | 10.6 | 31.1 | 44.2 | 18.8 |
| 2010–2050 | −7.5 | 68.7 | 232.0 | 425.4 | 99.5 |
| **Panel C: Percent of Texas Prison Population by Race/Ethnicity** | | | | | |
| 2010 | 31.0 | 36.2 | 32.3 | 0.5 | 100.0 |
| 2020 | 25.3 | 35.9 | 38.1 | 0.7 | 100.0 |
| 2030 | 20.7 | 34.6 | 43.8 | 0.9 | 100.0 |
| 2040 | 17.4 | 32.9 | 48.6 | 1.1 | 100.0 |
| 2050 | 14.4 | 30.6 | 53.7 | 1.3 | 100.0 |

**Panel D: Number and Percent of Net Change in Prison Population 2010–2050**

| | Number | Percent |
|---|---|---|
| NH White | −3,602 | −2.3 |
| NH Black | 38,524 | 25.0 |
| Hispanic | 115,842 | 75.2 |
| NH Asian & Other | 3,301 | 2.1 |
| Total | 154,065 | 100.0 |

*Source*: Projections by the authors and 2010 data and rates derived from Texas Department of Criminal Justice 2001, 2011.
*NH refers to nonHispanic; values for categories labeled NH are only for the non-Hispanic persons in each race category. Hispanic includes Hispanics of all races.

in 2010 to 1.9 percent in 2050. Overall because the number of nonHispanic White juvenile offenders is projected to decrease, all of the increase in the number of juvenile offenders is projected to be due to minority population members.

The overall increase in the number of adult prisoners will be greater than the increase in youth offenders (see Table 7.24). The number of adult defenders is projected to nearly double from 154,795 in 2010 to 308,860 in 2050, by 99.5 percent. Although the data show a population with increasing diversity, the diversification of the adult population base results in less diversification in the adult incarcerated population. By 2050, the percentage of prisoners who will be nonHispanic White will be 14.4 percent (down from 31.0 percent in 2010), 30.6 percent are projected to be nonHispanic Black (down from 36.2 percent in 2010), 53.7 percent are projected to be Hispanic (an increase from 32.3 percent in 2010), and 1.3 percent are projected to be nonHispanic Asian and Other (up from 0.5 percent in 2010). Similar to the findings for juvenile offenders, all of the increase in the number of adult prisoners is projected to be due to increases in minority populations.

Table 7.25 shows the projected increases in costs for both juvenile and adult facilities. Since these are projected on a per capita basis, the percentage increases reflect the rates of increase in the associated populations. The costs of increased numbers of incarcerated persons are substantial in absolute terms. For example, the projected increase in the costs of housing youth offenders will be from $259.4 million in 2010 to $487.5 million in 2050 (in 2010 constant dollars), an increase of $228 million from 2010 to 2050. Similarly, the costs of incarcerating adult prisoners will increase from about $3.5 billion in 2010 to $6.9 billion in 2050, an increase of nearly $3.5 billion dollars. In the absence of change in factors that reduce the growth in the number of offenders such as increased levels of education, Texas will be faced with substantial increases in incarceration costs in the coming decades.

## SUMMARY

In this chapter we have examined the growth in enrollment and in associated costs for the provision of several critical state services. The data point to substantial growth in the numbers of persons served by such programs and to a related and substantial increase in the costs of providing such services. Overall, they point to a number of major conclusions:

1.   The aging, diversifying, and growing Texas population will present clear challenges to the provision of health care services in Texas in the coming decades. Due to the aging of the population the number of health

Table 7.25

Expenditures (in 2010 Dollars) for Texas Juvenile Justice Department Services and
Adult Prison Costs in Texas by Race/Ethnicity in 2010 and Projected to 2050 Using
the Population Projection That Assumes 2000–2010 Rates of Net Migration

| Year | NH* White | NH Black | Hispanic | NH Asian & Other | Total |
|---|---|---|---|---|---|
| **Panel A: Texas Juvenile Justice Department Costs** | | | | | |
| 2010 | $ 51,960,716 | $ 86,453,897 | $ 118,971,584 | $ 2,001,488 | $ 259,387,685 |
| 2020 | 50,167,174 | 92,692,302 | 160,508,965 | 3,561,090 | 306,929,531 |
| 2030 | 53,832,237 | 100,568,289 | 184,682,784 | 3,950,990 | 343,034,300 |
| 2040 | 50,167,174 | 108,600,235 | 252,083,553 | 5,640,558 | 416,491,520 |
| 2050 | 48,035,719 | 114,734,667 | 315,663,298 | 9,019,694 | 487,453,378 |
| **Panel B: Adult Prison Costs** | | | | | |
| 2010 | $ 1,075,853,916 | $ 1,255,734,128 | $ 1,118,595,068 | $ 17,383,194 | $ 3,467,566,306 |
| 2020 | 1,041,669,956 | 1,478,445,096 | 1,575,620,732 | 27,239,644 | 4,122,975,428 |
| 2030 | 1,013,556,672 | 1,696,832,666 | 2,151,304,614 | 43,323,578 | 4,905,017,530 |
| 2040 | 1,010,823,747 | 1,915,063,429 | 2,832,743,724 | 63,327,691 | 5,821,958,591 |
| 2050 | 995,165,433 | 2,118,711,126 | 3,713,574,337 | 91,328,969 | 6,918,779,865 |

*Source*: Projections by the authors and 2010 data and rates from Texas Comptroller of Public Accounts 2011b.
*NH refers to nonHispanic; values for categories labeled NH are only for the nonHispanic persons in each race category. Hispanic includes Hispanics of all races.

related incidences will increase substantially. Whereas the population
is projected to increase by 119.5 percent from 2010 to 2050, the number
of health incidences requiring medical assistance is expected to increase
by 136.8 percent, or by 84.3 million, from 2010 to 2050. Because of the
baseline changes in the population, these incidences will increasingly involve Hispanic, nonHispanic Asian and Others, and nonHispanic Black
residents. The number of incidences involving nonHispanic Whites will increase by 18.3 percent from 2010 to 2050, while the increase in the number
of incidences involving nonHispanic Black persons will be 123.9 percent,
the increase involving Hispanics will be 317.5 percent, and the increase
involving nonHispanic Asian and Others will be 556.1 percent.

2. The older age structure of nonHispanic White and nonHispanic
Black persons will lead to a disproportionate number of incidences in
disease/disorders related to aging. For example, although representing
28.1 percent of all incidences, nonHispanic Whites will account for 35 percent of all coronary incidences, 43 percent of all emphysema cases, nearly
48 percent of all cancer incidences, and nearly 50 percent of all auditory
incidences. NonHispanic Black persons, who account for 12 percent of
all incidences, will account for 14 percent of all incidences involving high

blood pressure, 15 percent of all stroke incidences, 16.4 percent of all kidney related incidences, and 18.6 percent of all incidences involving blindness by 2050.

3.  The number of persons with disabilities will increase faster than the overall population and the number of health incidences. Although the population is projected to increase by 119.5 percent from 2010 to 2050 and the percentage of all health incidences to increase by 136.8 percent, the number of conditions associated with disability will increase by 198.8 percent, including a 46.1 percent increase from 2010 to 2050 for nonHispanic White, 183.3 percent for nonHispanic Black, 462.7 percent for Hispanic, and 787.5 percent for nonHispanic Asian and Other persons.

4.  Texas had 284,156 health care personnel of various types in 2010. Texas will need to add 54,421 physicians and an additional 195,543 registered nurses between 2010 and 2050 and increase the total of all health care workers from 284,156 in 2010 to 600,036 by 2050, an increase of 315,880 health care personnel, to provide the current level of care. This represents an increase of 111.2 percent from 2010 to 2050, while health related institutions are projected to increase enrollment by 105.7 percent. Texas is likely to require net inmigration of health care personnel from other states to meet its needs in the coming years. Alternatively, increased levels of participation in health related professions among the state's rapidly growing minority populations could result in a 34.5 percent increase in the number of medical personnel produced by Texas health related institutions from 2010 to 2050.

5.  If the projections under the 1.0 scenario occur, the increase in the size, and the aging of the population, will result in a substantial increase in the number of physician contacts and associated costs. Although the population under this scenario is projected to increase by 119.5 percent, the number of households by 127.6 percent, and the total number of incidences of disease and disorders by 136.8 percent, the number of physician contacts will increase by more than 143.9 percent and associated costs by 148.6 percent. The number of hospital days will increase by 173.7 percent and associated costs by 176.3 percent. The number of nursing home residents will increase by 324.7 percent and costs by the same 324.7 percent (since costs are determined by a constant cost per day, rather than the variable costs by age associated with physician visits and hospital care).

6.  The aging of the population particularly impacts the increase in medically related contacts and costs. Of the total increase in contacts from

2010 to 2050 (of 92,030,469), 41,456,512 contacts will be due to populations 65 years of age or older. The elderly population is projected to be
20.9 percent of Texas' total population by 2050 but will account for 45 percent of the increase in physician contacts from 2010 to 2050. Similarly, of
the total cost increases from 2010 to 2050 (of $19.7 billion), nearly $9.5 billion or 48.1 percent will be costs associated with persons 65 years of age
or older. Nursing home care shows especially dramatic increases. Using
per capita per day average rates, the number of nursing home patients is
projected to increase by nearly 296,000 from 2010 to 2050, with associated
costs increasing from $288.3 million in 2010 to $1.2 billion in 2050, an
increase of nearly 325 percent. These increases are likely to substantially
impact public and private health care budgets and health care insurance in
the coming decades.

7.   Medicaid and CHIP services are federally funded programs in which
the federal government pays for more than 70 percent of the costs while
the state pays the remainder of the costs. Because of the state's relatively
younger and poorer population, growth in the involvement of Texans
in these programs has exceeded levels of population growth. Although
Medicaid costs increased by 35.5 percent and CHIP costs by 42.8 percent, nationally from 2005 to 2010, Texas costs for Medicaid increased by
37.5 percent and its CHIP expenditures increased by 146.8 percent. These
are critical programs for the state's poorest residents, with nearly 79 percent
of CHIP recipients and 78 percent of Medicaid recipients being minority population members. Overall, the number of CHIP recipients is projected to increase from roughly 575,000 in 2010 to nearly 1.2 million by
2050 (106.9 percent) and Medicaid recipients from 3.4 million in 2010 to
7.6 million in 2050 (125.3 percent). Total costs for CHIP will increase from
$1.1 billion in 2010 to nearly $2.3 billion in 2050, with the related state costs
increasing from $315 million to $652 million. Total costs for Medicaid will
increase from $27.2 billion in 2010 to $61.3 billion in 2050, with state costs
increasing from $8.1 billion to $18.3 billion. These programs are likely to
continue to be a focus of the state as it attempts to meet the needs of a
rapidly growing population.

8.   Millions of Texans are medically uninsured. In 2010, Texas had the
highest percentage of uninsured persons of any state in the nation with
more than 6 million Texans lacking health insurance (see Table 7.13).
Equally dramatic is the fact that under the current system, in the absence
of any reforms, nearly 14.8 million Texans (26.7 percent of all Texans) will
be uninsured in 2050, an increase of nearly 8.8 million or 145.9 percent
from 2010 to 2050.

9.   Although, the effects of the Affordable Care Act have yet to impact medical care substantially, an analysis by Cline and Murdock (2012) suggests that its implementation could substantially reduce the number of uninsured in Texas. Analysis of the results in Tables 7.13 and 7.14 suggests that this act could reduce the number of uninsured in Texas in 2050 from 14.8 million to 7.9 million, a reduction of more than 6.9 million persons. This will reduce the percentage of uninsured Texans in 2050 from 26.7 percent to 14.2 percent, from more than one-in-four to one-in-seven Texans.

10.   Programs that provide direct financial and food assistance to households with limited financial resources are projected to be impacted by changing demographics in Texas. Temporary Assistance for Needy Families (TANF) and the Supplemental Nutrition Assistance Program (SNAP) are projected to show increases in both the number of participants and costs from 2010 through 2050. These are programs in which a majority of the costs are borne by the federal government. For example, in 2010, the TANF program provided $801.3 million in assistance to Texas families of which $247.1 or 31 percent was provided by the state. Similarly, while the SNAP program provided $5.9 billion in assistance to Texans, $501 million (8.4%) of which was paid by the state. Assuming enrollment rates at the same levels as in 2010, the number of TANF recipients is projected to increase from 116,740 in 2010 to 243,239 in 2050, or by 108.4 percent. The number of participants in SNAP will increase more rapidly, from 3.5 million in 2010 to 8.6 million in 2050, an increase of 141.7 percent. Projected total costs for TANF increase from $801.3 million in 2010 to nearly $1.7 billion in 2050 and Texas' costs increase from $247.1 to $514.9 million from 2010 to 2050. Total costs for providing SNAP services will increase from $5.9 to nearly $14.4 billion, and Texas' costs are projected to increase from $501.1 million in 2010 to $1.2 billion in 2050.

11.   Change will also occur in the Texas juvenile and adult correctional systems. Although Texas has shown more rapid growth in juvenile and adult correctional programs in the past (see Murdock et al. 2003), slower growth is projected based on recent data due to policy and demographic changes. The number of juveniles in correction facilities is projected to increase from 9,979 in 2010 to 18,753 in 2050, a percent increase of 87.9 percent, while the number of adult offenders in Texas prisons will increase from 154,795 to 308,860, or by 99.5 percent. Those incarcerated will increasingly be members of minority populations.

12.   Although the numbers in both juvenile and adult correctional facilities will increase more slowly than the 119.5 percent increase in the total population for 2010 to 2050, the growth is still projected to be substantial

and costly. Assuming the same costs per person in such facilities in the future as in 2010, the costs for incarcerating juvenile offenders will increase from $259.4 million in 2010 to nearly $487.5 million in 2050 (in 2010 dollars) and the costs of incarcerating the adult prison population will increase from nearly $3.5 billion in 2010 to $6.9 billion in 2050 (in 2010 dollars), numerical increases of $228.1 million and nearly $3.5 billion, respectively.

The data in this chapter indicate that the future population of Texas is likely to show continuing patterns of substantial need. Due to the fact that aging and poorer minority populations are growing more rapidly than other components of the population, medical services are likely to involve increasing numbers of personnel and substantial increases in treatment costs. Meeting such needs will also substantially increase the demand for medical personnel and Texas may wish to take steps to educate a larger share of its own residents to address such demand. The elderly population in Texas, like that in the nation as a whole, will grow substantially and its medical and long-term care needs will require additional infrastructure and personnel requirements that will require significant increases in expenditures. Although this is not a challenge for Texas alone, addressing such needs will likely challenge the state's medical facilities and personnel as well as state government.

Large numbers of the Texas population are impoverished and need assistance in meeting basic needs. If the education, income, and other resources of Texans can be improved, the number of those with such needs will decrease and Texas will become more prosperous. In the absence of such progress, Texas will face substantial challenges in meeting the human needs of its most vulnerable citizens. It will face substantial increases in costs for programs such as TANF, SNAP, Medicaid, and CHIP, and additional resources to serve those without adequate medical coverage and care. It will also be required to pay for the needs of an increasing prison population. Addressing such needs is among the most daunting challenges facing Texas.

# CHAPTER 8

# The Effects of Demographic Change on Selected Transportation Services and Demand

In this chapter we analyze the effects of projected patterns of population and household change on transportation related services. We do not explore the effects of population change on all transportation modes, but focus primarily on the forms of personal transportation used on a daily basis. We specifically examine the effects of change in the size of the population as well as change in the population's age, sex, and race/ethnicity characteristics and change in the household composition on the number of licensed drivers, yearly vehicle miles of travel, number of crashes, vehicle ownership, and changes in modes of daily work commuting.

In 1950, less than half of the population in Texas was licensed to drive (a licensure rate of 362.7 drivers per 1,000 people [Table 8.1]). At that time, drivers were largely male and most households owned only one vehicle. The number of drivers increased rapidly from the 1950s through the 1970s, as more people were able to afford the cost of purchasing and maintaining a vehicle. At the same time, public and private policies, such as the development of modern freeways, suburban development, and limited development of public transportation systems made the car necessary for most transportation needs. Finally, and probably more significantly, the increase in the number of drivers coincided with the rapid increase in the number of women entering the labor force beginning in the 1960s (Pisarski 2006). Today, an almost equal number of women and men are licensed to drive in Texas, although there are some variations by race/ethnicity.

In a society dependent upon the automobile for most forms of inter- and intra-urban transportation, the lack of a vehicle can limit a person's

Table 8.1

Total Population, Total Licensed Drivers, Licensed Drivers per
1,000 People in Texas, and Percent Change, 1950–2010

| | Number | | Percent Change from Previous Decade | | Licensed Drivers Per 1,000 Population | |
|---|---|---|---|---|---|---|
| Year | Population | Drivers | Population | Drivers | Drivers | Percent Change |
| 1950 | 7,711,194 | 2,796,862 | — | — | 362.7 | — |
| 1960 | 9,579,677 | 4,352,168 | 24.2 | 55.6 | 454.3 | 25.3 |
| 1970 | 11,196,730 | 6,380,057 | 16.9 | 46.6 | 569.8 | 25.4 |
| 1980 | 14,229,191 | 9,287,826 | 27.1 | 45.6 | 652.7 | 14.6 |
| 1990 | 16,986,510 | 11,136,694 | 19.4 | 19.9 | 655.6 | 0.4 |
| 2000 | 20,851,820 | 13,462,023 | 22.8 | 20.9 | 645.6 | −1.5 |
| 2010 | 25,145,561 | 15,157,650 | 20.6 | 12.6 | 602.8 | −6.6 |

Source: U.S. Department of Transportation 1991, 2001–2010, 2011b; U.S. Census
Bureau 1991b, 2001b, 2011c.

economic and social interactions. For example, workers with cars are able
to travel further distances in a shorter amount of time so that they have
more job opportunities. People who own vehicles are more likely to drive
to reach work or other destinations than those who use any other form
of transportation (Polzin et al. 2001; Pucher and Renne 2003). The single
best predictor of vehicle ownership is income, and because of household
income differences between nonHispanic White households and other
groups, households headed by persons from minority groups are less likely
to own a vehicle than nonHispanic White households and the driver's licensure rates among minorities is lower than that of nonHispanic Whites
(Giuliano and Dargay 2006; Dargay et al. 2007; Pisarski 2006).

The differences in vehicle ownership and driver's licensure rates influence the types of transportation that individuals use for various purposes.
Persons who are nonHispanic Black, because of a variety of factors including lack of resources to purchase and maintain a vehicle and a large
proportion of nonHispanic Black persons living in major urban areas
where public transit is available, were more likely to take public transportation on the journey to work than any other group in 2000 and 2010
(U.S. Census Bureau 2011a, 2002; Kim 2009; Giuliano 2003; Polzin et al.
2001). At the same time, Hispanics have higher carpooling rates than any

other group. This is likely a result of a combination of factors, including working in occupations conducive to carpooling and having a larger proportion of households with only one vehicle or no vehicles at all leading to ridesharing with family and friends. In addition, Hispanics have a larger proportion of persons who live in places where public transportation may not be available (Cline et al. 2009). These differences in transportation behaviors mean that although population growth alone will have significant impacts on the transportation system and transportation infrastructure, changes in the composition of the population will also affect the rate of increase of that change and the types of transportation services demanded.

## HISTORIC CHANGE IN THE CHARACTERISTICS
## OF THE DRIVING POPULATION

The growth in the number of drivers in Texas began to slow in the 1980s (Table 8.1). Since the 1980s, the percent increase in licensed drivers has been at or below the change in the population so that by 2010, there were 602.8 licensed drivers for every 1,000 people. The most recent period, 2000–2010, saw the smallest increase in the number of drivers when compared with any previous decade, and the percent increase was well below the change in the population as a whole (an increase of 12.6 percent between 2000 and 2010, while the population increased by 20.6 percent).

The number of licensed drivers has increased more rapidly for people of older ages over the past twenty years in Texas and in the United States overall (Table 8.2). In the 2000–2010 decade, whereas the total number of drivers increased by 1.7 million (12.6 percent), the number of drivers less than 45 years of age declined by 259,035 (–3.2 percent). And over a twenty year period, the number of drivers in the younger age groups saw a much smaller increase than the number of drivers 45 years old and older.

The deceleration in the growth of licensed drivers in the most recent decades, and the decline in the number of younger drivers, is due in large part to increases in the minority population. In 2010, there were an estimated 702.0 nonHispanic White drivers per 1,000 nonHispanic Whites compared to 498.8 Hispanic drivers per 1,000 Hispanics. All other minority groups also lag the licensure rates of nonHispanic Whites. As a result, whereas 48.9 percent of the population age 15 and older was nonHispanic White in 2010, 52.8 percent of licensed drivers were nonHispanic White (Table 8.3: Panel C).

The effects of the racial and ethnic diversification of the population can be seen in the age characteristics of drivers as well. The majority of drivers age 45 years and older were nonHispanic White in 2010 while all other age groups had no racial/ethnic majority (Table 8.3: Panel C). Relative to

Table 8.2

Licensed Drivers in Texas and the United States by Age in 1990,
2000, and 2010 and Numeric and Percent Change, 1990–2010

| | Licensed Drivers | | | Percent Change | | |
|---|---|---|---|---|---|---|
| Age | 1990 | 2000 | 2010 | 1990–2000 | 2000–2010 | 1990–2010 |
| **Texas** | | | | | | |
| 15–19 | 595,420 | 771,147 | 713,345 | 29.5 | −7.5 | 19.8 |
| 20–29 | 2,518,608 | 2,696,169 | 2,763,663 | 7.0 | 2.5 | 9.7 |
| 30–44 | 3,976,226 | 4,571,863 | 4,303,136 | 15.0 | −5.9 | 8.2 |
| 45–64 | 2,731,128 | 3,895,912 | 5,292,040 | 42.6 | 35.8 | 93.8 |
| 65–79 | 1,111,165 | 1,266,379 | 1,656,077 | 14.0 | 30.8 | 49.0 |
| 80+ | 204,147 | 260,553 | 429,389 | 27.6 | 64.8 | 110.3 |
| Total | 11,136,694 | 13,462,023 | 15,157,650 | 20.9 | 12.6 | 36.1 |
| **United States** | | | | | | |
| 15–19 | 9,249,046 | 9,743,519 | 9,556,240 | 5.3 | −1.9 | 3.3 |
| 20–29 | 36,791,828 | 33,551,534 | 35,899,449 | −8.8 | 7.0 | −2.4 |
| 30–44 | 56,536,675 | 61,307,460 | 55,188,228 | 8.4 | −10.0 | −2.4 |
| 45–64 | 42,177,752 | 58,696,700 | 75,739,404 | 39.2 | 29.0 | 79.6 |
| 65–79 | 20,711,422 | 21,764,592 | 25,856,814 | 5.1 | 18.8 | 24.8 |
| 80+ | 1,548,526 | 5,561,217 | 7,874,804 | 259.1 | 41.6 | 408.5 |
| Total | 167,015,250 | 190,625,023 | 210,114,939 | 14.1 | 10.2 | 25.8 |

*Source*: U.S. Department of Transportation 1991, 2001, 2011b.

their representation in the population overall, Hispanics and nonHispanic Blacks have fewer drivers at all ages than nonHispanic Whites (again reflecting the gaps in the licensure rates between nonHispanic Whites and other groups).

The number of drivers age 65 years and older has increased along with increases in the number of people age 65 years and older. In 2010, 13.7 percent of all drivers were 65 years old or older (Table 8.3: Panel B). As the baby boom generation (those born in the years of 1946 through 1964) moves into older ages, and as improvements in the health of the elderly allow people to live with better health into older ages, the number of elderly drivers will increase significantly in future years. This increase

Table 8.3

Licensed Drivers in Texas by Race/Ethnicity and Age, 2010

| Age | NH* White | NH Black | Hispanic | NH Asian & Other | Total |
|---|---|---|---|---|---|
| **Panel A: Number of Drivers** | | | | | |
| 15–19 | 338,466 | 61,011 | 242,657 | 41,294 | 683,428 |
| 20–29 | 1,160,860 | 319,128 | 1,131,457 | 159,804 | 2,771,249 |
| 30–44 | 1,890,451 | 507,830 | 1,662,763 | 287,981 | 4,349,025 |
| 45–64 | 3,092,752 | 576,301 | 1,345,728 | 264,624 | 5,279,405 |
| 65–79 | 1,163,783 | 128,338 | 294,093 | 60,973 | 1,647,187 |
| 80+ | 354,134 | 22,303 | 42,316 | 8,603 | 427,356 |
| Total | 8,000,446 | 1,614,911 | 4,719,014 | 823,279 | 15,157,650 |
| **Panel B: Percent of Drivers by Age (Within Race/Ethnicity)** | | | | | |
| 15–19 | 4.2 | 3.8 | 5.1 | 5.0 | 4.5 |
| 20–29 | 14.5 | 19.8 | 24.0 | 19.4 | 18.3 |
| 30–44 | 23.6 | 31.4 | 35.2 | 35.0 | 28.7 |
| 45–64 | 38.7 | 35.7 | 28.5 | 32.1 | 34.8 |
| 65–79 | 14.5 | 7.9 | 6.2 | 7.4 | 10.9 |
| 80+ | 4.5 | 1.4 | 1.0 | 1.1 | 2.8 |
| Total | 100.0 | 100.0 | 100.0 | 100.0 | 100.0 |
| **Panel C: Percent of Drivers by Race/Ethnicity (Within Age)** | | | | | |
| 15–19 | 49.5 | 8.9 | 35.5 | 6.1 | 100.0 |
| 20–29 | 41.9 | 11.5 | 40.8 | 5.8 | 100.0 |
| 30–44 | 43.5 | 11.7 | 38.2 | 6.6 | 100.0 |
| 45–64 | 58.6 | 10.9 | 25.5 | 5.0 | 100.0 |
| 65–79 | 70.7 | 7.8 | 17.9 | 3.6 | 100.0 |
| 80+ | 82.9 | 5.2 | 9.9 | 2.0 | 100.0 |
| Total | 52.8 | 10.7 | 31.1 | 5.4 | 100.0 |

*Source*: Derived from U.S. Department of Transportation 2011a, 2011b.
*NH refers to nonHispanic; values for categories labeled NH are only for the non-Hispanic persons in each race category. Hispanic includes Hispanics of all races.

in the number of drivers age 65 years and older will impact transportation services and demand in many different ways. For instance, the majority of persons in this population group is no longer working or may be working part time, which means that their travel will not be restricted primarily to peak commute times, and thus they will increase the miles traveled during off-peak times. In addition, while most accident rates are higher for the youngest population, more people in older age groups will increase the number of elderly involved in traffic accidents, including fatality crashes.

## CHANGE IN DRIVING PATTERNS OF THE TEXAS POPULATION

There are several ways of measuring transportation use and behaviors. One measure of roadway transportation use is vehicle miles traveled. Vehicle miles traveled (or VMT) measures the distance a vehicle travels, regardless of the number of people in the vehicle and can be reported as a yearly figure (VMT) or a daily figure (DVMT). Over the years, VMT has grown in both Texas and the nation as a result of growth in the population, the number of drivers, and the number of vehicles in Texas and the United States. In Texas, yearly VMT grew from 220.1 million in 2000 to a peak of 243.4 million in 2007 before dropping to 234.0 million in 2010 (U.S. Department of Transportation 2011b). However, when examined on a per capita basis, change in VMT was relatively stable between 2002 and 2007 prior to dropping during the recession years. In addition, the gap in the per capita VMT in Texas and the United States as a whole has steadily declined since the 1990s, and since 1998 Texas per capita VMT has been below that of the per capita miles traveled in the United States as a whole. Although much of the decline in the aggregate vehicle miles of travel can be attributed to the economic downturn, change in the per capita VMT and the closure in the gap in per capita VMT between Texas and the United States may be indicative of other factors affecting the driving population and travel behavior.

The number of households owning no cars increased by 71,953 or 14.7 percent between 1990 and 2010 (Table 8.4), but the percent increase was not as large as the growth in the number of households overall (47.0 percent between 1990 and 2010). In 2010, an estimated 6.3 percent of all Texas households did not own a vehicle. This percentage is lower than that of the previous two decades.

While the decline in the percentage of households without vehicles has been small overall, the most significant change has been the decline in the percentage of households headed by a person age 65 years and older where no car is present. In 1990, 17.0 percent of households headed by an older person owned no vehicle. By 2010, 11.9 percent of these households owned no vehicle, a drop of 5.1 percent. Changes in the number of households

Table 8.4

Households and Households Without Vehicles (in Thousands),
by Age of Householder in Texas, 1990 and 2010

| Age of Householder | 1990 Households | | | 2000 Households | | | 2010 Households | | |
| | | Without Vehicles | | | Without Vehicles | | | Without Vehicles | |
| | Total | Number | % | Total | Number | % | Total | Number | % |
| --- | --- | --- | --- | --- | --- | --- | --- | --- | --- |
| 15–64 | 4,933.5 | 295.8 | 6.0 | 6,057.8 | 361.3 | 6.0 | 7,284.2 | 366.8 | 5.0 |
| 65+ | 1,137.4 | 193.5 | 17.0 | 1,335.6 | 186.8 | 14.0 | 1,638.7 | 194.4 | 11.9 |
| All Households | 6,070.9 | 489.2 | 8.1 | 7,393.4 | 548.1 | 7.4 | 8,922.9 | 561.2 | 6.3 |

*Source*: U.S. Census Bureau 1992, 2002, 2011d, 2011e.

owning no vehicles by age are indicative of the changing composition of Texas households. The number of households without vehicles in the 65 years and older age group grew by only 0.5 percent over the twenty year period from 1990 to 2010, while there was an increase of 24.0 percent in the number of households without vehicles headed by persons aged 15 to 64 (compared to a change in all households headed by householders from the same age groups of 44.1 and 46.6 percent, respectively).

The overwhelming majority of workers in Texas drove alone to work on a typical day in 2010 (Table 8.5). The percentage of workers driving alone increased only slightly, from 77.6 percent in 2000 to 80.1 percent in 2010, with nonHispanic Whites more likely to drive alone than any other group. Over time, the percentage of people driving alone or using other modes of transportation (including working from home) has increased while the percentage that carpool or use public transportation has declined overall and for all racial/ethnic groups, except nonHispanic Asians and Others. Still, the gaps in transportation behavior between nonHispanic Whites and all other groups mean that change in the demographic characteristics of the population will change the forms and perhaps the overall demand for transportation in Texas.

## THE EFFECTS OF FUTURE DEMOGRAPHIC
## CHANGE ON FUTURE TRANSPORTATION USE

In order to project how changes in the future demographic composition of the population are likely to influence the number of drivers in Texas, drivers licensing rates by age, sex, and race/ethnicity were applied to the population projections presented in Chapter 2. The licensure rates by age and

Table 8.5

Percent of All Texas Commuters by Transportation
Mode on the Journey to Work, 2000 and 2010

| Mode | NH* White | NH Black | Hispanic | NH Asian & Other | Total |
|---|---|---|---|---|---|
| **2000** | | | | | |
| Drove Alone | 82.7 | 74.6 | 68.0 | 76.3 | 77.6 |
| Carpooled | 10.3 | 15.5 | 23.3 | 15.1 | 14.5 |
| Public Transit | 0.9 | 5.3 | 2.7 | 2.0 | 1.9 |
| Other | 6.1 | 4.6 | 6.0 | 6.6 | 6.0 |
| Total | 100.0 | 100.0 | 100.0 | 100.0 | 100.0 |
| **2010** | | | | | |
| Drove Alone | 83.0 | 80.5 | 76.4 | 76.4 | 80.1 |
| Carpooled | 8.2 | 9.8 | 15.5 | 13.7 | 11.2 |
| Public Transit | 0.8 | 3.9 | 1.7 | 2.3 | 1.5 |
| Other | 8.0 | 5.8 | 6.4 | 7.6 | 7.2 |
| Total | 100.0 | 100.0 | 100.0 | 100.0 | 100.0 |
| **Change** | | | | | |
| Drove Alone | 0.3 | 5.9 | 8.4 | 0.1 | 2.5 |
| Carpooled | −2.1 | −5.7 | −7.8 | −1.4 | −3.3 |
| Public Transit | −0.1 | −1.4 | −1.0 | 0.3 | −0.4 |
| Other | 1.9 | 1.2 | 0.4 | 1.0 | 1.2 |

*Source*: U.S. Census Bureau 2002, 2011d; 2012d; Ruggles et al. 2010.
*NH refers to nonHispanic; values for categories labeled NH are only for the non-
Hispanic persons in each race category. Hispanic includes Hispanics of all races.

sex were obtained from the U.S. Department of Transportation, Federal
Highway Administration, Highway Statistics Series (2009, 2010, 2011b).
These data do not include licensure rates by race and ethnicity. Therefore,
data for Texas from the 2009 National Household Travel Survey (NHTS
[U.S. Department of Transportation 2011a]) were used to estimate the race/
ethnicity of Texas drivers by age. The NHTS is a periodic survey of travel
and transportation behaviors in the United States. The proportions of drivers by race/ethnicity and age from the 2009 survey were multiplied by the

2010 estimates of licensed drivers by age in Texas to derive the estimates of drivers by age and race/ethnicity. These estimates were then used in combination with the 2010 population to calculate licensure rates by age and race/ethnicity.

Panel A of Table 8.6 shows the number of licensed drivers by race/ethnicity in 2010 and projected through 2050 assuming no change in licensure rates by age and race/ethnicity and assuming 2000–2010 rates of age and race/ethnicity specific net migration. Assuming current rates of licensure by race/ethnicity and age, there will be a projected total of 33.3 million drivers by 2050 (up from 15.2 million in 2010 [Table 8.6: Panel A]). The overwhelming majority of all Texans will continue to drive, but without improvements in the socioeconomic status of minority groups, the driving population will increase slowly. The number of licensed drivers will increase by 119.4 percent (Table 8.6: Panel D), compared to a 119.5 percent increase for the population.

The rapid increase in the Hispanic and all other minority populations is reflected in the changing characteristics of drivers. In 2010, an estimated 52.8 percent of all licensed drivers were nonHispanic White (Table 8.6: Panel B). By 2020, the majority of drivers will be minority and by 2050, the majority of drivers will be Hispanic (50.5 percent [see Table 8.6: Panel B]). These changes in the demographic characteristics of drivers have implications for other driving related characteristics.

The change in the number and characteristics of licensed drivers will influence changes in transportation demand and the demand on transportation related infrastructure. Assuming 2010 licensure rates by race/ethnicity, the number of Texas drivers will more than double between 2010 and 2050, and assuming the 2010 average VMT by race/ethnicity of the driver, aggregate yearly VMT will increase substantially from 204.2 billion VMT in 2010 to 408.3 billion VMT in 2050 (Table 8.7). In 2010, there were 20.5 local street, freeway, and roadway miles per 1,000 drivers in Texas (or 311,249 road miles [U.S. Department of Transportation 2011b]). The increase in drivers will require the addition of 371,753 road miles just to maintain the 2010 capacity levels, more than doubling the number of local streets, urban freeways, and highways in Texas by 2050.

Although population growth alone will significantly impact the growth in the number of drivers and VMT, the overall driving rate and average VMT will decline as a result of increases in the minority population. The number of drivers per 1,000 persons will increase slightly, peaking in 2030 and then dropping to the 2010 level by 2050 (Table 8.7). Assuming average yearly vehicle miles traveled by race/ethnicity of the driver, VMT will decline from an average of 13,475 miles in 2010 to 12,276 per year by 2050, a decline in average VMT of 8.9 percent. Thus, on a daily basis, Texas drivers

Table 8.6

Projection of Drivers in Texas Using 2010 Age and Race/
Ethnicity Licensure Rates for 2010 and the Population Projection
That Assumes 2000–2010 Rates of Net Migration

| Year | NH* White | NH Black | Hispanic | NH Asian & Other | Total |
|------|-----------|----------|----------|------------------|-------|
| **Panel A: Number of Drivers** | | | | | |
| 2010 | 8,000,452 | 1,614,917 | 4,719,022 | 823,279 | 15,157,670 |
| 2020 | 8,436,301 | 2,022,078 | 6,830,572 | 1,336,998 | 18,625,949 |
| 2030 | 8,668,904 | 2,420,128 | 9,492,457 | 2,126,997 | 22,708,486 |
| 2040 | 8,697,630 | 2,791,185 | 12,707,721 | 3,206,471 | 27,403,007 |
| 2050 | 8,580,822 | 3,150,187 | 16,807,607 | 4,723,181 | 33,261,797 |
| **Panel B: Percent by Race/Ethnicity** | | | | | |
| 2010 | 52.8 | 10.7 | 31.1 | 5.4 | 100.0 |
| 2020 | 45.3 | 10.9 | 36.7 | 7.1 | 100.0 |
| 2030 | 38.2 | 10.7 | 41.8 | 9.3 | 100.0 |
| 2040 | 31.7 | 10.2 | 46.4 | 11.7 | 100.0 |
| 2050 | 25.8 | 9.5 | 50.5 | 14.2 | 100.0 |
| **Panel C: Numeric Change** | | | | | |
| 2010–2020 | 435,849 | 407,161 | 2,111,550 | 513,719 | 3,468,279 |
| 2020–2030 | 232,603 | 398,050 | 2,661,885 | 789,999 | 4,082,537 |
| 2030–2040 | 28,726 | 371,057 | 3,215,264 | 1,079,474 | 4,694,521 |
| 2040–2050 | −116,808 | 359,002 | 4,099,886 | 1,516,710 | 5,858,790 |
| 2010–2050 | 580,370 | 1,535,270 | 12,088,585 | 3,899,902 | 18,104,127 |
| **Panel D: Percent Change** | | | | | |
| 2010–2020 | 5.4 | 25.2 | 44.7 | 62.4 | 22.9 |
| 2020–2030 | 2.8 | 19.7 | 39.0 | 59.1 | 21.9 |
| 2030–2040 | 0.3 | 15.3 | 33.9 | 50.8 | 20.7 |
| 2040–2050 | −1.3 | 12.9 | 32.3 | 47.3 | 21.4 |
| 2010–2050 | 7.3 | 95.1 | 256.2 | 473.7 | 119.4 |

*Source*: Projections by the authors and 2010 data and rates derived from U.S. Department of Transportation 2009, 2010, 2011a, 2011b.
*NH refers to nonHispanic; values for categories labeled NH are only for the non-Hispanic persons in each race category. Hispanic includes Hispanics of all races.

Table 8.7

Population, Licensed Drivers, and Yearly Vehicle Miles of Travel
in 2010 and Projected to 2050 Using the Population Projection
That Assumes 2000–2010 Rates of Net Migration

| | | | | Yearly Vehicle Miles of Travel | |
| | | | Drivers Per 1,000 | | Total |
| Year | Population | Drivers | Population | Per Driver | (in Billions) |
| --- | --- | --- | --- | --- | --- |
| 2010 | 25,145,561 | 15,157,650 | 602.8 | 13,475 | 204.2 |
| 2020 | 30,583,311 | 18,625,949 | 609.0 | 13,075 | 243.2 |
| 2030 | 37,282,785 | 22,708,486 | 609.1 | 12,688 | 288.1 |
| 2040 | 45,316,711 | 27,403,007 | 604.7 | 12,446 | 341.1 |
| 2050 | 55,205,530 | 33,261,797 | 602.5 | 12,276 | 408.3 |

*Source*: Projections by the authors and 2010 data and rates derived from U.S. Department of Transportation 2009, 2010, 2011a, 2011b.

will drive an average of 33.6 miles per day in 2050 compared to 36.9 miles per day in 2010.

## AGE EFFECTS ON TRANSPORTATION

Growth in the number of drivers on the road will increase demand on the current infrastructure and have implications for other factors including public safety. Although technological improvements and public policies have improved automobile safety over the years, decreasing crash incident rates over time, accidents will still occur. Younger drivers have higher incident rates but older drivers may experience worse outcomes in injury crashes simply as a result of being more frail (and thus more prone to injury) prior to any incident. Tables 8.8 and 8.9 show the projections of the total number of drivers involved in crashes and the number of drivers by age and crash severity in 2010 and projected for 2050. We assume that the crash rates in 2010 by age of driver continue unchanged throughout the projection period.

In order to take into account major fluctuations in crash rates, we averaged data on the ages of drivers in crashes for 2009, 2010, and 2011 to establish crash rates for 2010. We assumed those crash rates prevailed throughout the projection period and applied them to our projection of drivers by age and race/ethnicity. Given these assumptions (Table 8.8), the

Table 8.8

Drivers Involved in Crashes by Severity of Crash in 2010 and
Projections through 2050 Using the Population Projection
That Assumes 2000–2010 Rates of Net Migration

| Year/Time Period | Fatality | Injury | Non-Injury | Total |
|---|---|---|---|---|
| **Crashes** | | | | |
| 2010 | 4,229 | 271,957 | 452,408 | 728,594 |
| 2020 | 5,124 | 327,725 | 545,067 | 877,916 |
| 2030 | 6,186 | 393,039 | 653,389 | 1,052,614 |
| 2040 | 7,431 | 470,585 | 781,827 | 1,259,843 |
| 2050 | 9,015 | 570,229 | 947,113 | 1,526,357 |
| **Numeric Change** | | | | |
| 2010–2020 | 895 | 55,768 | 92,659 | 149,322 |
| 2020–2030 | 1,062 | 65,314 | 108,322 | 174,698 |
| 2030–2040 | 1,245 | 77,546 | 128,438 | 207,229 |
| 2040–2050 | 1,584 | 99,644 | 165,286 | 266,514 |
| 2010–2050 | 4,786 | 298,272 | 494,705 | 797,763 |
| **Percent Change** | | | | |
| 2010–2020 | 21.2 | 20.5 | 20.5 | 20.5 |
| 2020–2030 | 20.7 | 19.9 | 19.9 | 19.9 |
| 2030–2040 | 20.1 | 19.7 | 19.7 | 19.7 |
| 2040–2050 | 21.3 | 21.2 | 21.1 | 21.2 |
| 2010–2050 | 113.2 | 109.7 | 109.3 | 109.5 |

*Source*: Projections by authors and 2010 data and rates derived from the Texas Department of Transportation 2011.

number of drivers involved in crashes is projected to increase from 728,594 in 2010 to 1.5 million in 2050, or more than double between 2010 and 2050 (109.5 percent). Due to the age characteristics of the driving population (with proportionally fewer drivers at the younger ages with higher crash rates), these changes are less than the growth in the driving population overall (which will increase by 119.4 percent over the same period). Under these assumptions, fatality crashes will grow the fastest (at a rate of 113.2 percent)—a change of 4,786 between 2010 and 2050. Because of increases in the number of elderly drivers, the proportion of drivers age

Table 8.9

Drivers Involved in Crashes by Age and Severity of Crash in
2010 and Projected for 2050 Using the Population Projection
That Assumes 2000–2010 Rates of Net Migration

| Age | Fatality | Injury | Non-Injury | Total |
|---|---|---|---|---|
| **Panel A: 2010 Crashes by Age** | | | | |
| 15–19 | 368 | 11,265 | 17,195 | 28,828 |
| 20–29 | 1,119 | 29,258 | 46,700 | 77,077 |
| 30–44 | 1,180 | 29,577 | 50,146 | 80,903 |
| 45–64 | 1,171 | 25,869 | 43,355 | 70,395 |
| 65–79 | 296 | 5,762 | 9,240 | 15,298 |
| 80+ | 95 | 1,489 | 2,101 | 3,685 |
| Total | 4,229 | 103,220 | 168,737 | 276,186 |
| **Panel B: 2050 Crashes by Age** | | | | |
| 15–19 | 661 | 20,245 | 30,901 | 51,807 |
| 20–29 | 2,238 | 58,542 | 93,440 | 154,220 |
| 30–44 | 2,480 | 62,135 | 105,346 | 169,961 |
| 45–64 | 2,368 | 52,292 | 87,638 | 142,298 |
| 65–79 | 907 | 17,667 | 28,332 | 46,906 |
| 80+ | 361 | 5,679 | 8,012 | 14,052 |
| Total | 9,015 | 216,560 | 353,669 | 579,244 |
| **Panel C: Percent by Age in 2010** | | | | |
| 15–19 | 8.7 | 10.9 | 10.2 | 10.4 |
| 20–29 | 26.5 | 28.3 | 27.7 | 27.9 |
| 30–44 | 27.9 | 28.7 | 29.7 | 29.3 |
| 45–64 | 27.7 | 25.1 | 25.7 | 25.5 |
| 65–79 | 7.0 | 5.6 | 5.5 | 5.5 |
| 80+ | 2.2 | 1.4 | 1.2 | 1.4 |
| Total | 100.0 | 100.0 | 100.0 | 100.0 |
| **Panel D: Percent by Age in 2050** | | | | |
| 15–19 | 7.3 | 9.3 | 8.7 | 8.9 |
| 20–29 | 24.8 | 27.0 | 26.4 | 26.6 |
| 30–44 | 27.5 | 28.7 | 29.8 | 29.3 |
| 45–64 | 26.3 | 24.1 | 24.8 | 24.6 |
| 65–79 | 10.1 | 8.2 | 8.0 | 8.1 |
| 80+ | 4.0 | 2.7 | 2.3 | 2.5 |
| Total | 100.0 | 100.0 | 100.0 | 100.0 |

*Source*: Projections by authors and 2010 data and rates derived from the Texas Department of Transportation 2011.

65 years and older among all drivers involved in crashes will increase from 6.9 percent of all drivers involved in crashes in 2010 to 10.6 percent in 2050 (see Table 8.9). This increase will be particularly evident in the number of fatality crashes. Elderly drivers will account for 14.1 percent of all drivers involved in fatality crashes in 2050 compared to 9.2 percent in 2010.

## IMPACT OF POPULATION CHANGE ON VEHICLE OWNERSHIP

In Table 8.10 we examine the effects of changes in the race/ethnicity characteristics of householders on the number of households with and without vehicles. The percentages of all households with and without vehicles by race/ethnicity and age of the householder in 2010 were multiplied by the number of households by age and race/ethnicity of the householder for 2050. The first column shows the number of households in 2010 and 2050 and the second and third columns show the number and percentage of households without vehicles within an age and race/ethnicity specific age group. Finally, the last two columns show the percentage of all households and households without vehicles by age and race/ethnicity. In 2010, 6.3 percent of all households in Texas owned no vehicle. Assuming no change in the rates of household vehicle ownership by race/ethnicity and age, the percentage of all households owning no vehicles will increase to 8.3 percent of all households in 2050. This is an increase of 1.1 million households (from 561,201 in 2010 to 1,686,837 in 2050). The percent change in the number of households without vehicles is much greater than the change in total households (200.6 percent compared to 127.6 percent).

The effect of continued diversification of elderly households (combined with the increase in households headed by frail elderly) will be to substantially increase the number of households with no vehicle available and headed by a person age 65 years and older. In 2010, only 34.6 percent of households without vehicles were headed by a householder age 65 years and older. This will increase to 51.7 percent of all households without vehicles (compared to only 27.6 percent of households overall) by 2050. The number of these households will increase from 194,444 in 2010 to 871,770 in 2050 (a numeric increase of 677,326). This is an increase of 348.3 percent, much larger than the 242.2 percent change in the total number of households with a householder age 65 years and older.

In 2010, nonHispanic White households accounted for the largest share of elderly householders owning no vehicles (16.2 percent of all households without vehicles and 46.8 percent of householders headed by a person age 65 years and older). Assuming no change in vehicle ownership rates by age and race/ethnicity of the householder, by 2050, 27.5 percent of all households without vehicles will be headed by an Hispanic elderly person (or 53.3 percent of all households without vehicles headed by a person age

Table 8.10

Zero Vehicle Households by Age and Race/Ethnicity of Householder
in 2010 and Projections for 2050 Using the Population Projection
That Assumes 2000–2010 Rates of Net Migration

| Age, Race/Ethnicity of Householder | Households | | | Percent of Households | |
|---|---|---|---|---|---|
| | | Without Vehicles | | | |
| | All | Number | Percent | All | Without Vehicles |
| **Panel A: 2010** | | | | | |
| 15 to 64 years: | 7,284,203 | 366,757 | 5.0 | 81.6 | 65.4 |
| NH* White | 3,658,967 | 96,915 | 2.6 | 41.0 | 17.3 |
| NH Black | 919,140 | 112,742 | 12.3 | 10.3 | 20.1 |
| Hispanic | 2,312,308 | 139,562 | 6.0 | 25.9 | 24.9 |
| NH Asian & Other | 393,788 | 17,538 | 4.5 | 4.4 | 3.1 |
| 65 years and older: | 1,638,730 | 194,444 | 11.9 | 18.4 | 34.6 |
| NH White | 1,144,613 | 90,976 | 7.9 | 12.8 | 16.2 |
| NH Black | 148,968 | 34,362 | 23.1 | 1.7 | 6.1 |
| Hispanic | 301,849 | 63,258 | 21.0 | 3.4 | 11.3 |
| NH Asian & Other | 43,300 | 5,848 | 13.5 | 0.5 | 1.0 |
| All Households | 8,922,933 | 561,201 | 6.3 | 100.0 | 100.0 |
| **Panel B: 2050** | | | | | |
| 15 to 64 years: | 14,697,885 | 815,067 | 5.5 | 72.4 | 48.3 |
| NH White | 3,355,621 | 89,156 | 2.7 | 16.5 | 5.3 |
| NH Black | 1,511,465 | 181,932 | 12.0 | 7.4 | 10.8 |
| Hispanic | 7,670,727 | 453,309 | 5.9 | 37.8 | 26.9 |
| NH Asian & Other | 2,160,072 | 90,670 | 4.2 | 10.7 | 5.3 |
| 65 years and older: | 5,607,211 | 871,770 | 15.5 | 27.6 | 51.7 |
| NH White | 2,250,089 | 188,753 | 8.4 | 11.1 | 11.2 |
| NH Black | 652,174 | 149,628 | 22.9 | 3.2 | 8.9 |
| Hispanic | 2,209,767 | 464,307 | 21.0 | 10.9 | 27.5 |
| NH Asian & Other | 495,181 | 69,082 | 14.0 | 2.4 | 4.1 |
| All Households | 20,305,096 | 1,686,837 | 8.3 | 100.0 | 100.0 |

*Source*: Projections by the authors and 2010 estimate and rates derived from U.S. Census Bureau 2011d, 2011e.
*NH refers to nonHispanic; values for categories labeled NH are only for the non-Hispanic persons in each race category. Hispanic includes Hispanics of all races.

65 years and older). Overall, whereas households headed by Hispanics will account for 48.7 percent of total households, they will account for 54.4 percent of all households without vehicles by 2050.

## DEMOGRAPHIC IMPACT ON WORKERS' MODES OF COMMUTING

Data in Table 8.11 can be used to examine the effects of racial/ethnic change in the workforce on change in the transportation mode used on the journey to work. The projections shown in Table 8.11 assume that the transportation mode use rates by age, sex, and race/ethnicity of persons in the workforce in 2010 continue throughout the projection period. Transportation mode use rates were computed using the 2009–2011 American Community Survey, Public Use Microdata Sample (U.S. Census Bureau 2012d and Ruggles et al. 2010). We applied these rates to the labor force projections shown in Chapter 4.

More than 8.8 million commuters drove alone on a typical workweek in 2010 (Table 8.11). By 2050, this number will more than double to nearly 18.3 million. Although the number of carpoolers and persons using public transportation is smaller than the number of commuters driving alone, the percentage increase in the number of carpoolers and persons using public transportation on the journey to work is larger. The number of carpoolers will increase by 144.8 percent and public transit users will increase by 145.7 percent over the forty-year period compared to a 106.0 percent increase in the number of commuters driving alone (see the bottom panel, last column of Table 8.11). The changing racial/ethnic composition of the labor force can be seen in the change in the number of commuters overall and in the change in the frequency of use of different modes of commuting. From 2010 to 2050, the largest numeric increase occurs for Hispanic commuters, while nonHispanic Asian and Other commuters see the largest percentage increase during that time period. At the same time, reflecting declines in the population overall, and in the working age population in particular, the percentage of nonHispanic White commuters will decline from 2010 to 2050.

The first two panels (A and B) in Table 8.12 show how modes of commuting as a percentage of all journey-to-work trips will change. In 2050, 78.2 percent of all commuters will drive to work alone (down from 80.1 in 2010). At the same time, carpooling and public transit use on the journey to work will increase so that by 2050, 13.0 percent of all commuters are projected to carpool and another 1.8 percent of all commuters will use public transportation (compared to 11.2 percent and 1.5 percent, respectively, in 2010). Over time, the percentage using some "other" form of transportation (such as walking, bicycling, or working from home) will decrease only slightly.

The bottom two panels in Table 8.12 show the percentage of commuters

Table 8.11

Journey to Work by Race/Ethnicity of Commuter and Transportation
Mode in 2010 and Projected to 2050 Using the Population
Projection That Assumes 2000–2010 Rates of Net Migration

| Mode | NH* White | NH Black | Hispanic | NH Asian & Other | Total |
|---|---|---|---|---|---|
| **2010** | | | | | |
| Drove Alone | 4,551,505 | 943,486 | 2,900,284 | 463,544 | 8,858,819 |
| Carpooled | 448,970 | 115,149 | 588,880 | 83,088 | 1,236,087 |
| Public Transit | 46,012 | 45,232 | 63,006 | 14,001 | 168,251 |
| Other | 439,226 | 67,453 | 246,217 | 46,488 | 799,384 |
| Total | 5,485,713 | 1,171,320 | 3,798,387 | 607,121 | 11,062,541 |
| **2050** | | | | | |
| Drove Alone | 4,284,014 | 1,642,632 | 9,806,190 | 2,520,099 | 18,252,935 |
| Carpooled | 418,928 | 193,379 | 1,963,715 | 449,998 | 3,026,020 |
| Public Transit | 42,590 | 77,095 | 218,378 | 75,308 | 413,371 |
| Other | 427,808 | 116,277 | 844,628 | 249,780 | 1,638,493 |
| Total | 5,173,340 | 2,029,383 | 12,832,911 | 3,295,185 | 23,330,819 |
| **Numeric Change, 2010–2050** | | | | | |
| Drove Alone | −267,491 | 699,146 | 6,905,906 | 2,056,555 | 9,394,116 |
| Carpooled | −30,042 | 78,230 | 1,374,835 | 366,910 | 1,789,933 |
| Public Transit | −3,422 | 31,863 | 155,372 | 61,307 | 245,120 |
| Other | −11,418 | 48,824 | 598,411 | 203,292 | 839,109 |
| Total | −312,373 | 858,063 | 9,034,524 | 2,688,064 | 12,268,278 |
| **Percent Change, 2010–2050** | | | | | |
| Drove Alone | −5.9 | 74.1 | 238.1 | 443.7 | 106.0 |
| Carpooled | −6.7 | 67.9 | 233.5 | 441.6 | 144.8 |
| Public Transit | −7.4 | 70.4 | 246.6 | 437.9 | 145.7 |
| Other | −2.6 | 72.4 | 243.0 | 437.3 | 105.0 |
| Total | −5.7 | 73.3 | 237.9 | 442.8 | 110.9 |

Source: Projections by the authors and 2010 data and rates derived from U.S. Census Bureau 2012d; Ruggles et al. 2010.
*NH refers to nonHispanic; values for categories labeled NH are only for the non-Hispanic persons in each race category. Hispanic includes Hispanics of all races.

## Table 8.12

Journey to Work Mode as a Percent of All Commuters by Race/
Ethnicity in 2010 and Projected to 2050 Using the Population
Projection That Assumes 2000–2010 Rates of Net Migration

| Mode | NH* White | NH Black | Hispanic | NH Asian & Other | Total |
|---|---|---|---|---|---|
| **Panel A: Commute as a Percent of All Commuters (Within Race/Ethnicity)** | | | | | |
| **2010** | | | | | |
| Drove Alone | 83.0 | 80.5 | 76.4 | 76.4 | 80.1 |
| Carpooled | 8.2 | 9.8 | 15.5 | 13.7 | 11.2 |
| Public Transit | 0.8 | 3.9 | 1.7 | 2.3 | 1.5 |
| Other | 8.0 | 5.8 | 6.4 | 7.6 | 7.2 |
| Total | 100.0 | 100.0 | 100.0 | 100.0 | 100.0 |
| **2050** | | | | | |
| Drove Alone | 82.8 | 80.9 | 76.4 | 76.5 | 78.2 |
| Carpooled | 8.1 | 9.5 | 15.3 | 13.7 | 13.0 |
| Public Transit | 0.8 | 3.8 | 1.7 | 2.3 | 1.8 |
| Other | 8.3 | 5.8 | 6.6 | 7.5 | 7.0 |
| Total | 100.0 | 100.0 | 100.0 | 100.0 | 100.0 |
| **Panel B: Commute as a Percent of All Commuters (Across Race/Ethnicity)** | | | | | |
| **2010** | | | | | |
| Drove Alone | 51.4 | 10.7 | 32.7 | 5.2 | 100.0 |
| Carpooled | 36.3 | 9.3 | 47.6 | 6.8 | 100.0 |
| Public Transit | 27.3 | 26.9 | 37.4 | 8.4 | 100.0 |
| Other | 54.9 | 8.4 | 30.8 | 5.9 | 100.0 |
| Total | 49.6 | 10.6 | 34.3 | 5.5 | 100.0 |
| **2050** | | | | | |
| Drove Alone | 23.5 | 9.0 | 53.7 | 13.8 | 100.0 |
| Carpooled | 13.8 | 6.4 | 64.9 | 14.9 | 100.0 |
| Public Transit | 10.3 | 18.7 | 52.8 | 18.2 | 100.0 |
| Other | 26.1 | 7.1 | 51.5 | 15.3 | 100.0 |
| Total | 22.2 | 8.7 | 55.0 | 14.1 | 100.0 |

*Source*: Projections by the authors and 2010 data and rates derived from U.S. Census
Bureau 2012d; Ruggles et al. 2010.
*NH refers to nonHispanic; values for categories labeled NH are only for the non-
Hispanic persons in each race category. Hispanic includes Hispanics of all races.

by each mode of transportation. Hispanics accounted for only 34.3 percent of commuters but were 47.6 percent of carpoolers. If these rates of use continue during the projection period, 64.9 percent of carpoolers will be Hispanic by 2050 (compared to 55.0 percent of commuters overall).

NonHispanic Blacks are more likely than any other group to use public transportation. In 2010, 3.9 percent of nonHispanic Black commuters rode public transportation on the journey to work and by 2050, about 3.8 percent will commute using this same form of transportation. Because of their population size relative to other groups, nonHispanic Blacks accounted for only 26.9 percent of transit commuters in 2010. In fact, public transit riders on the journey to work in Texas in 2010 were the most racially/ethnically diverse of those using any transportation mode to work. No racial/ethnic group accounted for the majority of transit commuters in 2010 and the largest group (Hispanics) accounted for only 37.4 percent of public transit riders. By 2050, this diversity will change so that Hispanics will account for the majority (52.8 percent) of public transit riders on the journey to work.

## ALTERNATIVE PROJECTION SCENARIOS

In order to further illustrate the impact of changing demographic composition without concomitant improvements in the socioeconomic characteristics of minority groups, we present an additional simulation in Table 8.13. In this simulation, we compare a summary of the current, baseline projections presented earlier in this chapter to a projection scenario that assumes that nonHispanic White transportation-related characteristics and transportation use behaviors prevail for all racial/ethnic groups. The first column shows a summary of the transportation-related statistics for 2050 under the assumption that current rates by race/ethnicity prevail, while the second column shows how these same items will change assuming the nonHispanic White rates for all groups.

Taken together, these changes show that racial/ethnic diversity will lessen the dependence of commuters on the automobile and increase the demand for more public forms of transportation (including sharing rides or using public transportation). There will be 3.5 million fewer drivers in Texas than if nonHispanic White licensure rates prevail. This is only a 10.6 percent difference, but coupled with lower average VMT, it would result in a decline of more than a quarter, or 110.3 billion miles driven per year. Thus Texas drivers would drive, on average, 1,812 miles per year less in 2050 than they would drive if all groups were licensed at the same rates and drove as much as nonHispanic Whites in 2010. Under the assumption that nonHispanic White rates apply to all groups, the number of households without vehicles would decline by more than half (from 561,201 to 229,062, a difference of 332,139 households). The number of commuters driving alone in 2050

Table 8.13

Drivers, Vehicle Ownership, and Commute Mode in
2050 Using Alternative Rate Assumptions

| Factor | Assuming 2010 Differentials in 2050 | Assuming NH* White Rates for All Groups in 2050 | Difference |
|---|---|---|---|
| Drivers | 33,261,797 | 36,811,415 | −3,549,618 |
| Vehicle Miles Traveled | | | |
| Yearly Aggregate (Billions) | 408.3 | 518.6 | −110.3 |
| Yearly Per Driver | 12,276 | 14,088 | −1,812 |
| Daily Per Driver | 33.6 | 38.6 | −5.0 |
| Zero Vehicle Households | 561,201 | 229,062 | 332,139 |
| Commuters (Number) | 23,330,819 | 23,853,603 | −522,784 |
| Driving Alone | 18,252,935 | 19,752,154 | −1,499,219 |
| Carpooling | 3,026,020 | 1,988,859 | 1,037,161 |
| Riding Public Transit | 413,371 | 199,722 | 213,649 |
| Commuters (Percent) | | | |
| Driving Alone | 78.2 | 82.8 | −4.6 |
| Carpooling | 13.0 | 8.3 | 4.7 |
| Riding Public Transit | 1.8 | 0.8 | 1.0 |

*Source*: Projections by the authors and 2010 data and rates derived from U.S. Census Bureau 2011d, 2011e, 2012d; Ruggles et al. 2010; U.S. Department of Transportation 2009, 2010, 2011a, 2011b.
*NH refers to nonHispanic; values for categories labeled NH are only for the non-Hispanic persons in each race category. Hispanic includes Hispanics of all races.

would be 1.5 million less than the number of commuters driving alone if nonHispanic White rates prevailed for all groups. At the same time, public transportation use under the current scenario (that is assuming the 2010 rates of use by race/ethnicity, age, and sex remain for all groups) is 51.7 percent greater than the scenario assuming nonHispanic White transportation use rates. In other words, 213,649 more people will be using public transportation in 2050 under current trends than if everyone commuted and/or drove as nonHispanic Whites did in 2010.

## SUMMARY

In this chapter we provided an overview of how projected demographic change is likely to impact transportation use in Texas. Unlike many other factors explored in this volume, many of the transportation impacts are both positive and negative. We summarize these changes and the impact on public policy below:

1.   The most significant impact of demographic change on Texas transportation is a result of continued population growth alone. The number of drivers on Texas roads will more than double from 15.2 million in 2010 to 33.3 million in 2050, increasing the yearly vehicle miles traveled from 204.2 billion in 2010 to 408.3 billion in 2050. As a result of this growth and in order to maintain the 2010 level of street, freeway, and highway infrastructure, cities, counties, and the state will need to add 371,753 miles of road by 2050. The number of people commuting to work on a typical work day will more than double between 2010 and 2050, from 11.1 million in 2010 to 23.3 million by 2050. Although the majority of work commuters in 2050 (18.3 million or 78.5 percent) will drive alone on the journey to work, the number of public transit riders on the journey to work will increase at a higher rate than the number driving alone (145.7 percent compared to 106 percent), from 168,251 in 2010 to 413,371 in 2050. Population growth will increase demand on all forms of transportation services, impacting an already stressed transportation infrastructure.

2.   The effect of racial/ethnic change, assuming no change in the patterns of minority groups' use of transportation, will be to reduce the rate of growth in the number of drivers and vehicle miles traveled, resulting in 3.5 million fewer drivers and 110.3 billion fewer vehicle miles traveled in 2050 than if all racial/ethnic groups were licensed and drove the same amount as nonHispanic Whites in 2010. While population growth alone will increase congestion and reduce air quality, the demographic compositional changes, without changes in transportation use behaviors, will reduce the rate of growth in congestion and deterioration in air quality.

3.   On a per driver basis, the number of miles driven per year will decrease from 13,475 to 12,276. If all racial/ethnic groups drove the same number of miles as nonHispanic Whites in 2010, then the number of miles driven per driver per year would increase to 14,088. The slower growth in the number of drivers and average vehicle miles driven per driver, coupled with increases in average vehicle mileage, will place further pressure on a transportation financing structure that is currently dependent primarily on the gas tax.

4.   Racial/ethnic change, without changes in transportation behaviors, will increase the demand for public transportation. The number of transit riders on the journey to work will increase by 245,120 or 145.7 percent.

Population growth and change in the racial/ethnic composition of the population without improvements in the socioeconomic characteristics of that population will lead to an increase of 1.1 million households that do not own a vehicle (doubling the number present in 2010).

5.   An aging and more racially/ethnically diverse elderly population with fewer resources will mean that additional public transportation and related services (such as para-transit for the disabled and medical-related transportation) will be needed to help support those in urban and rural areas who might not otherwise have transportation to reach medical appointments and other needs. In 2010, 11.9 percent of all elderly households had no vehicle present. By 2050, 15.5 percent of elderly households will have no vehicle present (which will account for half of all households without vehicles).

6.   Change in the composition of the population will increase the number of carpoolers on the journey to work. If current commute rates prevail throughout the projection period, 13.0 percent of all commuters will carpool on the journey to work (compared to 11.2 percent in 2010). This means that 3.0 million workers will carpool on the journey to work in 2050. If all commuters used the same commute modes as nonHispanic Whites did in 2010, then the number of carpoolers would be 1.5 million fewer and the percentage carpooling would decline to 4.7 percent of all commuters.

7.   The aging of the population will have an impact on public safety. The sheer growth in the number of drivers will increase the number of crashes overall. However, the aging of the population coupled with relatively fewer drivers at the younger ages (due, in part, to a more diverse racial/ethnic population) will slow down the growth in the number of crashes. While the number of drivers will increase by 119.4 percent between 2010 and 2050, the number of drivers involved in crashes will increase at the reduced rate of 109.5 percent. Crash rates are generally highest at the youngest ages. At the same time, increases in the number of elderly drivers will increase the number of elderly drivers involved in vehicular accidents and, because these drivers are more likely to have other health issues, the number of fatality accidents among elderly drivers will increase (from 9.2 percent of all fatality accidents in 2010 to 14.1 percent of all fatality accidents in 2050). Policies to improve driver safety and awareness for elderly drivers may be necessary.

In summary, the changing Texas population will have a diverse range of effects on the Texas transportation system. The growth in minority populations, in the absence of change in their patterns of use of different forms of transportation, will reduce overall vehicle miles travelled compared to what would otherwise occur with either greater growth in the nonHispanic White population or if patterns for Hispanics and other minorities came to reflect current patterns for nonHispanic Whites. The growth in minority populations will, on the other hand, increase demand on public transportation systems. Since the rate of use of different modes of transportation largely reflects households' levels of socioeconomic resources, much of the future will be determined by change in the future socioeconomic characteristics of minority populations. As a result, the extent to which the differences in socioeconomic resources are reduced among racial/ethnic groups may be particularly significant for transportation in Texas in the coming decades.

CHAPTER 9

# Conclusions and Implications for the Future of Texas

This work has examined the demographic future of Texas and the socioeconomic implications of that future. It evaluated the implications of demographic change for households, housing, the labor force, and economic and private sector development in Texas. It has also examined the effects of this future on elementary, secondary, and higher education and on the need for financial assistance for students attending college, and on health care. A variety of social, rehabilitation, and income assistance programs including Medicaid, TANF, SNAP, CHIP, juvenile and adult correctional services, and employee training programs has also been examined. It evaluated the impacts of underlying demographic change on these factors and has often examined how change in the socioeconomic conditions impacting Texas could be altered, if socioeconomic differences, historically linked to age, race/ethnicity, and household composition, were to be reduced or eliminated.

In this final chapter we examine three issues in detail. We do not attempt to provide yet an additional summary of chapter findings since these were provided at the end of each chapter. Rather this chapter attempts to increase the breadth and depth of our analysis of the implications of Texas' demographic and socioeconomic future.

In doing so we examine three critical sets of questions:

1. Will the demographic and related socioeconomic patterns delineated in this book change in the manner projected?
2. Will recent demographic and socioeconomic patterns of change, if continued, substantially and positively alter Texas' socioeconomic future?
3. Will closure of socioeconomic differentials between minority and nonHispanic White racial/ethnic groups substantially and positively alter Texas' socioeconomic future?

In large part, the analysis of these key questions involves a final attempt to address readers' concerns as to whether the patterns and impacts delineated will occur and how pervasive and persistent the relationships are between demographic and socioeconomic change. We also address issues related to whether the problems resulting from the trends delineated above will resolve themselves without concerted actions to change them. Finally, we examine whether closure in socioeconomic differences among racial/ethnic groups is critical to improving Texas' socioeconomic future.

In addressing the first question, we examine whether projected demographic and socioeconomic patterns are likely to occur in the manner and in the direction projected over the period from now to 2050. These patterns include: (1) the predominance of minority population growth in future population growth in Texas; (2) the relationship between minority status and the socioeconomic resources available at the individual and aggregate levels; and (3) the relationship between education and socioeconomic resources, with increased levels of education, increasing socioeconomic resources, and reduced levels of education leading to lower levels of socioeconomic resources. These issues are addressed through an examination of baseline demographic data and trends and related socioeconomic change.

The second question involves analyzing historical patterns of change in key socioeconomic factors among racial/ethnic groups in Texas and evaluating how these patterns of change, if continued, will alter the long-term patterns of socioeconomic change for racial/ethnic groups and the overall level of growth in key socioeconomic characteristics of Texas' population. Specifically, we examine the levels of change for racial/ethnic groups in Texas in regard to the socioeconomic factors of mean household income, median household income, per capita income, aggregate household income, educational attainment, and occupational change. With these data we address the questions of to what extent have socioeconomic differences among racial/ethnic groups been reduced over time and will such trends, if continued, eliminate many of the concerns discussed in this volume related to decreasing future levels of socioeconomic resources in Texas?

In the next section of this chapter we examine the third issue of how closure between the socioeconomic characteristics of Texas' minority and nonHispanic White populations would affect Texas' socioeconomic future. Alternative patterns of change that would bring increasing levels of closure are examined. Three futures are examined. In one of these, the 2010 socioeconomic characteristics of each racial/ethnic group in 2010 are applied to the 2050 population projections. This provides baseline data that allow us to determine the extent to which differentials in relative population growth among the racial/ethnic groups are likely to alter future socioeconomic conditions for racial/ethnic groups and for Texas as a whole. In examining the second future we apply the average of three decade rates (1980–2010) for socioeconomic factors to 2010 values to project them to 2050. In the third, we assume that the differences between socioeconomic factors for minority groups and nonHispanic Whites come to complete closure to 2050 nonHispanic White rates by 2050. The purpose of this analysis is to provide readers with an indication of the overall change that would occur in the socioeconomic characteristics of racial/ethnic groups in Texas and for the state overall under conditions of socioeconomic closure between racial/ethnic groups in Texas.

In the final section of this chapter we provide overall conclusions regarding Texas' future depending on what Texas does or does not do in the coming decades. This section delineates what Texas' future may be in the absence of change and its potential patterns of socioeconomic change if closure occurs in key socioeconomic differences among Texans. It also suggests those realities that will shape Texas' socioeconomic future and how they may be altered to attain both continued economic growth and improved socioeconomic conditions for all Texans.

## QUESTION 1: WILL THE DEMOGRAPHIC AND RELATED SOCIOECONOMIC PATTERNS CHANGE IN THE MANNER PROJECTED?

Addressing this question involves an evaluation of three patterns asserted in the analysis in preceding chapters. These patterns and the analysis of each of these patterns are presented below.

### The Continuation of Minority Population Growth

As noted throughout this volume, Texas' current population growth is primarily minority population growth. The nonHispanic White population accounted for 16.6 percent of Texas' population growth from 1990 to 2000 and for 10.8 percent of Texas population growth from 2000 to 2010. The proportion of the total population that was nonHispanic White declined from 60.6 percent in 1990, to 52.4 percent in 2000, and to 45.3 by 2010. Projections for 2010 to 2050 (see Chapter 2, Tables 2.4–2.8) suggest that the nonHispanic White population will account for no more than 2.1 percent of net population change between 2010 and 2050 and will represent only 21.8 percent of the Texas population in 2050 (under the scenario assuming 2000–2010 rates of net migration).

What is the likelihood that greater minority than nonHispanic White population growth will continue in the future? Clearly there is no absolute certainty that any given level of future population change will be achieved, but a reversal of more than 30 years of consistent patterns of change is unlikely.

Several characteristics of nonHispanic White populations and their patterns of change make a substantial renewal of nonHispanic White population growth unlikely. One of these factors is that the nonHispanic White population is an aging population. In 2010 (see Table 2.8), 15.4 percent of Texas nonHispanic White population was 65 years of age or older compared to 10.3 percent of the total population, 7.6 percent of the nonHispanic Black, 6.5 percent of the nonHispanic Asian and Other, and 5.6 percent of the Hispanic population. Another 29.8 percent of nonHispanic White population members were 45–64 compared to 24.0 percent of the nonHispanic Black, 21.4 percent of the nonHispanic Asian and Other, and 17.5 percent of the Hispanic population. This means that 45.2 percent of the persons in nonHispanic White populations are largely beyond the childbearing years compared to 31.6 percent of the nonHispanic Black, 27.9 percent of the nonHispanic Asian and Other, and 23.1 percent of the Hispanic population. By 2050 (under the scenario assuming 2000–2010 patterns of net migration) 51.4 percent of nonHispanic White population members will be 45 years of age or older.

A second factor impacting the potential growth of nonHispanic White populations is the fact that nonHispanic White birth rates have been below replacement levels for more than two decades. This replacement level of fertility (2.1 births per woman, an average sufficient to replace the woman and her mate and take into account the fact that some women do not have or cannot have children) has not occurred among nonHispanic White population members in the United States since the late 1980s (Martin et al. 2012, Mather 2012). Finally, the average nonHispanic White woman in Texas is now 42 years of age (U.S. Census Bureau 2011d). By contrast Hispanic fertility, although lower than a decade ago, is still substantially above replacement levels (at 2.53 children per woman in 2009 [Martin et al., 2012]) and the average Hispanic woman is 28 years of age. Higher birth rates for nonHispanic Whites are unlikely to occur and, even if they did, the size of the childbearing cohorts is decreasing so that the potential to reverse nonHispanic White population change through birth related growth is decreasing. By contrast, growth through Hispanic fertility is likely to continue.

Similarly, neither fertility nor immigration is likely to significantly alter the relative size of minority and nonHispanic White populations. In preparing its 2012 population projections of the United States population, the Census Bureau (U.S. Census Bureau 2012b and 2012c) projected both fertility and immigration by race/ethnicity for the United States through 2060. The Census Bureau projects nonHispanic White fertility in the United States to remain at 1.83 children per woman from 2012 to 2050 (the end year for our projections for Texas) and Hispanic fertility to fall from 2.53 in 2012 to 2.23 in 2050. Thus, even in 2050, the Census Bureau expects

Hispanic fertility to be nearly 22 percent higher than that for nonHispanic Whites and to remain above replacement levels. The Census Bureau also projects all groups except Asians and Others to have higher fertility than nonHispanic Whites and for all other groups (other than Hispanics) to have fertility below the 2.1 replacement level. Similarly, the United States Census Bureau (2012) projects that even with reduced rates of immigration, by 2050, annual immigration rates for Hispanics will be approximately 507,000 per year compared to 189,000 for nonHispanic Whites. Although these data are national data, there is little evidence to suggest that Texas' race/ethnicity specific fertility rates or immigration rates will be lower than those for the nation and Texas projections clearly validate the likely lack of impact of either fertility or mortality on the relative size of future non-Hispanic White populations. In fact, if one examines the alternative population projection scenarios shown in Chapter 2 (see Tables 2.4–2.8), the scenario that assumes no inmigration so that all growth is through natural increase, produces the highest proportion of nonHispanic Whites. However, even this unlikely pattern will lead to a total population that is only 33.6 percent nonHispanic White in 2050.

In summary, the data available from the nation's leading demographers and our own analyses suggest that the nonHispanic White population will continue to decline as a proportion of all Texans (and all Americans) and that minority population groups, particularly Hispanics, will account for an increasing proportion of all Texans. Although the exact numbers are likely to vary from those presented here, because of the uncertainty inherent in all projections (see Murdock and Ellis 1990; Murdock et al. 2003), there is little doubt that Texas will become increasingly diverse and decreasingly nonHispanic White in the coming decades.

### Minority Status and Socioeconomic Resources

As noted in the literature review of analyses of minority status and socioeconomic resources (see Chapter 1), there are clear and persistent relationships between minority, particularly nonHispanic Black and Hispanic, status and reduced levels of socioeconomic resources that have been evident for decades. There is, of course, nothing that is completely determinative of the relationships that currently exist between minority status and income and other types of socioeconomic resources. However, this literature provides strong and consistent evidence that such racial/ethnic differences have been pervasive. At the same time, the literature indicates that education enhances the competitiveness of all persons and can substantially reduce many of the socioeconomic differences among racial/ethnic groups. This same literature also suggests that educational enhancements and other factors have not brought full closure between minority and majority income levels and levels of other socioeconomic factors. As shown in the discussion of educational attainment and socioeconomic resources below, the minority disadvantage is persistent, at least at some levels, for many socioeconomic factors, and hence the eventual disappearance of such differences cannot be taken as a given no matter what public and private practices and policies prevail.

*Educational Attainment and Socioeconomic Resources*
The literature in Chapter 1 also clearly shows that educational attainment is a major factor mitigating the disadvantages related to racial/ethnic differences. Table 9.1 provides data on mean household income in 2010 within educational attainment and occupational categories for nonHispanic White, nonHispanic Black, Hispanic, and nonHispanic Asian and Other households in Texas. These data show that for every racial/ethnic group within (1) managerial and professional, (2) technical, sales and administrative, and (3) service industries increased education leads to increased incomes. Only in occupations where education is less of a differentiator of type of work and reimbursement, such as operatives and laborers and precision production, craft, and repairers occupations are there reversals in these patterns. These occur for Hispanic and nonHispanic Black populations. Despite these exceptions, the total mean income differences are large at different educational levels. NonHispanic White households have mean household incomes of $50,533 when householders have less than a high school level of education compared to mean incomes of $144,714 when householders have a graduate degree. These values for the same educational levels are $31,072 and $94,490 for nonHispanic Black households, $38,221 and $108,473 for Hispanic households, and $50,815 and $123,035 for nonHispanic Asian and Other households. Education is clearly a factor of substantial importance in increasing socioeconomic resources.

At the same time, it must be acknowledged that education alone does not eliminate all of the income and other socioeconomic differences between racial/ethnic groups. For all educational levels for all occupations shown in Table 9.1, mean household incomes are lower for nonHispanic Black and Hispanic householders in the same occupations and at the same levels of education when compared with nonHispanic White and nonHispanic Asian and Other householders. These differentials suggest that there may be differences in the specific positions and types of activities performed within occupational categories by persons from different racial/ethnic groups. In addition, income varies not only by occupation and education but also by the number of generations over which a group has experienced higher levels of education and accumulated financial resources. The number of such generations tends to be larger for nonHispanic White than for minority households. Also, some minority racial/ethnic groups may

Table 9.1

Mean Household Income by Race/Ethnicity, Educational Attainment, and Occupation in 2010

| Occupations | Less Than High School | High School/ GED | Bachelor's Degree | Graduate/ Prof Degree |
|---|---|---|---|---|
| **NH* White** | | | | |
| Managerial & Professional | $ 72,446 | $ 84,504 | $ 120,792 | $ 149,819 |
| Technical, Sales, & Admin. | 52,930 | 64,179 | 112,843 | 130,471 |
| Service | 35,233 | 46,108 | 78,468 | 86,444 |
| Farming, Forestry, & Fishing | 47,269 | 59,941 | 103,702 | 108,433 |
| Precision Prod., Craft, & Repairers | 55,079 | 68,247 | 94,875 | 119,057 |
| Operatives and Laborers | 48,819 | 61,211 | 77,581 | 89,720 |
| Total | 50,533 | 64,975 | 114,698 | 144,714 |
| **NH Black** | | | | |
| Managerial & Professional | $ 47,483 | $ 52,186 | $ 84,758 | $ 99,073 |
| Technical, Sales, & Admin. | 33,980 | 43,933 | 75,416 | 80,852 |
| Service | 23,902 | 33,052 | 56,955 | 65,987 |
| Farming, Forestry, & Fishing | 32,374 | 32,243 | 87,493 | 90,173 |
| Precision Prod., Craft, & Repairers | 42,767 | 53,192 | 82,885 | 69,805 |
| Operatives and Laborers | 37,811 | 46,296 | 66,181 | 63,707 |
| Total | 31,072 | 42,465 | 78,933 | 94,490 |
| **Hispanic** | | | | |
| Managerial & Professional | $ 52,178 | $ 61,992 | $ 88,036 | $ 116,400 |
| Technical, Sales, & Admin. | 40,131 | 50,127 | 81,005 | 91,155 |
| Service | 31,601 | 37,145 | 64,772 | 68,359 |
| Farming, Forestry, & Fishing | 31,194 | 35,158 | 45,096 | 63,449 |
| Precision Prod., Craft, & Repairers | 42,302 | 51,527 | 63,695 | 63,345 |
| Operatives and Laborers | 41,273 | 47,455 | 54,282 | 57,806 |
| Total | 38,221 | 47,760 | 81,548 | 108,473 |
| **NH Asian & Other** | | | | |
| Managerial & Professional | $ 84,172 | $ 73,016 | $ 103,737 | $ 130,603 |
| Technical, Sales, & Admin. | 52,764 | 60,719 | 86,039 | 105,469 |
| Service | 40,857 | 43,341 | 63,605 | 76,454 |
| Farming, Forestry, & Fishing | 50,801 | 42,306 | 52,129 | 67,507 |
| Precision Prod., Craft, & Repairers | 54,594 | 63,451 | 70,778 | 92,041 |
| Operatives and Laborers | 47,939 | 49,015 | 60,895 | 65,074 |
| Total | 50,815 | 55,496 | 93,474 | 123,035 |

Source: Ruggles et al. 2010; U.S. Census Bureau 2011f.
*NH refers to nonHispanic; values for categories labeled NH are only for the nonHispanic persons in each race category. Hispanic includes Hispanics of all races.

continue to face barriers that cannot be completely overcome by educational attainment. Nevertheless it is clear that education pays for members of all racial/ethnic groups.

## QUESTION 2: WILL RECENT DEMOGRAPHIC AND SOCIOECONOMIC PATTERNS OF CHANGE, IF CONTINUED, SUBSTANTIALLY AND POSITIVELY ALTER TEXAS SOCIOECONOMIC FUTURE?

*Baseline Patterns of Change*

The degree to which socioeconomic differences have been altered over time is evident in Table 9.2, which shows median household, mean household, per capita, and aggregate household income levels by race/ethnicity of the householder for 1980, 1990, 2000, and 2010 and percent change in these income levels by race/ethnicity for the decade periods from 1980 to 2010. In this table all income values shown are in 2010 constant dollars so they are directly comparable across time. The data in this table show that total median household income increased by nearly $4,900 from 1980 to 2010, with total mean household income increasing by more than $15,500 and total per capita income by nearly $6,200. Incomes have increased for all racial and ethnic groups from 1980 to 2010, with increases varying from $3,600 to more than $12,400 for median household income, from $8,700 to more than $25,000 for mean household income, and from $3,800 to nearly $12,300 for per capita income. There are clear increases and continuing differences between racial/ethnic groups over time.

In all cases, for every decade from 1980 to 2010, incomes are lower for nonHispanic Black and Hispanic households than for nonHispanic White and nonHispanic Asian and Other households. The largest increases occur for nonHispanic Asian and Other and nonHispanic White populations. It is also apparent that during the period of limited general economic growth from 2000 to 2010, median and mean household income levels declined for nonHispanic Black and Hispanic households and for the population overall while continuing to increase for nonHispanic White and nonHispanic Asian and Other households.

Finally, if one examines relative income disparity for these factors, the data (not shown but computed from income data for 1980 to 2010) fail to show any substantial decrease in disparity between nonHispanic White and nonHispanic Black and Hispanic racial/ethnic groups over time. Non-Hispanic Black median household income levels in 1980 were 59 percent of the income level for nonHispanic White households in 1980 and similarly 59.7 percent of such levels in 2010. For mean and per capita income levels, there were declines for nonHispanic Black households, with non-Hispanic Black households having mean incomes that were 63.8 percent

Table 9.2

Median, Mean, and Per Capita Income Levels (in 2010 Dollars) by Race/Ethnicity for 1980–2010 and Percent Change for 1980–1990, 1990–2000, 2000–2010, Average Change for the Three Decades, and the Largest Decade Growth for Any Period from 1980–2010

| Race/Ethnicity | Income Levels | | | | Percent Change 1980–2010 | | | | |
|---|---|---|---|---|---|---|---|---|---|
| | 1980 | 1990 | 2000 | 2010 | 1980–1990 | 1990–2000 | 2000–2010 | Avg. | Largest |
| **Median Household Income** | | | | | | | | | |
| NH* White | $ 50,095 | $ 51,729 | $ 59,721 | $ 61,049 | 3.2 | 15.5 | 2.2 | 7.0 | 15.5 |
| NH Black | 29,579 | 30,031 | 37,129 | 36,466 | 1.5 | 23.6 | -1.8 | 7.8 | 23.6 |
| Hispanic | 33,370 | 32,320 | 37,828 | 37,019 | -3.1 | 17.0 | -2.1 | 3.9 | 17.0 |
| NH Asian/Other | 47,660 | 48,383 | 56,625 | 60,110 | 1.5 | 17.0 | 6.2 | 8.2 | 17.0 |
| Total | 44,749 | 45,046 | 50,559 | 49,646 | 0.7 | 12.2 | -1.8 | 3.7 | 12.2 |
| **Mean Household Income** | | | | | | | | | |
| NH White | $ 58,060 | $ 65,313 | $ 80,765 | $ 82,052 | 12.5 | 23.7 | 1.6 | 12.6 | 23.7 |
| NH Black | 37,037 | 38,754 | 50,063 | 49,284 | 4.7 | 29.0 | -1.6 | 10.7 | 29.0 |
| Hispanic | 39,744 | 40,581 | 49,429 | 48,459 | 2.1 | 21.8 | -2.0 | 7.3 | 21.8 |
| NH Asian/Other | 54,470 | 62,309 | 75,010 | 79,573 | 14.4 | 20.4 | 6.1 | 13.6 | 20.4 |
| Total | 52,920 | 57,753 | 69,618 | 68,429 | 9.1 | 20.5 | -1.7 | 9.3 | 20.5 |

Table 9.2, continued

| Race/Ethnicity | Income Levels | | | | Percent Change 1980–2010 | | | | |
|---|---|---|---|---|---|---|---|---|---|
| | 1980 | 1990 | 2000 | 2010 | 1980–1990 | 1990–2000 | 2000–2010 | Avg. | Largest |
| **Per Capita Income** | | | | | | | | | |
| NH White | $ 22,531 | $ 26,622 | $ 33,173 | $ 34,826 | 18.2 | 24.6 | 5.0 | 15.9 | 24.6 |
| NH Black | 12,085 | 13,550 | 18,138 | 18,545 | 12.1 | 33.9 | 2.2 | 16.1 | 33.9 |
| Hispanic | 10,345 | 11,039 | 13,638 | 14,169 | 6.7 | 23.5 | 3.9 | 11.4 | 23.5 |
| NH Asian/Other | 17,604 | 19,660 | 24,203 | 24,634 | 11.7 | 23.1 | 1.8 | 12.2 | 23.1 |
| Total | 18,697 | 21,087 | 24,841 | 24,870 | 12.8 | 17.8 | 0.1 | 10.2 | 17.8 |
| **Aggregate Household Income (in $Billions)** | | | | | | | | | |
| NH White | $ 210.7 | $ 274.0 | $ 362.7 | $ 396.9 | 30.1 | 32.4 | 9.4 | 24.0 | 32.4 |
| NH Black | 20.5 | 26.8 | 42.9 | 53.5 | 30.9 | 60.1 | 24.8 | 38.6 | 60.1 |
| Hispanic | 30.9 | 47.9 | 91.0 | 134.1 | 55.1 | 89.9 | 47.4 | 64.1 | 89.9 |
| NH Asian/Other | 3.5 | 7.4 | 21.4 | 34.5 | 110.8 | 187.7 | 61.1 | 119.9 | 187.7 |
| Total | 265.5 | 356.1 | 517.9 | 619.0 | 34.1 | 45.4 | 19.5 | 33.0 | 45.4 |

*Source:* Projections by the authors and 2010 data and rates derived from Ruggles 2010; U.S. Census Bureau 2011g.

*NH refers to nonHispanic; values shown are only for the nonHispanic persons in each race category. Hispanic includes Hispanics of all races.

of nonHispanic White levels in 1980 but only 60.1 percent of nonHispanic White levels in 2010. Similarly, nonHispanic Black per capita income levels were 53.6 percent of nonHispanic White levels in 1980 and 53.3 percent in 2010.

When median income levels for Hispanics are compared to nonHispanic White median income levels, the results show that Hispanic median income levels were 66.6 percent of those for nonHispanic Whites in 1980 and 60.6 percent in 2010. For mean income levels the percentage of Hispanic to nonHispanic White income was 68.5 percent in 1980 and 59.1 percent in 2010. For per capita income, Hispanic levels were 45.9 percent in 1980 but only 40.7 percent in 2010. The data show that, no matter what time period is examined, there has not been substantial closure in income levels over the period from 1980 through 2010, with this lack of closure being particularly evident for nonHispanic Black and Hispanic populations.

The data for three decade periods from 1980–2000 for nonHispanic Asians and Others compared to nonHispanic Whites show very similar incomes in 1980 that became even more similar by 2010. NonHispanic Asian and Others median, mean, and per capita incomes were 95.1, 93.8, and 78.1 percent, respectively, of nonHispanic White incomes in 1980 but 98.5, 97.0, and 70.7 in 2010. Only the per capita income values showed some decline due to the larger household size of nonHispanic Asian and Other households.

The data on aggregate household income show increases impacted both by change in relative incomes among racial/ethnic groups and by change in levels of population growth. Despite the continuing disparities noted above, large relative increases are evident for each of the growing minority populations. The aggregate household income for Asians and Others increased by 885.7 percent, that for Hispanics by 334.0 percent, and that for nonHispanic Black households by 161.0 percent from 1980 to 2010. The increase for nonHispanic White households was 88.4 percent. The data in this part of Table 9.2 clearly demonstrate that aggregate income increases in an area are a function of both growth in the number of households and the level of household growth in different racial/ethnic groups.

The level of progress in closing socioeconomic gaps and the continuing disparities are also evident in the data for education and occupational change in Tables 9.3 and 9.4. Examinations of the data in Table 9.3 for attainment of high school or higher levels of education and a bachelor's or higher level of education show both relative educational progress and persistent disparity. For example, at the high school or higher level of educational attainment, the percentage of nonHispanic White persons 25 years of age or older with a high school level of education or higher increased by 22.0 percent from 1980 to 2010. The percentage of nonHispanic Black population members with a high school degree or higher increased

Table 9.3

Number and Percent of Persons 25+ Years of Age in Texas by Race/Ethnicity and Education Level, 1980–2010, and Change for 1980–1990, 1990–2000, 2000–2010, Average Percent Change 1980–2010, and Largest Decade Percent Change 1980–2010

| Attainment Level and Race/Ethnicity | Decade Numeric and Percent | | | | | | | | Percent Change 1980–2010 | | | | |
| | 1980 | | 1990 | | 2000 | | 2010 | | 1980–1990 | 1990–2000 | 2000–2010 | Avg. | Largest |
| | Number | % | Number | % | Number | % | Number | % | | | | | |
| **Less than high school/GED** | | | | | | | | | | | | | |
| NH* White | 1,708,620 | 30.0 | 1,269,087 | 18.5 | 953,459 | 12.8 | 647,925 | 8.0 | -25.7 | -24.9 | -32.0 | -27.5 | -24.9 |
| NH Black | 390,520 | 46.9 | 378,550 | 33.9 | 328,585 | 24.1 | 239,653 | 13.6 | -3.1 | -13.2 | -27.1 | -14.5 | -3.1 |
| Hispanic | 846,720 | 64.5 | 1,179,784 | 55.4 | 1,731,468 | 50.7 | 2,050,831 | 40.5 | 39.3 | 46.8 | 18.4 | 34.8 | 46.8 |
| NH Asian/Other | 24,840 | 24.8 | 45,138 | 21.2 | 101,046 | 18.6 | 105,611 | 12.5 | 81.7 | 123.9 | 4.5 | 70.0 | 123.9 |
| Total | 2,970,700 | 37.4 | 2,872,559 | 27.9 | 3,114,558 | 24.3 | 3,044,020 | 19.3 | -3.3 | 8.4 | -2.3 | 0.9 | 8.4 |
| **High school/GED** | | | | | | | | | | | | | |
| NH White | 1,592,280 | 27.9 | 1,849,137 | 27.0 | 1,922,526 | 25.7 | 2,049,060 | 25.3 | 16.1 | 4.0 | 6.6 | 8.9 | 16.1 |
| NH Black | 226,520 | 27.2 | 315,212 | 28.2 | 409,822 | 30.0 | 535,695 | 30.4 | 39.2 | 30.0 | 30.7 | 33.3 | 39.2 |
| Hispanic | 244,780 | 18.6 | 437,389 | 20.6 | 750,001 | 22.0 | 1,306,455 | 25.8 | 78.7 | 71.5 | 74.2 | 74.8 | 78.7 |
| NH Asian/Other | 23,420 | 23.4 | 38,424 | 18.1 | 94,394 | 17.4 | 146,453 | 17.3 | 64.1 | 145.7 | 55.2 | 88.3 | 145.7 |
| Total | 2,087,000 | 26.3 | 2,640,162 | 25.6 | 3,176,743 | 24.8 | 4,037,663 | 25.6 | 26.5 | 20.3 | 27.1 | 24.6 | 27.1 |

Table 9.3, continued

| Attainment Level and Race/Ethnicity | Decade Numeric and Percent | | | | | | | | Percent Change 1980–2010 | | | | |
|---|---|---|---|---|---|---|---|---|---|---|---|---|---|
| | 1980 | | 1990 | | 2000 | | 2010 | | 1980–1990 | 1990–2000 | 2000–2010 | Avg. | Largest |
| | Number | % | Number | % | Number | % | Number | % | | | | | |
| **Some college/associates** | | | | | | | | | | | | | |
| NH White | 1,239,200 | 21.7 | 2,003,686 | 29.3 | 2,352,191 | 31.5 | 2,640,291 | 32.6 | 62.1 | 17.1 | 12.2 | 30.5 | 62.1 |
| NH Black | 139,140 | 16.7 | 289,619 | 25.9 | 417,804 | 30.6 | 639,662 | 36.3 | 108.1 | 44.3 | 53.1 | 68.5 | 108.1 |
| Hispanic | 148,400 | 11.3 | 355,244 | 16.7 | 625,832 | 18.3 | 1,124,159 | 22.2 | 139.4 | 76.2 | 79.6 | 98.4 | 139.4 |
| NH Asian/Other | 20,480 | 20.5 | 49,430 | 23.2 | 131,469 | 24.2 | 201,348 | 23.8 | 141.4 | 166.0 | 53.2 | 120.2 | 166.0 |
| Total | 1,547,220 | 19.5 | 2,702,979 | 26.2 | 3,527,296 | 27.6 | 4,605,460 | 29.2 | 74.7 | 30.5 | 30.6 | 45.3 | 74.7 |
| **Bachelor's degree** | | | | | | | | | | | | | |
| NH White | 645,420 | 11.4 | 1,182,796 | 17.3 | 1,515,104 | 20.3 | 1,846,584 | 22.8 | 83.3 | 28.1 | 21.9 | 44.4 | 83.3 |
| NH Black | 41,420 | 5.0 | 92,024 | 8.3 | 146,402 | 10.6 | 230,842 | 13.1 | 122.2 | 59.1 | 57.7 | 79.7 | 122.2 |
| Hispanic | 38,880 | 3.0 | 106,558 | 5.0 | 206,895 | 6.1 | 425,357 | 8.4 | 174.1 | 94.2 | 105.6 | 124.6 | 174.1 |
| NH Asian/Other | 13,480 | 13.5 | 46,653 | 21.9 | 127,849 | 23.4 | 225,794 | 26.6 | 246.1 | 174.0 | 76.6 | 165.6 | 246.1 |
| Total | 739,200 | 9.3 | 1,428,031 | 13.8 | 1,996,250 | 15.7 | 2,728,577 | 17.3 | 93.2 | 39.8 | 36.7 | 56.6 | 93.2 |
| **Graduate/professional degree** | | | | | | | | | | | | | |
| NH* White | 512,340 | 9.0 | 543,114 | 7.9 | 725,387 | 9.7 | 915,193 | 11.3 | 6.0 | 33.6 | 26.2 | 21.9 | 33.6 |
| NH Black | 34,720 | 4.2 | 41,845 | 3.7 | 63,608 | 4.7 | 116,302 | 6.6 | 20.5 | 52.0 | 82.8 | 51.8 | 82.8 |
| Hispanic | 34,620 | 2.6 | 48,756 | 2.3 | 97,840 | 2.9 | 156,977 | 3.1 | 40.8 | 100.7 | 60.4 | 67.3 | 100.7 |
| NH Asian/Other | 17,780 | 17.8 | 33,159 | 15.6 | 89,208 | 16.4 | 167,930 | 19.8 | 86.5 | 169.0 | 88.2 | 114.6 | 169.0 |
| Total | 599,460 | 7.5 | 666,874 | 6.5 | 976,043 | 7.6 | 1,356,402 | 8.6 | 11.2 | 46.4 | 39.0 | 32.2 | 46.4 |

Table 9.3, continued

| Attainment Level and Race/Ethnicity | Decade Numeric and Percent | | | | | | | | Percent Change 1980–2010 | | | | |
| --- | --- | --- | --- | --- | --- | --- | --- | --- | --- | --- | --- | --- | --- |
| | 1980 | | 1990 | | 2000 | | 2010 | | 1980–1990 | 1990–2000 | 2000–2010 | Avg. | Largest |
| | Number | % | Number | % | Number | % | Number | % | | | | | |
| **High school/GED and higher** | | | | | | | | | | | | | |
| NH White | 3,989,240 | 70.0 | 5,583,733 | 81.5 | 6,515,208 | 87.2 | 7,451,128 | 92.0 | 40.0 | 16.7 | 14.4 | 23.7 | 40.0 |
| NH Black | 441,800 | 53.1 | 738,700 | 66.1 | 1,037,636 | 75.9 | 1,522,501 | 86.4 | 67.2 | 40.5 | 46.7 | 51.5 | 67.2 |
| Hispanic | 466,680 | 35.5 | 947,947 | 44.6 | 1,680,568 | 49.3 | 3,012,948 | 59.5 | 103.1 | 77.3 | 79.3 | 86.6 | 103.1 |
| NH Asian/Other | 75,160 | 75.2 | 167,666 | 78.8 | 442,920 | 81.4 | 741,525 | 87.5 | 123.1 | 164.2 | 67.4 | 118.2 | 164.2 |
| Total | 4,972,880 | 62.6 | 7,438,046 | 72.1 | 9,676,332 | 75.7 | 12,728,102 | 80.7 | 49.6 | 30.1 | 31.5 | 37.1 | 49.6 |
| **Bachelor's degree and higher** | | | | | | | | | | | | | |
| NH White | 1,157,760 | 20.4 | 1,725,910 | 25.2 | 2,240,491 | 30.0 | 2,761,777 | 34.1 | 49.1 | 29.8 | 23.3 | 34.1 | 49.1 |
| NH Black | 76,140 | 9.2 | 133,869 | 12.0 | 210,010 | 15.3 | 347,144 | 19.7 | 75.8 | 56.9 | 65.3 | 66.0 | 75.8 |
| Hispanic | 73,500 | 5.6 | 155,314 | 7.3 | 304,735 | 9.0 | 582,334 | 11.5 | 111.3 | 96.2 | 91.1 | 99.5 | 111.3 |
| NH Asian/Other | 31,260 | 31.3 | 79,812 | 37.5 | 217,057 | 39.8 | 393,724 | 46.4 | 155.3 | 172.0 | 81.4 | 136.2 | 172.0 |
| Total | 1,338,660 | 16.8 | 2,094,905 | 20.3 | 2,972,293 | 23.3 | 4,084,979 | 25.9 | 56.5 | 41.9 | 37.4 | 45.3 | 56.5 |

*Source:* U.S. Census Bureau 1992, 2002, 2011a; Ruggles et al.2010.

*NH refers to nonHispanic; values for categories labeled NH are only for the nonHispanic persons in each race category. Hispanic includes Hispanics of all races.

by 33.3 percent. The increase for Hispanics was 24.0 percent, and the increase for nonHispanic Asians and Others was 12.3 percent. Although the differences decreased between nonHispanic Black and Hispanic and nonHispanic White and nonHispanic Asian and Other populations, the absolute differences remained large, especially for Hispanics. Whereas 92 percent of nonHispanic White, 87.5 percent of nonHispanic Asian and Other, and 86.4 percent of nonHispanic Black persons 25 years of age or older had high school or higher levels of education in 2010, only 59.5 percent of Hispanics 25 years of age or older had a high school or higher level of education in 2010.

The data in the bottom panel of Table 9.3 show that disparities at the college level remained substantial for both nonHispanic Black and Hispanic populations. Whereas 46.4 percent of nonHispanic Asian and Other and 34.1 percent of nonHispanic White populations had a bachelor's degree or higher level of education, only 19.7 percent of nonHispanic Black and 11.5 percent of the Hispanic population members had a bachelor's degree or higher level of education in 2010. In fact, the disparity between nonHispanic Black and nonHispanic White populations with a bachelor's degree or higher level of education increased from 11.2 percent in 1980 to 14.4 percent in 2010 and the percentage difference for Hispanic relative to nonHispanic White populations was 14.8 percent in 1980 but 22.6 percent in 2010. For virtually all higher levels of educational attainment, the disparities between nonHispanic White and Hispanic and nonHispanic Black populations continue to be extensive. Disparities among racial/ethnic groups at key levels of educational attainment continued and at the higher levels of education expanded from 1980 to 2010.

The data in Table 9.4 show similar patterns when differences in occupational attainment are examined. For example, whereas all racial/ethnic groups have shown increased percentages employed in managerial and professional occupations, the disparity in the proportion of nonHispanic Black population members in such occupations compared to nonHispanic Whites was 13.7 percent in 1980 (24.3 percent for nonHispanic White persons in such occupations compared to 10.6 percent of the nonHispanic Black population) and 13.5 percent in 2010 (35.4 for nonHispanic White populations versus 21.9 percent for nonHispanic Black populations). The disparity between the nonHispanic Asian and Other and nonHispanic White populations showed an advantage for nonHispanic Asians and Others of 1.8 percent in 1980 (26.1 for nonHispanic Asians and Others and 24.3 for nonHispanic Whites) and 3.6 percent in 2010 (when the values were 39.0 percent for Asians and Other and 35.4 for nonHispanic White populations). The disparity between nonHispanic White and Hispanic populations increased substantially from 14.3 percent in 1980 (10.0 percent for Hispanics vs. 24.3 percent for nonHispanic Whites) to 20.6 percent in

Table 9.4

Percent of Persons 25+ Years of Age in Texas by Race/Ethnicity and Occupation, 1980–2010 and Change from 1980–1990, 1990–2000, 2000–2010, Average Percent Change 1980–2010, and Largest Decade Percent Change 1980–2010

| Occupation and Race/Ethnicity | Decade Numeric and Percent | | | | | | | | Percent Change 1980–2010 | | | | |
| | 1980 | | 1990 | | 2000 | | 2010 | | 1980–1990 | 1990–2000 | 2000–2010 | Avg. | Largest |
| | Number | % | Number | % | Number | % | Number | % | | | | | |
| --- | --- | --- | --- | --- | --- | --- | --- | --- | --- | --- | --- | --- | --- |
| **Managerial and professional** | | | | | | | | | | | | | |
| NH* White | 1,140,420 | 24.3 | 1,543,427 | 29.2 | 1,923,086 | 33.1 | 2,145,208 | 35.4 | 4.9 | 3.9 | 2.3 | 3.7 | 4.9 |
| NH Black | 78,920 | 10.6 | 124,589 | 14.1 | 208,189 | 19.3 | 302,861 | 21.9 | 3.5 | 5.2 | 2.6 | 3.8 | 5.2 |
| Hispanic | 117,300 | 10.0 | 210,546 | 11.6 | 374,442 | 13.8 | 599,458 | 14.8 | 1.6 | 2.2 | 1.0 | 1.6 | 2.2 |
| NH Asian/Other | 22,760 | 26.1 | 52,586 | 28.1 | 117,373 | 34.1 | 209,796 | 39.0 | 2.0 | 6.0 | 4.9 | 4.3 | 6.0 |
| Total | 1,359,400 | 20.3 | 1,931,148 | 23.7 | 2,623,090 | 27.8 | 3,257,323 | 27.0 | 3.4 | 4.1 | -0.8 | 2.2 | 4.1 |
| **Technical, sales, and administrative** | | | | | | | | | | | | | |
| NH White | 1,540,620 | 32.7 | 1,760,413 | 33.4 | 1,849,683 | 31.8 | 1,821,102 | 29.9 | 0.7 | -1.6 | -1.9 | -0.9 | 0.7 |
| NH Black | 157,360 | 21.1 | 233,975 | 26.6 | 314,681 | 29.3 | 388,669 | 28.1 | 5.5 | 2.7 | -1.2 | 2.3 | 5.5 |
| Hispanic | 266,340 | 22.8 | 429,373 | 23.7 | 644,865 | 23.9 | 951,476 | 23.5 | 0.9 | 0.2 | -0.4 | 0.2 | 0.9 |
| NH Asian/Other | 22,340 | 25.5 | 52,109 | 27.9 | 103,758 | 30.1 | 150,702 | 28.0 | 2.4 | 2.2 | -2.1 | 0.8 | 2.4 |
| Total | 1,986,660 | 29.7 | 2,475,870 | 30.3 | 2,912,987 | 28.7 | 3,311,949 | 27.4 | 0.6 | -1.6 | -1.3 | -0.8 | 0.6 |

Table 9.4, continued

| Occupation and Race/Ethnicity | Decade Numeric and Percent | | | | | | | | Percent Change 1980–2010 | | | | |
|---|---|---|---|---|---|---|---|---|---|---|---|---|---|
| | 1980 | | 1990 | | 2000 | | 2010 | | 1980–1990 | 1990–2000 | 2000–2010 | Avg. | Largest |
| | Number | % | Number | % | Number | % | Number | % | | | | | |
| **Service** | | | | | | | | | | | | | |
| NH White | 399,340 | 8.5 | 478,549 | 9.1 | 561,538 | 9.7 | 632,755 | 10.4 | 0.6 | 0.6 | 0.7 | 0.6 | 0.7 |
| NH Black | 168,220 | 22.6 | 180,298 | 20.5 | 194,094 | 18.0 | 252,666 | 18.3 | -2.1 | -2.5 | 0.3 | -1.4 | 0.3 |
| Hispanic | 174,300 | 14.9 | 310,246 | 17.1 | 475,315 | 17.5 | 792,843 | 19.5 | 2.2 | 0.4 | 2.0 | 1.5 | 2.2 |
| NH Asian/Other | 11,020 | 12.6 | 25,952 | 13.9 | 40,105 | 11.6 | 68,128 | 12.6 | 1.3 | -2.3 | 1.0 | 0.0 | 1.3 |
| Total | 752,880 | 11.2 | 995,045 | 12.2 | 1,271,052 | 10.7 | 1,746,392 | 14.5 | 1.0 | -1.5 | 3.8 | 1.1 | 3.8 |
| **Farming, forestry and fishing** | | | | | | | | | | | | | |
| NH White | 123,420 | 2.6 | 117,530 | 2.2 | 109,585 | 1.9 | 104,928 | 1.7 | -0.4 | -0.3 | -0.2 | -0.3 | -0.2 |
| NH Black | 10,460 | 1.4 | 8,904 | 1.0 | 9,412 | 0.9 | 10,649 | 0.8 | -0.4 | -0.1 | -0.1 | -0.2 | -0.1 |
| Hispanic | 45,620 | 3.9 | 67,849 | 3.7 | 81,746 | 3.0 | 127,930 | 3.1 | -0.2 | -0.7 | 0.1 | -0.3 | 0.1 |
| NH Asian/Other | 680 | 0.8 | 1,765 | 0.9 | 2,308 | 0.7 | 2,820 | 0.5 | 0.1 | -0.2 | -0.2 | -0.1 | 0.1 |
| Total | 180,180 | 2.7 | 156,048 | 2.4 | 203,051 | 3.0 | 246,327 | 2.0 | -0.3 | 0.6 | -1.0 | -0.2 | 0.6 |
| **Precision production, craft and repairers** | | | | | | | | | | | | | |
| NH* White | 679,360 | 14.5 | 557,305 | 10.6 | 590,670 | 10.2 | 541,161 | 8.9 | -3.9 | -0.4 | -1.3 | -1.9 | -0.4 |
| NH Black | 70,180 | 9.4 | 56,574 | 6.4 | 68,956 | 6.4 | 72,175 | 5.2 | -3.0 | 0.0 | -1.2 | -1.4 | 0.0 |
| Hispanic | 183,500 | 15.7 | 256,930 | 13.0 | 396,879 | 14.6 | 586,754 | 14.4 | -2.7 | 1.6 | -0.2 | -0.4 | 1.6 |
| NH Asian/Other | 8,620 | 9.9 | 16,192 | 8.7 | 23,946 | 6.9 | 32,050 | 5.9 | -1.2 | -1.8 | -1.0 | -1.3 | -1.0 |
| Total | 941,660 | 14.0 | 867,001 | 10.6 | 1,080,451 | 11.3 | 1,232,140 | 10.2 | -3.4 | 0.7 | -1.1 | -1.3 | 0.7 |

Table 9.4, continued

| Occupation and Race/Ethnicity | Decade Numeric and Percent | | | | | | | | Percent Change 1980–2010 | | | | |
|---|---|---|---|---|---|---|---|---|---|---|---|---|---|
| | 1980 | | 1990 | | 2000 | | 2010 | | 1980–1990 | 1990–2000 | 2000–2010 | Avg. | Largest |
| | Number | % | Number | % | Number | % | Number | % | | | | | |
| **Operatives and laborers** | | | | | | | | | | | | | |
| NH White | 683,600 | 14.5 | 571,462 | 10.8 | 533,509 | 9.2 | 513,643 | 8.4 | -3.7 | -1.6 | -0.8 | -2.0 | -0.8 |
| NH Black | 209,940 | 28.1 | 162,747 | 18.5 | 170,460 | 15.8 | 195,585 | 14.1 | -9.6 | -2.7 | -1.7 | -4.7 | -1.7 |
| Hispanic | 309,360 | 26.5 | 365,408 | 20.1 | 500,830 | 18.5 | 679,600 | 16.7 | -6.4 | -1.6 | -1.8 | -3.3 | -1.6 |
| NH Asian/Other | 18,220 | 20.8 | 26,560 | 14.2 | 39,533 | 11.5 | 42,661 | 7.9 | -6.6 | -2.7 | -3.6 | -4.3 | -2.7 |
| Total | 1,221,120 | 18.2 | 1,126,177 | 13.8 | 1,244,332 | 12.4 | 1,431,489 | 11.9 | -4.4 | -1.4 | -0.5 | -2.1 | -0.5 |
| **Unemployed** | | | | | | | | | | | | | |
| NH White | 134,300 | 2.9 | 249,015 | 4.7 | 236,210 | 4.1 | 325,249 | 5.3 | 1.8 | -0.6 | 1.2 | 0.8 | 1.8 |
| NH Black | 50,520 | 6.8 | 113,891 | 12.9 | 111,489 | 10.3 | 161,212 | 11.6 | 6.1 | -2.6 | 1.3 | 1.6 | 6.1 |
| Hispanic | 71,980 | 6.2 | 195,956 | 10.8 | 235,758 | 8.7 | 323,626 | 8.0 | 4.6 | -2.1 | -0.7 | 0.6 | 4.6 |
| NH Asian/Other | 3,800 | 4.3 | 11,685 | 6.3 | 17,567 | 5.1 | 32,673 | 6.1 | 2.0 | -1.2 | 1.0 | 0.6 | 2.0 |
| Total | 260,600 | 3.9 | 570,547 | 7.0 | 601,024 | 6.1 | 842,760 | 7.0 | 3.1 | -0.9 | 0.9 | 1.0 | 3.1 |

*Source*: Ruggles et al. 2010; U.S. Census Bureau 2011f.

*NH refers to nonHispanic; values for categories labeled NH are only for the nonHispanic persons in each race category. Hispanic includes Hispanics of all races.

2010 (14.8 percent for Hispanics vs. 35.4 percent for nonHispanic Whites). In fact, the disparities are particularly pronounced between Hispanics and all other racial/ethnic groups.

The data in Tables 9.2 through 9.4 clearly show that all racial/ethic groups have shown increases in real incomes, in educational attainment, and in occupational mobility. At the same time, they suggest that in a relative sense the comparative competitiveness of nonHispanic Black and Hispanic minority populations compared to nonHispanic White populations did not change substantially in the period from 1980 to 2010, while nonHispanic Asians and Others have come to outperform all other groups in educational and occupational attainment while continuing to have incomes that are somewhat lower than those for nonHispanic Whites.

*Projections Using Baseline Patterns*
Given the historical patterns described above, the critical question is whether there is any indication in recent patterns to suggest that, although there has not been substantial closure between the socioeconomic characteristics of racial/ethnic groups in Texas in recent history, patterns might emerge that will substantially alter socioeconomic differentials among racial/ethnic groups. Specifically we examine whether Texas future socioeconomic patterns will change if any of three different levels of historical patterns from 1980 to 2010 were to prevail from 2010 to 2050.

In the first scenario, we examine the mean rate of change for the socioeconomic factors over the three decades, 1980–1990, 1990–2000, and 2000–2010. We then multiply these average rates of change by the projections of populations and households by race/ethnicity from 2010 to 2050 to determine future levels for the socioeconomic factors of per capita income, median household income, mean household income, aggregate household income, and occupational change. Because of change in the definition of educational attainment between 1980 and the subsequent decade periods (from a definition based on years of education to degrees attained) that made it impossible to appropriately compare data for 1980 to that for later periods, the analysis for education uses an average over two decades, 1990–2000 and 2000–2010.

In the second scenario, we use the highest rate of change for each socioeconomic factor for each racial/ethnic group for any decade period from 1980 to 2010 and apply it to the appropriate racial/ethnic group for each of the four decades of change of 2010 to 2020, 2020 to 2030, 2030 to 2040, and 2040 to 2050 to delineate the socioeconomic implications of such a change over time. This is a scenario of relatively robust growth.

In the third scenario, we take the most recent patterns of change, those from 2000–2010, and project the implications of the continuation of these patterns for the period from 2010 through 2050. The rationale for this scenario is the premise that the best predictor of the near term future is often the most recent past.

These three alternatives provide a means of assessing the extent to which the continuation of recent historical patterns are likely to produce future closure in the socioeconomic differences that exist among racial/ethnic groups in Texas. They allow us to address the issue of whether a concerted effort is necessary, or whether baseline change will be sufficient, to resolve the socioeconomic issues resulting, in large part, from demographic change.

The results for each of these projection scenarios are shown in Tables 9.5 through 9.7. Table 9.5 provides alternative projections of median, mean, per capita, and aggregate household income levels for each of the decades through 2050 for each of the alternative projection scenarios. The scenario assuming the 2000–2010 historical data (the last two columns in the table) shows, when compared to 2010, negative change in median household and mean household income levels for nonHispanic Black and Hispanic households for every decade from 2010 through 2050, slow growth for the incomes of nonHispanic Whites, and decreased income overall by 2050. Only nonHispanic Asians and Others continue to show substantial growth from 2010 through 2050. But, for this group as well, median and mean household and per capita and aggregate household income, show the slowest growth from 2010 through 2050 under this scenario.

If this scenario characterizes the future, Texas economic growth will suffer and the disparity among racial/ethnic groups will increase. When total aggregate household income is compared for the scenario assuming 2000–2010 rates and that for the scenario assuming an average rate of growth over the three decades, the total decline in aggregate household income is $586.4 billion per year, and the difference when compared to the scenario using the highest rate of growth from the three decade period from 1980 to 2010 to project the period from 2010 to 2050 is $1,568.8 trillion per year. For nonHispanic White populations, the projection of aggregate income based on the average change in the three decades will be 50.8 percent greater than that based on the 2000–2010 decade and that based on the largest increase for any decade will be 119.5 percent greater than that based on 2000–2010. For nonHispanic Black populations these increases will be 60.2 and 195.4 percent greater, for Hispanics 43.6 and 138.3 percent greater, and for nonHispanic Asians and Others 31.6 and 65.8 percent greater than those for the 2000 to 2010 decade. A broad-based continuing economic recovery from the patterns of the 2000 to 2010 decade is essential to the future of Texas economy and to the socioeconomic improvement of all racial/ethnic groups in Texas.

The results for the remaining two alternative scenarios are displayed in columns two through five of Tables 9.5 through 9.7. They provide projected

Table 9.5

Median, Mean, Per Capita, and Aggregate Income Levels by Race/Ethnicity in 2010 and Projected Through 2050 Assuming Average Percent Change for the Three Decades Between 1980 and 2010, Largest Percent Change for Any Decade, and Percent Change for the 2000–2010 Decade

| | | | | Projections Based on: | | | |
| Race/Ethnicity | Average Percent Change | | | Largest Percent Change | | 2000–2010 Percent Change | |
| | 2010 | 2030 | 2050 | 2030 | 2050 | 2030 | 2050 |
| **Median Household Income**[a] | | | | | | | |
| NH[b] White | $ 61,049 | $ 69,868 | $ 79,961 | $ 81,400 | $ 108,535 | $ 63,794 | $ 66,663 |
| NH Black | 36,466 | 42,371 | 49,232 | 55,742 | 85,209 | 35,175 | 33,930 |
| Hispanic | 37,019 | 39,977 | 43,172 | 50,713 | 69,472 | 35,452 | 33,952 |
| NH Asian/Other | 60,110 | 70,418 | 82,494 | 82,334 | 112,776 | 67,737 | 76,331 |
| Total | 49,646 | 53,387 | 57,409 | 62,542 | 78,789 | 47,868 | 46,155 |
| **Mean Household Income** | | | | | | | |
| NH White | $ 82,052 | $ 103,997 | $ 131,811 | $ 125,466 | $ 191,852 | $ 84,688 | $ 87,409 |
| NH Black | 49,284 | 60,444 | 74,132 | 82,075 | 136,686 | 47,760 | 46,284 |
| Hispanic | 48,459 | 55,809 | 64,274 | 71,896 | 106,666 | 46,577 | 44,769 |
| NH Asian/Other | 79,573 | 102,725 | 132,612 | 115,319 | 167,123 | 89,550 | 100,777 |
| Total | 68,429 | 79,653 | 92,906 | 98,253 | 141,288 | 65,642 | 64,026 |

Table 9.5, continued

| | Projections Based on: | | | | | | |
| | Average Percent Change | | | Largest Percent Change | | 2000–2010 Percent Change | |
| Race/Ethnicity | 2010 | 2030 | 2050 | 2030 | 2050 | 2030 | 2050 |
|---|---|---|---|---|---|---|---|
| **Per Capita Income** | | | | | | | |
| NH White | $ 34,826 | $ 46,207 | $ 61,447 | $ 55,745 | $ 89,436 | $ 37,627 | $ 40,748 |
| NH Black | 18,545 | 23,944 | 30,870 | 32,512 | 56,918 | 18,919 | 19,274 |
| Hispanic | 14,169 | 16,908 | 20,685 | 21,781 | 34,328 | 14,111 | 14,408 |
| NH Asian/Other | 24,634 | 36,343 | 48,344 | 40,799 | 60,926 | 31,682 | 36,739 |
| Total | 24,870 | 28,989 | 34,172 | 35,758 | 51,967 | 23,890 | 23,549 |
| **Aggregate Household Income (in Billions of Dollars)** | | | | | | | |
| NH White | $ 396.9 | $ 564.3 | $ 738.9 | $ 680.7 | $ 1,075.5 | $ 459.5 | $ 490.0 |
| NH Black | 53.5 | 97.7 | 160.4 | 132.7 | 295.7 | 77.2 | 100.1 |
| Hispanic | 134.1 | 299.3 | 635.1 | 385.6 | 1,053.9 | 249.8 | 442.3 |
| NH Asian/Other | 34.5 | 119.5 | 352.1 | 134.2 | 443.8 | 104.2 | 267.6 |
| Total | 619.0 | 1,080.8 | 1,886.5 | 1,333.2 | 2,868.9 | 890.7 | 1,300.1 |

*Source:* Projections by the authors and 2010 data and rates derived from 2010; U.S. Census Bureau 2011g.

[a] All monetary values are in 2010 constant dollars.

[b] NH refers to nonHispanic; values shown are only for the nonHispanic persons in each race category. Hispanic includes Hispanics of all races.

values for one scenario (results shown in columns 2 and 3) that utilizes the average over the three-decade period (1980–2010) for income and occupation and the two decade period (1990–2010) for education and another scenario (results shown in columns 4 and 5) based on the decade (for each variable) that had the largest percent change for each racial/ethnic group. For each scenario these values are multiplied by the 2010 race/ethnicity specific values to project them to 2050.

The differences in values in these two sets of data in Table 9.5 are substantial. For example, the mean household income level in 2050 assuming that the largest percent change for any decade (from 1980–2010) prevailed will be $191,852 for nonHispanic Whites in 2050 compared to $131,811 for 2050 if the average rates for the decades from 1980 to 2010 prevailed. Similarly 2050 mean household income values will be $136,686 for non-Hispanic Black households under the assumption that the highest rates of closure prevailed through 2050 but $74,132 if the average rate of change from 1980–2010 prevailed. Mean income levels will be $106,666 for Hispanics for 2050 assuming the highest rates of closure from the period from 1980–2010 prevailed but $64,274 if the average rates of change of 1980 through 2010 prevailed. For nonHispanic Asians and Others these two income values will be $167,123 and $132,612. It is evident that differentials in rates of growth have substantial effects on total income.

A comparison of the data in Table 9.5 for alternative income measures shows that higher rates of growth lead to some increases in closure between nonHispanic Black and Hispanic and nonHispanic White incomes under a limited number of circumstances. Under the scenario assuming the average rates of change for the three decades from 1980–2010, mean household income levels for nonHispanic Black households are 56.2 percent of those of nonHispanic White households and Hispanic income levels are 48.8 percent of nonHispanic White levels in 2050, compared to 60.1 percent and 59.1 percent, respectively, in 2010. There is an increase rather than a decrease in relative incomes. However, assuming that the highest rates of percent change occur, nonHispanic Black mean household incomes will be 71.2 percent of those for nonHispanic White but Hispanic income will be 55.6 percent of that for nonHispanic White households in 2050 compared to the 60.1 for nonHispanic Black and 59.1 percent for Hispanic households in 2010. Hispanic incomes continue to decrease relative to those for nonHispanic Whites.

When mean household income for Asian and Other populations are compared to those for nonHispanic White population, the comparisons show that nonHispanic Asians and Others' higher levels of education (see Table 9.6) are evident in their income levels. For example, Asian and Other incomes levels were 97 percent of those for nonHispanic Whites in 2010 but will be 100.6 percent in 2050 under the scenario assuming the average of the

Table 9.6

Educational Attainment Levels by Race/Ethnicity for Persons 25+ for 2010 and Projected
Through 2050 Assuming Average Percent Change for the Two Decades Between 1990 and 2010,
Largest Percent Change for Any Decade, and Percent Change for the 2000–2010 Decade

| Attainment Level | Average Percent Change | | | Largest Percent Change | | Percent Change 2000–2010 | |
|---|---|---|---|---|---|---|---|
| | 2010 | 2030 | 2050 | 2030 | 2050 | 2030 | 2050 |
| **Less Than High School** | | | | | | | |
| NH* White | 8.0 | 5.2 | 4.9 | 5.0 | 4.7 | 4.8 | 4.4 |
| NH Black | 13.6 | 6.5 | 4.4 | 5.7 | 3.8 | 5.9 | 4.0 |
| Hispanic | 40.5 | 29.4 | 21.4 | 25.2 | 16.2 | 25.2 | 16.2 |
| NH Asian/Other | 12.5 | 8.6 | 5.8 | 5.0 | 2.2 | 5.2 | 2.4 |
| Total | 19.3 | 16.1 | 13.5 | 13.8 | 10.2 | 13.8 | 10.2 |
| **High School/GED but Less Than Bachelor's Degree** | | | | | | | |
| NH White | 57.9 | 56.3 | 55.6 | 55.2 | 54.2 | 56.7 | 56.1 |
| NH Black | 66.7 | 68.4 | 66.9 | 67.3 | 64.0 | 68.6 | 66.7 |
| Hispanic | 48.0 | 54.8 | 58.6 | 56.7 | 59.4 | 58.3 | 62.6 |
| NH Asian/Other | 41.1 | 39.5 | 37.1 | 26.1 | 14.9 | 37.0 | 31.6 |
| Total | 54.8 | 55.5 | 55.8 | 54.5 | 52.4 | 56.9 | 57.2 |
| **Bachelor's Degree** | | | | | | | |
| NH White | 22.8 | 25.3 | 25.9 | 26.2 | 26.8 | 25.4 | 25.9 |
| NH Black | 13.1 | 16.2 | 18.0 | 16.6 | 18.4 | 15.6 | 16.6 |
| Hispanic | 8.4 | 12.0 | 15.9 | 13.4 | 18.2 | 13.3 | 18.2 |
| NH Asian/Other | 26.6 | 29.5 | 32.1 | 40.0 | 48.8 | 31.4 | 34.0 |
| Total | 17.3 | 18.9 | 20.8 | 20.8 | 24.5 | 19.6 | 22.1 |
| **Graduate/Professional Degree** | | | | | | | |
| NH White | 11.3 | 13.2 | 13.6 | 13.6 | 14.3 | 13.1 | 13.6 |
| NH Black | 6.6 | 8.9 | 10.7 | 10.4 | 13.8 | 9.9 | 12.7 |
| Hispanic | 3.1 | 3.8 | 4.1 | 4.7 | 6.2 | 3.2 | 3.0 |
| NH Asian/Other | 19.8 | 22.4 | 25.0 | 28.9 | 34.1 | 26.4 | 32.0 |
| Total | 8.6 | 9.5 | 9.9 | 10.9 | 12.9 | 9.7 | 10.5 |
| **High School/GED or Higher** | | | | | | | |
| NH White | 92.0 | 94.8 | 95.1 | 95.0 | 95.3 | 95.2 | 95.6 |
| NH Black | 86.4 | 93.5 | 95.6 | 94.3 | 96.2 | 94.1 | 96.0 |
| Hispanic | 59.5 | 70.6 | 78.6 | 74.8 | 83.8 | 74.8 | 83.8 |
| NH Asian/Other | 87.5 | 91.4 | 94.2 | 95.0 | 97.8 | 94.8 | 97.6 |
| Total | 80.7 | 83.9 | 86.5 | 86.2 | 89.8 | 86.2 | 89.8 |
| **Bachelor's Degree or Higher** | | | | | | | |
| NH White | 34.1 | 38.5 | 39.5 | 39.8 | 41.1 | 38.5 | 39.5 |
| NH Black | 19.7 | 25.1 | 28.7 | 27.0 | 32.2 | 25.5 | 29.3 |
| Hispanic | 11.5 | 15.8 | 20.0 | 18.1 | 24.4 | 16.5 | 21.2 |
| NH Asian/Other | 46.4 | 51.9 | 57.1 | 68.9 | 82.9 | 57.8 | 66.0 |
| Total | 25.9 | 28.4 | 30.7 | 31.7 | 37.4 | 29.3 | 32.6 |

*Source*: Projections by the authors and 2010 data and rates derived from U.S. Census Bureau 1992, 2002, 2011a;
Ruggles et al. 2010.
*NH refers to nonHispanic; values for categories labeled NH are only for the nonHispanic persons in each race
category. Hispanic includes Hispanics of all races.

three decades and would be 115.3 percent of nonHispanic White income levels under the scenario assuming the 2000–2010 rates. However, because of variability in the patterns of decennial growth for nonHispanic White income levels, nonHispanic Asian and Others incomes are only 87 percent of nonHispanic White levels when the decade of highest income growth is used for each racial/ethnic group. There are large differences between nonHispanic Asian and Other and both of the other minority populations under all scenarios.

When per capita income is examined, nonHispanic Black per capita incomes in 2050 are 50.2 percent of nonHispanic White incomes assuming the average rates of change over the three decades from 1980–2010 but 63.6 percent of nonHispanic White per capita incomes assuming that the maximum decennial rate of growth occurs. Hispanic per capita incomes in 2050 are 33.6 percent of nonHispanic White incomes in 2050 assuming the average of three decade values and 38.4 percent of nonHispanic White levels in 2050 assuming the highest decade rate. These compare to differences of 53.3 percent between nonHispanic Black and nonHispanic White per capita incomes and 40.7 percent between Hispanic and nonHispanic White populations in 2010. Although there is some relative increase in per capita income for nonHispanic Black persons, when more robust assumptions of future growth are assumed, Hispanic income continues to lag that of other racial/ethnic groups. Comparisons of nonHispanic Asians and Others to other racial/ethnic groups show higher income levels for all types of incomes relative to nonHispanic Black and Hispanic populations and show substantial continuing lower incomes when compared with nonHispanic White populations. This suggests that some of the higher values compared to nonHispanic White populations shown in the mean household income levels may be due to larger household sizes and larger numbers of household members who are contributing to total household incomes in nonHispanic Asian and Other households.

What these comparisons make evident is because of larger average household size, the average minority household will have fewer resources per person in 2050 than in 2010 despite larger relative total household income. At the same time it is evident that for nonHispanic Black and Hispanic households even income from multiple household members has not substantially closed the income gaps. These findings suggest a mixed set of results related to future closure in the socioeconomic characteristics of the Texas population.

The data in Tables 9.6 and 9.7 show similar patterns to those shown in Table 9.5 in that minority achievement of higher educational levels and involvement in higher income occupations increase by larger amounts under the assumption that the highest rates of growth from 1980 through 2010 continue from 2010 through 2050. They also show (as was evident

Table 9.7

Occupation by Race/Ethnicity for Persons 25+ for 2010 and Projected for 2020–2050
Assuming Average Percent Change for the Three Decades Between 1980 and 2010, Largest
Percent Change for Any Decade, and Percent Change for the 2000–2010 Decade

| Occupation | Average Percent Change | | | Largest Percent Change | | Percent Change 2000–2010 | |
|---|---|---|---|---|---|---|---|
| | 2010 | 2030 | 2050 | 2030 | 2050 | 2030 | 2050 |
| **Managerial and Professional** | | | | | | | |
| NH* White | 35.4 | 42.1 | 47.7 | 45.2 | 55.0 | 38.8 | 40.9 |
| NH Black | 21.9 | 30.2 | 38.0 | 31.7 | 41.8 | 27.3 | 32.8 |
| Hispanic | 14.8 | 18.0 | 21.2 | 18.2 | 21.4 | 16.6 | 18.2 |
| NH Asian/Other | 39.0 | 45.7 | 51.3 | 42.8 | 44.5 | 47.6 | 54.4 |
| Total | 27.0 | 30.7 | 33.5 | 31.8 | 34.8 | 28.7 | 30.2 |
| **Technical, Sales, and Administrative** | | | | | | | |
| NH White | 29.9 | 26.2 | 21.7 | 27.4 | 23.8 | 25.7 | 21.1 |
| NH Black | 28.1 | 29.0 | 27.2 | 32.2 | 33.6 | 25.2 | 21.9 |
| Hispanic | 23.5 | 22.5 | 20.9 | 23.3 | 22.1 | 22.3 | 20.8 |
| NH Asian/Other | 28.0 | 27.3 | 25.6 | 31.3 | 33.2 | 22.6 | 17.0 |
| Total | 27.4 | 25.0 | 22.3 | 26.5 | 25.2 | 23.9 | 20.5 |
| **Service** | | | | | | | |
| NH White | 10.4 | 11.0 | 11.1 | 10.5 | 10.0 | 11.7 | 12.5 |
| NH Black | 18.3 | 13.6 | 9.2 | 16.1 | 12.8 | 18.2 | 17.6 |
| Hispanic | 19.5 | 22.1 | 24.1 | 23.7 | 27.4 | 23.8 | 28.4 |
| NH Asian/Other | 12.6 | 11.6 | 10.2 | 14.4 | 15.6 | 14.0 | 14.4 |
| Total | 14.5 | 16.1 | 17.5 | 17.1 | 20.1 | 17.8 | 21.5 |
| **Farming, Forestry, and Fishing** | | | | | | | |
| NH White | 1.7 | 1.2 | 0.8 | 1.1 | 0.7 | 1.4 | 1.1 |
| NH Black | 0.8 | 0.4 | 0.2 | 0.5 | 0.3 | 0.6 | 0.4 |
| Hispanic | 3.1 | 2.6 | 2.1 | 3.0 | 2.6 | 3.4 | 3.6 |
| NH Asian/Other | 0.5 | 0.4 | 0.3 | 0.7 | 1.0 | 0.3 | 0.2 |
| Total | 2.0 | 1.7 | 1.3 | 1.8 | 1.7 | 2.1 | 2.2 |
| **Precision Production, Craft, and Repairers** | | | | | | | |
| NH White | 8.9 | 6.0 | 3.9 | 7.0 | 5.2 | 6.6 | 4.7 |
| NH Black | 5.2 | 3.1 | 1.6 | 4.0 | 2.8 | 3.4 | 2.1 |
| Hispanic | 14.4 | 13.0 | 11.3 | 15.5 | 15.9 | 13.8 | 13.0 |
| NH Asian/Other | 5.9 | 3.8 | 2.4 | 4.3 | 3.0 | 4.1 | 2.6 |
| Total | 10.2 | 8.5 | 7.3 | 10.1 | 10.2 | 9.1 | 8.4 |
| **Operatives and Laborers** | | | | | | | |
| NH White | 8.4 | 5.5 | 3.3 | 5.5 | 3.4 | 6.9 | 5.4 |
| NH Black | 14.1 | 7.8 | 3.9 | 9.7 | 6.0 | 11.0 | 8.2 |
| Hispanic | 16.7 | 11.7 | 7.8 | 12.0 | 8.3 | 13.5 | 10.7 |
| NH Asian/Other | 7.9 | 3.8 | 1.7 | 3.6 | 1.6 | 3.5 | 1.5 |
| Total | 11.9 | 8.2 | 5.5 | 8.6 | 5.9 | 9.9 | 7.9 |

*Source*: Ruggles et al. 2010.
*NH refers to nonHispanic; values for categories labeled NH are only for the nonHispanic persons in each race category. Hispanic includes Hispanics of all races.

in Table 9.5) that disparities between minority and nonHispanic White household income will decrease if the rates of socioeconomic growth for nonHispanic Black and Hispanic households can be increased over time. However, the data also indicate that despite some progress, equity is not achieved between nonHispanic White and nonHispanic Black and Hispanic populations by 2050.

High levels of disparity in education are apparent no matter what the rate of growth. For example in 2050, the percentage of the nonHispanic White adult population with a bachelor's degree (see Table 9.6) under the 2000–2010 scenario is 25.9 percent compared to 18.2 percent for Hispanics, a difference of 7.7 percent, while under the highest growth scenario, assuming the highest percent change for any (1980–2010) decade, the percentage of nonHispanic Whites with a bachelor's degree is 26.8 percent compared to 18.2 percent for Hispanics, a difference of 8.6 percent. Similarly, when these scenarios are examined for employment in managerial and professional occupations (see Table 9.7), the difference between nonHispanic White and Hispanic involvement in such occupations is 22.7 percent for the scenario assuming 2000–2010 rates of growth compared to 33.6 percent assuming the highest rate of growth for any decade.

It is evident that even assuming the highest rates of closure in the past three decades, the disparity between nonHispanic Black and Hispanic and nonHispanic White populations will continue to be large. *In other words, under any of the scenarios examined here, nonHispanic Black and Hispanic socioeconomic resources will not come to equal those for nonHispanic Whites by 2050.*

What is also apparent is that nonHispanic Asian and Other populations had high levels of education in 2010, which are expected to continue to increase over time. These higher levels of education are a result both of selective patterns of immigration and high levels of attainment among native born Asian and Other groups. This population group continues to show high levels of educational attainment that are positively impacting their levels of socioeconomic resources.

Why are the continuing disparities between nonHispanic Black and Hispanic and nonHispanic White populations so problematic for Texas? In addition to the critically important factors related to equity, these disparities will reduce the overall wealth and socioeconomic resources of Texas as a whole. This is both because the disparities are large and because these populations are a plurality of Texas population today and will be a majority of Texas population in the near future. If such disparities are not eliminated over the long run, Texas will be poorer and less competitive.

Rapid increases in populations that lack access to opportunities or do not have the characteristics that lead to improved socioeconomic conditions (such as higher levels of education) are likely to increase levels of overall socioeconomic disadvantage. As shown in earlier chapters, the projected patterns of change in Texas' population indicate that population growth (Table 2.7) will be largely a result of increases in populations that, due to a variety of historical, discriminatory and other factors, have more limited socioeconomic resources (see Table 5.2). This suggests that total population growth in Texas, in the absence of closure in the socioeconomic conditions of minority racial/ethnic groups to those of nonHispanic Whites, will lead to reduced overall socioeconomic resources for Texas.

This is evident when one examines the long-term socioeconomic impacts in the absence of socioeconomic closure. This was discussed in Chapter 4. However, it is clearly evident in the bar chart shown in Figure 9.1. This figure shows the percent increase in the projected number of households from 2010 to 2050 relative to the percent increases in the socioeconomic resources of households. If all households with householders from all racial/ethnic groups had the same rates of growth in these socioeconomic factors as the total rate of growth in their number of households, then all of the bars would show increases in socioeconomic factors equal to that for the number of households. What is evident in this figure is that assuming that the projected population and number of households of the different racial/ethnic groups increase as indicated in the projections in Chapter 2 and 3, and that they have the socioeconomic characteristics and differences that prevailed in 2010 as shown in Chapter 5, aggregate household income, aggregate net worth, consumer expenditures, and state tax revenues will not increase as rapidly as the population and average household income and net worth per household will decline in absolute terms from 2010 to 2050. Levels of all of these factors will decrease on a per capita basis compared to the levels in 2010. Only the percent increase in the number of households in poverty will increase more rapidly than household growth because, under current patterns of differences in socioeconomic resources by race/ethnicity, the types of households increasing most rapidly are those with the highest rates of poverty. The absence of closure in the levels of socioeconomic differences among groups impacts not only individuals and households, but also the state's economy overall.

## QUESTION 3: WILL CLOSURE OF SOCIOECONOMIC DIFFERENTIALS BETWEEN MINORITY AND NONHISPANIC WHITE RACIAL/ETHNIC GROUPS SUBSTANTIALLY AND POSITIVELY IMPACT TEXAS SOCIOECONOMIC FUTURE?

The patterns of closure in the socioeconomic differences among racial/ethnic groups that will occur if historical patterns of change for 1980 to 2010 prevail from 2010 and 2050 were presented above. They revealed that

Figure 9.1

Percent Change in Socioeconomic Resources Compared
to Percent Change in Households, 2010 to 2050*

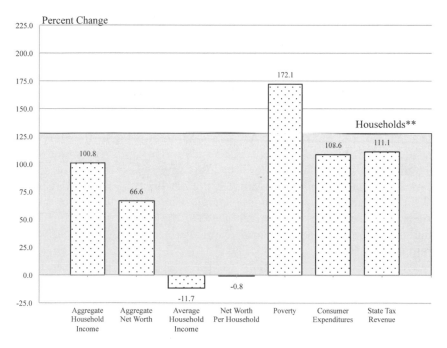

* Projections are shown for the scenario assuming 2000–2010 net migration rates.
** Shaded background indicates household change (127.6 %)

substantial disparities will continue to exist in 2050 because no recent period shows growth in nonHispanic Black or Hispanic socioeconomic characteristics sufficient to close the socioeconomic disparities between these
groups and nonHispanic White households in Texas by 2050. In this section, we examine the differences in the state's socioeconomic resources under three different scenarios of change in rates of closure between racial/
ethnic groups' socioeconomic resources.

In one scenario, we examine the effects of population growth alone on
socioeconomic change. This projection involves multiplying 2010 rates for
socioeconomic factors by the number of persons by race/ethnicity pro-

jected for 2050 (under the population projection scenario that assumes 2000–2010 rates of net migration). It provides base values for 2050 assuming that 2010 racial/ethnic socioeconomic differences apply in 2050.

In a second scenario, we assume the effects of an average of rates of percent change for 1980–1990, 1990–2000, and 2000–2010 for income and occupational variables and an average of 1990–2000 and 2000–2010 values for educational variables. This is a scenario that assumes a continuation of long-term patterns of socioeconomic change.

In the third scenario, we examine the impacts of complete closure of socioeconomic rates for racial/ethnic minorities in 2050 to those projected for nonHispanic White populations in 2050 by 2050. This provides data on the effects of such closure on minority groups and data on the overall statewide effects of closing the socioeconomic differences between minorities and nonHispanic White populations.

In the projections under this scenario, the values for some socioeconomic characteristics of nonHispanic Asians and Others are higher than those for nonHispanic Whites. Projected values for nonHispanic Asians and Others are used without modification in cases where the value of the socioeconomic factor for this population is greater than that for nonHispanic Whites but are increased to nonHispanic White levels if they are lower. As a result, total projected percentages for these factors may be slightly higher than the projected percent change values for nonHispanic White populations.

We do not provide projections for the scenario of highest decennial growth from 1980 to 2010 used in the analysis above because we wish to show the implications of broad patterns of growth in this part of the analysis, and those shown for the complete closure scenario encompass those for such a scenario. The use of the complete closure scenario, rather than the highest decade of growth scenario, allows us to evaluate the maximum impact of socioeconomic closure compared to the two more probable alternative bases.

The data from this analysis are shown in Table 9.8 and Figures 9.2 through 9.4. The first column presents the 2010 values for each of the variables as reported in the 2010 census. The second column shows the values of applying the 2010 rates for socioeconomic factors to the projected 2050 populations. The third column provides projections in which the average values for the three baseline decades of 1980–1990, 1990–2000, and 2000–2010 for occupational and income data, and the two baseline decades of 1990–2000 and 2000–2010 for educational change, were used to project socioeconomic factors from 2010 to 2050. The fourth and final column shows projected values for 2050 assuming closure of minority rates to those for nonHispanic Whites in 2050 by 2050.

A comparison of the values in columns 1 and 2 of Table 9.8 shows the

Table 9.8

Selected Socioeconomic Characteristics of the Texas Population in 2010; Projections for 2050 Assuming 2010 Rates, Projections for 2050 Assuming the Average Rates of Change by Race/Ethnicity for the Decades of 1980–1990, 1990–2000, and 2000–2010, and Projections for 2050 Assuming Closure of Projected Minority Rates to Projected NonHispanic White Rates by 2050

| Socioeconomic Factor[a] | Values and Rates in 2010 | Projected Values Assuming 2010 Levels | Projected Values Assuming Average Rates | Projected Values Assuming Closure to nonHispanic White Rates by 2050 |
|---|---|---|---|---|
| Employment in Mgmt. & Prof. | 3,257,323 | 8,766,549 | 12,302,912 | 17,086,277 |
| Employment as Operative or Laborer | 1,431,489 | 4,852,684 | 2,023,485 | 1,445,345 |
| Employed in Mgmt. & Prof. (%) | 27.0 | 23.9 | 33.5 | 46.5 |
| Employed as Operative or Laborer (%) | 11.9 | 13.2 | 5.5 | 3.9 |
| Median Household Income | $49,646 | $41,957 | $57,409 | $104,620 |
| Per Capita Income | $24,870 | $21,564 | $34,172 | $48,520 |
| Mean Household Income | $66,333 | $58,574 | $92,906 | $131,916 |
| Aggregate Household Income[b] | $592.0 | $1,189.4 | $1,886.5 | $2,678.6 |
| Population in Poverty | 4,399,571 | 11,274,223 | 10,954,430 | 6,401,313 |
| Population in Poverty (%) | 17.8 | 20.9 | 20.3 | 11.9 |
| Aggregate State Tax Revenue[b] | $34.2 | $72.2 | $104.1 | $147.8 |
| Mean Household Tax | $3,838 | $3,556 | $5,125 | $7,278 |
| Aggregate Consumer Expenditures[b] | $438.7 | $915.4 | $1,277.5 | $1,813.9 |
| Mean Consumer Expenditures | $49,165 | $45,081 | $62,915 | $89,332 |
| Population 25+ < High School/GED[b] | 3,044,020 | 9,570,659 | 4,968,674 | 1,612,343 |
| Population 25+ Bachelor's Degree | 2,728,577 | 5,468,516 | 7,628,783 | 9,892,751 |
| Population 25+ Grad./Prof. Degree | 1,356,402 | 2,846,315 | 3,667,727 | 5,896,597 |
| Population 25+ < High School/GED (%) | 19.3 | 26.0 | 13.5 | 4.4 |
| Population 25+ Bachelor's Degree (%) | 17.3 | 14.9 | 19.1 | 26.9 |
| Population 25+ Grad./Prof. Degree (%) | 8.6 | 7.7 | 9.9 | 16.1 |

[a] All monetary values are in 2010 constant dollars.

[b] Billions of 2010 constant dollars.

[c] Because of change in how educational attainment was defined in 1980 (based on years of education) compared to later periods (degree attainment levels) the values for education are based on an average of 1990–2000 and 2000–2010 decades.

## Figure 9.2

### Per Capita Income, Mean Household Income, and Mean Consumer Expenditures Per Household in 2050 Under Alternative Assumptions of Socioeconomic Closure Between Minority and NonHispanic White Households

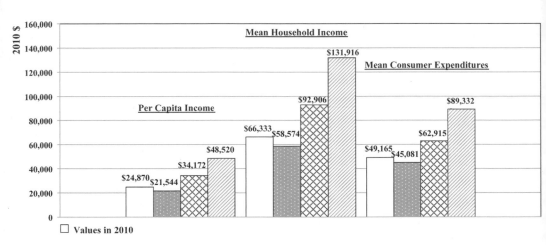

☐ Values in 2010

▦ Values and Rates in 2050 Assuming 2010 Socioeconomic Rates by Race/Ethnicity Apply to 2050 Population

⊠ Values and Rates in 2050 Assuming Average Rates of Closure Between Minority and NonHispanic White Rates by Race/Ethnicity for Three Decades from 1980–2010 for Each Decade, 2010-2050

▨ Values and Rates in 2050 Assuming Closure of Minority Rates to NonHispanic White Rates for 2050 by 2050

change that will occur assuming 2010 socioeconomic characteristics apply to the projected patterns of population growth in 2050. This comparison shows that if 2010 socioeconomic characteristics continue, the population will become poorer and more economically disadvantaged in 2050 than it was in 2010. Thus, the percentage of persons employed in management and professional positions will decrease from 2010 to 2050, while the percentage in operator and laborer positions will increase. Income levels will decline with median, per capita, and mean income levels declining, respectively, from 2010 levels of $49,646, $24,870, and $66,333 to 2050 levels of $41,957, $21,544, and $58,574. The poverty rate will increase from 17.8 in 2010 to 20.9 percent in 2050 and the percentage of persons with a graduate degree will decline from 8.6 percent in 2010 to 7.7 percent in 2050. Although aggregate values for some factors increase because of population

Figure 9.3

Percent of Persons in the Labor Force in Management/
Professional and Operative/Laborer Positions,
Households in Poverty, and Levels of Educational
Attainment Under Alternative Assumptions of Closure
Between Racial/Ethnic Groups in Texas by 2050

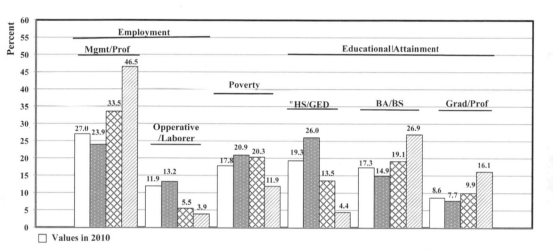

☐ Values in 2010

▦ Values and Rates in 2050 Assuming 2010 Socioeconomic Rates by Race/Ethnicity Apply to 2050 Population

⊠ Values and Rates in 2050 Assuming Average Rates of Closure Between Minority and NonHispanic White Rates by
Race/Ethnicity for Three Decades from 1980–2010 for Each Decade, 2010-2050

▨ Values and Rates in 2050 Assuming Closure of Minority Rates to NonHispanic White Rates for 2050 by 2050

growth, they do not increase at rates equivalent to population change, and
as a result, mean tax revenues per household decline from $3,838 in 2010
to $3,556 in 2050 and mean consumer expenditures decline from $49,165
in 2010 to $45,081 in 2050. These data again reinforce what has been noted
throughout this volume—that in the absence of socioeconomic improvements, Texas' population will be poorer and less competitive in the future
than it is today.

We compare projections in the second column, which projects patterns
for 2050 assuming 2010 rates for socioeconomic factors, to those in column three, which shows projections based on an average percent change
for decade periods from 1980–2010, and those in column four, which

## Figure 9.4

Aggregate Household Income, Consumer Expenditures, and
State Tax Revenues in 2050 (in Billions of 2010 Constant
Dollars) Under Alternative Assumptions of Socioeconomic
Closure Between Minority and NonHispanic White Households

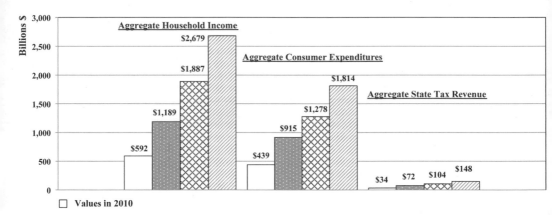

☐  Values in 2010

▦  Values and Rates in 2050 Assuming 2010 Socioeconomic Rates by Race/Ethnicity Apply to 2050 Population

▨  Values and Rates in 2050 Assuming Average Rates of Closure Between Minority and NonHispanic White Rates by
Race/Ethnicity for Three Decades from 1980–2010 for Each Decade, 2010-2050

▧  Values and Rates in 2050 Assuming Closure of Minority Rates to 2010 NonHispanic White Rates for 2050 by 2050

provides projections based on assuming closure between minority and
nonHispanic White rates to 2050 nonHispanic White rates by 2050. These
comparisons indicate how significant growth and closure could be to Texas'
socioeconomic future. The number of persons employed in management
and professional occupations when assuming the average rates (shown in
column 3) will increase by nearly 3.6 million from the levels assuming 2010
rates continue to 2050, and the increase will be more than 8.3 million assuming closure between nonHispanic White and minority rates by 2050.
The percentage of persons employed in such occupations will increase from
23.9 percent assuming 2010 rates applied to 2050 population, to 33.5 percent under the average rate scenario, to 46.5 percent under the complete
closure scenario.

Assuming these same three scenarios, median household income (in 2010
constant dollars) increases from $41,957 to $57,409 to $104,620; per capita
income increases from $21,544 to $34,172 to $48,520; and mean income

increases from \$58,574 to \$92,906 to \$131,916. Similarly, poverty rates will decline from 20.9 percent, to 20.3 percent, to 11.9 percent. Aggregate tax revenues will increase from \$72.2 billion, to \$104.1 billion, to \$147.8 billion; aggregate household income will change from \$1,189.4 billion, to \$1,886.5 billion, to \$2,678.6 billion; and aggregate consumer expenditures will increase from \$915.4 billion, to \$1,277.5 billion, to \$1,813.9 billion. The percentage of persons with bachelor's and graduate degrees will increase across these three scenarios. The percentage of persons 25 years of age or older with bachelor's degrees will increase from 14.9 percent, to 19.1 percent, to 26.9 percent, and the percentage with a graduate degree will increase from 7.7 percent, to 9.9 percent, to 16.1 percent. What the data for these items from these scenarios indicate is that overall closure in the socioeconomic characteristics of Texas' diverse population to the level projected for nonHispanic Whites will bring both improvement in the conditions of the minority populations, whose households would experience positive economic change, and in the private sector markets and public sector revenues of Texas. Such closure would be a major factor positively impacting all Texans.

## CONCLUSIONS AND IMPLICATIONS

This volume has described the future of Texas through an examination of a variety of private and public sector factors likely to be impacted by the state's future population growth and associated socioeconomic change. We believe the analysis makes evident several characteristics of that future. These are discussed below.

First, as noted above, it is evident that future population growth in Texas is going to be largely a function of Hispanic population growth. Projections presented in Chapter 2 show that under the scenario in which the nonHispanic White population shows the largest increase, it will account for only 2.1 percent of net population growth from 2010 to 2050. Similarly, nonHispanic Black growth will account for between 6.9 and 8.0 percent of net growth (depending on the scenario of growth assumed) and nonHispanic Asians and Others for between 4.8 and 19.5 percent of net growth. Hispanics are projected to account for a minimum of 70.7 percent of the net growth (under the scenario assuming a continuation of migration levels of the decade from 2000 to 2010 through 2050). Under the most likely future patterns of demographic change, Texas' population will be increasingly diverse and Hispanic.

A second and equally evident fact is that the nonHispanic Black and Hispanic components of this future population are projected to continue to show reduced income, higher rates of poverty, and lower levels of education compared to other components of the population. These characteristics, coupled with the size of nonHispanic Black and Hispanic populations, and their rates of population growth, mean that Texas' overall levels of socioeconomic resources are likely to decline. Although some believe that nonHispanic Asian and Other populations, that often have higher educational and other socioeconomic characteristics compared to other minority populations, could reverse the state's overall socioeconomic patterns, the size of this population is likely to be too small to substantially alter the overall socioeconomic characteristics of the state's future population, and as shown here, they too have selected characteristics such as per capita incomes that are lower than those for nonHispanic Whites.

The above set of factors lead to a third reality about Texas' future: that in the absence of improvements in the socioeconomic conditions of non-Hispanic Black and Hispanic Texans, the state will be poorer and less competitive overall. This is indicated in the data presented throughout this volume and is particularly evident as shown in Figures 9.1 through 9.4. The data throughout this volume show that low levels of education, low income, and high rates of poverty create severe problems for the individuals directly impacted and also create problems for the state as a whole. A less well educated workforce makes the state less attractive to out-of-state private corporations. Lower income and higher poverty populations impact state service demand and increase costs in areas such as education, Medicaid, and a variety of human service programs. Populations with such characteristics are also more likely to live in circumstances that make it more likely that they will become incarcerated. Lower income populations are less likely to purchase housing units, to create substantial increases in private sector revenues, and to increase state taxes and other revenues at the rate of persons with higher incomes. Although closing the socioeconomic gaps for Texas minority populations will be difficult, it is clear that the state is better off if they become better off.

The data in this volume make a fourth reality equally apparent. If current patterns of change (even patterns that assume the most positive rates of growth experienced in the last 30 years) are continued in the future, existing socioeconomic disparities are unlikely to close over the next 40 years. Analyses in Tables 9.2 through 9.7 show that no recent period produced patterns of socioeconomic change that, if continued, will reduce socioeconomic differences sufficiently to significantly reduce racial/ethnic disparities and prevent a decline in per capita resources in the state. Although the analysis assuming the most rapid economic growth in any decade in recent (1980–2010) Texas history improved conditions and led to modest closure in socioeconomic resources, it does not eliminate such disparities or lead to sufficiently significant rates of socioeconomic growth.

An analysis of Table 9.1 reveals that a fifth reality may assist Texas in addressing the realities noted above, and this is that increased levels of education can play a large role in improving the socioeconomic characteristics of minority as well as nonHispanic White populations in Texas. The data in Table 9.1 show that, although not the total answer, education plays a major role in increasing income for all racial/ethnic groups. Its data indicate that, no matter what one's occupation or race/ethnicity, increased education leads to increased income. This does not mean that income differences by race/ethnicity will not continue, but rather that education increases income for all racial/ethnic groups in virtually all occupations. This suggests that closing educational gaps between nonHispanic Blacks and Hispanics and nonHispanic Whites could substantially improve the socioeconomic futures of these minority groups but also could improve the socioeconomic future of the State of Texas.

The data in Table 9.8 and Figures 9.2 through 9.4 point to a final reality; that is, changes in the economy that lead to increases in the socioeconomic resources of minority populations to the levels of those of nonHispanic Whites will lead to substantial increases in the state's socioeconomic resources. Closure between minority and nonHispanic Whites to the level projected for nonHispanic Whites in 2050 shows significant increases in socioeconomic factors. Closure of minority to 2050 nonHispanic White levels in 2050 by 2050 will lead to increases of 8.3 million persons in professional occupations, increases of $27,000 in per capita income per year, increases in aggregate household income of nearly $1,489.2 billion, increases in aggregate consumer expenditures of more than $898.5 billion, and increases in aggregate state tax revenues of more than $75.6 billion compared to the levels of these socioeconomic factors if current patterns continue (i.e., under the scenario that applies 2010 rates to the projected 2050 population). Achieving circumstances that lead to closing the gaps so that minority populations have the same socioeconomic resources as nonHispanic Whites will substantially benefit the state as a whole. In other words, improving minority socioeconomic resources improves conditions for all Texans.

In summary, then, minority population growth, particularly Hispanic growth, is likely to dominate future population growth in Texas. Non-Hispanic Black and Hispanic populations are likely to continue to have limited socioeconomic resources and those limited resources, if not mitigated, will lead to a state that is poorer and less competitive. A continuation of historic patterns of change, even those that lead to substantial levels of overall economic growth, will not close the socioeconomic gaps between racial/ethnic groups in Texas sufficiently to reduce the overall socioeconomic effects of rapid growth without socioeconomic closure. Increased levels of education, although not closing socioeconomic gaps entirely, do lead to improved socioeconomic conditions for all racial/ethnic groups.

Finally, closing socioeconomic differences between minority racial/ethnic groups and nonHispanic Whites leads to substantial socioeconomic improvements not only for minority populations but also for the state overall.

The key question is how can Texas effect such change? Clearly continued economic growth is essential and will help to alter the negative implications of population growth in the absence of improved socioeconomic conditions for all Texans. At the same time, we must consider ways to enhance the rate of growth in factors, particularly levels of education, that we know will positively impact the growth in household income and overall state income and other socioeconomic resources for all racial/ethnic and socioeconomic groups. Education is not the key; but, as the analysis above shows, it is a key to changing the future of Texas. We must be willing to consider and promote programs that help to bring the levels of socioeconomic resources of disadvantaged populations up to the levels of nonHispanic White populations without diminishing the socioeconomic resources of either the disadvantaged or advantaged. This is a major challenge for Texas' future. In fact, we argue that it is **The Texas Challenge.**

# References

Abdullah, Abdul J., H. Doucouliagos, and E. Manning. 2011. *Education and Income Inequality: A Meta-Regression Analysis*. Paper presented at MAER-NET Colloquium (September 16–18, 2011), Wolfson College. University of Cambridge, United Kingdom.

Ashenfelter, Orley, and C. Rouse. 1999. *Schooling, Intelligence and Income in America: Cracks in the Bell Curve*. Working Paper 6902 (January). Cambridge, MA: National Bureau of Economic Research.

Acs, Gregory, K. Bracewell, E. Sorenson, and M. Turner. 2013. *The Moynihan Report Revisited*. (June 2013). Washington, DC: The Urban Institute.

Baretz-Snowden, J., D. Rock, J. Pollock, and G. Wilder. 1988. *Educational Progress of Language Minority Children: Findings from the NAEP 1985–86 Special Study*. Princeton, NJ: National Assessment of Educational Progress/Educational Testing Service.

Bartik, Timothy J. 2011. *Investing in Kids: Early Childhood Programs and Local Economic Development*. Kalamazoo, MI: W. E. Upjohn Institute.

Bartik, Timothy J., W. Gormley, and S. Adelstein. 2011. *Earnings Benefits of Tulsa's Pre-K Program for Different Income Groups*. Upjohn Institute working paper: 11–176. Kalamazoo, MI : W. E. Upjohn Institute for Employment Research. Accessed December 2011, http://research.upjohn.org/up_workingpapers/176.

Beaton, A. E. 1986. *National Assessment of Educational Progress 1983–84*. Princeton, NJ: Technical Report. Educational Testing Service.

Becker, Gary S. 1967. *Human Capital and the Personal Distribution of Income*. Ann Arbor: University of Michigan Press.

Bowman, Mary Jean, and C. A. Anderson. 1963. "Concerning the Role of Education in Development." In *Old Societies and New States*, edited by C. Geetz. Glencoe, IL: Free Press.

Caffrey, Christine, M. Sengupta, E. Park-Lee, A. Moss, E. Rosenhoff, and L. Harris-Kojetin. 2012. *Residents Living in Residential Care*

*Facilities: United States, 2010*. U.S. Department of Health and
Human Services. Center for Disease Control and Prevention,
National Center for Health Statistics. Washington DC: U.S.
Department of Health and Human Services.

Card, David. 1999. "The Casual Effect of Education on Earnings." In
*Handbook of Labor Economics* 3:1801–34, edited by O. Ashenfelter
and D. Card. Amsterdam: Elsevier Science.

Carter, Susan B., S. S. Gartner, M. R. Haines, A. L. Olmstead, and
G. Wright (eds.). 2006. *Historical Statistics of the United States:
Earliest Times to the Present*. New York: Cambridge University
Press.

Centers for Medicare and Medicaid Services. 2013. Medicaid Statistical
Information System (MSIS), Medicaid Financial Management
Reports, 2002–2010. Baltimore, MD: Centers for Medicare and
Medicaid Services. Accessed January 2013, http://medicaid.gov
/Medicaid-CHIP-Program-Information/By-Topics/Data-and-Systems
/MBES/CMS-64-Quarterly-Expense-Report.html.

Cheeseman Day, Jennifer, and E. C. Newburger. 2002. "The Big Payoff:
Educational Attainment and Synthetic Estimates of Work-Life
Earnings." *Current Population Reports* (July). U.S. Department of
Commerce Economics and Statistics Administration. Washington
DC: U.S. Census Bureau.

Cline, Michael, and Steve H. Murdock. 2012. *Estimates of the Impact of
the Affordable Care Act on Texas Counties*. Prepared for Methodist
Healthcare Ministries. Houston: Hobby Center for the Study of
Texas, Rice University.

Cline, Michael, Corey Sparks, and Karl Eschbach. 2009. "Understanding
Carpool Use Among Hispanics in Texas." *Transportation Research
Record* 2118:39–46.

Cohn, D'Vera, and T. Bahrampour. 2006. "Of U.S. Children Under
5, Nearly Half are Minorities." *The Washington Post* (10 May).
Accessed January 2011, http://www.washingtonpost.com/wp-dyn
/concent/article/2006/05/09/AR2006050901841.html.

Cohn, E., and J. T. Addison. 1998. "The Economic Returns to Lifelong
Learning." *Education Economics* 6(3): 253–308.

Dargay, Joyce D., D. Gately, and M. Sommer. 2007. "Vehicle Ownership
and Income Growth, Worldwide: 1960–2030." *Energy Journal* 28(4):
143–170.

Davern, M. E., and P. J. Fisher. 2001. "Household Net Worth and
Asset Ownership: 1995." *Current Population Reports* (February).
U.S. Department of Commerce, Economics and Statistics
Administration. Washington DC: U.S. Census Bureau.

Denison, Edward F. 1962. *The Sources of Economic Growth in the United*

*States and Alternatives Before Us*. Supplementary Paper No. 13. New York: Committee on Economic Development.

Denny, Kevin, C. Harmon, and S. Redmond. 2000. *Functional Literacy, Educational Attainment and Earnings—Evidence from the International Adult Literacy Survey* (April). The Institute for Fiscal Studies, WP 00/09.

Duncan, Greg, J. Ludwig, and K. Magnuson. 2007. "Reducing Poverty through Pre-School Intervention." *The Future of Children* 17: 143–160.

Ekstrom, R. B., M. E. Goertz, J. M. Pollack, and D. A. Rock. 1986. "Who Drops Out of High School and Why? Findings from a National Study." *Teachers College Record* 87:356–373.

Giuliano, Genevieve. 2003. "Travel, Location and Race/Ethnicity." *Transportation Research Part A* 37: 351–372.

Giuliano, Genevieve, and J. Dargay. 2006. "Car Ownership, Travel and Land Use: A Comparison of the U.S. and Great Britain." *Transportation Research Part A: Policy and Practice* 40(2): 106–124.

Glaze, Lauren E. 2010. *Correctional Population in the United States, 2010*. Washington DC: U.S. Department of Justice.

Gordon, Robert J., and I. D. Becker. 2012. *Controversies about the Rise of American Inequality: A Survey*. Working Paper No. 13982. New York: NBER.

Gottschalk, A. O. 2008. "Net Worth and the Assets of Households: 2002." *Current Population Reports* (April). U.S. Department of Commerce, Economics and Statistics Administration. Washington DC: U.S. Census Bureau.

Hanoch, Giora. 1967. "An Economic Analysis of Earning and Schooling." *Journal of Human Resources* 2 (Summer): 310–29.

Haynes, Sam W., ed. 2013. *Major Problems in Texas History* (Second Edition). Arlington: University of Arlington Press.

Health Care and Education Reconciliation Act (ACA). 2010. Public Law 111–152.

Health Management Associates. 2012a. "CHIP Enrollment: June 2011; Data Snapshot." *Kaiser Commission on Medicaid and the Uninsured, 2012*. Naples, Florida: Health Management Associates. Accessed February 2012, http://www.kff.org/medicaid/enrollmentreports.cfm.
———. 2012b. "Medicaid Enrollment: June 2011; Data Snapshot." *Kaiser Commission on Medicaid and the Uninsured, 2012*. Naples, Florida: Health Management Associates. Accessed February 2012, http://www.kff.org/medicaid/enrollmentreports.cfm.

Hobby Center for the Study of Texas. 2012. *Population Projections for Texas and Counties in Texas, 2010–2050*. Houston, TX: Hobby Center for the Study of Texas, Rice University.

Hopwood v. Texas 1996. 78F 3d 932 (5th Cir. 1996 rev'g861F Supp. 551 (W.D. TX 1994) Cert. denial 116.S. Ct. 258.

Isaacs, Julia B. 2012. *Starting School at a Disadvantage: The School Readiness of Poor Children* (March). Executive Summary. Washington DC: The Brookings Institution.

———. 2011. *The Recession's Ongoing Impact on America's Children: Indicators of Children's Economic Well-Being Through 2011.* Washington DC: The Brookings Institution.

———. 2010. *Child Poverty During the Great Recession: Predicting State Child Poverty Rates for 2010* (December). Washington DC: The Brookings Institution, Executive Summary.

Isaacs, Julia B., and K. Magnuson. 2011. *Income and Education as Predictors of Children's School Readiness* (December 14, 2011). Washington DC: Brookings Institution.

Jacob, Brian A., and J. Ludwig. 2009. "Improving Educational Outcomes for Poor Children." In *Changing Poverty, Changing Politics*. Maria Cancian and Sheldon Danziger, Eds. New York: Russell Sage Foundation.

Johnson, Kenneth M., and D. T. Lichter. 2010. "Growing Diversity Among America's Children and Youth: Spatial and Temporal Dimensions." *Population and Development Review* 36(1): 151–176.

Julian, Tiffany A., and R. A. Kominski. 2011. "Education and Synthetic Work-Life Earnings Estimates." *American Community Survey Reports*. ACS-14. Washington DC: U.S. Census Bureau. Accessed April 2012, http://www.census.gov/prod/2011pubs/acs-14.pdf.

Kelly, Patrick J. 2005a. "Income of U.S. Workforce Projected to Decline if Education Doesn't Improve." *Policy Alert*. San Jose, CA: National Center for Public Policy and Higher Education.

——— 2005b. *As America Becomes More Diverse: The Impact of State Higher Education Inequality*. Boulder, CO: National Center for Higher Education Management Systems (NCHEMS). Accessed May 2008, http:www: higheredinfo.org/raceethnicity.

Kim, S. 2009. "Immigrants and Transportation: An Analysis of Immigrants' Work Tips." *Cityscape: A Journal of Policy and Development Research* 11(3): 155–169.

Legislative Budget Board. 2001. *Summary of Legislative Budget Estimates*. Austin TX: Legislative Budget Board.

Maralani, Vida. 2013. "The Demography of Social Mobility: Black-White Differences in the Process of Educational Reproduction." *American Journal of Sociology* 118(6): 1509–1558.

Martin, Joyce A., Brady E. Hamilton, Stephanie J. Ventura, Michelle J.K. Osterman, Elizabeth C. Wilson, and T.J. Mathews. 2012. Births:

Final Data for 2010. National Vital Statistics Reports, Vol. 61(1). Hyattsville, MD: National Center for Health Statistics.

Mather, Mark. 2012. *Fact Sheet: The Decline in U.S. Fertility*. Washington DC: Population Reference Bureau.

———. 2009. "Children in Immigrant Families Chart New Path." *Reports on America*. Washington DC: Population Reference Bureau.

McKinsey & Company. 2009. *The Economic Impact of the Achievement Gap in America's Schools, Summary of Findings*. Social Sector Office. New York.

Milne, A., D. E. Myers, A. S. Rosenthal, and A. Ginsberg. 1986. "Single Parents, Working Mothers, and the Educational Achievement of School Children." *Sociology of Education* 59:125–139.

Milne, A., and J. Gombert. 1983. "Students with a Primary Language Other Than English: Distribution and Service Rates." Pp. 133–138 in *Bilingual Education*, edited by K. Baker and A. DeKanter. Lexington, MA: Heath.

Mincer, Jacob. 1974. *Schooling, Experience and Earnings*. New York: Columbia University Press.

Murdock, Steve H. 1995. *An America Challenged: Population Change and the Future of the United States*. Boulder, CO: Westview Press.

Murdock, Steve, M. Cline, J. Prozzi, R. Ramirez, A. Meers, J. McCray, and R. Harrison. 2008. *Impacts of Current and Future Demographic Change on Transportation Planning in Texas*. In cooperation with the U.S. Department of Transportation Federal Highway Administration. Institute for Socioeconomic and Demographic Research. San Antonio: The University of Texas at San Antonio.

Murdock, Steve, M. Cline, and M. Zey. 2013. "The History of Texas' Population." In *Major Problems in Texas History* (Second Edition), edited by S. Haynes. Arlington: University of Texas-Arlington Press.

———. 2012. *The Children of the Southwest*. Washington DC: First Focus. Retrieved December 2012 (http://www.firstfocus.net/library /reports/the-children-of-the-southwest).

Murdock, Steve H., N. Hoque, S. White, B. Pecotte, X. You, and J. Balkan. 2003. *The New Texas Challenge: Population Change and the Future of Texas*. College Station: Texas A&M University Press.

Murdock, Steve H., N. Hoque, M. Michael, S. White, and B. Pecotte. 1997. *The Texas Challenge: Population Change and the Future of Texas*. College Station: Texas A&M University Press.

———. 1996. *Texas Challenged: The Implications of Population Change for Public Service Demand in Texas*. Austin: Texas Legislative Council.

————. 1995. *An Assessment of the Implications of Population Change for Public Service Demand and Costs in Texas.* College Station: The Center for Demographic and Socioeconomic Research and Education, Department of Rural Sociology, Texas A&M University.

Murdock, Steve, and David R. Ellis. 1990. *Applied Demography: An Introduction to Basic Concepts, Methods, and Data.* Boulder CO: Westview Press.

National Assessment of Educational Progress (NAEP). 1985. *The Reading Report Card.* Princeton NJ: Educational Testing Service.

National Center for Health Statistics. 2012a. "United States, Healthcare Cost and Utilization Project (HCUP). Nationwide Inpatient Sample (NIS)." In *2010 National Statistics for Outcomes by Patient and Hospital Characteristics.* Accessed November 2012, http://www.cdc.gov/nchs/data/hus/hus11.pdf.

————. 2012b. *United States, Medical Expenditure Panel Survey* [MRDF]. Agency for Healthcare Research and Quality. Atlanta GA: Centers for Disease Control and Prevention. Accessed November 2012, http://meps.ahrq.gov/mepsweb/data_stats/download_data_files.jsp.

————. 2012c. *United States, National Health Interview Survey* [MRDF]. Inter-University Consortium for Political and Social Research, University of Michigan.

————. 2011. *Health, United States, 2011: With Special Feature on Socioeconomic Status and Health.* Atlanta GA: Centers for Disease Control and Prevention. Accessed December 2012, http://www.cdc.gov/nchs/data/hus/hus11.pdf.

National Center for Public Policy and Higher Education. 2005. *Income of U.S. Workforce Projected to Decline if Education Doesn't Improve.* San Jose, CA: National Center for Public Policy and Higher Education.

Passel, Jeffrey S., D. Cohn, and A. Gonzalez-Barrera. 2012. *Net Migration from Mexico Falls to Zero-and Perhaps Less.* Washington DC: Pew Hispanic Center. Retrieved December 2012 (http://www.pewhispanic.org/files/2012/04/Mexican-migrants-report_final.pdf).

Passel, Jeffrey, and D. Cohn. 2008a. *Trends in Unauthorized Immigration: Undocumented Inflow Now Trails Legal Inflow* (October). Washington DC: Pew Hispanic Center. Accessed February 2009, http://pewhispanic.org/files/reports/94.pdf.

————. 2008b. *U.S. Population Projections: 2005–2050* (11 February). Washington DC: Pew Hispanic Center. Accessed February 2008, http://pewhispanic.org/files/reports/85.pdf.

Patient Protection and Affordable Care Act (ACA). 2010. Public Law 111–148.

Perez, Anthony D., and C. Hirschman. 2009. "The Changing Racial and

Ethnic Composition of the U.S. Population: Emerging American Identities." *Population and Development Review* 35: 1–51.

Pisarski, Alan. 2006. *Commuting in America III*. Washington D.C.: Transportation Research Board.

Polzin, Steven E., X. Chu, and J.R. Rey. 2001. "Mobility and Mode Choice of People of Color for Non-Work Travel." *TRB Transportation Research Circular E-C026*.

Psacharopoulos, George. 1984. "The Contributions of Education to Economic Growth: International Comparisons." In *International Comparison of Productivity and Causes of the Slowdown* (Ed: J. W. Kendrick). Cambridge: American Enterprise Institute/Ballinger: 335–60.

Psacharopoulos, G., and J. B. G. Tilak. 1992. "Education and Wage Earnings." In *The Encyclopedia of Educational Research*, editor-in-chief: M. C. Alkin. American Educational Research Association: 419–23. New York: Macmillan.

Pucher, John, and J. L. Renne. 2003. "Socioeconomics of Urban Travel: Evidence from the 2001 NHTS." *Transportation Quarterly* 57(3), 49–77.

Reardon, Sean F. 2011. "The Widening Academic Achievement Gap Between the Rich and Poor: New Evidence and Possible Explanations." In *Social Inequality and Economic Disadvantage*, edited by Richard Murnane and Greg Duncan. Washington DC: The Brookings Institution.

Romer, Paul M. 1990. "Human Capital and Growth: Theory and Evidence." *Carnegie-Rochester Series on Public Policy* 32: 251–86.

Rosen, S. 1989. "Human Capital." In *The New Palgrave Dictionary of Economics*. Vol 2, edited by J. Eatwell, M. Milgrate, and P. Newman. London: Macmillan.

Ruggles, Stephen J., T. Alexander, K. Genadek, R. Goeken, M. B. Schroeder, and M. Sobek. 2010. *Integrated Public Use Microdata Series: Version 5.0* [MRDF]. University of Minnesota, Minneapolis.

Ryan, Camille, and J. Siebens. 2012. "Educational Attainment in the United States: 2009." *Current Population Reports* (February). U.S. Department of Commerce, Economics and Statistics Administration. Washington DC: U.S. Census Bureau.

Schultz, T. W. 1968. "Resources for Higher Education: An Economist's View." *Journal of Political Economy* 76: 327–47.

———. 1963. *The Economic Values of Education*. New York: Columbia University Press.

Sickmund, Melissa. 2002. "Juvenile Residential Facility Census, 2000: Selected Findings." *Juvenile Offenders and Victims National Report Series Bulletin*. Office of Justice Programs, Office of Juvenile and

Delinquency Prevention. Washington DC: U.S. Department of Justice.

Texas Comptroller of Public Accounts. 2012a. *Texas Economy in Focus*. Austin: Texas Comptroller. Accessed January 2012, http://www .texasahead.org/economy/indicators/ecoind.

———. 2012b. *Texas Net Revenue by Source*. Austin: Texas Comptroller. Accessed April 2012, http://www.texasahead.org/economy/indicators /ecoind.

———. 2011a. *2010 Annual Cash Report*. Austin: Texas Comptroller. Accessed March 2012, http://www.window.state.tx.us/finances/pubs /cafr.

———. 2011b. *Spending by Agency*. Austin: Texas Comptroller. Accessed April 2012, http://www.texastransparency.org/moneygoes/Spending _by_Agency.php.

———. 2011c. *Tax Exemptions and Tax Incidence*. Austin: Texas Comptroller. Accessed March 2012, http://www.window.state.tx.us /taxinfo/incidence.

———. 2002a. *2000 Annual Cash Report*. Austin: Texas Comptroller. Accessed April 2012, http://www.window.state.tx.us/finances/pubs /cafr.

———. 2002b. *1998 Annual Cash Report*. Austin: Texas Comptroller. Accessed January 2012, http://www.window.state.tx.us/comptrol /san/fm_manuals/cr98_manual/tab0598.html.

———. 2001. *Tax Exemptions and Tax Incidence*. Austin: Texas Comptroller. Accessed January 2012, http://www.window.state.tx.us /taxinfo/incidence.

———. 1995. *Texas Financial Update*. Texas Bond Review Board. Austin: Texas Comptroller.

Texas Department of Criminal Justice. 2011. *Statistical Report Fiscal Year 2010*. Huntsville: Texas Department of Criminal Justice. Accessed April 2012, http://www.tdcj.state.tx.us/publications/index .html.

———. 2001. *Statistical Report 2000*. Huntsville: Texas Department of Criminal Justice. Accessed April 2012, http://www.tdcj.state.tx.us /publications/index.html.

Texas Department of Human Services. 2011. *TDHS Annual Report Data: Fiscal Years 2005–2009*. Austin: Texas Department of Human Services.

———. 2009–2011a. Monthly Client Files for 2009, 2010, and 2011 [MRDF]. Austin: Texas Department of Human Services.

———. 2009–2011b. Monthly Medical Eligibility Files for 2009, 2010, and 2011 [MRDF]. Austin: Texas Department of Human Services.

———. 2001 *Expanded TDHS Annual Report Data: Fiscal Years 1995–*

*1999*. Program Budget and Statistics, Client Self Support. Austin: Texas Department of Human Services.

———. 1999–2001a. Monthly Client Files for 1999, 2000, and 2001 [MRDF]. Austin: Texas Department of Human Services.

———. 1999–2001b. Monthly Medical Eligibility Files for 1999, 2000, and 2001 [MRDF]. Austin: Texas Department of Human Services.

———. 2000. *Expanded TDHS Annual Report Data 2000*. Program Budget and Statistics, Client Self Support. Austin: Texas Department of Human Services.

Texas Department of State Health Services. 2012a. *Births for 2006, 2007, 2008, 2009, 2010 and Deaths for 1999, 2000, 2001 and 2009 and 2010 Used for Computation of Fertility and Survival Rates for Population Projections*. Office of Vital Statistics. Austin: Texas Department of State Health Services.

———. 2012b. Health Care Personnel 2010 [MRDF]. Center for Health Statistics. Austin: Texas Department of State Health Services.

Texas Department of Transportation. 2011. *Ages of Drivers in Crashes 2009, 2010, and 2011*. Accessed March 2013, http://www.dot.state.tx .us/txdot_library/drivers_vehicles/publications/crash_statistics.

Texas Education Agency. 2012a. *Academic Excellence Indicator System, 2009–10 AEIS Reports*. Austin: Texas Education Agency. Accessed April 2012, http://www.tea.state.tx.us/perfreport/aeis/2010/index .html.

———. 2012b. Public Education Information Management System (PEIMS) 2009–10 [MRDF]. Austin: Texas Education Agency. Accessed April 2012, http://www.tea.state.tx.us/index4.aspx?id=3012.

———. 2011a. *2000–10 State Performance Report*. Elementary and Secondary Program Enrollment and Expenditures, Academic Excellence Indicator System. Austin: Texas Education Agency.

———. 2011b. *Academic Excellence Indicator System, 2009 10 AEIS Reports*. Austin: Texas Education Agency. Accessed April 2012, http://www.tea.state.tx.us/perfreport/aeis/2010/index.html.

———. 2011c. Demographic Data for Public School Students for 1980–2010 [MRDF]. Austin: Texas Education Agency.

———. 2011d. *Enrollment for Instructional Programs and Special Populations by Race/Ethnicity, 2009–10 and 2010–11*. Austin: Texas Education Agency.

———. 2011e. *Enrollment in Texas Public Schools 2011–2012*. Division of Research and Analysis Department of Assessment and Accountability. Austin: Texas Education Agency. Accessed April 2012, http://www.tea.state.tx.us/acctres/home_index.html.

———. 2011f. *Pocket Edition: Texas Public School Statistics*. Austin: Texas Education Agency.

————. 2011g. *Public Education Information System Budget and Actual Financial Reports, 2009–2010.* Austin: Texas Education Agency. Accessed March 2012, http://www.tea.state.tx.us/perfreport/aeis /2010/index.html.

————. 2002. *Pocket Edition: Texas Public School Statistics.* Austin: Texas Education Agency. Accessed April 2012, http://www.tea.state .tx.us/perfreport/pocked.

————. 2001a. *1999–2000 State Performance Report.* Elementary and Secondary Program Enrollment and Expenditures, Academic Excellence Indicator System. Austin: Texas Education Agency.

————. 2001b. *Academic Excellence Indicator System, 1999–2001 AEIS Reports.* Austin: Texas Education Agency. Accessed March 2012, http://www.tea.state.tx.us/perfreport/aeis/2001/index.html.

————. 2001c. Demographic Data for Public School Students for 1980–2000 [MRDF]. Austin: Texas Education Agency.

————. 2001d. *Pocket Edition: Texas Public School Statistics.* Austin: Texas Education Agency.

————. 2001e. *Public Education Information System Budget and Actual Financial Report, 1999–2000.* Austin: Texas Education Agency.

Texas Health and Human Services Commission. 2013a. *Maximus A010 CHIP Monthly Enrollment File for 02/2013.* Strategic Support System, Data Quality & Dissemination/Human Services Programs. Austin: Texas Health and Human Services Commission.

————. 2013b. *Medicaid Enrollment Statistics.* Strategic Support System, Data Quality & Dissemination/Human Services Programs, March 30, 2012, TANF Strip Tape (TP550100cntiers). Austin: Texas Health and Human Services Commission.

————. 2013c. *Program Specific Enrollment Estimates from Medicaid Enrollment Statistics.* Texas Health and Human Services Commission. Accessed January 2012, http://www.hhsc.state.tx.us /research/MedicaidEnrollment/MedicaidEnrollment.asp.

————. 2013d. SNAP Data Tape (FSQTREV_w_TIERS 1202_G). Strategic Decision Support Department, SFY 2011 SNAP Annual Report_PUBLIC.xls. Austin: Texas Health and Human Services Commission.

Texas Higher Education Coordinating Board. 2011a. *An Overview of Article III, Senate Bill 1, 81st Legislature.* Austin: Texas Higher Education Coordinating Board.

————. 2011b. *Sources and Uses of Funds, Universities, Health-Related Institutions, Lamar State Colleges and Texas State Technical Colleges FY 2010.* Austin: Texas Higher Education Coordinating Board.

————. 2011c. Demographic Data for Public Community College and

University Students for 1980–2010 [MRDF]. Austin: Texas Higher Education Coordinating Board.

———. 2011d. *Financial Aid Report for 2011*. Austin: Texas Higher Education Coordinating Board.

———. 2010. *2010 Financial Aid Database Manual 2009–10*. Austin: Texas Higher Education Coordinating Board. Accessed January 2013, Financial_Aid_Database_Manual_2010_HECB-2036.

———. 2002a. *2000–2001 College Student Budgets*. Austin: Texas Higher Education Coordinating Board. Accessed January 2003, http://www.thecb.state.tx.us/reports/pdf/0111.pdg.

———. 2002b. *Statistical Report 2000*. Austin: Texas Higher Education Coordinating Board. Accessed January 2003, http://www.thecb.state.tx.us/DataAndStatistics/.

———. 2001a. *An Overview of Article III, Senate Bill 1. 76th Legislature, 2000*. Austin: Texas Higher Education Coordinating Board.

———. 2001b. Demographic Data for Public Community College and University Students for 1980–2000 [MRDF]. Austin: Texas Higher Education Coordinating Board.

———. 2001c. Enrollment of Texas Residents in Texas Public Community Colleges and Universities, School Years 1999–2000, 2000–2001 [MRDF]. Austin: Texas Higher Education Coordinating Board.

———. 1990. *Statistical Report 1990*. Austin: Texas Higher Education Coordinating Board.

Texas Juvenile Probation Commission. 2011. *The State of Juvenile Probation Activity in Texas, Calendar Years 2009 & 2010*. Austin: Texas Juvenile Probation Commission. Accessed January 2013, http://www.tjjd.texas.gov.

———. 2001. *The State of Juvenile Probation Activity in Texas, Calendar Year 2000*. Austin: Texas Juvenile Probation Commission. Accessed January 2013, http://www.tjjd.texas.gov.

Texas Workforce Commission. 2011. *Workforce Investment Act Title I-B Program Year 2010 Annual Report*. Austin: Texas Workforce Commission.

———. 2010. *Workforce Investment Act Participant Demographics*. Austin: Texas Workforce Commission.

Tolley, G. S., and E. Olson. 1971. "The Interdependence between Income and Education." *Journal of Political Economy* 79: 460–480.

Turner, Margery, R. Santos, D. Levy, D. Wissoker, C. Aranda, and R. Pitingolo. (2013). *Housing Discrimination Against Racial and Ethnic Minorities 2012*. Washington DC: U.S. Department of Housing and Urban Development.

U.S. Bureau of Labor Statistics. 2012. 2012 National Projections of the Labor Force of the United States [MRDF]. Washington DC: U.S. Bureau of Labor Statistics.

———. 2011. 2010 Consumer Expenditure Survey [MRDF]. Washington DC: U.S. Bureau of Labor Statistics.

———. 2002. 2000 Consumer Expenditure Survey [MRDF]. Washington DC: U.S. Bureau of Labor Statistics.

U.S. Bureau of Labor Statistics and U.S. Census Bureau. 2002. *Current Population Survey: Annual Demographic Survey*. Washington DC: U.S. Bureau of Labor Statistics.

U.S. Census Bureau. 2012a. 2012 Population Estimates of the United States [MRDF]. Washington DC: U.S. Census Bureau.

———. 2012b. *Methodology and Assumptions for the 2012 National Projections*. Washington DC: U.S. Census Bureau.

———. 2012c. 2012 Population National Projections. [MRDF]. Washington DC: U.S. Census Bureau.

———. 2012d. 2009–2011 American Community Survey Public Use Microdata Sample (PUMS) File [MRDF]. Washington DC: U.S. Census Bureau.

———. 2011a. 2010 American Community Survey [MRDF]. Washington DC: U.S. Census Bureau.

———. 2011b. 2010 Census Redistricting Data (Public Law 94-171) [MRDF]. Washington DC: U.S. Census Bureau.

———. 2011c. 2010 Census Summary File 1 [MRDF]. Washington DC: U.S. Census Bureau.

———. 2011d. 2010 Census Summary File 2 [MRDF]. Washington DC: U.S. Census Bureau.

———. 2011e. 2006–2010 American Community Survey [MRDF]. Washington DC: U.S. Census Bureau.

———. 2011f. 2010 American Community Survey Public Use Microdata Sample (PUMS) [MRDF]. Washington DC: U.S. Census Bureau.

———. 2011g. 2006–2010 American Community Survey Public Use Microdata Sample (PUMS) [MRDF]. Washington DC: U.S. Census Bureau.

———. 2008a. National Population Projections [MRDF]. Washington DC: U.S. Census Bureau. Accessed February 2009, http://www.census.gov/population/www/projections/2008projections.html.

———. 2008b. Survey of Income and Program Participation [MRDF]. Wave 7, 2008 Panel, 2012. Washington DC: U.S. Census Bureau.

———. 2003a. *2000 Census of Population and Housing, Summary File 4: Technical Documentation*. Washington DC: U.S. Census Bureau.

———. 2003b. Census 2000 Summary File 4 [MRDF]. Washington DC: U.S. Census Bureau.

————. 2002. Census 2000 Summary File 3 [MRDF]. Washington DC: U.S. Census Bureau.

————. 2001a. Census 2000 Redistricting Data (Public Law 94-171) [MRDF]. Washington DC: U.S. Census Bureau.

————. 2001b. Census 2000 Summary File 1 [MRDF]. Washington DC: U.S. Census Bureau.

————. 2001c. Census 2000 Summary File 2 [MRDF]. Washington DC: U.S. Census Bureau.

————. 1992. Census of Population and Housing, 1990: Summary Tape File 3 [MRDF]. Washington DC: U.S. Census Bureau.

————. 1991a. Census 1990 Redistricting Data (Public Law 94-171) [MRDF]. Washington DC: U.S. Census Bureau.

————. 1991b. Census of Population and Housing, 1990: Summary Tape File 1 [MRDF]. Washington DC: U.S. Census Bureau.

————. 1991c. Census of Population and Housing, 1990: Summary Tape File 2 [MRDF]. Washington DC: U.S. Census Bureau.

————. 1983. Census of Population and Housing, 1980: Summary Tape File 3 [MRDF]. Washington DC: U.S. Census Bureau.

————. 1982. Census of Population and Housing, 1980: Summary Tape File 2 [MRDF]. Washington DC: U.S. Census Bureau.

U.S. Census Bureau and U.S. Bureau of Labor Statistics. 2011. *Educational Attainment-People 25 Years Old and Over, by Total Money Earnings in 2010, Work Experience in 2010, Age, Race, Hispanic Origin, and Sex.* Current Population Survey, Annual Social and Economic Supplement. Washington DC: U.S. Census Bureau.

U.S. Department of Agriculture. 2013. *Supplemental Nutrition Assistance Program (SNAP) State Activity Reports, 2005–2010.* Food and Nutrition Service Program Accountability and Administration Division. Washington DC: U.S. Department of Agriculture. Accessed December 2013, http://www.fns.usda.gov/pd/snapmain.htm.

————. 2012. *Food Stamp Program Participation and Costs.* Washington DC: U.S. Department of Agriculture. Accessed December 2012, http://www.fns.usda.gov/pd/.

————. 2002. *Food Stamp Program Participation and Costs.* Washington DC: U.S. Department of Agriculture. Accessed December 2002, http://www.fns.usda.gov/pd/fssummar.htm.

U.S. Department of Health and Human Services. 2013a. *Administration for Children and Families, Caseload Data for 2005–2010.* Washington DC: U.S. Department of Health and Human Services. Accessed January 2013, http://www.acf.hhs.gov/programs/ofa/programs/tanf /data-reports.

————. 2013b. *TANF Financial Data FY Reports, 2005–2010.* Washington DC: U.S. Department of Health and Human Services.

————. 2012a. *Federal Matching Percentages*. Washington DC: U.S. Department of Health and Human Services. Accessed December 2012, http://aspe.hhs.gov/health/fmap.htm.

————. 2012b. Medical Expenditure Panel Survey, 2010 [MRDF]. Agency for Healthcare Research and Quality. Washington DC: U.S. Department of Health and Human Services. Accessed December 2012, http://meps.ahrq.gov/mepsweb/data_stats/download_data _files.jsp.

————. 2012c. *Medicaid Financial Management Reports, 2002–2010*. Medicaid Statistical Information System (MSIS). Washington DC: U.S. Department of Health and Human Services.

————. 2012d. *Medicaid Statistical Information System, 2009–2010*. Washington DC: U.S. Department of Health and Human Services.

————. 2012e. *United States: AFDC/TANF State-by-State Welfare Caseloads Since 1963*. Washington DC: U.S. Department of Health and Human Services. Accessed December 2012, http://aspe.hhs.gov /_/office_specific/hsp.cfm.

————. 2011a. *Administration for Children and Families, Caseload Data for 2005–2010*. Washington DC: U.S. Department of Health and Human Services. Accessed November 2011, http://www.acf.hhs.gov /programs/ofa/programs/tanf/data-reports.

————. 2011b. *Fourth Quarter ACF-196 Report, Fiscal Year 2010*. Washington DC: U.S. Department of Health and Human Services. Accessed November 2011, http://www.acf.hhs.gov/programs/ofs /data/.

————. 2010. *2009 HCFA Statistics*. Washington DC: U.S. Department of Health and Human Services.

————. 2002a. *Federal Matching Percentages*. Washington DC: U.S. Department of Health and Human Services. Accessed December 2002, http://aspe.hhs.gov/health/fmap.htm.

————. 2002b. *United States: AFDC/TANF State-by-State Welfare Caseloads Since 1963*. Washington DC: U.S. Department of Health and Human Services. Accessed December 2002, http://www.acf.dhhs .gov/news/stats/caseload.htm.

————. 2001. *Fourth Quarter ACF-196 Report, Fiscal Year 2000*. Washington DC: U.S. Department of Health and Human Services. Accessed December 2001, http://www.acf.hhs.gov/programs/ofs /data/q400/q4fy00.xls)

————. 2000a. *HCFA-2082 Report, 1999–2000*. Washington DC: U.S. Department of Health and Human Services.

————. 2000b. *1999 HCFA Statistics*. Washington DC: U.S. Department of Health and Human Services.

U.S. Department of Justice. 2013. *Easy Access to the Census of Juveniles in Residential Placement: 1997–2010*. Office of Justice Programs, Office of Juvenile Justice and Delinquency Prevention. Washington DC: U.S. Department of Justice. Accessed December 2013, http://www.ojjdp.gov/ojstatbb/ezacjrp/.

U.S. Department of Transportation. 2011a. *2009 National Household Travel Survey*. Bureau of Transportation Statistics, Federal Highway Administration. Washington DC: Federal Highway Administration.

———. 2011b. 2010 Highway Statistics Series. Federal Highway Administration, Office of Highway Policy Information. Washington DC: U.S. Department of Transportation.

———. 2010. 2009 Highway Statistics Series. Federal Highway Administration, Office of Highway Policy Information. Washington DC: U.S. Department of Transportation.

———. 2009. 2008 Highway Statistics Series. Federal Highway Administration, Office of Highway Policy Information. Washington D.C.: U.S. Department of Transportation.

———. 2008. 2007 Highway Statistics Series. Federal Highway Administration, Office of Highway Policy Information. Washington D.C.: U.S. Department of Transportation.

———. 2007. 2006 Highway Statistics Series. Federal Highway Administration, Office of Highway Policy Information. Washington D.C.: U.S. Department of Transportation.

———. 2006. 2005 Highway Statistics Series. Federal Highway Administration, Office of Highway Policy Information. Washington D.C.: U.S. Department of Transportation.

———. 2005. 2004 Highway Statistics Series. Federal Highway Administration, Office of Highway Policy Information. Washington D.C.: U.S. Department of Transportation.

———. 2004. *2001 National Household Travel Survey*. Bureau of Transportation Statistics, Federal Highway Administration. Washington D.C.: U.S. Department of Transportation.

———. 2003. 2002 Highway Statistics Series. Federal Highway Administration, Office of Highway Policy Information. Washington D.C.: U.S. Department of Transportation.

———. 2002. 2001 Highway Statistics Series. Federal Highway Administration, Office of Highway Policy Information. Washington D.C.: U.S. Department of Transportation.

———. 2001. 2000 Highway Statistics Series. Federal Highway Administration, Office of Highway Policy Information. Washington D.C.: U.S. Department of Transportation.

————. 1991. 1990 Highway Statistics Series. Federal Highway
Administration, Office of Highway Policy Information. Washington
D.C.: U.S. Department of Transportation.

Workforce Investment Act of 1998. Pub.L 105-220, 112 Stat. 936 (U.S.C.
2801, et seq).

# Index